'Through a series of bravura r— ...uunaonarata, Gurcharan Das makes a learned and passionate attempt to inform how the great Indian epic might illuminate our present-day moral dilemmas. Readers will find his analyses of dharma insightful, challenging, and honest—doing full justice to the world's most complex, exciting and honest poem.

This admirable book offers precisely the kind of reflection that the epic itself invites—moral, political and public. It shows why the *Mahabharata* is a classic: because it is ever timely. This superb book is knowledgeable, passionate, and even courageous. Grounded in a secure knowledge of the narrative, it raises key moral problems—from the doctrine of just war to affirmative action to the nature of suffering—and it makes striking attempts to link these with contemporary discussions and issues, both public and personal.'
—Sheldon Pollock, William B. Ransford Professor of Sanskrit and Indian Studies, Columbia University

'The book is a wonderful combination of the scholarly and the personal, the academic and the meditative. The basic plan works beautifully, building a rich mix of his very, very careful and detailed reading of the text, his other wide reading, and his life in business; an extraordinary blend. I found the use of evolutionary biology and the Prisoner's Dilemma to explain the pragmatism of the *Mahabharata* absolutely brilliant.'
—Wendy Doniger, Mircea Eliade Professor of the History of Religions, University of Chicago

'I was very moved by this richly articulated, contemporary meditation on the *Mahabharata* and the great human themes it embodies—above all the question of what life means and what one might do to endow it with purpose, within the inherently ambiguous and painful contexts in which we always find ourselves. The book is a kind of miracle: a deeply sensitive man suddenly decides to leave his usual routines and familiar roles and to spend some years simply reading the *Mahabharata* and seeing what the ancient epic has to tell him; he engages profoundly with the text, with the bewildering profusion of its messages, its tormented heroes, and the dramatic events it describes; and he then finds the space and the right words for a thoughtful, highly personal, philosophically informed, sceptical, sustained response. Such things

happen only rarely in our generation, and we should all be grateful to Gurcharan Das for this gift.'
—David Shulman, Renee Lang Professor of Humanistic Studies, The Hebrew University of Jerusalem

'How can we live with moral balance in an arbitrary and uncertain world? In this wise, passionate, and illuminating book, Gurcharan Das turns to the classical Indian epic the *Mahabharata* for answers—and finds, instead, a life of questioning, an ethical temper tolerant and suspicious of ideology, in which certainty is no virtue and respect for the projects of others is the appropriate response to life's complexities. Gurcharan Das's book is a fitting tribute to Ingalls's scholarly integrity and Rawls's insights about pluralism and respect. It is also one of the best things I've read about the contribution of great literature to ethical thought.'
—Martha Nussbaum, Ernst Freund Distinguished Service Professor of Law and Ethics, University of Chicago

'Gurcharan Das is the rare author who can speak to businessmen, modern-day savants and the uninitiated. This book is a scholarly discussion of the intellectual framework of the subtleties of dharma, as espoused by the *Mahabharata*. It brings out Gurcharan Das at his intellectual best. A must-read to resolve the moral dilemmas of life.'
—N.R. Narayana Murthy, Chairman of the Board and Chief Mentor, Infosys Technologies Ltd

'This book is a triple treat. It provides a subtle reading of episodes in the *Mahabharata*. It uses those readings to raise consistently provocative questions about the character of dharma. And it addresses important questions about the character of our ethical lives . . . It wears its learning lightly, prompting one to think, and hence it is a pleasure and a provocation.'
—Pratap Bhanu Mehta, President, Centre for Policy Research, New Delhi

'*The Difficulty of Being Good* is a remarkable tour de force that connects an ageless philosophical epic to the travails of contemporary society. This book is for the liberal Hindu who does not want his religion co-opted, for the modern Indian who wants to build a fair and inclusive society and for the global citizen who is rendered asunder by moral absolutism. The dharmic challenges we face every day resonate throughout Gurcharan's book. Reading this book has been an enriching experience.'
—Nandan Nilekani, Chairman, Unique Identification Authority of India

'The *Mahabharata* is one of the outstanding achievements of the human intellect and imagination and Gurcharan Das addresses its moral conflicts based on a close reading of classical texts and an informed understanding of modern philosophical arguments, making this book both instructive and enjoyable.'
—Andre Bétéille, FBA, Professor Emeritus of Sociology, University of Delhi

'Gurcharan Das is a delightful story teller. He also invariably has a point.'
—Rajat Kanta Ray, Vice-Chancellor, Visva-Bharati University, Santiniketan

'Storytelling is an ancient art in India but the stories always had a higher moral purpose. Gurcharan Das has mastered both the art and the purpose. In this elegantly written book, he weaves many tales, both personal and epic, to present a moral philosophy for individuals, corporations, and governments of the twenty-first century.

The recent global economic crisis has revealed deep corruption and lack of moral insight at the highest echelons of the economy … showing that it is difficult to be good, a constant moral struggle exemplified in the characters of the *Mahabharata* and in the stories and moral tales narrated with such charm and force by Gurcharan Das.'
—Patrick Olivelle, Chair in the Humanities, Professor of Sanskrit, University of Texas

'Gurcharan Das's personal search for dharma in the ancient epic uncovers buried signposts to a desirable future polity. *The Difficulty of Being Good* is a significant Indian contribution to a new, universal Enlightenment that is not Western in origin or character. It is a delight to read a book that wears its learning so elegantly and presents its arguments with such panache.'
—Sudhir Kakar, author and psychoanalyst

'The book is entertaining and thought-provoking, and will help many people see connections between the *Mahabharata* and contemporary issues—even when they encounter the epic for the first time. It is a book for both those for whom it has always been part of their cultural memory and for those who are reading for the first time this critical composition from India's rich and complex history. It offers insights and suggestions even for scholars of Indian thought, literature and history.'
—Chakravarthi Ram-Prasad, Professor of Comparative Religion and Philosophy, Lancaster University

'This book has done the rare thing of successfully invoking the *Mahabharata* to help address the questions that one faces in one's life. Unlike many attempts to make the *Mahabharata* "relevant" to modern life, this one takes the text seriously as a historical document and does not gloss over the explicit uncertainties and uncomfortable ambiguities that the text conveys. It is written in the expository memoir style that Gurcharan Das used so effectively in *India Unbound*. The style personalizes the questions and the quest for answers. It makes the work come alive and holds one's interest throughout. The added service that the author provides is to show how the authors of the *Mahabharata* engaged in the same sorts of central ethical issues (with sometimes remarkably similar responses) as Western thinkers both ancient and modern.

This book is a work of great insight. The Sanskritist, the philosopher, and the intelligent lay reader will all benefit from spending time with this work. There are few works on classical Indian thought for which this is true. Das is to be congratulated for so effectively speaking to such diverse audiences.'
—Richard W. Lariviere, Professor of Sanskrit and Provost and Vice Chancellor, University of Kansas

'It took me on a huge intellectual and emotional journey. And with Gurcharan Das as guide, even familiar paths seemed to lead through fresh landscapes ... The secular humanism and intellectual humility that shines through this beautiful book shows that—along with everything else—the *Mahabharata* can provide just what the modern world needs. Das's rehabilitation of Yudhishthira is inspiring ... showing convincingly that [others] misunderstand his role. I came away feeling more whole.'
—Dr Ian Proudfoot, Sanskrit scholar, Australian National University

PENGUIN BOOKS

THE DIFFICULTY OF BEING GOOD

GURCHARAN DAS is the author of the international bestseller *India Unbound* and a columnist for six Indian newspapers, including the *Times of India*. He also writes occasionally for *Newsweek*, the *New York Times*, the *Wall Street Journal* and *Foreign Affairs*. Gurcharan Das graduated from Harvard University where he studied philosophy with John Rawls and Sanskrit under Daniel Ingalls. he was CEO of Procter & Gamble India before he took early retirement to become a full-time writer. He lives in Delhi.

ALSO BY GURCHARAN DAS

NOVEL
A Fine Family

PLAYS
Three Plays: Larins Sahib, Mira, 9 Jakhoo Hill

NON-FICTION
The Elephant Paradigm: India Wrestles with Change
India Unbound: From Independence to the Global Information Age
India Grows at Night: A Liberal Case for a Strong State

GENERAL EDITOR
The Story of Indian Business
Arthashastra: The Science of Wealth
Thomas R. Trautmann
The East India Company: The World's Most Powerful Corporation
Tirthankar Roy
Merchants of Tamilakam: Pioneers of International Trade
Kanaklatha Mukund
Three Merchants of Bombay: Doing Business in Times of Change
Lakshmi Subramanian
The Mouse Merchant: Money in Ancient India
Arshia Sattar
The Marwaris: From Jagat Seth to the Birlas
Thomas A. Timberg
Caravans: Indian Merchants on the Silk Road
Scott C. Levi

GURCHARAN DAS

THE DIFFICULTY OF BEING GOOD

ON THE SUBTLE ART OF DHARMA

PENGUIN BOOKS

PENGUIN BOOKS
Published by the Penguin Group
Penguin Books India Pvt. Ltd, 7th Floor, Infinity Tower C, DLF Cyber City,
Gurgaon 122 002, Haryana, India
Penguin Group (USA) Inc., 375 Hudson Street, New York, New York 10014, USA
Penguin Group (Canada), 90 Eglinton Avenue East, Suite 700, Toronto, Ontario,
M4P 2Y3, Canada
Penguin Books Ltd, 80 Strand, London WC2R 0RL, England
Penguin Ireland, 25 St Stephen's Green, Dublin 2, Ireland (a division of Penguin
Books Ltd)
Penguin Group (Australia), 707 Collins Street, Melbourne, Victoria 3008, Australia
Penguin Group (NZ), 67 Apollo Drive, Rosedale, Auckland 0632, New Zealand
Penguin Books (South Africa) (Pty) Ltd, Block D, Rosebank Office Park, 181 Jan
Smuts Avenue, Parktown North, Johannesburg 2193, South Africa

Penguin Books Ltd, Registered Offices: 80 Strand, London WC2R 0RL, England

First published in Allen Lane by Penguin Books India 2009
Published in Penguin Books 2012

Copyright © Gurcharan Das 2009, 2012

15 14 13

The views and opinions expressed in this book are the author's own and
the facts are as reported by him which have been verified to the extent
possible, and the publishers are not in any way liable for the same.

ISBN 9780143418979

For sale in the Indian Subcontinent only

Typeset in PalmSprings by SÜRYA, New Delhi
Printed at Thomson Press India Ltd, New Delhi

A PENGUIN RANDOM HOUSE COMPANY

For my two teachers:
John Rawls, who taught me philosophy, and
Daniel Ingalls, who taught me Sanskrit

Contents

ACKNOWLEDGEMENTS

My happiest task is to thank friends, acquaintances and relatives who encouraged, educated, inspired and generally kept me in line during my dharma journey. I could write an amusing essay about how they did this but rather than embarrass them, I shall merely acknowledge their contribution by naming them below in alphabetical order. I apologize if I have missed anyone. Dániel Balogh, Andre Bétéille, Jacob Blakesley, Dipesh Chakrabarty, Krishan Chopra, Bhagwan Choudhry, Steven Collins, Lance Dane, Bunu Basnyat Das, Kim Kanishka Das, Puru Pulakesin Das, Robin Desser, Wendy Doniger, Stephen Espie, James Fitzgerald, Paul Friedrich, Robert Goldman, B.N. Goswamy, Vineet Haksar, Alf Hiltebeitel, David Housego, Ronald Inden, Arun and Vasanti Jategaonkar, W.J. Johnson, Sudhir Kakar, Matthew Kapstein, Daniel Kurtz-Phelan, P. Lal, Richard Lariviere, T.N. Madan, Kevin McGrath, Pratap Bhanu Mehta, Tanya Menon, Udayan Mitra, Lynn Nesbit, Jim Nye, Martha Nussbaum, Ralph Nicholas, Philip Oldenburg, Patrick Olivelle, Isabelle Onians, Gieve Patel, Stephen Phillips, Sheldon Pollock, Ian Proudfoot, Vaughan Pilikian, Chakravarthi Ram-Prasad, A.K. Ramanujan, Raju Rana, Lloyd Rudolph, Susanne Rudolph, David Shulman, Ravi Singh, John D. Smith, Manjushree Thapa, Romila Thapar, Tom Teal, Uma Waide and Mike Witzell.

A NOTE ON RENDERING SANSKRIT INTO ENGLISH

I like to show off my learning as much as the next person but since this book is for a wider audience I have tried to be reader-friendly in rendering Sanskrit words into English. Scholars traditionally use daunting diacritical marks to distinguish between long and short vowels in Sanskrit. I have dispensed with these irritations. Sanskrit also employs three forms of 's' and in the interest of simplicity I have reduced them simply to 'sh' and 's'. Thus, I have rendered, for example, the transliterated 'Krsna' of the scholars as the more familiar 'Krishna'. However, when quoting a scholar in the notes, I had to naturally stick to the original transliterated words. Occasionally, I had to break this rule when distinguishing in the text between two apparently identical words, such as Krishna, the god, and Krisnā, the epithet of Draupadi (the long 'a' at the end denoting the feminine).

I was tempted to drop the final short 'a' of Sanskrit as modern Indian languages tend to. Thus, Krishna becomes 'Krishan', Arjuna becomes 'Arjun', Dharma becomes 'Dharam' and Hastinapura becomes 'Hastinapur'. This is how Indian readers know the epic names. However, I decided against this for I felt that the *Mahabharata* is, after all, a Sanskrit text and it would take something away from its epic quality.

To avoid cluttering the text with italics I also made the practical decision of not italicizing the most frequently used Sanskrit words. These words are dharma, karma, brahmin and kshatriya.

I have also preferred not to translate 'dharma' and 'kshatriya' as van Buitenen did and fell far short of the mark. Dharma, in any case, is at the heart of the poem; it is not only untranslatable, but the *Mahabharata*'s characters are still trying to figure it out at the epic's end.

THE CENTRAL STORY OF
THE MAHABHARATA

The *Mahabharata* is the story of a futile and terrible war of annihilation between the children of two brothers of the Bharata clan. Set in and around Hastinapura, 'elephant city', in the fertile region around modern-day Delhi, it recounts the rivalry between the Pandavas, the five sons of Pandu, and the Kauravas, the hundred sons of his brother, Dhritarashtra.

The conflict begins when Dhritarashtra, the elder of two princes, is passed over as king because he is blind. Pandu assumes power, but he has been cursed to die if he has sex. Kunti, his wife, comes to the rescue of the dynasty. When she was young, she had looked after the ill-tempered sage Durvasa with extraordinary hospitality. He had rewarded her with a boon—a mantra by which she could invoke any god and have a child by him. Kunti uses the boon to obtain three sons—Yudhishthira, Bhima and Arjuna—from the gods Dharma, Vayu and Indra respectively. She also teaches the mantra to Pandu's second wife, Madri, who has the younger twins, Nakula and Sahadeva, by the Ashvins (the divine stars of sunrise and sunset). Despite their divine parentage, the children are called 'Pandavas', the sons of Pandu.

After a series of wars, Pandu retires to the forest and becomes a wandering hermit—leaving Dhritarashtra to rule the imperial city. Soon a rivalry develops over the succession. Prince Duryodhana, the eldest son of Dhritarashtra, disputes the right of the eldest Pandava, Yudhishthira, to take over the throne. Angry and vengeful, Duryodhana attempts to assassinate his cousins, who are forced to flee for their lives. While they are away, the five Pandavas jointly marry Princess Draupadi and also meet their cousin Krishna, who is God, and who becomes their friend and companion for life.

In the hope of averting conflict, King Dhritarashtra divides the kingdom, giving the barren half to the Pandavas. Despite their disadvantages, the accomplished Pandavas work hard and prosper. They rule justly, enhance their status through conquests and alliances, and build a striking, grand capital called Indraprastha (which some archaeologists believe is buried under present-day Delhi). Soon they are widely acknowledged to have become the paramount power. To commemorate his rise to imperial power, Yudhishthira performs the ancient *rajasuya* ceremony of consecration where dozens of rulers come laden with expensive gifts and pay tribute to acknowledge his imperial claim.

Intensely envious of his cousins' success, Duryodhana devises a scheme with his uncle, Shakuni, to usurp their half of the kingdom in a game of dice. Yudhishthira loses everything, including himself and his family, in a grand gambling match in the Hastinapura assembly. His wife, Queen Draupadi, is dragged into the assembly, where Duryodhana's brother, Duhshasana, attempts to disrobe her. But an extraordinary thing happens. Each time her garment is stripped off, another appears, and this goes on until a pile of clothes is heaped in the middle of the hall.

As a result, the Pandavas are allowed to retain their patrimony, provided they go into exile for twelve years and spend a thirteenth in disguise in society without being discovered. During their wanderings, they face hardship, encounter sages and enchanted spirits, and have many adventures. In the thirteenth year, they move to the capital city of the kingdom of

Virata, where they have perilous and hilarious escapades. To avoid being discovered, they assume disguises: Yudhishthira becomes a dice master at the royal court; Draupadi, the queen's handmaiden; Bhima, a cook in the royal kitchen; Nakula, a groom in the stables; Arjuna dresses like a woman and gets the job of a eunuch to guard the ladies' chambers and teach the royal women dancing; and Sahadeva looks after the royal cattle. Duryodhana sends spies to find them, but the Pandavas are undetected during their year of masquerade.

After thirteen years in exile, the Pandavas return to reclaim their inheritance. They have fulfilled the terms of the agreement and now expect the restoration of their kingdom. But Duryodhana refuses. Elaborate peace negotiations ensue. Krishna personally leads the final embassy to the court of Hastinapura in a last-ditch effort to broker a peace, hoping that his godly stature and neutrality (somewhat compromised though it is) will help to reach a settlement between the warring cousins. But the intractable Duryodhana is unmoved.

Krishna tells the Pandavas, 'War is the only course left.' The mood of the epic then changes to dread and foreboding at the approaching horror of the war. Both sides make furious preparations. Yudhishthira assembles seven armies against eleven of the Kauravas. All the great kingdoms of the time are allied to one or the other side.

As the war is about to begin, the epic's focus is on Arjuna, the greatest warrior of his age, who stands at the head of his troops. His debonair and confident charioteer, Krishna, halts their chariot between the two armies. As he surveys the field full of his kinsmen, Arjuna is filled with a strange pity. He puts down his magical Gandiva bow and refuses to fight. Krishna doesn't have much success in persuading Arjuna until he resorts to his authority as God. The awestruck Pandava sees the most amazing sights, and can only say, 'I salute you. I salute you in front and from behind and on all sides.'

The first ten days of the war are indecisive. The ancient patriarch of the Bharatas, Bhishma, leads the Kaurava army in repelling the Pandavas successfully. Bhishma is the eldest son of Shantanu, the Bharata king and ancestor of the Pandavas and Kauravas. He would have succeeded to the throne had his father not fallen in love with Satyavati, the daughter of the chief of a tribe of fishermen. As a condition of their marriage, the bride's father was adamant that the kingship should descend on Satyavati's children. To make his father happy, Bhishma renounced his right to the kingdom and vowed to remain celibate to avoid potential disputes in succeeding generations.

Although he has come out of retirement, Bhishma begins to decimate the armies of the Pandavas, who realize that their 'grandfather' must be eliminated if they are to win. Since Bhishma had told them that he would never strike a woman—or someone who had been a woman—the Pandavas call upon their ally, Shikhandi—who had changed her sex—to appear before Bhishma. Seeing him/her, Bhishma lays down his bow, and Arjuna pierces him with twenty-five arrows. Bhishma falls from his chariot, not on the ground but on a bed of the arrows with which he had been transfixed. Because of his remarkable vow of celibacy, Bhishma had received the gift of choosing his time of death. So, he prefers to lie on his bed of arrows through to the end of the war.

After Bhishma falls, Drona becomes leader of the Kaurava armies. He has been the revered teacher of martial arts to both the Pandavas and the Kauravas. Like Bhishma, he accepts his post reluctantly because of his affection for the Pandavas, especially his favourite pupil, Arjuna. On the thirteenth day of the war, Drona is able to divert Arjuna to the southern end of the battlefield, and he creates an impenetrable military formation, the *chakra vyuha*, in the form of a lotus-like circular array. In it, he places the greatest Kaurava warriors, and they advance menacingly against Yudhishthira.

The only one in the Pandava forces besides Arjuna who knows how to penetrate the *chakra vyuha* is his sixteen-year-old son, Abhimanyu. Yudhishthira turns to him, but the young warrior warns his uncle, 'My father taught me how to enter but not how to come out.' Abhimanyu's arrowhead pierces the *chakra vyuha*, and he smashes his way in. Once he is inside, powerful Jayadratha, ruler of Sindhu, quickly moves his troops and seals the breach. Bhima and the others are unable to enter, and Abhimanyu is trapped behind enemy lines. The boy fights valiantly, single-handedly causing so much destruction that Duryodhana is frightened. It takes the top six Kaurava generals (including Karna, Drona, Kripa and Ashwatthama) to subdue the 'lion's cub'.

When Arjuna hears of his son's death, he weeps bitterly, blaming himself for not teaching the boy how to exit the military formation. He vows to kill Jayadratha before sunset the next day—if not, he says, he will immolate himself. Krishna censures him for this rash oath. On the following day, Arjuna rages over the battlefield, inflicting terrible losses on the enemy. But he makes no headway against Jayadratha, who is well guarded. Finally, he reaches Jayadratha at the end of the day. But it is too late—he must still subdue six warriors who are protecting Jayadratha—an impossible task in the few minutes before sunset. Krishna saves the day—he plays a trick on the king of Sindhu, making him believe that the sun has set. Jayadratha lets down his guard and Arjuna pierces him with a fierce arrow.

Drona is also killed through trickery. The Pandavas kill an elephant named Ashwatthama—also the name of Drona's son—and spread the word about his death. When Drona encounters Yudhishthira, he asks if the rumour is true; Yudhishthira replies that Ashwatthama—he says 'elephant' under his breath—is indeed dead. Hearing this, Drona lays down his weapons, assumes a yogic posture, and Dhrishtadyumna, Draupadi's brother, cuts off his head. This is the only time that Yudhishthira told what was understood as a lie, and his chariot, which always moved slightly above the ground, sinks to the earth.

After Drona, Duryodhana appoints Karna as commander-in-chief of the Kauravas on the sixteenth day of the war. Unknown to the Pandavas, Karna is the eldest son of Kunti, their mother, and the sun god. Long before her marriage to Pandu, she had accidentally invoked the god through a boon, and found herself with an unwanted child, which was born with protective armour and earrings of immortality. Ashamed and desperate to hide her affair, Kunti set the infant afloat on a river, praying for his safety. Adhiratha, a charioteer, picked up the baby and took it home to his childless wife, Radha, who brought him up with great affection. Although he grows up a charioteer's son, the prince by birth acquires extraordinary martial skills and yearns to be a champion warrior. At a tournament of princes, he challenges Arjuna, but is disqualified because of his low birth. Duryodhana, however, is delighted to discover someone who can match Arjuna. From that day he makes Karna a lifelong ally and friend.

The lowly epithet, 'charioteer's son', nevertheless continues to dog him. Karna vies for Draupadi's hand at her *swayamvara*, where young, ambitious noblemen have come from afar. To help her decide, Draupadi's father poses a difficult test—the winner must string an extremely stiff bow and with it hit a golden target suspended in the sky. All the princes fail except Karna, but the beautiful and haughty princess rejects him, saying, 'I do not choose a charioteer!'

Krishna realizes that victory will be difficult with Karna on the opposite side. So he reveals to him the secret of his royal birth and asks him to defect. As Kunti's son, he says, Karna is the eldest 'Pandava'. If he crosses over, he will become king. Knowing his weakness for Draupadi, Krishna entices him with the prospect of enjoying her—sharing her as a wife with his brothers. This is a tempting offer. It is his chance to rise from being Duryodhana's retainer to king of the realm—and to be acknowledged as a genuine kshatriya or peer. Even so Karna refuses to switch sides, saying that his 'real' parents are the low caste family who have brought him up, not the royal family to which he had been born.

The seventeenth day of the war goes well for the Kauravas. Karna betters Yudhishthira twice. The tide, however, begins to turn in the afternoon. Just before sundown, the epic's two greatest heroes meet. Karna shoots a dazzling arrow that is spitting fire, at Arjuna's head. Krishna presses down their chariot in the nick of time. The arrow misses Arjuna's head but knocks off his crown. As Arjuna gets ready to retaliate, the left wheel of Karna's chariot gets stuck in the bloody mire of the ground. As he descends to lift it out, Karna reminds Arjuna that the rules of battle do not permit an enemy to strike a warrior who is not prepared. Arjuna hesitates but Krishna urges him on, 'Waste no more time, go on, shoot . . .' Arjuna lets loose his Anjalika weapon at the helpless Karna, striking him on the head—'the beautiful head, with a face that resembled a lotus of a thousand petals fell down on the earth like the thousand rayed sun at the close of the day'. Once again, the Pandavas have won unfairly.

The war is almost over now. All the great warriors on the Kaurava side are dead. In despair, Duryodhana leaves the battlefield and hides in a lake nearby. The Pandavas manage to find him and choose Bhima to fight the last duel. As the duel begins, Krishna doubts if Bhima will be able to defeat his adversary in a fair fight—he will need some sort of dodge. Arjuna gets the point, and slaps his left thigh, signalling to Bhima to strike a blow, unfairly, below the navel. Bhima hurls his mace at Duryodhana's thigh, smashing it.

As he lies dying, Duryodhana enumerates the god Krishna's many misdeeds, accusing him of perfidy in the way he had all the Kaurava commanders killed. Krishna's defence is that once the peace talks failed, and Duryodhana refused to part with five villages to the Pandavas, the only thing that mattered was victory. Krishna now becomes grave and tells the victors: 'Kauravas were great warriors and you could not have defeated them in a fair fight. So, I had to use deceit, trickery and magic on your behalf . . . It is evening, let us go home and rest.'

The same night, Ashwatthama, Drona's son, vows revenge. Only three Kauravas have survived, and they manage to flee from the jubilant Pandavas, taking refuge in a forest. Ashwatthama sees a guileful owl swoop down on crows sleeping in a tree. 'This owl has tutored me in war,' he says, and with his companions he sets off for the victorious camp of the sleeping Pandava armies. They set the camp on fire, and Ashwatthama slays all the Pandava warriors in an orgy of slaughter. The five Pandava brothers and Draupadi survive miraculously, but all of Draupadi's children are killed. Eventually Ashwatthama is punished for his heinous deed—he has to wander the earth, alone and anonymous, for three thousand years.

The only one who rejoices at Ashwatthama's act is Dhritarashtra. When the Pandavas come to console the blind king over the death of his children, Dhritarashtra rises to embrace Bhima, but Krishna, sensing devious thoughts in the old man, instantly substitutes an iron image of Bhima. The powerfully built king embraces the statue with all his desperate strength, and crushes it to pieces. (It was Bhima who had killed his favourite son, Duryodhana.) Despite the enmity, Yudhishthira behaves magnanimously towards Dhritarashtra after the devastating eighteen-day war.

A sense of horror and melancholy dominates the victors' mood. Almost everyone is dead and there is no joy in ruling over an empty kingdom. Yudhishthira, in particular, is inconsolable. Deeply troubled by the hollowness of a victory which was achieved by crooked means, he decides to abdicate the throne and retire to the forest—creating a crisis for the state. Gradually, however, Yudhishthira becomes reconciled to the tragedy of war and to his royal duties. Bhishma, the patriarch, is then brought from his bed of arrows to lecture the reluctant king on the dharma of a monarch.

The end of the epic is a time of twilight. After ruling for thirty-six years, the Pandavas feel weary and disillusioned. Krishna dies a banal death. As he is resting on the bank of a river, a hunter mistakes his foot for a bird, killing him with an arrow. After that the Pandavas decide that it is time to leave the world. They crown Abhimanyu's son Parikshit (Arjuna's grandson) to continue the dynasty at Hastinapura. The five brothers, along with Draupadi, set out for the 'city of the gods' in the Himalayas. On the way, they fall one by one, except Yudhishthira, who alone reaches heaven.

DRAMATIS PERSONAE

(In alphabetical order)

Abhimanyu, son of Arjuna and Subhadra

Adhiratha, adoptive father of Karna

Arjuna, son of Pandu and Kunti, fathered by the god Indra

Ashwatthama, son of Drona

Bharata, son of Dushyanta and Shakuntala, who gave the name to the dynasty from whom the Pandavas and the Kauravas are descended

Bhima, son of Pandu and Kunti, fathered by Vayu (the wind god)

Bhishma, son of Shantanu and Ganga, great-uncle of the Pandavas and Kauravas

Dharma, the god Dharma, father of Yudhishthira

Dhrishtadyumna, son of Drupada, brother of Draupadi

Dhritarashtra, father of the Kauravas, husband of Gandhari, brother of Pandu; fathered by Vyasa by levirate (with Ambika)

Draupadi, daughter of Drupada, wife of the Pandavas

Drona, teacher of the Pandavas and Kauravas

Drupada, king of Panchala, father of Dhrishtadyumna and Draupadi

Duhshasana, second son of Dhritarashtra

Duryodhana, eldest son and heir of Dhritarashtra; also called Suyodhana

Ganga, the river Ganges, mother of Bhishma

Gandhari, princess of Gandhara, wife of Dhritarashtra, mother of the Kauravas

Janamejaya, great-grandson of Arjuna, at whose snake sacrifice the *Mahabharata* is narrated

Karna, son of Kunti by the sun god, adopted by the charioteer Adhiratha and Radha

Kaurava, any descendant of Kuru, but specifically the children of Dhritarashtra

Kripa, teacher of the Kauravas and Pandavas

Krishna, son of the Vrishni king Vasudeva by Devaki; brother of Subhadra, Arjuna's second wife

Kunti, Pandu's wife, mother of the three Pandavas, Yudhishthira, Arjuna and Bhima

Kuru, ancestor of the Bharatas, eponym of the Kauravas

Madri, Pandu's second wife, who bore him Nakula and Sahadeva by the Ashvins; she cremated herself with Pandu, entrusting her children to Kunti

Nakula, son of Pandu by Madri, fathered by the Ashvins

Pandava, the five sons of Pandu

Pandu, father of the Pandavas; husband of Kunti, brother of Dhritarashtra; fathered by Vyasa by levirate (with Ambalika)

Parikshit, son of Abhimanyu by Uttara; grandson of Arjuna; father of Janamejaya

Radha, foster mother of Karna

Sahadeva, youngest of the Pandavas, son of Pandu and Madri; fathered by the Ashvins

Shakuni, son of the Gandhara king Subala, brother of Gandhari, maternal uncle of Duryodhana and the Kauravas; also called Saubala

Shantanu, great-grandfather of the Pandavas and Kauravas; grandfather of Pandu and Dhritarashtra; father of Bhishma (with Ganga); husband of Satyavati

Shikhandi, daughter of Drupada, later became a man; ally of the Pandavas

Subhadra, daughter of Vasudeva and sister of Krishna; wife of Arjuna

Vidura, adviser to Dhritarashtra, son of Vyasa by a commoner, uncle of the Pandavas and Kauravas

Vikarna, a son of Dhritarashtra

Vyasa, epithet of Krishna Dvaipayana, legendary author of the *Mahabharata*: premarital son of Satyavati; by levirate, father of Dhritarashtra (by Ambika), Pandu (by Ambalika), and Vidura (by a commoner)

Yudhishthira, eldest son of Kunti, fathered by Dharma; heir of Pandu; also called Ajatshatru

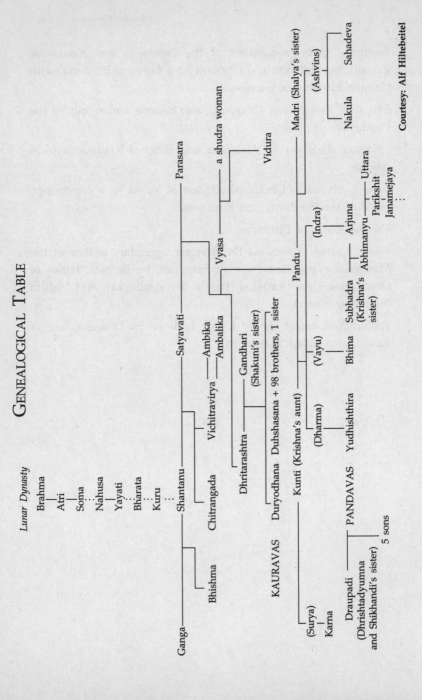

GENEALOGICAL TABLE

Lunar Dynasty

Brahma
Atri
Soma
Nahusa
Yayati
Bharata
Kuru
Shantanu — Satyavati — Parasara

Ganga

Bhishma

Chitrangada

Vichitravirya — Ambika
— Ambalika

Vyasa — a shudra woman

Dhritarashtra
Gandhari (Shakuni's sister)

Pandu — Madri (Shalya's sister)

Vidura

KAURAVAS

Duryodhana Duhshasana + 98 brothers, 1 sister

Kunti (Krishna's aunt)

(Surya)

Karna

(Dharma)

Yudhishthira

PANDAVAS

Draupadi (Dhrishtadyumna and Shikhandi's sister)

5 sons

(Vayu)

Bhima

Subhadra (Krishna's sister)

(Indra)

Arjuna

Abhimanyu — Uttara

Parikshit

Janamejaya
...

(Ashvins)

Nakula   Sahadeva

Courtesy: Alf Hiltebeitel

CHRONOLOGY

c. 2500–1500 BC*	Indus Valley civilization
c. 1500 BC	Rig Veda is composed
c. 1200–900 BC	Yajur Veda, Sama Veda, Atharva Veda
c. 950 BC	Kurukshetra War in the *Mahabharata* probably takes place
c. 650–400 BC	Early Upanishads are composed
c. 483 BC	Death of Gautama, the Buddha
c. 468 BC	Death of Mahavira, the founder of Jainism
c. 400 BC–300 AD	*Mahabharata* is composed (according to conventional scholarly wisdom; I prefer the dating of 150 BC–0 AD)
c. 300–100 BC	Dharma texts (*Dharma Sutras*) are composed
327–25 BC	Alexander the Great invades Punjab, India
c. 324 BC	Chandragupta founds the Maurya dynasty (324–185 BC)
c. 265–232 BC	Ashoka reigns
c. 200 BC–200 AD	*Ramayana* is composed
c. 185 BC	Pushyamitra founds the Shunga dynasty (185–73 BC)
c. 100 AD*	Manu composes his famous text on dharma
c. 320–550 AD	Gupta dynasty rules from Pataliputra (Patna)

c. 400 AD	Kalidasa writes the play *Shakuntala* based on a story in the *Mahabharata*
788–820 AD	Shankara, philosopher, writes a commentary on the Gita
820–890 AD	Anandavardhana, Kashmiri author, comments on the *Mahabharata*'s aesthetics
c. 1650–1670	Nilakantha Chaturdhara's vulgate text and commentary on the *Mahabharata*

Note: Although it is increasingly politically correct to use BCE/CE instead of BC/AD in textbooks in the USA and UK, I have retained the old-fashioned (albeit Christian) designation of BC/AD since many readers are still not familiar with the former. BCE stands for 'Before Christian Era' or 'Before Common Era' and is a substitute for BC or 'Before Christ'. CE stands for 'Common Era' or 'Christian Era' and replaces AD or 'Anno Domini' ('in the year of the Lord'). Both usages refer to identical dates based on the globally accepted Gregorian calendar.

PRELUDE

I take an academic holiday

What is here is found elsewhere.
What is not here is nowhere.
                    —*Mahabharata* I.56.34–35

In the spring of 2002 I decided to take an academic holiday. My wife thought it a strange resolve. She was familiar with our usual holidays, when we armed ourselves with hats and blue guides and green guides and trudged up and down over piles of temple stones in faraway places like Khajuraho and Angkor Wat. She also knew of our visits to our beach house near Alibagh, where we went away with a dozen books and did nothing else but read. But she was puzzled at the prospect of an academic holiday.

As she moved to get up from her chair, I hastened to explain. I had studied philosophy and read the great books of the West during college. But I had never read the classics of my own country. The closest I had come was to take Daniel Ingalls's Sanskrit classes at Harvard as an undergraduate.[1] Now, forty years later, I yearned to go back and read the texts of classical India, if not in the original, at least with a scholar of Sanskrit nearby. My wife gave me a sceptical look, and after a pause she said, 'It's a little late in the day for a mid-life crisis, isn't it?' I looked at her—she was still a handsome woman with extremely fine skin. 'Why don't we go to the Turkish coast instead?' she added.

After an absorbing career in multinational companies in six countries, I had taken early retirement at fifty to become a full-time writer. My wife and I had settled in Delhi, where I began to write a Sunday column for the *Times of India* and other newspapers. I travelled widely across the country in the 1990s and from these travels emerged a book, *India Unbound*. In it I wrote about India's economic rise and concluded that it was increasingly possible to believe that soon, perhaps for the first time in history, Indians would emerge from a struggle against want into an age when the large majority would be at ease.

Prosperity had indeed begun to spread across India, but goodness had not. I was angered and troubled in early 2009 by a scandal that posed a challenge to our conception of worldly success. B. Ramalinga Raju had built through talent, skill and dedication an outstanding and respected software company, and then committed the greatest fraud in Indian corporate history by swindling his company of Rs 7,136 crore. As a result, the public— both Indian and foreign investors—had lost around Rs 23,000 crore in the value of their shares, and the 50,000 employees of Satyam faced an uncertain future.

I had met Raju ten years earlier. I had looked him in the eye and I had seen sincerity, competence and great purpose. Soon after, I had run into one of his customers in the US and she spoke glowingly about Satyam's dedication to quality, reliability and integrity. There is no tribute greater than a satisfied, passionate customer, and it explained to my foggy mind, at least in part, why India had become the world's second fastest growing economy. Why should a person of such palpable achievement, who lacked nothing in life, turn to crime? What was the nature of moral failure in the case of the investment bankers on Wall Street who brought the world economy to its knees in 2008? Greed is too easy an answer. There must be more to it.

I wondered if the Sanskrit epic, the *Mahabharata*, held any answers. The epic is obsessed with questions of right and wrong— it analyses human failures constantly. Unlike the Greek epics, where the hero does something wrong and gets on with it, the action stops in the *Mahabharata* until every character has weighed in on the moral dilemma from every possible angle. In the Indian epic, harmony and happiness come to a society only through behaviour based on dharma—a complex word that means variously virtue, duty and law, but is chiefly concerned with doing the right thing. Would I be able to recover a meaningful ideal of civic virtue from India's foundational text?

Moral failure pervaded our public life and hung over it like Delhi's smog. One out of five members of the Indian parliament elected in 2004 had criminal charges against him.[2] A survey by a Harvard professor had found that one out of every four teachers in government primary schools is absent and one out of four is simply not teaching.[3] A World Bank study found that two out of five doctors do not show up at state primary health centres and that 69 per cent of their medicines are stolen.[4] A cycle rickshaw driver in Kanpur routinely pays a fifth of his daily earnings in bribes to the police. A farmer cannot hope to get a clear title to his land without bribing a revenue official and that too after a humiliating ordeal of countless visits to the revenue office.

In despair, I watched teachers—once revered as gurus and moral guides—fail their students; and political leaders, who had the duty to uphold the law, become lawbreakers. The abuse of power is a routine matter in the world's largest democracy, and the entire political class has united in recent years in order to prevent political and electoral reform. It was an amazing spectacle to see the country turning middle class alongside the most appalling governance. In the midst of a booming private economy, Indians despair over the delivery of the simplest public goods. Social scientists think of governance failures as a problem of institutions, and the solution, they say, lies in changing the structure of incentives to enhance accountability. True, but these failings also have a moral dimension.

∽

When I announced my plan to spend the next few years reading the *Mahabharata*, my mother, who lived 400 km away at her guru's ashram by the river Beas, reminded me that my restlessness was not inappropriate to the third stage of the Hindu life. Called *vanaprastha*, literally 'one who goes to the forest', such a person spends his time in reflection and searches for life's meaning. She said that I was suffering from '*vanaprastha* melancholy'.

In the classical Indian way of life, the first stage is *brahmacharya*—the period of adolescence when one is a student and celibate. In the worldly second stage, called *garhasthya*, 'householder', a person produces, procreates, provides security for the family while engaging in worldly pleasure. At the third stage, one begins to disengage from worldly pursuits, and in the fourth and final stage, *sannyasa*, one renounces the world in quest of spiritual release from human bondage.[5]

My mother had commended my decision to take early retirement so that I might, as she put it, 'have a rich and prolonged third stage'. Now that I was speaking about dharma and my restlessness, she insinuated that I had detached myself insufficiently from worldly concerns. While I was not expected to become a 'forest-dweller', she felt that my mental makeup remained that of a 'lowly second stage householder'.

I explained in my defence that I was attracted to the old idea of life's stages partly because the dharma texts recognized the value of the second stage, which was the indispensable material basis of civilization. It was important to remember this in a country that has long been mesmerized by the romantic figure of 'the renouncer', even before the Buddha came along.[6] My mother, however, was spot on in recognizing 'my third stage melancholy'.

During my second stage, I had felt as though I was waking up each morning, going to work, and feeding my family—only to repeat it the following day, as my children would after me and their children after them. What was the point of it all? Now in my third stage, I wanted to find a better way to live.

Meanwhile, my friends and acquaintances were incredulous. 'So, what is this I hear about wanting to go away to read old books?' one asked me at a dinner party. 'Don't tell me you are going to turn religious on us!' exclaimed another. My wife began to explain my idea of an 'academic holiday' to some of the guests, who reciprocated with suitable looks of sympathy. 'Tell us, what books are you planning to read?' asked a retired civil servant. A self-proclaimed 'leftist and secularist', who had once been a favourite of former prime minister Indira Gandhi, he had the gruff, domineering accent of an English aristocrat, not surprising in a former civil servant of the old school. I admitted reluctantly that I had been thinking of reading the *Mahabharata*, the *Manusmriti*, the *Kathopanishad* perhaps, and . . .

'Good Lord, man!' he exclaimed. 'You haven't turned saffron, have you?'

The remark upset me. Saffron is, of course, the colour of Hindu right-wing nationalism, and I wondered what sort of secularism is it that regards the reading of Sanskrit texts as a political act. I was disturbed that I had to fear the intolerance of my 'secular' friends as much as the bigotry of the Hindu Right, which had become a force in Indian politics over the past two decades with the rise of the Bharatiya Janata Party.

'Why are you going to read them?' my persecutor demanded.

'Well, perhaps, to learn to be good,' I answered with a weak smile.

'No such thing as Hindu ethics,' he scoffed. 'It all comes down to who you are in the pecking order. Frankly, it is too passive for my taste—all this non-violence business of Gandhi's. It's also too negative—keeping one's anger in check, *not* doing wrong, *not* injuring. Give me Marx any day—now that is about changing the world!'

Surrounded by narrow and rigid positions on both sides, it was becoming increasingly difficult to be a 'liberal Hindu'. The extremism of the 'secularists' was a reaction to the intolerance of the Hindu nationalists who regarded Muslims as their natural enemies. But the contempt of the secularists for religion per se prevented them from gaining sympathy. What sort of ideas, I wondered, might help to give meaning to life when one is in the midst of fundamentalist persons of all kinds who believe that they have a monopoly on truth and some are even willing to kill to prove that?

Hinduism is not a 'religion' in the usual sense. It is a civilization based on a simple metaphysical insight about the unity of the individual and the universe and has self-development as its objective. It employs innovative mental experiments of yoga that evolved in the first half of the first millennium BC, and does not have the notion of a 'chosen people', or a jealous God; it does not proselytize, does not hunt heretics. It could not be more different from the great Semitic religions—Christianity, Judaism and Islam.[7] Hence, I felt I could interrogate its texts in order to learn to live a secular life in a better way.

I was born a Hindu in the Punjab and had a Hindu upbringing. Like many in the Indian middle class, I went to an English medium school that gave me a 'modern education'. Both my grandfathers belonged to the Arya Samaj, a reformist sect that had come up in the nineteenth century. My ancestors did not have the living memory of their own political heritage and this must have been difficult. They had lived under Muslim rulers since the thirteenth century and had regarded political life as something filled with deprivation and fear. After the Muslims, they saw the rise of the Sikh kingdom of Ranjit Singh, and after its collapse around 1850, the powerful British arrived with Christian missionaries in tow. Thus, three powerful, professedly egalitarian and proselytizing religions surrounded us—Islam, Sikhism and Christianity. As a result, they were eager to receive the Gujarati reformer Dayanand Saraswati, who established the Arya Samaj. He advocated a return to the Vedas, a diminished role for brahmins and vigorous social reform. He 'modernized' our Hinduism.

'Arya' in Sanskrit means 'noble' among other things. European scholars in the nineteenth century took this ancient word from the Vedic texts to propagate a racial theory of 'Aryan' origins of Hindu culture and society based on a common Indo–European language system. We, in the new Punjabi middle class, embraced this idea enthusiastically, for it related us racially to the European Aryans. The Arya Samaj had a positive side in helping to create a nationalist sentiment among us for freedom and independence from Britain. In contrast, the invention of an Aryan race in nineteenth century Europe had tragic consequences, culminating in the ideology of Nazi Germany.[8] Half a century after the Second World War, the word 'Aryan' evokes repulsive memories of Nazism and is thoroughly discredited in the West. In India, however, it has been revived, curiously enough, with the rise of Hindu nationalism and the ascent of the Bharatiya Janata Party.

My father, however, turned away from the Arya Samaj and became a passionate mystic. When he was studying to be an engineer, he was drawn to a kindly guru, who taught him the *bhakti* path of direct union with God through devotion and meditation. The guru belonged to the Radhasoami sect, descended intellectually from the medieval *bhakti* and Sufi traditions of Kabir, Nanak, Rumi and Mirabai. My father found his discourses 'modern' for they appealed to his rational, engineer's temper. His own decision, he once told me, was made in the scientific spirit of Blaise Pascal's wager. If you believe in God, Pascal had said, and He turns out to exist, then you have obviously made a good decision; however, if He does not exist, and you still believe in Him, you haven't lost anything; but if you don't believe in Him and he does exist, then you are in serious trouble.

Amidst this, my maternal grandmother remained a traditional Hindu in Lyallpur, where I was born. Her dressing room was filled with the images of her many gods, prominent among them being Krishna and Rama, and she would say in the same breath that there are millions of gods but only one God. Her gods and goddesses were symbols of reality rather than reality itself (as the theologian Paul Tillich explained to me in a class at Harvard), and they helped her to reach one God. Her eclecticism did not stop there. She would visit the Sikh gurdwara on Mondays and Wednesdays, a Hindu temple on Tuesdays and Thursdays and she saved Saturdays and Sundays for discourses by holy men, including Muslim pirs, who were forever visiting our town. In between, she made time for Arya Samaj ceremonies.

Amidst this religious chaos I grew up with a liberal attitude that was a mixture of scepticism and sympathy for the Hindu way of life. One of its attractive features is of multiple goals to the good life. The first goal is to come to grips with *kama*, 'human desire'. I find it reassuring that pleasure has a valued place in the good life. A second goal is *artha*, 'material well-being', which makes sense, for how can one be happy in conditions of extreme deprivation? A third objective of life is *dharma* or moral well-being. The final goal is *moksha*, 'spiritual liberation' from our fragmented, finite and suffering existence. I have always felt that Indians are sensible, like Aristotle, in believing in multiple paths to a flourishing life.

ॐ

When my wife and I returned from the dinner party, we did what everyone does. We gossiped about who was there, who said what, and to whom. I was still smarting from the remark about Hindutva, and I burst out accusingly, 'I wish you hadn't blabbered about my plans! You know what people are like—half of Delhi will be talking about it in twenty-four hours!'

Soon I calmed down, though, and realized that many Indians thought of classical Sanskrit texts either in religious or political terms. Mine, however, was a project in self-cultivation. I wanted to know how to live my life and I had a feeling that the answer might lie in examining the four ends of life. My first book, *India Unbound*, had examined the second goal of *artha*; the next one would be about dharma. I began to feel more secure about my endeavour—less concerned with what others would say or think about it. My wife also turned out to be a good sport, and began to see our 'academic holiday' as an opportunity to attend lectures on Renaissance painting and Chinese ceramics while I went off to read the Sanskrit texts. So, in the fall of 2002, we found ourselves at the University of Chicago.

I was an implausible student—a husband, a father of two grown-up boys, and a taxpayer with considerably less hair than his peers. Wintry and windy Chicago also seemed an unusual choice for 'a forest-dweller' at life's third stage. The city of Benares, the home of classical learning in north India, would have been a more conventional choice. But I did not want to escape into 'our great classical past'. I wanted to learn about that past with full consciousness of the present—and also to learn something about the present in encountering the past.[9] Sanskrit pandits in Benares seemed to me impossibly rigid and they would not have approved of my desire to 'interrogate' the texts.

It was a stray remark by the poet A.K. Ramanujan that finally pushed me to Chicago. 'If you don't experience eternity at Benares,' he said, 'you will at Regenstein.' He was referring to the Regenstein Library with its fabulous collection of South Asian texts under the able stewardship of Jim Nye. Chicago was a logical choice. Indology had been in terminal decline at Harvard, my old alma mater, ever since Daniel Ingalls's death. The University of Chicago had four Sanskrit scholars—two big names,

Sheldon Pollock and Wendy Doniger, both students of Ingalls, and Sanskrit-knowing Buddhist scholars like Steve Collins, Mathew Kapstein and Dan Arnold.

I had two criteria in mind in selecting a reading list. I wanted a text from each of the major genres and I wanted it to illuminate one of the four aims of life. When it came to desire, *Kamasutra*, the text on erotic love and sex, was the obvious choice. The *Arthashastra*, a text of politics and economics, would help me with the second goal of *artha*. In the epic genre, I chose the *Mahabharata* because of dharma—its heroes were more human and fallible, unlike the *Ramayana*. The Upanishads were the clear choice for studying the fourth end of *moksha*. In my second year I planned to read the *Manusmriti*, the law book by Manu, which tries to reconcile the first three ends. The stories from the *Kathasaritsagara* would instruct me on how to live. To understand yoga, I would read the *Yoga Sutras* of Patanjali. If there was time, Kalidasa's *Shakuntala* would be my drama text.

I wanted to read the texts in Sanskrit, but that would have needed a lifetime—given my shallow grasp of the language. I was hungry and impatient. So, I decided on the next best course. I would arrive early in the morning at Regenstein and follow the drill I had learned from Daniel Ingalls. I would pull out from the shelf a volume of the *Mahabharata*'s Critical Edition. With Whitney's grammar on my right and Apte's dictionary on my left, I would read a small passage. It was hard labour, but Wendy Doniger consoled me, saying: 'Reading Sanskrit is good for the soul.' I would tire after an hour or so, and then I would turn to van Buitenen's translation and read it for the rest of the morning. If I had a doubt, I would go back to the original. It was an unhurried pursuit. I did not want information. I wanted to be cultivated, and thus I read at leisure with lingering appreciation.

By the end of my first year, I had become dangerously addicted to the *Mahabharata* and had fallen hopelessly behind in the rest of my reading. The epic is a splendid and moving story, exciting, ironic and witty, and with a cast of characters that I became increasingly attached to. I was also intrigued by its boast:

What is here is found elsewhere.
What is not here is nowhere.[10]

In the summer I returned to India and went to visit my mother. On the way the train stopped at a sleepy station, about a hundred miles north of Delhi. I stepped on to the platform and discovered that this was no ordinary station—it was historic Kurukshetra, where the *Mahabharata*'s futile war of annihilation had been fought. In the burning heat of the summer afternoon, I began to imagine the brutal magnificence of the raging, ruthless battles. I saw a dithering Arjuna, the greatest warrior of his age, put down his Gandiva bow and refuse to fight—leaving his debonair and confident charioteer, Krishna, who is also God, with a problem on his hands. I visualized ruthless Drona grinding the exhausted Pandava armies into the dust. Suddenly he turns anxiously to his pupil, Yudhishthira, to ask if the rumour about his son's death is true. Yudhishthira—who had never spoken false—tells a white lie and his fabulous chariot, which always travelled slightly above the ground, sinks into the dust. The train began to move and I jumped in. As I settled back, I felt that the epic might indeed have something to teach me about the right way to live in the world.

The *Mahabharata* tells the story of a futile and terrible war of annihilation between the children of two brothers of the Bharata family. The rival cousins, the Kauravas and the Pandavas, both lay claim to the throne. To resolve the feud, the kingdom is divided, but the jealous Kauravas are not content, and plot to usurp the other half of the kingdom through a rigged game of dice. Yudhishthira, the eldest Pandava, loses everything in the game—his kingdom, his brothers, his wife and, indeed, himself—

to his rival Duryodhana. Yudhishthira's wife, Queen Draupadi, is dragged before Duryodhana in the assembly of the nobles, where his brother Duhshasana tries to strip her:

> *When her dress was being stripped off, lord of the people, another one appeared every time. A terrible roar went up from all the kings, a shout of approval, as they watched that greatest wonder on the earth . . . [In the end] a pile of clothes was heaped up in the middle of the hall, when Duhshasana, tired and ashamed, at last desisted and sat down.*[11]

With this act of 'cosmic justice', the assembly should have been forced to confront the question of dharma, the central problem of the *Mahabharata*. But the elders fail to address it, and the failure hangs over the entire epic, leading to a destructive and terrible war between the rivals.

Dharma, the word at the heart of the epic, is in fact untranslatable. Duty, goodness, justice, law and custom all have something to do with it, but they all fall short. Dharma refers to 'balance'—both moral balance and cosmic balance. It is the order and balance within each human being which is also reflected in the order of the cosmos. Dharma derives from the Sanskrit root dhr, meaning to 'sustain'.[12] It is the moral law that sustains society, the individual and the world. In the dharma texts, it commonly means the whole range of duties incumbent on each individual according to his *varna*, 'status', or *ashrama*, 'stage of life'.[13] The *Mahabharata*, however, will also challenge this latter meaning. This conceptual difficulty, such complexity, is part of the point.[14] Indeed, the *Mahabharata* is in many ways an extended attempt to clarify just what dharma is—that is, what exactly should we do when we are trying to be good in the world.

When I began my quest for dharma, I did not imagine that I would be undertaking an enterprise quite so bizarre. I tried to picture the look of shocked incomprehension on Yudhishthira's face when he loses his kingdom and his wife in the dice game and this happens at the very moment of his greatest triumph when he is consecrated 'king of kings'. He could only suppose that his world had gone awry. Gradually, I began to realize that the dice game may be symbolic of the quixotic, vulnerable human condition in which one knows not why one is born, when one will die, and why one faces reverses on the way. The only thing certain, the *Mahabharata* tells us, is that *kala* (time or death) is 'always cooking us'.[15]

> *In this cauldron fashioned from delusion, with the sun as fire and day and night as kindling wood, the months and seasons as the ladle for stirring, Time (or Death) cooks all beings: this is the simple truth.*[16]

Could one depend on dharma to protect one in this uncertain world? If so, how does a person go about finding dharma? In a life and death debate with the Yaksha, a tree spirit, who controls the waters of a lake, thirsty Yudhishthira is asked this very question. The right answer will save him and his brothers; the wrong answer will mean their death. He tells the Yaksha that in seeking dharma 'reason is of limited use for it is without foundation;[17] neither are the sacred texts helpful as they are at odds with one another; nor is there a single sage whose opinion could be considered authoritative. The truth about dharma is hidden in a cave.'[18]

To help me to search in this cave, I had to depend on a gambling addict and a loser. A curious choice for a guide, you might think. Yudhishthira is so fraught with frailties to be almost an 'un-hero'. His world is off balance and the god, Krishna, 'constantly feeds this imbalance, fostering disorder'.[19] Although he is a warrior, he lacks physical prowess, distrusts martial values and feels helpless. What redeems him, however, is that he insists on not being anything other than himself. Alone, he confronts the possibility that the universe might not care about dharma.

Originally, the epic set out to narrate a tale of triumph but, in fact, ended in telling a story of defeat. Early versions of the epic used to go by the name *Jaya*, meaning 'victory', and the bard, it seems, did want to narrate a story of triumph. Indeed, the epic announces unambiguously at the beginning of Book One:

The king who seeks conquest should listen to this history named Jaya *for he will conquer the whole earth and defeat his enemies.*[20]

I felt something was clearly wrong when the epic begins with a remarkable murderous rite performed by King Janamejaya, the great-grandson of the valiant hero of the *Mahabharata*, Arjuna. He is holding a sacrifice to kill all the world's snakes in order to avenge his father, Parikshit, who has been killed by a snake.[21] Not a promising start for a heroic epic. The story is also wacky— it is about a war between the 'children of a blind pretender fighting the sons of a man too frail to risk the act of coition'.[22] The winner of the war is reluctant, pacific Yudhishthira, who does not want to fight but who, in fact, gives the order for the war to begin. Then he goes on to win the war, not by skill and excellence but by deception and trickery. After the bloody victory, he suffers inconsolably and bitterly, his mind in torment, consumed by guilt and shame for what has happened:

I have conquered this whole earth . . . But ever since finishing this tremendous extermination of my kinsmen, which was ultimately caused by my greed, a terrible pain aches in my heart without stopping . . . This victory looks more like defeat to me.[23]

The victory 'looks more like defeat' to Yudhishthira because he is left wondering what the ridiculous war has been all about. They try to calm his burning grief but not very convincingly. Yudhishthira has seen through the disturbing chaos of the world— too much envy, hypocrisy, greed, ego and revenge on one side, and too much deceit on the other and instigated by no less than Krishna, the God.[24] Yudhishthira's mournful regret at the war's end is the all-too-familiar sadness for the defective human condition. The *Mahabharata* is a profoundly ironic text with a 'very modern sense of the absurd'.[25]

Yudhishthira persists in his Faustian search for dharma until the end. He hopes to find goodness in heaven but he encounters the villainous Duryodhana instead. In hell, he finds his virtuous wife and his brothers rather than the wicked. The old look of incomprehension appears on his face, which reminded me of Sisyphus, the Greek hero, who was punished for betraying secrets of the gods to men, and who was condemned to push a huge rock up a hill. Each time he nears the peak, the stone rolls down to the bottom and Sisyphus must begin all over again. Yudhishthira has the same look on his face as Sisyphus when he sees the rock rolling back down. It is the realization that life may well be absurd and futile.

I had hoped that my search for dharma might help to lift me out of my own third stage melancholy. For thirty years I had gone to work each morning. I had fed and looked after my family. My wife and I had raised two children. Gradually, I had moved up the corporate hierarchy with higher pay and more responsibility. At fifty, I asked myself, what had I really achieved? What had all this been for? Is this all there was to life?

I had been tremendously competitive throughout my corporate life, but I could not reconcile to my boss's view, who felt 'it is not enough to do well. Someone has to lose, and you must be the one to win'. Duryodhana would have approved of my boss's big-chested sentiments, but I wondered, once one's youth, vigour and the thrill of winning are gone, what happens then? How long could an adult be expected to be motivated by a 0.5 per cent gain in the monthly market share of Vicks Vaporub or Pampers? I felt weary by the time I was fifty, and it was this feeling of futility that drove me, in part, to early retirement. My kshatriya-like craving to win was disappearing and my job had begun to resemble the futile labours of Yudhishthira. I identified with

Karna's sense of mortality in the *Mahabharata*, who says, 'I see it now: this world is swiftly passing.'[26]

Thoughts such as these—of life's futility, of one's mortality, and the relentless passage of time—tend to drive one to religion. Instead, they made me ask, like Iris Murdoch, if virtue is the main thing of worth in our life.[27] The familiar pain of being alive and being human made me admire Yudhishthira's commitment to dharma all the more—to *satya*, 'truth', *ahimsa*, 'non-violence' and *anrishamsya*, 'compassion'.[28] I wondered if acts of goodness might be one of the very few things of genuine worth in this world, and might give meaning to my life.

In my second year of study, I focused more and more on the *Mahabharata*. My other readings suffered but this book began to take shape. I realized that each major hero in the epic embodies a striking virtue or a failing—and the hero's story is an attempt to clarify this moral idea, whose significance goes well beyond the narrative to the very heart of dharma. Duryodhana has many flaws, but the driving one is envy, and in Chapter 1, I examine this destructive vice in our private and public lives. Arjuna's despair over killing his kinsmen is a celebrated protest against war in Chapter 4, and I raise the question if it is possible to have 'just' wars. Bhishma's selflessness in Chapter 5 made me wonder if it is possible for a human being to 'be intent on the act and not its fruits'; I asked myself if a person's ego could shrink that far—in other words, is *karma yoga* as hopelessly idealistic as Marx's notion of equality? Karna's anxiety over his social position in Chapter 6 trumps his finer qualities and made me think about the place of inequality and caste in human society. Ashwatthama's awful revenge in Chapter 8 set me thinking about forgiveness and retributive justice in our lives. Yudhishthira's remorse after the war in Chapter 9 made me examine the related ideas of grief, reconciliation and non-violence. And so on. As I pored over the narrative of each hero, I realized that my own understanding of dharma was growing deeper. To the sceptical reader, I might suggest dipping into Chapter 4 or 6 to get a quick idea about what I am doing in this book, although my favourites are Chapter 5 and 10.

∾

The *Mahabharata* is unique in engaging with the world of politics. India's philosophical traditions have tended to devalue the realm of human action, which is supposed to deal with the world of 'appearances', not of reality or of the eternal soul. Indeed, a central episode in the epic dramatizes the choice between moral purity and human action. King Yudhishthira feels guilty after the war for 'having killed those who ought not to be killed'. He feels trapped between the contradictory pulls of ruling a state and of being good, and wants to leave the world to become a non-violent ascetic. To avert a crisis of the throne, the dying Bhishma, his grandfather, tries to dissuade him, teaching him that the dharma of a political leader cannot be moral perfection. Politics is an arena of force. An upright statesman must learn to be prudent and follow a middle path. A king must wield *danda*, 'the rod of force', embodied in retributive justice in order to protect the innocent.[29]

The *Mahabharata* is suspicious of ideology. It rejects the idealistic, pacifist position of Yudhishthira as well as Duryodhana's amoral view. Its own position veers towards the pragmatic evolutionary principle of reciprocal altruism: adopt a friendly face to the world but do not allow yourself to be exploited. Turning the other cheek sends a wrong signal to cheats. With my background in Western philosophy, I was tempted to view the ideas of the epic, especially dharma, from a modern viewpoint. More than once I had to warn myself to beware of transposing contemporary ideas on to another historical context, but I am not sure I succeeded in this.[30]

I sometimes wonder why a pre-modern text like the *Mahabharata* ought to matter in our postmodern world. What sort of meaning does the past hold for us? What is the relationship between the original historical meaning of the text (assuming we can discover it) and its meaning to our present times? Take, for example, the game of dice. If the episode is merely an enactment of an ancient ritual then it obviously has limited moral significance. But the *Mahabharata* seeks other explanations, for example, in Yudhishthira's weakness for gambling, which suggests that the epic believes that the game does have moral meaning. The point is that we should not be guilty of reading too much 'into' the text, but try to read 'out' as much as we can for our lives. There may also be more than one meaning. I find myself sometimes using expressions such as: 'What is the epic telling us?' The fact is that the epic may be saying a multiplicity of things to different readers at different times in history. There is no one meaning. Hence, one should not expect too much coherence in it, especially when it comes to the ambiguous and even unsolvable nature of political power. The good news is that it is perfectly permissible to interrogate the text as I have done, and the *Mahabharata* would even applaud it.[31]

Of course, the *Mahabharata* is also a thrilling story. I wanted to share my excitement of the narrative—its simple and direct language comes through even in translation. As I pick up the thread of the story in each chapter, I quote extensively in order to give the reader a 'feel' for the text. I also follow the epic's example: I stop the action from time to time in order to examine more closely the moral idea that the action has thrown up, trying to understand how the idea relates to our daily lives in both a personal and a broader social and political sense. For the reader's convenience, I have provided a summary of the central story at the beginning of the book, as well as a dramatis personae and a tree of the Bharata family. I have also narrated the story of the historical evolution of the word dharma at the end of the book. The *Mahabharata* winds its way leisurely, with a steady aim, through masses of elaborate treatises on law, philosophy, religion, custom, even geography and cosmography, together with a formidable array of episodes and legends, piled up at various distances along its course.[32]

Interwoven with the main events of the narrative are fascinating subplots: the romance of Nala and Damayanti, written with such simplicity that I was able to read it in my first year Sanskrit class with Daniel Ingalls; the legend of Savitri, whose devotion to her dead husband persuades Yama, the god of death, to restore him to life; descriptions of places of pilgrimage; and many other myths and legends. Indeed, the *Mahabharata* is a virtual encyclopaedia of ancient India. It is an important source of information about the life of the times and the evolution of Hinduism and the influence of Buddhism.[33] Thus, it is said, 'the *Mahabharata* is not a text but a tradition'.

The clash of ideas is especially dramatic and noisy in India, a country where cultural memories are preserved with more loyalty and steadfastness than almost anywhere else. The centuries during which the epic took shape were a period of transition from the religion of Vedic sacrifice to the sectarian, internalized worship of later Hinduism, and different sections of the poem express varying and sometimes contradictory beliefs. Clashes in India do not lead to rejections or radical reversals but result in accretions and steady proliferation. This is the synthetic Indian way. The epic has been retold in written and oral vernacular versions throughout South and Southeast Asia and has always enjoyed immense popularity.[34] Its various incidents have been portrayed in Indian miniature paintings and in sculpted relief in temples across India and far away in Borobudur in Indonesia and Angkor Wat in Cambodia.

The entire *Mahabharata* is made up of almost 100,000 couplets— its length is seven times that of the *Iliad* and the *Odyssey* combined—divided into eighteen *parvans* or 'books'.[35] Its author is said to be the sage Vyasa (literally 'the compiler'), who appears as a character in the poem. More likely it was composed by a great number of bardic poets and revised by priests who added substantially to the ever-expanding text over a long period and was passed on for generations by oral tradition. Professional *suta*s, 'bards', were the original poets and singers when Brahminism had not separated its priest caste greatly from other Aryans. The brahmin redaction, which is all that now remains, took its present form between 200 BC and AD 200.'[36] Comparing over a hundred different versions from different parts of the country, Sanskrit scholars in the twentieth century published a Critical Edition of the epic under V.S. Sukthankar's leadership at the Bhandarkar Oriental Research Institute in Pune.[37]

Homer's *Iliad* and *Odyssey* have invited many acts of homage from translators in many languages. John Keats, the English poet, was so taken with an Elizabethan verse translation of 'deep-browed' Homer that he published a sonnet in its honour, entitled 'On First Looking into Chapman's Homer'. It had left him with a combined sense of shock and uplift, and he felt like:

some watcher of the skies
When a new planet swims into his ken.

The *Mahabharata* has not been so fortunate. It has had no Chapman, no Lattimore. The only full-scale English translation is by K.M. Ganguly from the late nineteenth century and it is 'grating and refractory'. The University of Chicago Press's project remains incomplete, although a fine translation of Books 11 and 12 by James Fitzgerald has appeared recently in a fourth volume. Ten volumes have appeared in the incomplete parallel text Clay Sanskrit Library edition (CSL), of which my favourites are the battle books, translated by Vaughan Pilikian (*Drona*), Adam Bowles (*Karna*) and Justin Meiland (*Shalya*).

The best starting point is John D. Smith's abridged translation in a single volume of Penguin Classics (2009). It is accurate, lucid, and often elegant. For a quick appetizer, however, I suggest a short English prose version either by R.K. Narayan or C.V.

Narasimhan, which capture the weft and warp of the story, although neither has the majestic music of the original as Pilikian's poetic translation of Drona's book (CSL) or W.J. Johnson's verse version of the tenth book, *Sauptikaparvan*.

∾

The *Mahabharata* is about our incomplete lives, about good people acting badly, about how difficult it is to be good in this world. It turned out to be a fine guide in my quest to make some sort of sense out of life at its third stage. I set out with the assumption that 'nature does not give a man virtue; the process of becoming a good man is an art'. I am not sure if the *Mahabharata* has taught me the art of which Seneca speaks. If anything it has probably made me more ambivalent. Even at the end, the Pandava heroes are still looking for dharma which is hidden in a cave.

Nevertheless, although human perfection may be illusory, dharma may be 'subtle', and there are limits to what moral education can achieve, the epic leaves one with the confidence that it is in our nature also to be good. This thought more than any other helped to assuage my 'third stage melancholy'. The *Mahabharata* believes that our lives should not have to be so cruel and humiliating. This explains its refrain, 'dharma leads to victory!' Although it is spoken with irony at times, the epic genuinely desires that our relationships be more honest and fair. What comes in the way is our tendency to deceive ourselves, rationalize our actions, and readily find fault in others while remaining blind to the same fault in ourselves. Since the epic is a narrative, the personal viewpoint dominates. But the story stops often enough when the impersonal viewpoint takes over. Goethe pointed out long ago that the impersonal viewpoint within us produces a desire for goodness, fairness and equality, while the personal one wishes the opposite, seeking only one's own gain, often at the expense of others.[38] This conflict between our divided selves underlies the dilemmas that are faced both by the epic's heroes and by us. Hence, it leaves us with an 'awareness of the possibilities of life'.[39]

My academic holiday turned out to be a much-needed corrective to my stereotypical view of the 'spirituality' of India in contrast to the 'rationality' of the West.[40] From the beginning, the West has sought for what was 'wondrous in the East' and it seemed to find it in India's religious and spiritual identity. This focus on the exotic neglected the 'deep-seated heterogeneity of Indian traditions'.[41] Indians, for their part, have been happy to embrace this self-image of 'spirituality' as a way to recover their self-esteem after long years of colonial history. It makes them feel superior to the 'materialistic' West. But they have paid a price. In their obsession with *moksha*, the 'spiritual' end, they sometimes lose sight these days of the three worldly goals—*dharma*, *artha*, and *kama*—which are needed to lead a more balanced life. These are the very pursuits that the *Mahabharata* commends to its listeners:

> *When this great incomparable tale, esteemed*
> *By dispassionate men of wide erudition,*
> *Is studied in detail, their spreading insight*
> *Into the three pursuits will conquer the earth.*[42]

1

DURYODHANA'S ENVY

*'What man of mettle will stand to see his
rivals prosper and himself decline?'*

*Why should one like you envy Yudhishthira? . . . Be content with what
you have, stay with your own dharma—that is the way to happiness.*

—Dhritarashtra to Duryodhana,
Mahabharata II.5.3, 6[1]

'I am scorched by envy'

The *Mahabharata* is set in and around Hastinapura, 'city of the
elephant', in the fertile region around modern-day Delhi. It is the
story of the rivalry between cousins, the Pandavas and the
Kauravas, who are descended from King Bharata. The Pandavas
are the five sons of the pale and sickly Pandu; the Kauravas are
the hundred sons of his blind brother, Dhritarashtra. The conflict
begins when Dhritarashtra, the elder of the two princes, is
passed over as king because of blindness. Pandu assumes power.
But Pandu has been cursed to die if he has sex. So, he turns to
niyoga—employing a surrogate to obtain an heir. In this way,
Pandu has five sons from his two wives—Yudhishthira, Bhima,
Arjuna, Nakula and Sahadeva. After a series of wars, he renounces
the throne to become a religious hermit—leaving blind
Dhritarashtra to rule the imperial city.

1

Soon there is rivalry over the succession. Prince Duryodhana, the eldest son of Dhritarashtra, disputes the right of the eldest Pandava, Yudhishthira, to take over the throne. Angry and vengeful, Duryodhana threatens, abuses, and attempts to assassinate the Pandavas, who are forced to flee the kingdom. During their exile the five brothers jointly marry Princess Draupadi and meet their cousin Krishna, who is God, and who becomes their friend and companion for life.

In the hope of stopping the conflict between the cousins, Dhritarashtra divides the kingdom, giving the barren half to the Pandavas. Despite their disadvantages, the accomplished Pandavas work hard, clear a forest to live in, and prosper. They rule justly and enhance their status through conquests and alliances, and they build a striking, grand capital called Indraprastha, which some archaeologists believe is buried under present-day Delhi. Soon they are widely acknowledged to have become the paramount power, and the Kauravas grow jealous again.

To commemorate his rise to imperial power, Yudhishthira performs *rajasuya*, the ancient ceremony of consecration. Dozens of rulers come laden with expensive gifts to acknowledge his imperial claim. Duryodhana comes as well to participate in his cousin's festivities. As a close relative, he has been assigned, ill-advisedly it turns out, the responsibility of overseeing the collection of tribute.

We join the action in Book Two of the *Mahabharata* as Prince Duryodhana is returning home from the grand and opulent ceremony, accompanied by his uncle, Shakuni Saubala. He is sulking as he remembers his humiliation when he fell into the pool in the amazing palace of the Pandavas.

> *He thought it was land and fell into the water with his clothes on . . . Mighty Bhimasena saw him that way, as did Arjuna and the twins, and they burst out laughing. A choleric man, he did not suffer their mockery; to save face he did not look at them.*[2]

'Scorched by envy' of his cousin Yudhishthira, Duryodhana is sunk in gloomy thought.[3] Seeing him thus, Shakuni asks, 'What is the reason that you travel with so many sighs?'[4] Duryodhana replies:

> *I saw the earth entire under Yudhishthira's sway, conquered by the majesty of the weapons of the great spirited Arjuna. I saw their grand sacrifice, Uncle . . . Rancour has filled me, and burning day and night I am drying up like a shrunken pond in the hot season.*[5]

The memory of 'those manifold riches which the kings heaped' upon Yudhishthira as they 'waited upon him like tax-paying commoners' makes him prey to envy.[6] He says:

> *For what man of mettle in this world will have patience when he sees his rivals prosper and himself decline? . . . When I see their fortune and that splendid hall and the mockery of the guards, I burn as if with fire.*[7]

Shakuni consoles him, saying that it is useless to brood over the good fortune of his cousins. They cannot be defeated in battle; they are far superior warriors, and have made important alliances which give them immense power. One needs clever means. Shakuni suggests a gambling match.

> *[Yudhishthira] loves to gamble but does not know how to play. If the lordly king is challenged he will not be able to resist. I am a shrewd gambler, and I don't have any match on earth . . . Challenge him to a game of dice . . . I will [play on your behalf and] defeat him.*[8]

Duryodhana likes the idea, and together they hatch a conspiracy. He asks his uncle to work on his father. Thus, a few days later king Dhritarashtra summons his son:

> *My son, what is the reason that you are so sorely aggrieved? Shakuni here tells me that you looked pale and yellow and wan and that you are brooding . . . You wear fine clothes, you eat [the*

*best of] meats, purebred horses carry you. [You have] costly beds
and charming women, well-appointed houses and all the recreation
you want ... Why do you pine, my son?*[9]

Duryodhana tells his father that these pleasures do not satisfy
him for he bears an awesome grudge against his more successful
cousin. 'Having seen the all-surpassing wealth of the Pandava, I
find no peace in my burning heart,' he says. Words come
cheaply to the blind king, and he counsels his son to abide by the
dharma of the kshatriya, behave and fight honourably, and not
pursue wealth.

*Do not hate the Pandavas! One who hates takes on as much grief
as in death. Why should one like you envy Yudhishthira, a simple
man who has the same goals as you, the same friends, and does not
hate you? Why do you, my son, a prince, his equal in birth and
prowess, covet your brother's fortune ... Be content with what
you have, stay with your own dharma—that way lies happiness.*[10]

Duryodhana counters his father with the big-chested ethic of the
warrior, which is to put down his enemies before they become
dangerous, and to win at any cost. That is the true dharma of the
kshatriya, he says.

*Low is the man, they say, who is incapable of indignation ...
Discontent is at the root of prosperity. That is why I want to be
dissatisfied. Only he who reaches for the heights, king, is the
ultimate politician. Should we not pursue selfish ways when we
have power or are rich?*[11]

Duryodhana, thus, makes a virtue of his envy, cloaking it in a
philosophy of egoism and the amoral pursuit of power:

*No one, lord of the people, is born anyone's enemy ... If one
watches in his folly the rise of his enemy's side, the other will cut
his root, like a swelling disease. An enemy, however tiny, whose
might grows on and [who eventually] destroys one, is like an*

*anthill [who] destroys the tree . . . As long as I fail to recover the
power from the Pandavas I shall be in danger.*[12]

Gradually he succeeds in persuading his father, who has always
had a weakness for his eldest son. The king summons his
counsellor and half-brother, Vidura, before whom he disguises
his decision as an act of fate. 'It is ordained,' he says, and
commands him to go and invite Yudhishthira for a 'friendly
game of dice'. Vidura is not taken in by this hypocritical talk. He
is hugely distressed, and leaves dejectedly on his mission.

Yudhishthira smells trouble as soon as he receives the invitation.
He knows that Shakuni cheats. But he cannot refuse his uncle,
who is like a father to him. He says:

> It sounds like the most dangerous dice players will be there, sure
> to resort to tricks and deceit . . . [But] I shall not refuse to play
> dice at Dhritarashtra's command; a son must respect his father . . .
> I shall not be able to refuse; that is my eternal vow.[13]

Besides, a game of dice is part of the ritual of imperial
consecration, required of the king in the Vedic *rajasuya* ceremony.
So, Yudhishthira agrees reluctantly, uneasy about the match.[14]

Indeed, the game of dice is a grand affair in a specially built
hall of a thousand pillars adorned by gems and filled with kings
and noblemen. Duryodhana announces that his uncle Shakuni
will play on his behalf. It is clear to Yudhishthira that the
'friendly game of dice' is, in fact, a duel, but he cannot refuse a
challenge and must stand by his word, even when the challenge
is dodgy.

They begin to play. Starting modestly with a handful of pearls,
the stakes rise quickly. Yudhishthira slowly slips into a gambler's
frenzy, blind to the consequences, forgetting himself. He hears
only the clatter of the rolling dice, followed by Shakuni's chant,
'Won!' and cheers from the Kauravas' side. He begins to lose,
and lose consistently. By the end of round ten, halfway through
the game, he has lost pearls, gold, his finely caparisoned chariot,

a thousand elephants, choice horses, male and female slaves, and an army of chariots and charioteers.

Vidura, standing beside King Dhritarashtra, sees disaster ahead. He tries to stop the game. Appealing to the blind king to give up his son's cause for the greater good of the kingdom, he argues:

> To save the family, abandon an individual. To save the village, abandon a family; to save the country, abandon a village. To save the soul, abandon the earth.[15]

But the hypocritical king is so delighted at seeing his son winning, he ignores his counsellor. Shakuni prods his rival to keep playing. Yudhishthira is spellbound, oblivious to the world around him. Besides, to pull out now would be dishonourable. Thus, the game enters a crucial stage. In the next four throws Yudhishthira loses all his wealth and his kingdom. Then he stakes his brothers one by one and loses them. Finally, he loses himself and becomes a slave of Duryodhana. Shakuni says:

> There is only your precious queen left, and there is also one throw of the dice remaining. Stake her and win yourself back with her.[16]

Yudhishthira agrees, saying 'I play you for her'. Feelings of revulsion and horror fill the assembly hall. The elders, in dismay, break into a sweat. Vidura buries his face in his hands. Only King Dhritarashtra is exhilarated. No one dares to stop the 'universal sovereign' from wagering his queen. Shakuni throws the dice and cries out joyfully, 'We have won!'

'A friendly game of dice'

'So much for a friendly game of dice!'[17] Although most of us do not go about trapping our neighbours in dice games, we do suffer universally from envy. I don't know anyone who is immune. Even as a child I remember envy used to make my world rotten. It has the terrible ability to wreak damage in public life as well, leaving everyone worse off. It was envy of the Jews which led, in part, to the Holocaust during World War II. In socialist societies, it is often behind extortionate tax rates. So, it is a good place to begin my dharma quest.

But before that I want to address a question that has been nagging at me—why did Yudhishthira agree to play this disastrous game, especially when he knew that Shakuni was a far better player and also cheated? It is not clear from the text if Shakuni cheated that day, but he had earlier confided in Duryodhana, 'I shall cheat him, my lord, win and seize his celestial fortune. Summon him!'[18]

Shakuni is confident that Yudhishthira will not refuse to play because he had taken an oath. The sage Vyasa, the narrator of the epic, had warned Yudhishthira during his royal consecration ceremony: 'At the end of thirteen years, bull of Bharatas, the entire race of kshatriyas will be wiped out and you will be the instrument of their destruction.'[19] As soon as he heard this, Yudhishthira grew depressed. He naively vowed not to say 'no', nor to refuse anything, hoping in this way to avoid conflict with others, and thus, to 'blunt the edge of fate'. It turned out, of course, to be a ruinous vow, for it gave Duryodhana and Shakuni the confidence to challenge him, knowing that he would not refuse.

A second explanation for his ruinous decision is that Yudhishthira knows that he is expected to play dice as a part of the ancient Vedic *rajasuya* ritual to consecrate him 'universal sovereign'.[20] The purpose of this ancient ritual was to re-create a social and cosmic order, heralding the 'birth' of the king.[21] The ritual game reproduces in miniature the model of the cosmos, allowing the players to fashion the cosmos in the right manner. The four sides of the dice also symbolize the four Ages. The king is the maker of the Age, and the ceremonial dice game played at his consecration, like the gambling of Shiva in mythology, determines what kind of cosmic age will come up next—a

Golden Age or the degraded Kali Age. The fate of the world, thus, hangs on this game of dice.[22] However, it is purely a ritual according to the manuals of the brahmins, and not this perversion that the epic dramatizes.

A third and simpler explanation is that Yudhishthira was addicted to gambling. Shakuni says that he 'loves to play but has little skill'.[23] In the next book of the epic, Yudhishthira will, indeed, confess to this weakness. And later, when the Pandavas are in disguise, he will play a gambling instructor to the king of Virata. Still, it is hard to believe that this most moral of human beings, incapable of telling a lie, cannot resist the sound of dice like the proverbial gambler of the Rig Veda: 'When I swear I will not play with them, I am left behind by my friends as they depart. But when the brown dice raise their voice as they are thrown down, I run at once to rendezvous with them, like a woman to her lover.'[24]

If Yudhishthira knew his weakness, why did he allow himself to get into a situation that could escalate into tragedy? Plato thought it was impossible for rational beings to do wrong knowingly.[25] But Aristotle disagreed, and he felt that Plato's view contradicted the observed facts about ordinary human beings. He believed that a person may have the knowledge but may not use it.[26] Indian thinkers seem to have shared Aristotle's practical view. They believed that 'people do, in fact, act against their moral convictions and this is an unhappy fact about ourselves'. [27]

Games have been used throughout history to understand human behaviour and even to help unravel moral dilemmas.[28] In this particular game everything seems to have gone wrong. The king was expected to preside over a ritual and not become a player in the gambling duel. It was in the wrong place—it should have been held in Yudhishthira's own assembly hall in the Pandavas' city of Indraprastha, not in the Kauravas' city of Hastinapura. According to the ritual, the king ought to have been ceremonially installed on a throne, after taking 'three Vishnu steps'. In the Vedic ceremony, the king takes a step 'in each of the five directions' to legitimize the physical battles over space that had been won by Arjuna, Bhima and the other Pandavas.[29]

What then is one to make of this dice game which was meant to create order but is destroying it? Is it a signal to the audience that the world of the *Mahabharata* has gone awry? It has become *vishama*, 'uneven', and even the god Krishna's attempts to 'even' it will only 'make it spiral downwards to destruction'.[30] Most of the characters in the epic hope that dharma will help to even it.

The loaded game of dice is a metaphor for the vulnerable human life in which death and *kala*, 'time', inevitably triumph. The *Mahabharata* keeps reminding us that *kala* is always 'cooking' us.[31] In an essay, David Shulman, the Sanskrit scholar, describes Yudhishthira's lonely and opaque situation by asking us to imagine if our world were 'impenetrably enigmatic; that blindness is far more than a metaphor for human perception ... Assume, too, that life is a dice game, governed by rules known to be deceptive, in which the least experienced, least adequate player is nevertheless pushed to the point of staking everything he has including, in the end, himself, with the certainty of losing ... Assume a world in which each of the players in this game must be seen to die in most cases violently and unfairly; in which, moreover, the poles of life and death are present in every move with the death pole always strangely privileged, cognitively and metaphysically, so that death is, in effect, the only possible outcome of the game. In such a world, one mostly fights for time.'[32]

The dice game foreshadows the apocalyptic war between the Pandavas and the Kauravas over a claim to the kingdom that is dubious on both sides. The 'least adequate player' is Yudhishthira—a good man, addicted to gambling. He does not want to fight the war, yet it is he who will give the order for the war to begin. He will win the war in the end, not only by skill and excellence, but by deception and trickery. After the victory, there will be no pleasure in ruling over an empty kingdom, as everyone will be dead.

Is this the epic's way of telling us that ours is an enigmatic, deficient and incompetent world where the ordinary human being does not know why he is born or when he will die, but only that he will? 'The *Mahabharata* sees a vice behind every virtue, a snake behind every horse, and a doomsday behind every victory, an uncompleted ritual behind every completed sacrifice.'[33]

Duryodhana's envy in this 'uneven world'

What makes for uncertainty in our lives is often our own frailties. The moral flaws of human beings make our world full of *vaishamya*, 'unevenness', and bring about the nasty surprises that make us vulnerable. Duryodhana is one of the chief causes of 'unevenness' in the *Mahabharata* and I felt that *my* education in dharma had to begin with him. He suffers from so many vices (pride, greed, anger, hatred, an excess of ego, etc.), but his most dangerous defect is envy—which is also the driving force of calamity in the *Mahabharata*.

Duryodhana realizes at his cousin's consecration that he feels inferior before the success of the Pandavas. 'What man of mettle will stand to see his rivals prosper and himself decline?' is his envious reaction to Yudhishthira's good fortune. It is his way of saying, 'Why not me?'—the age-old question of the envious person. Envy, of course, is 'inherent in the nature of man', according to Immanuel Kant.[34] Frankly, I have not met a single person who was free of envy, although some claimed to be. Put two human beings together and there will be envy. Envy is so pervasive, so natural, that one is often not aware of it. The universal human tendency to envy forces the *Mahabharata* towards a devastating conclusion. It believes that an envious person cannot be truthful. Such a person cannot be trusted for envy takes away some of an individual's liberty. And 'freedom is acquired by a good man, possessing the truth'.[35]

Envy involves an envier (Duryodhana), an envied or rival (Yudhishthira), and a possession (the Pandavas' talent for success). The possession can be an object (the throne) but it can also be a talent such as Arjuna's ability with the bow. In this case, Duryodhana's envy may have been incited by Yudhishthira's recent rise in wealth and power, but he is smart enough to know that his envy ultimately relates to the Pandavas' ability to acquire the possession. Hence, he does not merely want the throne but he also wants to destroy the Pandavas.

Duryodhana's envy makes him hate the Pandavas. That, too, one can understand, for 'hatred always accompanies envy'. Duryodhana thinks obsessively about the wealth and the power of the Pandavas. He grows anxious and mean-hearted, pale and sickly. He betrays another characteristic of envy. It is a colossal waste of mental energy and this is perhaps why writers across the ages have associated it with ill health. Horace, the Roman lyric poet, said that those who were inflicted by envy grew thin. Shakespeare's Cassius became 'lean and hungry'. Clearly, envy is a health hazard.

Duryodhana decides that he cannot be happy unless he can wreck the Pandavas' happiness. Schopenhauer, the German philosopher, captures this characteristic of envy in a devastating portrait:

Because they feel unhappy, [they] cannot bear the sight of someone they think is happy . . . in the boundless egotism of our nature there is joined more or less in every human breast a fund of hatred, anger, envy, rancour, and malice, accumulated like the venom in a serpent's tooth.[36]

The human tendency to evaluate one's well-being by comparing it with that of another is the cause of Duryodhana's distress.

Duryodhana is at least open about his envy, but his father's envy is hidden. It is so secretive, in fact, that the blind king himself is often not aware of it, let alone admit to it.[37] Dhritarashtra is a hypocrite—and hence, more dangerous. He has found clever ways of dealing with his envy so that the world will have a better opinion of him and, equally important, that he will retain a better opinion of himself. Even as he pretends to be virtuous, secretly he wants to see his son act out his own deepest desires.

Like Polonius in *Hamlet*, Dhritarashtra gives pious advice, counselling his son to be just and virtuous, but he is silently pleased with Duryodhana's plan to trap Yudhishthira in the dice game. 'It is the father who fails his son, and not the other way around.'[38] Dhritarashtra's envy slips out at unguarded moments. Bhima cannot forget the unrestrained rejoicing on the blind father's face as Yudhishthira keeps losing. At each throw of the dice, the hypocrite's mask falls. In the next chapter, he will 'generously' return his son's dishonest winnings (ostensibly as a boon to the virtuous Draupadi), but his real motive will be fear. He will be scared by evil omens.

Such hidden, hypocritical envy has often been considered more dangerous than Duryodhana's more open and honest feelings. The ancient Greeks realized that the very fact that one is successful and prosperous is a good reason for one to be envied. They thought man to be naturally envious—'envy being part of his basic character and disposition'.[39] So, they were open about it. Since envy could not be suppressed, the Greeks devised a way to deal with it by ostracizing successful people, especially popular politicians. Aristides the Just was shunned, according to Plutarch, because he was too good. 'I am fed up with hearing him being called too virtuous,' an Athenian is said to have remarked. They exiled their statesman Themistocles for living lavishly and putting on superior airs. Ostracism meant having to go away for ten years in order to give time for envy 'to cool off'. Socrates might have been put to death for the same reason—'envy for his great integrity and virtue'.[40]

The Greeks were not alone in driving out outstanding statesmen and generals. Winston Churchill, the popular wartime premier, was defeated in the 1945 elections. Many Conservatives interpreted his defeat as the result of envy and resentment, and a fear that he might acquire too much power or become too popular. De Gaulle suffered a similar fate in 1946.[41]

If the Greeks institutionalized how to deal with envy through ostracism, Indians coped with it by renouncing it. No one would be envious of worldly success if you renounce it, and hope for compensation in another world. Even before the Buddha, the 'Renouncer' had become a perennial hero in India. I have known a number of very successful Indians who worried constantly that things might be going *too* well. They feared that their good fortune would not last and soon there would be a reversal. For this reason, many parents in India place a small black dot on a child's face to ward off retaliation by the envious.

The Chinese, on the other hand, cope with envy by appearing to be excessively and hypocritically modest and seek to disparage their achievements. 'O sir, I am your mean and humble servant who just happened to hit upon this idea,' is not an uncommon refrain. If one sets too high a value on one's abilities, it makes one commit the social offence of regarding oneself as better than others. Thus, the well-known Chinese fear of 'losing face' is a ritualized attitude, in part, to avoid envy.[42]

'A kshatriya's duty is to prevail'

Duryodhana is not ashamed of his envy because it is part of a larger and consistent egoistic philosophical outlook. When he is feeling low, filled with hatred for the Pandavas, his father Dhritarashtra tries to comfort him, counselling him not to covet what belongs to Yudhishthira:

Envy of another is ignoble behaviour. Be content with what you have. Perform your own duty—therein lies happiness.[43]

Duryodhana disagrees. He replies that his duty is to win at all costs. A smart person pursues power and uses it to exact as much as possible from the weak. If he does not do that he leaves himself vulnerable to attack from an enemy:

> *A kshatriya's duty is to prevail, great king. Whether by virtuous means or not ... O bull among Bharatas, he should go out like a charioteer and whip every corner of the earth into submission.*[44]

Accordingly, he is not embarrassed about feeling envious because it is a form of discontent that will lead to ambition:

> *Discontent is the root of success; this is why I desire it. Only the person who reaches for the heights, noble lord, becomes the ultimate leader.*[45]

His envy goads him to act against his rivals, the Pandavas. No means are too foul for he has to win at any cost. He tries poisoning them, drowning them, and burning them alive; he lets serpents loose upon them. Trapping Yudhishthira in a game is merely the latest in a string of actions to wipe out his enemies. In Bhasa's classical play, *Dutavakya*, whose hero happens to be Duryodhana, he tells Krishna the same thing about what is necessary to gain power:

> *Kingship is enjoyed by brave princes after conquering their foes in battle. It cannot be had by begging, nor is it conferred upon the poor in this world. If they desire to become kings, let them venture forth on the battlefield, or else let them at their will enter a hermitage, sought for peace by men of tranquil minds.*[46]

Like Thrasymachus in Plato's *Republic*, Duryodhana sees morality as a veiled way to protect the interests of the powerful.[47] As he sees it, what people call 'dharma' is really a clever way of advancing those interests.

Duryodhana's view of the world is by no means unique. Conquerors and rulers throughout history have espoused it. It is called 'realism' or *'realpolitik'* by students of international politics. In India, its chief advocate was Kautilya, who wrote the classic treatise *Arthashastra*. In the West, this viewpoint was made famous by Thomas Hobbes, the English philosopher, who argued that if men do not conquer when they can, they only reveal weakness and invite attack. 'By a necessity of nature' (a phrase Hobbes made popular) they conquer when they can. Hobbes translated Thucydides's classic history of the Peloponnesian War, which is the foundation stone of 'Realist' thinking about international relations. In it, Athenian generals who were about to conquer Melos, a Spartan colony, said much the same to the people of Melos in 416 BC: 'They who have the odds of power exact as much as they can, and the weak yield to such conditions as they can get . . . [men] will everywhere reign over those such as they be too strong for . . .'[48]

The *Mahabharata* is clearly embarrassed by Duryodhana's *matsya nyaya*, 'big-fish-eats-small-fish' view of the world, which is the Indian equivalent of the law of the jungle, a metaphor for the vicious, violent aspects of human nature. Later when Arjuna will urge Yudhishthira not to renounce the throne, he will remind him that violence is the way of the world: 'I see no being which lives in the world without violence. Creatures exist at one another's expense; the strong eat the weak. The mongoose eats mice, as the cat eats the mongoose; the dog devours the cat, your majesty, and wild beasts eat the dog.'[49] Bhishma, their grandfather, will employ this anarchic image of disorder in the natural world in order to justify *danda*, 'retributive justice' and the rule of law and order, by a tough but just king.[50]

Other characters in the *Mahabharata* will contest Duryodhana's egoistic philosophy. Yudhishthira, in particular, will offer a competing view of the world, based on dharma, which he explains is a universal duty of righteousness, applicable to all and founded on non-violence, truth and a concern for others. So too will Vidura, whose moral thinking is based on the consequences of actions rather than duty. He reminds us on a number of occasions that there were evil portents when Duryodhana was born:

Wicked Duryodhana, killer of Bharata's line,
Shrieked, they say, the jackal's chilling scream,
The moment he was born. It is he who will cause
The destruction of you all![51]

If a kshatriya soldier's duty is to prevail at any cost, and if the prize is kingship, then the game of dice is not an unreasonable strategy. Duryodhana, however, does have a reasonable claim to the Hastinapura throne. Recall that there were two lines of succession. His father was the older son, but was born blind. Hence, the throne went to Pandu, his half-brother, who was the son of the second wife. His eldest son, Yudhishthira, was born a few minutes before Duryodhana, and this is at the heart of the Pandavas' legal claim to the kingdom. Since Pandu could not have sex, Yudhishthira was born from a god, who acted as proxy to give Kunti a son. On the other hand, Duryodhana was born naturally to Dhritarashtra and not by proxy. Hence, Duryodhana's claim to the kingdom might be stronger. In any case, this is academic. After Dhritarashtra divided the kingdom between the Kauravas and the Pandavas, Duryodhana's claim to the original, undivided kingdom disappeared.

Duryodhana might still argue that Yudhishthira was addicted to gambling—so, he was merely taking advantage of a weakness in the character of his adversary, who clearly made a bad decision to play. But Yudhishthira could easily counter, saying that he was innocently following an ancient Vedic *rajasuya* sacrifice, as a part of his consecration ceremony.[52] He was duped into playing against a cheat. Although Shakuni does admit that he cheats, Duryodhana could retort that there was no hard evidence of cheating on that day—Yudhishthira just happened to be playing against a better player. It is always tempting to see human beings as 'good' and 'bad', but this is not the *Mahabharata*'s way.[53] It never makes the choice easy.

Once the war begins, Duryodhana will grow as a character. He will prove himself to be a highly skilled commander and will rise in our esteem. He is brave and he possesses *shri*—an indispensable quality in a great, charismatic ruler. His flaw is his unwillingness to accept Krishna's divinity, at least according to the Vaishnav reading of the text;[54] he stands up to God, and asserts man's priority in the greater scheme of things.

In the end, there is something heroic about him as he lies dying on the battlefield. He evokes admiration as he defiantly recounts Krishna's wrongdoings. He proclaims that if the Pandavas had fought honestly, not deceitfully, he would have won. Unrepentant, and without self-pity, he declares:

> *Whose end is more admirable than mine? Who else could bring his life to a close with such nobility? I shall dwell in heaven with my brothers and friends. You will spend your days in despair, in sorrow.*[55]

Eternal sickness or healthy competitiveness?

The sort of envy evinced by Duryodhana was not unfamiliar to me when I was growing up in Simla. My mother had a great and unfulfilled desire to be a part of Simla's fashionable society. She envied those who belonged to 'the club', the glamorous Amateur Dramatic Club. She must have transmitted this to me, for I grew up with an acute concern over my position in society, comparing myself to those who had things that I did not possess, boys who were more attractive to girls than I was, and especially those who made it to the school cricket team.

My father, however, had a sunnier temperament, and he saw a positive side to envy. It fostered a healthy competitive spirit, a desire to better oneself. He pointed out the example of a daughter of a poor relative of ours. She had always been discriminated against by her family, who preferred and pampered her brother. Envy drove her to work hard at studies and aspire to a better life. She succeeded. She sat for a competitive exam, got into the coveted Indian Administrative Service, and went on to become a powerful civil servant. Her spoiled brother grew into a mediocrity. Drona, the archery teacher of the Kauravas and Pandavas, I recalled, had also exploited envy between the cousins to raise the level of their overall performance.

It is thus possible for the envier to want something but without wishing the envied to lose it at the same time. This positive sort of envy that my father alluded to leads to ambition, to want to emulate the successful, but without the malicious desire to deprive the rival of the possession. This is called 'benign' or 'emulative' envy and it is the one on display when one says to a friend, 'I envy you for such and such skill.' One obviously does not want to deprive the friend of the talent or the skill. Nor is one filled with pain in the case of benign envy.

While all this may be true, the *Mahabharata* would have thought this a marginal aspect of envy, probably deserving of a different name. The epic would have considered my father naïve. The epic says: 'The man who envies other people for their conduct, beauty, courage, family lineage, happiness, success and favour has an eternal sickness.'[56] To prove the point Duryodhana does grow physically sick after witnessing the enormous success of his cousins. So did my mother. She grew weak and was acutely depressed for several weeks. The doctor could not make anything of it. One day I overheard her tell my aunt that she thought that the cause of her depression was our attractive and sophisticated neighbour, who was also popular in Simla's 'high society'. She was an accomplished woman and each success of hers seemed to affect my mother in a negative way. Gore Vidal, I think, expressed my mother's emotion in a more brutal way: 'Whenever a friend succeeds a little,' he wrote, 'something in me dies.'[57]

John Rawls, my teacher at Harvard, would have characterized

my mother's sentiment as 'general envy' of Simla's high society. General envy, he explains, does not have a particular person as its object, and is experienced by the less advantaged for those better situated.[58] Duryodhana's 'special envy', on the other hand, is specific to the Pandavas. It covets the specific things that the other person possesses. Occasionally, general envy can become specific as my mother's did when it became concentrated on our neighbour.

When I grew up and entered the business world I encountered both the healthy envy (that my father spoke about) and the negative and destructive faces of envy. As a young manager, I felt envious of my rivals and it spurred me to improve, but on occasion, it threatened to get out of control too. Many of my customers were petty wholesalers of the merchant caste, who were objects of deep envy in the small towns of India. During my travels, I found that people were quite happy to borrow from them, but they scorned and abused them behind their back and never mixed with them socially. The Bania trader has always been more prosperous than the locals and was envied for his wealth in many parts of Asia and Africa. This envy occasionally turns violent, as it did in Idi Amin Dada's Uganda when thousands of Indian families were expelled in 1972.

The envy I encountered in the business world, however, was nothing compared to what I would see later in the academic world. 'The reason academic politics are so bitter is that so little is at stake,' Henry Kissinger was fond of saying.[59] There is a certain misery attached to the academic life, no doubt, in which envy plays a considerable part. As Max Weber noted, 'Do you think that, year after year, you will be able to stand to see one mediocrity after another promoted over you, and still not become embittered and dejected? Of course, the answer is always: "Naturally, I live only for my calling." Only in a very few cases have I found [young academics] able to undergo it without suffering spiritual damage.'[60]

The Jews have been victim to a general envy by the unsuccessful for the successful. Forced out of their homeland 2,000 years ago by Roman oppression, they spread across Europe and prospered spectacularly in many places, including Vienna and Berlin, till Hitler took over. Joseph Epstein tells us that in the 'Vienna of 1936, a city that was 90 per cent Catholic and 9 per cent Jewish, Jews accounted for 60 per cent of the city's lawyers, more than half its physicians, more than 90 per cent of its advertising executives, and 123 of its 174 newspaper editors. And this is not to mention the prominent places Jews held in banking, retailing, and intellectual and artistic life. The numbers four or five years earlier for Berlin are said to have been roughly similar.'[61]

Is it surprising that Nazism had its greatest resonance in these two cities? Before killing the Jews, Germans and Austrians felt the need to humiliate their victims: 'They had Jewish women cleaning floors, had Jewish physicians scrubbing the cobblestone streets of Vienna with toothbrushes as Nazi youth urinated on them and forced elderly Jews to do hundreds of deep knee bends until they fainted or sometimes died. All this suggests a vicious evening of the score that has the ugly imprint of envy on the loose. The Jews in Germany and Austria had succeeded not only beyond their numbers but also, in the eyes of the envious, beyond their right—and now they would be made to pay for it. Envy was being acted out, as never before.'[62] It led to the murder of six million Jews in the Second World War.

Today, I find envy laced through the statements of European and Indian intellectuals about America. Arundhati Roy's essay after the 11 September 2001 terrorist attack on the World Trade Center in New York and the Pentagon in Washington is an example. Like many anti-American intellectuals writing in the days after the attack, Roy claimed that it was the direct result of American foreign policy—the implication being that America somehow deserved what had happened. There is widespread anti-American sentiment in the world which regards the United States as arrogant, indifferent to human suffering, consumerist, and contemptuous of international law. Much of this is probably correct, but I find that some of it is inspired by envy of America's success.

What begins initially as envy of America slowly turns into a visceral hatred of the 'American Empire'. As a result of this India almost lost the Indo–US nuclear deal in 2008 and a historic opportunity to climb to world power status because of the intransigence of Leftist parties in the Parliament. Most Indians found it inexplicable that the Left could quibble over a treaty that was so obviously in their nation's self-interest. There is much to criticize about America's behaviour, but it should not come at one's own expense.

Envy of America, and anti-Americanism in general, often gets transferred to global institutions like the World Bank that are seen to be under American control. It came as a shock to me that the city of Delhi is endowed with more water than most cities. Delhi has 300 litres per person per day of treated water available compared to Paris with 150 or London with 171. Yet people in Paris and London get water twenty-four hours a day while Delhi's residents get it only for four hours on the average. The poor in Delhi (and our other cities) have to depend on water tankers, and when the tanker is late there is a scramble and even a riot. Recently, a tanker driver was late. Fearing for his life, he took off at high speed and crushed a child in the chaos.

Delhi's government, to its credit, decided to fix the problem in 2004. It enlisted the service of World Bank experts, who had solved similar problems in other countries. They came up with a plan to professionalize the water board and insulate it from politicians who were mostly responsible for the distribution problems. When the Left-leaning NGO Parivartan discovered that Delhi was about to take a World Bank loan and change its management, it mounted a huge and successful campaign in the media, claiming falsely 'privatization' and 'sell out to the World Bank'. I discovered later that Parivartan had been profoundly influenced by the employees of the water authority, who were afraid that better-performing employees might advance more rapidly in a professional system of management. It was thus envy of poor performers for high performers combined with an anti-Americanism (that was subconsciously rooted) that killed Delhi's water reforms. Sadly, Sheila Dikshit, the chief minister of Delhi, got scared by the 'fear' campaign unleased by the press, and dropped the excellent World Bank plan. With this died the prospect of water for twenty-four hours a day in Delhi.

An Indian morality play

In 2007, Anil Ambani was the fifth richest person in the world according to the Forbes list of billionaires, but he was consumed with a Duryodhana-like envy for his more accomplished older brother, Mukesh, who was placed a notch higher on the list. Each brother had his Shakuni, who was happy to rig a game of dice in order to win the prize and destroy the other brother. Sibling rivalry inside India's wealthiest family had been the longest-running soap opera in the country, having mesmerized millions for the past four years. It mattered to the nation because enterprises of the two brothers accounted for 3 per cent of India's GDP, 10 per cent of government tax revenues and 14 per cent of India's exports. Millions of shareholders worried if their epic fight might lay waste their lifelong savings. I saw in this corporate and family feud a morality play and I wondered if the *Mahabharata* could shed some light.

The first scene of the play opens in Mumbai's Kabutarkhana in 1964. The Ambani children are growing up in a single room in a fifth floor walk-up 'chawl' along with six members of their family. Their father, Dhirubhai Ambani, has just set himself up as a trader in synthetic yarn in the Pydhonie market. The son of a modest schoolteacher from a village near Porbandar in Gujarat (not far from where Mahatma Gandhi was born), Dhirubhai has returned from Aden with Rs 15,000 in capital.[63] He discovers that the demand for nylon and polyester fabrics is monumental whereas supply is scarce because of rigid government controls on production and imports. This is due to India's socialist, command economy, created by Jawaharlal Nehru. Businesses have to contend with dozens of controls, which Indians wryly call 'Licence Raj'.[64] Dhirubhai takes great risks and soon corners government licences in the black market, and begins to make large monopoly profits. His competitors cry 'foul'; his critics call him 'corrupt'. He understands what Leftist politicians do not— polyester is destined to become a fabric for the poor whereas they tax and control it as though it was a luxury of the rich. Hence, the mismatch between demand and supply and a black market.

Act Two: Dhirubhai ploughs his profits from trading into a technologically advanced factory to make synthetic textiles, which is up and running in record time thanks to his proximity to Prime Minister Indira Gandhi's secretary. The village boy soon becomes a master gamesman of the Licence Raj, manipulating a decaying and corrupt regime of controls to his advantage. He integrates backwards to create an outstanding petrochemicals company, which first makes the raw material for the textiles— polyester fibre—and then basic polymers and chemicals, until he reaches the magic raw material, petroleum.

By now his sons are grown up. They are back from business school in America and have plunged into his company, Reliance, which is growing at a scorching pace. Opponents predict its fall after the economic reforms in the 1990s, but Reliance continues to expand and soon it becomes India's largest company. It builds the world's largest oil refinery in the shortest time, thanks to the project management skills of Mukesh. Next, the company begins to explore for oil and gas. As luck would have it, Reliance makes the biggest petroleum find in the world in a decade—a mountain of gas off the shore of Andhra Pradesh. It is monumental and holds the promise of easing the import burden of a fast growing, energy-starved nation. From the 'prince of polyester' Dhirubhai has become the undisputed king of industrial India.[65]

Act Three opens in 2002 when the 'king' is dead. Three and a half million middle class shareholders (the largest in any enterprise in the world), who have become rich beyond their dreams, mourn his death. He leaves behind two highly accomplished sons, and power passes to the older, more sober Mukesh. The younger, flamboyant Anil marries a film star, Tina Munim. He loves glamour and cultivates powerful politicians, and this does not go down well with the serious, older brother. Mukesh tries to marginalize his brother, but Anil retaliates. Filled with monumental envy for 'the new king', he launches an attack on his brother. In the fight, governance failures are revealed for the first time (about the family's shareholding and the ownership structure of their new telecom venture). The stock plunges and the country watches in fear the unfolding of an awesome tragedy. Finally, their mother—an anguished, Kunti-like figure caught in the middle—intervenes and splits the kingdom as Dhritarashtra did in the *Mahabharata*. Three years later, both sons have prospered beyond their dreams and the value of the empire of each brother is more than double that of the undivided kingdom.

The Ambani saga raises troubling moral questions. It is a classic rags-to-riches story—the ascent of a simple village boy, who against all odds creates a world class, globally competitive enterprise that brings enormous prosperity to millions. But it is also a tale of deceit, bribery and the manipulation of a decaying and corrupt 'Licence Raj'. Ambani's defenders argue that since his enterprises brought so much good to society, what was the harm if he manipulated an evil system and bribed politicians and bureaucrats? The government itself realized its problems and has been dismantling the system since 1991. But Ambani's opponents counter, saying that it is never justified to break a law. Ends cannot justify the means. Others believe that the uncertain business world is full of danger and surprise, and a certain amount of deception is necessary for business success.

Anil's envy of Mukesh is as dangerous as Duryodhana's. He cannot bear the fact that his brother has far more power and fame than he does. He burns inside each time the media extols Mukesh's awesome managerial skills. Had the mother not intervened, the rivalry might have hurtled uncontrollably towards a Kurukshetra-like war, which might have destroyed the whole enterprise, and with it the lives of millions of people. The drama is by no means over. In 2009, Mukesh had moved up to the third richest person in the world while Anil had slid to number seven. There continued to be a huge amount of bad blood and dozens of court cases were pending between the two brothers. Mukesh too had a Duryodhana in him—he had denied his brother his fair share of the kingdom until the mother had to intervene.

Nevertheless, my father's view about the positive and competitive side of envy had also been vindicated. Envy had driven Anil to perform to great heights, and the value of the enterprises of each brother was far greater than if they had remained united. Dharma draws a fine line between the positive and negative sides of competition, and it is easily crossed as we have seen recently in the global financial crisis in 2008. Competition did put great pressure on investment bankers, rating agencies and other players to bend the rules of decent conduct in the market for US housing mortgages. But when they justified their acts as rational behaviour based on the healthy competition, they slipped into the arena of self-deception. To meet the relentless demand of the bottom line and the incentive of a huge but unseemly bonus, many senior executives compromised their character.

'Nobody shall be the favourite'

Envy also supplies the psychological foundations for our quest for justice, especially for equality.[66] And this too can take both good and bad forms. Freud wrote that our desire for justice is the product of childhood envy of other children, which makes one hunger for equal treatment and brings about a 'group spirit'. He adds, 'If one cannot be the favourite oneself, at all events nobody else shall be the favorite.'[67] The *Mahabharata* is aware of these psychological roots of human motivation. In it, Drona, the martial teacher, is as accomplished as he is insensitive, and makes the mistake of treating the brilliant Arjuna differently from the others. Duryodhana reacts predictably to the incipient teacher's pet. Since he cannot tolerate the lavish praise constantly heaped on his cousin, he does whatever he can to bring Arjuna down to his level.

Envy is thus a leveller, and it levels downwards. Instead of motivating one to better performance, as my father thought it could, envy prefers to see the other person fall. The envious person is willing to see both sides lose. 'Envy is collectively disadvantageous; the individual who envies another is prepared to do things that make them both worse off, if only the discrepancy between them is sufficiently reduced,' says John Rawls.[68] This is precisely what I experienced when I worked in Bombay in the 1980s. The factory next to ours, belonging to the Dutch electronics company Phillips, suffered from a debilitating strike that lasted almost a year. I worried—I did not want their militant union to contaminate ours—because their trade union leader had the same psychological make-up as Duryodhana's. He was overheard saying, 'I don't care if we sink this factory with our strike as long as the Dutch manager goes down with us.' The statement sent a shiver down my spine.

When this sort of attitude gets institutionalized and forms the mental make-up of a militant trade union movement, the result could be de-industrialization. This is what happened in West Bengal and Kerala after these two Indian states came under communist rule. The communist cadres preferred to sink the economy of the state rather than compromise with the capitalists. As a result, company after company left Bengal for other parts of India, and both states stopped receiving new investment. Even today, the memory of that militancy survives, and it is difficult for these two states to attract industry.

To avoid this sort of calamitous result, John Rawls argues that a just and sensible society ought to do something in order 'to mitigate if not prevent' the conditions that bring about envy. Since modern democracies cannot adopt the sensible Greek solution of exiling its successful citizens, they take the sting out of capitalist inequality by taxing the rich at a progressive rate. Universal and high quality education and health care can also help to create more equality of opportunity, and help to reduce envy. Rawls makes the excellent point that 'plurality of voluntary associations (churches, clubs, unions and other groupings) in a well-ordered society, each with its own secure internal life, tends to reduce the visibility, or at least the painful visibility, of variations in men's prospects'.[69] Alexis de Tocqueville, the French aristocrat who visited America in the 1830s, noted that there was greater envy in democratic, egalitarian America compared to feudal Europe but the American disposition to form associations was a 'safety valve'.

In a well-ordered society, one cannot merely dismiss envy as a human frailty. One ought to design institutions that help to diminish it, or, alternatively, face its consequences, as the French did in 1789 or as the Kauravas and the Pandavas did on the battlefield at Kurukshetra. Nietzsche thought the French Revolution was fired by the sentiment of envy of the masses against the classes. Sometimes resentment over social inequality is so great that it wounds one's self-respect.[70] Such envy is understandable, especially when it is exacerbated by ostentatious display by the well-off. It tends to demean the situation of those who have less. Although it is a psychological state, social institutions can and ought to mitigate such envy.

If the advantages of the better-off are a return for their contribution to improving the situation of the worst-off—this is Rawls's solution—the inequality will be perceived as just, and there will be fewer reasons to feel envious. If the lowest worker believes that his salary will grow significantly if his company performs well, then he will not resent an outstanding CEO who earns fifty times more than he does. Rawls believes that inequalities can be justified because the basis for inequality could be agreed to in a hypothetical situation by similarly placed rational human beings who are ignorant of their eventual place in society. The only caveat he places is that these rational human beings do not suffer from an excess of envy.[71]

I have always believed that it is none of my business how much Mukesh and Anil Ambani earn and how the brothers spend their money as long as they create vast numbers of new jobs and pay their taxes. I believe that in a poor country like India it is more important to remove poverty than to worry about inequality. However, this belief was shaken in a conversation I had with an employee of the scandal-ridden Satyam, a company that I alluded to in the Prelude. She said that she and many of her colleagues at Satyam continued to support B. Ramalinga Raju, the disgraced founder of their company, even after his fraud was exposed. It was only after she discovered that the IT czar owned a thousand designer suits, 321 pairs of shoes and 310 belts that she turned against him. 'When I was burning the midnight oil, he was buying belts!' she raged. So, inequality does matter, and the public anger at the 'obscene' salaries and bonuses on Wall Street was justified in 2008 when the world economy went into a recession.

If greed is the sin of capitalism, envy is the vice of socialism

The *Mahabharata* is just as interested as the nineteenth century Utopians in the best way to order society. Seeing Duryodhana's envy run amok, it will pose the question if there is another way to live. When he is in exile, Yudhishthira, through his example, will offer an alternative life of harmony and non-violence in contrast to Duryodhana's life of brutal competition, which many think was responsible for bringing the global economy to its knees in 2008. The earlier socialist dream was a reaction to the cruel excesses of the industrial revolutions in the West, and it envisioned a future of harmony rather than a life of excessive competition, exemplified most recently by Wall Street's investment bankers.

Capitalist greed gives one the permission to grow rich beyond one's dreams. Socialism seeks a society of equality. But Marxists seek this equality by 'soaking the rich'. In a perpetual class struggle, they wish to bring down the aristocracy, the rentier class and the bourgeoisie. In this there is more than a hint of the general envy of the poor for the rich. Leftists regard income inequality as a psychic wound that is uniquely worthy of state intervention. Lord Layard goes to the extent of saying that those who work too hard and excessive hours may improve their own income, but they create a problem for the others, who feel dissatisfied. The rat race forces people to spend less time with their families and in community activities, and reduces the overall contentment of the community. Hence, he makes a bizarre suggestion—tax those who work too hard. This will, he feels, tame the rat race, reduce envy, and improve overall human happiness.[72]

By creating more equality socialism was supposed to eliminate human envy. But the opposite happened. Oddly enough, as levelling increases in society, it actually increases envy.[73] The Soviet Union was pervaded with envy because tiny differences, such as a new tablecloth, got exaggerated in neighbours' eyes. If greed is the vice of capitalism, envy is the flaw of socialism. 'From each according to ability and to each according to his need' was the rallying cry of Marxism as it set out to create a classless, egalitarian society. Socialist societies, however, turned out to be the most envious in history. 'The searing heartburn of envy causes a choking feeling in the throat, squeezes the eyes out of their sockets,' says a character in Y. Olesha's 1929 novella set in the Soviet Union, where turning in your neighbour for his perceived advantage became a way of life.[74] Envy is felt more strongly between near equals than those widely separated in fortune. It does not make sense to envy the Queen of England.

As a libertarian, I have deep misgivings about the attempts of the state to create excessive equality. Envy will rise as the number of differences among people diminish; the fewer differences will result in fewer standards to measure one against, and since most will not measure up, there will be greater envy. I would opt for a more diverse society where more people will be good at something. I fear, like Immanuel Kant, in artificially enforcing excessive equality. Kant felt that 'inequality among men is a rich source of much that is evil, but also of everything that is good'. He believed that inequality among social classes is an impetus to liberty because it makes people strive to better themselves.

To be fair to my leftist egalitarian friends, I will concede that what drives many of them is not envy but resentment, a different moral idea. Many socialists do not suffer from envy for the better-off but they resent the inherently unjust distribution of income and power in our social arrangements. What upsets them is the unequal arrangements rather than those who are better off. Resentment, in this sense, is a rational and impersonal moral emotion, which can also drive one to change the world for the better.

Socialism in its various forms has often appealed to persons in comfortable circumstances, who suffer from guilt—that they are the cause of envy among the less advantaged.[75] Some of them believe that the aim of equality is to compensate people for undeserved bad luck—being born with poor native endowments, bad parents, disagreeable personalities, accidents and illness, and so on.[76] Hence, they look to the state as a great insurance company, which takes from people who have benefited from cosmic good luck to compensate those with bad luck.

Clearly, envy is related to inequality and societies have dealt with it in various ways. The ancient Greeks, who believed in 'moral luck', ostracized those who had too much of it; the Chinese act self-deprecatingly in order to reduce envy and thus 'save face'; Indians preach renunciation and hope for compensation in another world. In modern democracies, the Left's solution against envy is to have an extensive welfare state, and thereby diminish inequality. The Right is suspicious of egalitarianism because the impulse for equality usually curbs liberty. However, neither the Left nor the Right would quarrel with the goal of a just society in which inequalities are perceived to be fair and deserved and hence cause less envy.

Can dharma make us less vulnerable?

During my 'academic holiday' in Chicago, Martha Nussbaum, the philosopher, introduced me to a poem about envy by the Greek poet Pindar, which speaks about 'the way lies can make the world rotten'.[77] Pindar compares human beings to a vulnerable vine. The excellence of a young person is also vulnerable, like a plant that is constantly in need of nourishment and protection. Nussbaum asks if human reason might save a person from the vagaries of luck, human envy and other unexpected reverses in life. The answer of the ancient Greeks was, of course, 'yes'.

In the same vein, I wondered if dharma might play the same role in the *Mahabharata* as reason does among the ancient Greeks. Can a life lived according to dharma diminish the vulnerability of human beings to the 'unevenness' of the world engendered by Duryodhana's envy, for example? Yudhishthira hopes so, particularly as life has a way of presenting itself to him in the form of an enigmatic game of dice, 'governed by rules known to be deceptive, in which the least experienced, least adequate player is nevertheless pushed to the point of staking everything he has including, in the end, himself, with the certainty of losing'.[78] The look of shocked incomprehension on his face is a silent cry, wanting to know why tragedy has befallen him at the moment of his greatest triumph when he had been consecrated 'universal sovereign'. It is not unreasonable for him to look to dharma to insulate him from reverses and help him to navigate through the many crises of governance that will be fed by Duryodhana's *adharma*.

Dharma is easiest to spot by its absence: the *Mahabharata* employs the pedagogical technique of teaching about dharma via its opposite, *adharma*. Duryodhana's envy is *adharma*. Yet, it is a natural and universal emotion, common to all human beings. It is all-pervasive and hence the proverb: 'If envy were a fever the whole world would be ill'. It is also fearsome. When a person is unable to tolerate the good fortune of others, and when she cannot have what they do, she prefers to spoil it for everyone. This ability to make everyone worse off means that not only ordinary human beings but also rulers must take envy seriously, and not dismiss it merely as human frailty. We ought to be concerned about its terrible ability to damage both our personal and our public life. The *Mahabharata* does not think envy is a sin. It is just 'poor mental hygiene'.[79] It makes Duryodhana pale and sickly and shrivels his heart. It gives him a very low opinion of himself until Shakuni rescues him with the idea of trapping his rival in a dice game.

For one who goes through life rigging dice games, Duryodhana turns out to have a positive side. He grows on us. His integrity lies, oddly enough, in his adherence to principle. One may not agree with his egoistic philosophy, but he is consistent, unlike his hypocritical and cowardly father. There is something heroically Faustian in the way he stands up to Krishna, the God. As he lies dying on the battlefield, he elicits our grudging admiration.

Duryodhana's character points to an attractive feature of the *Mahabharata*, which refuses to slot people into rigid compartments. It is more relaxed in its boundaries, not judging human beings as inherently good or bad. Nor is it morally conservative, unlike Christian texts with their 'horror of sensuality' and their belief in a radically corrupt human nature that is a victim of 'original sin'.

2

DRAUPADI'S COURAGE

'Whom did you lose first, yourself or me?'

What is left of the dharma of kings? ... This ancient eternal dharma is lost among the Kauravas ... For this foul man, disgrace of the Kauravas, is molesting me, and I cannot bear it.

—Draupadi, as Duhshasana tries to disrobe
her in the assembly, *Mahabharata*, II.62.12[1]

'What son of a king would wager his wife?'

As soon as Shakuni cries *'jitam'*, Duryodhana realizes that he has won the game of dice—and with it Yudhishthira's wife Draupadi, the desperate Pandava king's final wager. 'Drunk with pride' he orders the messenger to go to the queen's chambers.[2]

... bring Draupadi
The beloved wife whom the Pandavas honour
Let her sweep the house and run our errands
What a joy to watch![3]

Vidura, Duryodhana's fearless counsellor, tries to dissuade him from claiming his prize.

You don't know it, fool, you are tied in a noose!

> ... you are a deer provoking a tiger's wrath ...
> She is not a slave yet. Bharata! I think she was staked
> when the king was no longer his own master.[4]

But Duryodhana refuses to listen. Impatiently, he commands the royal messenger, who speeds off on his master's orders. The messenger enters the queen's chambers, like 'a dog in a lion's den, crawling up to the Queen of the Pandavas'.[5] He says:

> Intoxicated on dice, Yudhishthira has lost you, O Draupadi ...
> You must come now to Dhritarashtra's house ...[6]

Hearing this, Draupadi rages:

> What son of a king would wager his wife?
> The king is befooled and crazed by the game.[7]

She tells the messenger to go back to the assembly and ask her husband:

> Whom did you lose first, yourself or me?[8]

When the messenger returns and puts the question to him, Yudhishthira does not stir, as though he has lost consciousness. Since he makes no reply, Duryodhana intervenes, 'Let Draupadi come here and ask the question herself. All the people want to hear what she has to say.' The messenger obediently returns to Draupadi and says:

> The kings in the hall are summoning you—it seems the fall of the
> Kurus has come! Princess, when you are led into that hall, the
> king will be too weak to protect our fortunes.[9]

Meanwhile, Duryodhana gets impatient, and orders his brother to fetch Draupadi.

> And quickly angry Duhshasana
> Came rushing to her with a thunderous roar;
> By the long-tressed black and flowing hair
> Duhshasana grabbed the wife of a king.[10]

And as she was dragged, she bent her body
And whispered softly, 'It is now my month!
This is my sole garment, man of slow wit,
You cannot take me to the hall, you churl!'[11]

But Duhshasana continues to drag her by the hair. She appeals to his good sense not to debase her. Duhshasana replies:

Come, come ... you are won ... enjoy the Kurus ...
With slaves one delights as one wishes.[12]

Draupadi warns him that he has lost his sanity.

'Whom did you lose first, yourself or me?'

When Draupadi enters, the assembly is in shock at the sight of the queen thus dragged. No one speaks. She throws a scornful glance at her husbands.

Not the kingdom lost, nor the riches looted
Not the precious jewels plundered did hurt
As much as did her sidelong glance.[13]

No one has answered her question, 'whom did you lose first, yourself or me', and the problem hangs uncomfortably over the entire assembly. Finally, Bhishma, the grandfather of the warring cousins, rises to speak. He is the eldest and most respected in the assembly. Having renounced the throne when he was young, he has lived his life selflessly, and looked after the affairs of the kingdom as trustee for two generations. Used to dealing with matters of state, he looks upon Draupadi's question as a legal challenge.

It is true, Bhishma begins, that a person who has lost himself in the game is no longer free to stake what no longer belongs to him. Since Yudhishthira did lose himself first, he was not competent to stake Draupadi. If that is so, then she is free. On the other hand, Bhishma continues, a wife does belong to a husband, in the sense that a wife is expected to act upon a husband's orders, which means that even if he is not free, she is legally his and he is allowed to stake her.[14] Moreover, no one forced Yudhishthira to gamble. He knew that Shakuni has no equal in dicing. He played voluntarily and never complained that Shakuni was cheating. Bhishma concludes in great distress that the matter is complex, and he cannot resolve Draupadi's dilemma:

> *As dharma is subtle, my dear, I fail*
> *To resolve your question in the proper way.*[15]

Draupadi is upset at Bhishma's reply. As Duhshasana hurls nasty insults at her, her eyes are filled with tears as she tells Bhishma that he is wrong:

> *. . . he was challenged, the king,*
> *By cunning, ignoble, and evil tricksters*
> *Who love to game; he had never much tried it.*
> *Why do you say he was left a choice?*

The elders remain silent, but Vikarna, a younger brother of Duryodhana, is so moved by Draupadi's grief that he gets up and rebukes them: 'We have to answer her question or we shall all go to hell,' he says.

> *Ye best of men, they recount four vices that are the curse of a king: hunting, drinking, dicing, and fornicating. A man with these addictions abandons dharma, and the world does not condone his immoderate deeds. The son of Pandu was intoxicated by one such vice when the cheating gamblers challenged him and when he staked Draupadi. The innocent Draupadi is, besides, the common wife of all of Pandu's sons. Yudhishthira staked her when he had already gambled away his own freedom. It was Saubala's idea to stake Draupadi. Considering all this, I do not think she has been won.*[16]

There is a roar of approval in the assembly. The nobles begin to praise young Vikarna and condemn Shakuni. Vikarna has, indeed, complicated things by suggesting that Yudhishthira was not competent to stake Draupadi as she was the wife of all the five Pandavas, not just his. Seeing the tide turning against the Kauravas, Karna now rises. Karna has never got over the humiliation of being rejected by Draupadi. He had won her fairly at her *swayamvara* in a difficult test that she had posed to all her suitors. But she rejected him, saying, 'I do not choose a charioteer!' She had chosen the handsome Pandava, Arjuna, instead.

When the clamour subsides, Karna argues that everyone in the assembly saw Yudhishthira make the bet, and everyone saw him lose all that he owned. Since Draupadi is part of 'all that he owned', she was won fairly, according to the law. Moreover, Draupadi was mentioned by name when the bet was placed and none of the Pandavas contested it at the time. Besides, he adds, a virtuous woman has only one husband. Draupadi shares the five Pandava brothers—making her a slut who ought to be stripped in public.[17]

The nobles are shocked. They know that Karna's last argument is false. They are aware that after winning Draupadi's heart with his extraordinary display of the bow, Arjuna had brought her home in the company of his brothers. At the door, they had shouted to Kunti, 'See what we have brought, mother.' Without looking up, Kunti had replied, 'Well, I hope you will share it equally.' And they did, and this is how she got five husbands.

'What is to be done'

In the second century BC, the Vedic exegete Jaimini, who worked on the most important dharma manuals, was fond of saying that all Vedic texts consisted of injunctions to act. He thus defined dharma in a practical, action-oriented way—'what is to be done'. But dharma also means 'law' and Draupadi makes a legal argument on the assumption that it is more likely to resonate with the rulers in the assembly. She is using a familiar strategy in the epic when she sends the messenger back with a question about the sequence of the stakes. *Prashna* is 'question' in Sanskrit, but it can also mean riddle or puzzle. It points to a 'baffling, ultimately insoluble crystallization of conflict articulated along opposing lines of interpretation'.[18]

It is curious that the messenger, deliberately or innocently, puts Draupadi's question in a way that is different from the way she had asked it. He asks, 'As the owner of whom did you lose us?' Thus, he sharpens the focus.[19] At the time of the epic, a husband's authority over his wife was complete; indeed, his honour depended on his legitimately 'owning' his woman's sexuality. To expect Bhishma or anyone else in the assembly on that day to answer differently would have required the person to step outside his moral paradigm of patriarchy.[20] But what is less clear is whether the husband loses this authority when he himself is no longer free. If Yudhishthira had lost himself first, he was no longer free; as a slave he did not own anything, and if he did not own her, then he could not stake her or lose her.[21] The question, as he puts it, also has a psychological focus, pointing to Yudhishthira's accountability. Was he a master of his faculties? Or was he temporarily deranged by the gambler's frenzy? When Vidura warns Duryodhana: 'I think she was staked when the king was no longer his own master,' he might be suggesting the possibility of a defence based on 'temporary insanity'. Draupadi herself observes that 'the king is befooled and crazed by the game'.

Draupadi disagrees with the Kauravas' claim that Yudhishthira knowingly joined the game, voluntarily staked his wife, and never complained about Shakuni cheating; thus, he lost in a fair contest. Draupadi believes that her husband was forced to respond to a 'challenge made by cheats'.[22] Shakuni was notorious for cheating, and her husband had warned him at the beginning of the game: 'Shakuni, don't defeat us by crooked means and cruelly.'[23] She sees more clearly than others that the game was a political conspiracy of Duryodhana and Shakuni, with the complicity of Dhritarashtra. It was an act of *realpolitik* to usurp the Pandavas' half of the kingdom—making Yudhishthira the victim of 'a vast right-wing conspiracy'.[24] Right-wing, because it was in support of the incumbent King Dhritarashtra's vested interest.

Draupadi will not leave it there. She will turn her legal challenge into a moral one. Knowing that dharma can mean both what is 'lawful' and what is 'right', the real question that she is leading to is: Is it right or fair that a woman, let alone a queen, become a slave because her husband staked her in a gambling game? Her assumption is that the law, too often, reflects the will of the powerful in society and diverges from the right thing to do. It is especially true for those who are vulnerable and powerless—the poor, the low castes, slaves and women—and historically it has been the role of the Left to fight to change that. This is the subtext of her second question, 'what is the dharma of the king?'

'This foul man, disgrace of the Kauravas, is molesting me, and I cannot bear it!'

Draupadi's arguments are not enough to overturn Karna's call to strip her. Duhshasana forcibly lays hold of her robe, and in the midst of the assembly begins to undress her.[25] Draupadi cries out:

> . . . *this foul man, disgrace of the Kauravas, is molesting me, and I cannot bear it any longer!*[26]

Then an extraordinary thing happens:

> *When her garment was being stripped off, lord of the people, another similar garment appeared every time. A terrible roar went up from all the kings, a shout of approval, as they watched that greatest wonder on earth . . . [And in the end] a pile of clothes was heaped*

> up in the middle of the hall, when Duhshasana, tired and ashamed,
> at last desisted and sat down.[27]

The men in the assembly raise a cry of 'Shame! Shame!' They
clamour for an answer to Draupadi's question. Widely respected
Vidura, born of a low caste woman, now rises, waves his hands,
and gradually silences the assembly. He says:

> Draupadi, having raised the question, now weeps piteously as she
> has none left to protect her. You have given no answer. If you do
> not do so, men in this hall, dharma will be offended . . . If a person
> comes with a grievance and raises a question about dharma, it
> must be resolved without partiality.[28]

Vidura quotes the sage Kashyapa about the immorality of
remaining silent when there is evil afoot. When honest persons
fail in their duty to speak up, they 'wound' dharma and commit
adharma.[29] Thus, the leader of the conspiracy earns half the
penalty; the immediate culprit a quarter; and the witnesses who
do not speak up are also guilty by a quarter.[30]

The kings and nobles, however, remain silent. Karna speaks to
Draupadi, 'Dear lady, you are the wife of a slave, without right
to property; you have no master, and are property yourself.'[31]
Turning impatiently to Duhshasana, he says, 'Take away this
serving girl to the inner apartments.'

Draupadi reflects on her fate in bitter puzzlement:

> Methinks that Time is out of joint—[the Kurus allow] their
> innocent daughter and daughter-in-law to be molested! What
> greater humiliation than that . . . a woman of virtue and beauty,
> now must invade the men's hall? What is left of the dharma of the
> kings?[32]

Crazed by success, Duryodhana looks invitingly at Draupadi
and exposes his left thigh. Bhima, her second husband, is enraged
by this insult and vows to break that thigh one day with a club.
Vidura warns the Kauravas that they have overplayed their

hand. Fate will catch up. At that moment, as though in response to his warning, a jackal howls, donkeys bray, and grisly birds shriek. The men in the assembly see in these omens portents of evil, and so does the blind Dhritarashtra. He reproaches his son, and turns to make amends to Draupadi. Referring to her as a righteous wife, he says:

> *Choose a boon from me, Panchali, whatever you wish; for you are to me the most distinguished of my daughters-in-law, bent as you are on dharma!*[33]

She asks for the Pandavas' freedom. The old king restores their kingdom and all they had lost. And there the story ends, at least for now. Meanwhile, Draupadi's unanswered question 'hovers over the entire *Mahabharata*: no one ever resolves it, and Yudhishthira is still trying to figure it out in the end.'[34]

'What is left of the dharma of the kings?'

Draupadi's never-ending sari that protected her from becoming naked is often the first picture that comes to Indian minds at the thought of the *Mahabharata*. Not surprisingly, this scene has been portrayed with great panache in cinema and the stage versions, including Peter Brook's. After the hugely successful television series, a company marketed a 'Draupadi Collection' of saris that presumably did not stretch infinitely.[35]

What did, in fact, happen that day? How did an inexhaustible stream of garment appear from nowhere to protect Draupadi? Popular versions of the epic, as well as many respectable ancient *bhakti* redactions, invariably show Krishna coming to her rescue. We shall never know what the original *Mahabharata* was like, but it seems clear to many scholars that the epic was reworked early on, as early as the first century BC, by Vaishnav redactors to glorify Krishna. The disrobing of Draupadi gave them an opportunity to bring in Krishna in order to save her.[36] As her clothes are being unravelled, she thinks of Krishna and appeals to him: 'Dost thou not see the humiliation the Kauravas are forcing upon me? ... O Krishna, save a distressed soul sinking amid the Kauravas.'[37] In the scholarly Pune Critical Edition of the epic, however, there is no Krishna, and the miracle is left unexplained. Franklin Edgerton, editor of Book Two of the epic, the *Sabhaparvan*, had the unenviable task of having to select from more than a hundred manuscripts. In the end he and his colleagues decided on the version without Krishna. He argued that it was 'cosmic justice' that protected her—she was a chaste and a just woman committed to dharma.[38]

Edgerton argues forcefully, 'No prayer by Draupadi; no explanation of the miraculous replacement of one garment by another; no mention of Krishna or any superhuman agency. It is apparently implied (though not stated) that cosmic justice automatically, or "magically" if you like, prevented the chaste Draupadi from being stripped in public. It is perhaps not strange that later redactors felt it necessary to embroider the story. Yet to me, at least, the original form, in its brevity, simplicity, and rapid movement appeals very forcefully.'[39] I tend to agree with Edgerton. I believe the narrative is stronger without Krishna. The text is briefer, simpler and quicker. It helps build Draupadi's character—it is her own agency, her own dharma, which is responsible for the miracle rather than God's intervention. It vindicates her courage as she stands up to the political and social order, reminding the rulers about the dharma of the king. No wonder feminists applaud this tough, eloquent and resilient heroine of the *Mahabharata*.

The public disrobing of Draupadi is consistent with the moral paradigm of patriarchy. This is a climactic moment for the Kauravas—they have 'defeated' and humiliated the Pandavas.[40] Karna's revolting remarks show how a patriarchal culture divides women into two types: angels and whores. Ever since the 'defeat' of the Pandavas, Draupadi is considered to be in the latter category; accordingly, if she has suffered a calamity, she deserves it. The stereotype of big-chested masculinity encourages the thought that a 'real man' does not need anyone. Instead of thinking that this unhappy person could have been 'me', one thinks that 'I am above all this' or 'I could never suffer that'.

All cultures, I suspect, contain the seeds of violence when it comes to female sexuality, and I learned something about Draupadi's situation from Tolstoy's famous novella *The Kreutzer Sonata*. The novella grew out of the Russian writer's own relationship with his wife, and it describes the events that lead to her murder. The husband has violent and humiliating sex with her, and he feels miserable each time he rapes her. Since she is merely an object of bestial desire, he decides that he must kill her to put an end to his misery. After her death, she becomes 'human' in his eyes, and he even begins to have compassionate feelings for her. The murdering husband concludes that women will never be treated as full human beings as long as sexual intercourse exists. They will always be humiliated. The Kauravas' wish to humiliate Draupadi and turn her into a slave may well be related to the disgust that many men feel towards the sexual act. Tolstoy's diaries describe how 'the tension mounts and mounts inside him until he has to use his wife, and then he despises her, despises himself, and wants to use force against her to stop the cycle from continuing.'[41]

The attempted disrobing of Draupadi is a clear insult to womanhood. And this affront upset the cosmic balance of dharma. Hence, there were omens and they changed the story's outcome. According to an ancient dharma text: 'Where women are honoured and worshipped, all gods become pleased; if women are unnecessarily insulted, a great disaster must be on the way.' The fact that Draupadi had five husbands has troubled Indians for centuries. They have never quite accepted Karna's fantasy about Draupadi's extraordinary libido. Nor have they fully bought the ingenuous story of Kunti telling her sons to share her equally. Historically, it was common for men, especially kings, to have more than one wife, but for a woman to legitimately have multiple husbands was unheard of. Yes, polyandry did exist on the margin among the Himalayan tribes, and it still does, but there is no evidence that this ever was an extensive practice. So, what is the *Mahabharata* trying to tell us?

I believe it is throwing a challenge to the audience's paradigm of patriarchy. The *Mahabharata*'s women are not meek. The Pandavas' mother, Kunti, saved the dynasty after discovering that her husband was incapable of coitus. It seems Pandu had once shot a deer as it was mating with a doe. He did not know that the deer was an ascetic in animal form, and as revenge the ascetic cursed Pandu to die the moment he made love to a woman. Kunti found an answer to continue the family line. She invoked a mantra given to her by a sage. 'May you be the mother of godly children!' the sage had said to her in gratitude for serving him selflessly. Thus, the five Pandavas were fathered by the gods: Yudhishthira by the god Dharma, Bhima by Vayu, the wind, Arjuna by Indra, and the twins, Nakula and Sahadeva, by the Ashvins. Despite the ambiguous parentage, the children were known as 'Pandavas' or 'sons of Pandu', which biologically, at least, they were not. To make up for this lapse, the epic also refers to them as Kaunteyas, the sons of Kunti.

Draupadi and Kunti are not the only assertive women in the epic. A third, Satyavati, had saved the Bharata dynasty earlier when Bhishma had refused her request to service her son's widows and produce an heir by the law of levirate. No virgin bride herself, Satyavati reveals that she has an illegitimate son from an alliance with a sage before her marriage to Bhishma's father. She summons this son, Vyasa, who turns out to be the author of the *Mahabharata*, and has him impregnate her daughters-in-law. Though the widows agree, they are not enamoured of Vyasa, who is old and ugly and smells of fish—his beard is red, his hair orange. In fact, they are both frightened—one screws her eyes shut while they are having sex; the other turns white with fear. Both become pregnant; the first gives birth to a blind child, Dhritarashtra, and the second to the pale and sickly Pandu.[42] He begets a bastard, the good Vidura, by a maid.

The surprising freedom enjoyed by the epic's feisty women is a feminist's dream, and some of this open-mindedness towards women may have existed in the society of those times.[43] The *Arthashastra*, a contemporary text of 300 AD, tells us that the Mauryan empire and post-Mauryan times were a cosmopolitan age, which allowed space to women in both the court and the village. Women archers were bodyguards of the king; women were spies in the intelligence services; women ascetics were a common sight; royal and upper class women generously donated to Buddhist monasteries. The *Mahabharata* reflects this autonomy.[44]

Oddly enough, Draupadi has come in for criticism for asking her famous question. In 1967, Iravati Karve, a distinguished anthropologist, wrote that Draupadi 'was only a young bride of the house, [yet] she spoke in the assembly of men, something she must have known she must not do. Over and above to pretend that she could understand the questions that baffled her elders— that was inexcusable arrogance . . . [which is why her husband] called her "a lady pundit", hardly a complimentary epithet.'[45] I find it difficult to agree with Karve. I think one admires Draupadi precisely because she is bold and courageous and attempts to save herself and the Pandavas.

Karve, however, argues that the question put Draupadi in greater jeopardy. She risked losing her husband as well as her freedom. 'Draupadi's question was not only foolish, it was terrible. No matter what answer was given, her position was desperate. If Bhishma told her her husband's rights over her did not cease, that even though he became a slave, she was in his power and he had the right to stake her, her slavery would have been confirmed. If Bhishma had argued that because of this slavery her husband had no more rights over her, then her plight would have been truly pitiable . . . if her relationship with her husband was destroyed she would have been truly widowed.'[46]

Karve's point is that in a patriarchal society a married woman's very existence and identity depended on her husband; to lose one's husband was akin to suicide. Obviously both alternatives were bad, but I think it is debatable if being a widow was a worse fate than becoming a slave of the Kauravas. In any case, what is important is that Draupadi did save the Pandavas from becoming slaves with her wit, courage and her knowledge of the law.

'Dharma is subtle'

Draupadi's insistent second question—'What is the dharma of the king?'—unsettles the assembly because it goes well beyond her initial legal question about whether she has been won fairly. This time the noble kshatriyas are forced to think about right and wrong, something they are not using to doing in their daily exercise of power. Since Draupadi's question suggests that she does not think that what is lawful is necessarily right, dharma must mean something other than what is customary. If Draupadi's words do not persuade them, the miracle—which covered the queen with an endless sari—certainly puts them on notice.

Bhishma has understood this distinction and hence he commends Draupadi for reminding everyone about dharma when everyone had forgotten it. Even though he does not have an answer, he praises her:

> Whereas the Kurus are set on greed and delusion . . . [righteous Draupadi] though you have suffered much, you still look to dharma . . . and the course of dharma is sovereign . . . [however] I cannot answer [your] question decisively, because the matter is subtle.[47]

The *Mahabharata* will keep returning to Bhishma's conclusion that 'dharma is subtle'. *Sukshma* is the word in Sanskrit. Draupadi,

Dhritarashtra, and others will repeat this phrase every time when they are in genuine difficulty. 'Dharma is subtle', I think, because it does not deal with matters of fact (like, say, the rivers of Asia). It deals with opinions about how we ought to behave.[48] The world of facts (and even the world of power) is more straightforward. Hence, moral dilemmas are confusing. When I make a moral judgement about somebody's action, I must make the same judgement about a similar act in similar circumstances—in other words, what kind of behaviour am I ready to prescribe to myself, given that I am prescribing it for everybody in the same situation?[49] This sort of reasoning does not come naturally to human beings.

Draupadi's insistent question also raises the issue about who has the authority to decide about dharma. It is curious that no one in the Hastinapura assembly that day appealed to God to decide who is right and who is wrong. This is because God is not expected to be an authority on dharma among Hindus, Buddhists or Jains. Human reason and the 'search for a rational basis of dharma is often compatible with these religious traditions'.[50] But if God is not an authority, then who is? Who is responsible for dharma? In his influential law book, Manu cited plural authorities for dharma two thousand years ago:

> *The root of dharma is the entire Veda, the tradition and customs of those who know the Vedas, the conduct of virtuous people, and what is satisfactory to oneself.*[51]

But the *Mahabharata*, in its typically sceptical way, challenges Manu and questions if the Vedas can be arbiters of true dharma:

> *In the opinion of the world the words of the Vedas are contradictory. How can there be scriptural authority over whether something is a true conclusion or not when such contradiction exists?*[52]

The epic also wonders if the wise can be relied upon to be authorities on dharma: 'intelligence appears differently in different men. They all take delight in their own different understanding of things'.[53]

If God is not the arbiter of dharma, and if the Vedas are contradictory, and if wise persons cannot agree about right and wrong, where does it leave the ordinary individual? Kulluka, who wrote a commentary in the fifteenth century on Manu's verse quoted above, declares that the 'satisfaction of the mind is the only authority in cases of conflicting alternatives'.[54] The classical poet, Kalidasa, who lived in the fifth century AD, was of the same view: 'In matters where doubt intervenes, the [natural] inclination of the heart of the good person becomes the "authority" or the decisive factor.'[55] This explains why the characters in the *Mahabharata* and in other texts of the classical Indian tradition prefer to depend on reason rather than on blind faith.[56]

One should not imagine for a moment, however, that the *Mahabharata* rejects God. It devotes much energy in the didactic books to explaining how one attains *moksha*, the fourth and supreme spiritual end of the Hindu life: liberation from human bondage. The *Mahabharata*, in fact, makes fun of non-believers:

> *I was a learned scholar who favoured reason and rejected the Vedas, devoted to the worthless sciences of logic and speculative reasoning. In assemblies of learned men I was an eloquent speaker employing reason and logic, decrying the recitation of the Vedas and speaking arrogantly to brahmins. I was an atheist, doubtful of everything, a fool who thought himself a great scholar. This present position of mine as a jackal is the result I have gained from this.*[57]

The idea of dharma based on one's reason, thus, sits side by side with deep faith in the existence of God in the *Mahabharata*. But it is left to individuals to decide how to best order their lives. Given the plurality of authorities, one has to depend on oneself. No wonder the epic says 'dharma is subtle'.

The concept of dharma evolved over time, its meaning shifting from a 'ritual ethics of deeds' to a more personal virtue based on one's conscience.[58] In earlier Vedic times dharma meant doing visible 'good deeds' endorsed by society, and Sanskrit scholars generally translate this earlier meaning of dharma as 'merit'. Often these deeds were specific to one's caste, and this concept is called *sva-dharma*. With the rise of yoga sects, Buddhism and Jainism, this meaning of dharma gradually changed to mean social harmony, the cultivation of an ethical self, and to actions required of all castes. In this sense, dharma has universal appeal and is called *sadharana-dharma*. In the latter sense, dharma has to do with basic traits rather than specific deeds, and the *Mahabharata* articulates these character traits in a number of places. It refers to 'not harming others, being truthful, not getting angry'.[59] Bhishma mentions a longer list of nine traits, which includes 'lack of malice and rectitude'.[60] While these are still visible deeds which accumulate good karma, they are now quite obviously inner traits or attitudes which determine one's character. This marked a change in the way that society thought about dharma and karma.[61]

Both these senses of dharma co-exist in the *Mahabharata*. Since they are often contradictory, they contribute to dramatic tension in the story. When Draupadi uses 'dharma', she has its former meaning in mind. Given her bias for action and for the kshatriya ethic, she usually thinks of dharma as *sva-dharma*. When Yudhishthira uses the word, he usually means universal, ethical dictates of his conscience and of *sadharana-dharma*. Draupadi and his brother Bhima use 'dharma' to awaken Yudhishthira's sense of his duty as a kshatriya warrior, usually to get him to act as we shall see in the book, when the Pandavas are in exile:

If we are to observe our own dharma . . . it is in war that our task lies . . . Others have stolen our kingdom . . . [Your idea of] dharma is not dharma, it is wrong dharma! . . . O king of men, by scrapping a lesser dharma, a man obtains a greater dharma, and he is judged to be wise.[62]

Thus, Yudhishthira finds himself in a moral dilemma. Should he obey his duty to his family, his kshatriya caste and kingship, or should he insist on observing the dictates of his own conscience and stick to his word? There is no easy answer and he suffers.

Duryodhana shows contempt for the newer ethical meaning, seeing in it a sign of weakness. But Arjuna is able to see both sides of dharma. When he puts down his bow and refuses to fight in the Gita, he is acting according to the dictates of his conscience. At other times, especially in the battle books, Arjuna is delighted to play the role of the most famous kshatriya warrior of his time. Being able to negotiate both senses of dharma, the universal and the particular, Arjuna goes on to become the most admired of the Pandavas, who is tough yet gentle.

Overall, the *Mahabharata*'s characters are aware of both meanings of dharma, but each one uses the word to suit specific ends. They repeat the epic's classic formula, 'Where there is dharma, there is victory!' But what they actually mean can be ambiguous. Unwilling to face the contradictions, they hope that both senses of dharma are possible, and that both together will bring victory. One can fight a 'just war' as a kshatriya soldier and still be, by and large, a good, honest and peaceful human being. Once in a while, our heroes do get into a muddle, and then they wriggle out by exclaiming, 'dharma is subtle'.

A woman and a slave are the property of others

When Draupadi saved the Pandavas from slavery on that fateful day in Hastinapura's assembly, she made us all aware that to be free is the essence of being human. But what if Draupadi had not succeeded in rescuing her family, and what if they and she had become slaves? It is an unthinkable prospect for us moderns, but slavery was the common fate of losers in the ancient world. Andromache, the beautiful and loyal wife of the renowned Trojan warrior Hector, became a slave. Homer tells us in the *Iliad*

how the lovely queen lost her freedom when her husband
was slain by Achilles. This led to the defeat of Troy by the
Greeks. Andromache's child, Astyanax, was thrown down the
Trojan walls by the Greeks, because they feared that he might
grow up and avenge his father and the city. Euripides wrote a
powerful drama about this. As a prize of war, he tells us that
Andromache is expected to sleep with the son of her husband's
killer. Just before going to bed with him she mourns her husband:
'Husband, you were too young to die and leave me widowed in
our home . . . Ah, Hector, you have brought utter desolation to
your parents. But who will mourn you as I shall? Mine is the
bitterest regret of all, because you did not die in bed and
stretching out your arms to me give me some tender word that
I might have treasured in my tears by night and day.'[63]

Both Draupadi and Andromache wrestled with the dilemmas
of becoming unfree. Both women were mature and faithful
women. Both faced a reversal in fortune and had to deal with a
fate that is especially cruel to women. In doing so, both women
displayed dignity and nobility as they strived to do the right
thing. They often bring out the contrast between heroic female
qualities and less-than-heroic male ones. Whereas the 'cosmic
justice' of dharma came to the aid of feisty Draupadi, who
fought back spiritedly, Andromache was not as fortunate.
Draupadi was clearly disappointed at Bhishma's suggestion that
a woman and a slave are not free and are the property of others.
So was I, frankly, for Bhishma is one of the more remarkable and
admirable characters in the *Mahabharata*. But to expect him to
have spoken out against slavery and patriarchy is to super-
impose contemporary values onto his world.

My own thoughts turned from Draupadi to mid-seventeenth-
century England when a scholar named John Locke wrote the
Second Treatise Concerning Civil Government. He did not sign his
name to it but only acknowledged his authorship in his will. In
the treatise, Locke speaks about human beings having certain

natural rights—such as the right to liberty—that existed in a state of nature. Civil society comes afterwards and so does political authority, whose purpose is to protect these rights. Locke expressed the radical view that is also found in the *Mahabharata* and the Gita that government is morally obliged to serve the people.[64]

Locke's ideas spread quickly, and by the eighteenth century, they contributed to an intellectual revolution, the Enlightenment. As a result slavery became a metaphor for everything that was evil in political and social relations among human beings. The metaphor, however, took root precisely at a time when Europeans were enslaving vast numbers of non-Europeans, so much so that by the mid-eighteenth century the slave trade came to underwrite the global economic system. Ironically, this economy based on involuntary servitude contributed to the spread of the very Enlightenment ideals of liberty and equality around the world and eventually undermined the notion that one human being could be the property of another.[65]

In 1776, Locke's ideas gave birth to the American Declaration of Independence, which stated that it was a 'self-evident' truth that all men are created equal, but it denied this truth to slaves and women. John C. Calhoun, the influential American Vice President, declared that slavery was a positive good: 'I hold that in the present state of civilization, where two races of different origin, and distinguished by color, and other physical differences, as well as intellectual, are brought together, the relation now existing in the slaveholding States between the two, is, instead of an evil, a good—a positive good.' The United States was thus born with the birth defect of slavery, which was approved by democratic majorities and enshrined in its constitution. Abraham Lincoln, in his 1858 debates with Stephen Douglas, had to refer to a principle of equality that lay beyond the American constitution in order to argue against slavery. It took a bloody civil war and the death of over a million persons, including 620,000 soldiers, to end slavery in the United States in 1865.

Ironically, John Locke himself believed that black Africans were inferior to Europeans and he authored the notorious 'Fundamental Constitutions of Carolina' in one of the southern states in America, in which a 'freeman' was allowed to have 'absolute power and authority over his negro slaves'. His famous contemporary, the respected philosopher David Hume, also suspected 'negroes to be naturally inferior to whites'. 'There scarcely ever was a civilized nation of that complexion, nor even any individual eminent either in action or speculation,' he wrote.

Even Immanuel Kant was guilty of the European blindness of regarding non-Europeans (particularly native Americans and Africans) as unequal human beings.[66] I wondered that if the greatest modern thinkers of the Western world—Locke, Hume and Kant—were not immune to racism, it did seem to suggest that slavery was not simply a matter of global economic inequality, but was about the very real difficulty that human beings have in being able to universalize the human experience to all persons.

Today, no state in the world permits slavery and it is hard to imagine anyone defending this institution. In India, we have expiated for our past sins against the 'untouchable' Dalits with an extensive programme of affirmative action. To this extent, humanity seems to have made progress and human beings have evolved morally. Nevertheless, slavery continues to exist in pockets in a furtive manner in parts of the world. When a ship carrying hundreds of people was turned away from Benin, Africa in March 2001, officials suspected that the children on board were human slaves. A few years earlier in Madhol, Sudan, an Arab trader had sold 132 former slaves, women and children, for $13,200 (in Sudanese money) to a member of Christian Solidarity International. These incidents drew attention to the persistence of the slave trade, and at this moment, according to Anti-Slavery International, roughly 20 million men, women and children are being held against their will as modern-day slaves.[67]

The great Indian bureaucrat

What makes Draupadi's second question about 'dharma of the king' admirable is her concern for accountability in public life. There will always be nasty types—Shakuni, Duryodhana, Duhshasana—but if public institutions are accountable, they will be punished. Today in India, we despair over the almost complete erosion of accountability in our bureaucracy—an institution that my grandfather used to be so proud of in the 1950s that he and his friends called it our 'steel frame'. Duryodhana's misbehaviour in the assembly reminded me of the innumerable and daily lapses of our corrupt public servants. As long as it is correctly noted in the file, their world is in order, and who cares about the real people outside.

Every year over 100,000 pilgrims gather annually on the banks of the Narmada river at a place called Dharaji, in the district of Dewas in Madhya Pradesh. They have been doing so for years and the date of this religious gathering is well known to the district authority. There is a dam nearby which releases water into the river for generating electricity at 690 cubic metres per second. On 7 May 2005, I read in the newspaper that sixty-two people had drowned at Dharaji. An enquiry revealed subsequently that the district authority had, indeed, sent a letter to the Indira Sagar power plant not to release the water between 7 p.m. and 9 p.m. on that day. But they had sent it by ordinary mail and it did not arrive on time. The enquiry also showed that telephones and faxes were functioning at both the district headquarters and the dam site. The bureaucrat who had conducted the enquiry, however, exonerated the district collector, Ashish Srivastava and the police superintendent, R.K. Chaudhary. He felt that the government was not negligent for it had done its job by drafting the letter and a copy was in the files.

A friend of mine from my schooldays, Arun Shourie, recounts his experience as minister of administrative reform. On 13 April 1999, a query came to his department from the ministry of steel:

'Can officers use inks other than blue or black?'[68] It seems two officers in Steel had made notings on official files in green and red inks, and this had raised eyebrows. There were serious consultations in Shourie's department and it was decided that since the matter concerned ink, the Directorate of Printing had to be consulted, and so an OM, an 'office memorandum', was sent to it on 3 May. On 21 May a reply came, saying that the matter had been deliberated in the Directorate and no rules were found about the use of different inks. However, they opined that heads of departments may be allowed to use colours while other officers must confine themselves to blue and black ink. They suggested that the department of personnel in the home ministry may be consulted on this matter.

It was now the department of personnel's turn to start holding meetings on the subject of inks, and after three weeks they wrote back on 6 July to say that the matter concerned the Manual of Office Procedures, and since this was regulated by the department of administrative reform, it was in their competence to decide. Like good bureaucrats, they had thrown the ball back. The matter was next discussed at a Senior Level Officers' meeting in the department of administrative reform; it was agreed that longevity of inks was an issue on government records and so, on 12 August, a letter was sent to the Director General, department of archives, asking for his opinion. On 27 August a reply came that as regards fountain pens blue/black ought to be prescribed but in the case of ballpoint pens blue, black, red and green could be permitted. But whatever ink was used its quality ought to comply with the Bureau of Indian Standards.

At the next Senior Officers' meeting, the chairman of the department of administrative reforms felt that before deciding on this matter, the manual of the armed forces, particularly the army, should be consulted. Accordingly, a letter was sent on 4 October to the joint secretary in the ministry of defence, who replied on 22 December that red colour ink is used by the chiefs of army, navy and air force; green colour is used by principal staff officers; and blue is used by all other officers. After several months of deliberations, the department of administrative reforms finally passed an order on 28 March, amending the Manual of Office Procedures: 'Initial drafting will be done in black or blue ink. Modifications in the draft at subsequent levels may be made in green and red ink by the officers so as to distinguish the corrections made.' Hierarchy was observed in the order: 'Only an officer of the level of joint secretary and above may use green or red ink in rare cases.'

Arun Shourie adds with irony, 'A good bureaucratic solution: discretion allowed but circumscribed.'

If Draupadi were to appear in India in the twenty-first century, she would remind our public officials that they are among the brightest in the world, having been selected through a very rigorous examination process. She would tell them that one-third of the world's poor reside in India and bureaucratic corruption is the main obstacle to their development. It is the poor who are most reliant on public services and the least capable of paying bribes. In 2005, Transparency International ranked India 90 out of 146 countries, with a score of 2.8 out of 10 (scores below 3 indicate 'rampant corruption'). Of the eleven public services surveyed, India's police are the most corrupt, with 80 per cent of the citizens admitting that they had paid bribes to get their work done. Of the citizens who had dealt with the legal system, 40 per cent had paid a bribe to influence the court. One in three parents reported paying a bribe in dealing with a government school or a primary health centre. So, Draupadi would remind the 20 million employees of the government that there is plenty to be done without worrying about the colour of ink on government files. As to government officials—they should stop and ponder over Draupadi's question about dharma each time they plan to entangle us in red tape.

Draupadi and my dharma education

In its first book, the *Adiparvan*, the *Mahabharata* predicts that the dice game would become a turning point of the entire epic:

> *I did not hope for victory, O Sanjaya, when I heard that poor Draupadi was dragged into the royal assembly with voice choked with tears, wearing only a single piece of clothing. She had five husbands but still she was as if without any protector and hence [she was] publicly humiliated.*

Draupadi did not let the Pandavas forget her humiliation, goading them on to fight and avenge her honour. This led to a horrific war between the Kauravas and the Pandavas, a war that was not only for the throne but was also for dharma, as the Gita tells us in its famous opening lines.[69]

Draupadi's questions were a defining moment in my own quest for dharma. I could understand that no one was able to resolve Draupadi's dilemmas on that day. Her legal question was a terrifying social and moral challenge to the society of her time, when everyone believed that a wife was a husband's property, and not an independent and free agent. 'If Draupadi's questions were properly answered, it would have required a "paradigm shift" in India's social thought.'[70] What I find appalling, however, is that women and the poor continue to be treated in many communities in contemporary India as though they were 'property'.

It is easy to dismiss Duryodhana as a villain, but there is clearly more to him. I admire him for his coherent, consistent worldview even though I do not share it. His amoral philosophy is unfortunately followed by too many contemporary political leaders, who also believe that *realpolitik* and 'balance of power' are the only basis for diplomacy and peace. Duryodhana thinks rightly that the dharma of the king is to further the interest of the state; but he is wrong in believing that it can be achieved only through security and power. In his geopolitical world there are only friends and foes and a ruler's neighbour is bound to be a foe. Since Yudhishthira is a neighbour who has become powerful, he is a foe. Hence, Duryodhana feels compelled to bring him down. If not, Yudhishthira might gobble his kingdom up one day. This dodgy view is sanctioned by the classic text on statecraft, *Arthashastra,* an indispensable primer of the kshatriya ruler. Of this, more later.

Neither Duryodhana nor his blind father counted on Draupadi's ability to change the agenda from power to dharma. Her admonition about 'the dharma of the kings' resonates with the assembly because they know that dharma is meant to guide the just ruler while protecting the interests of the state. Where dharma prevails, there will be the rule of law and justice, and the king who follows the path of dharma is known as 'dharma raja'.[71] Even the Machiavellian *Arthashastra* teaches the ideal king to 'establish the rule of dharma by commands and directives, and discipline among the people by the extension of education'.[72] The most powerful ruler or his minister could not place himself above dharma—his subjects would immediately know his violations and chastise him. Thus, a long and hallowed tradition supports Draupadi's reprimand to the Kaurava kings.

I believe that Draupadi's example is an inspiration to free citizens in all democracies. Her question about the dharma of the king should embolden citizens to question the dharma of public officials, especially when they confront the pervasive governance failures around them. These failures are commonplace and they range from sending troops to fight unnecessary wars in places like Iraq to the absence of schoolteachers in government schools in India. They test the moral fabric of society. When there is no other recourse, citizens must be prepared to follow the Pandavas and wage a Kurukshetra-like war on the corrupt.

Draupadi's call for accountability in public life is similar to Antigone's in Sophocles's tragedy of the same name.[73] In both cases, it is a clash between an individual and the power of the state. Creon, the ruler of Thebes, forbids his niece Antigone from giving her brother Polyneices an honourable burial because the latter is supposedly a traitor. However, Antigone, like Draupadi, appeals to a universal dharma, a sense of justice that is higher than the law of the state. She argues that Polyneices was not a criminal but a political prisoner, who was guilty of plotting to save the state and the people from a tyrant. Since her higher dharma trumps the king's writ, she must be allowed to honour her brother and give his dead body a decent burial. Although both Draupadi and Antigone have little hope of success, they are not afraid to challenge the ruler's brute power by appealing to a higher dharma. Since the king's law, as they see it, is defective, dharma must mean something other than what is legal or customary.

Draupadi's question also brought home to me the immorality of silence. Vidura accuses the nobles, kings and the wise elders— all the less-than-mad Kauravas, who stand by silently as Draupadi is dragged by her hair before their eyes. When honest persons fail in their duty to speak up, they 'wound' dharma, and they ought to be punished, says the sage Kashyapa. In answer to her heart-rending appeal, Bhishma ought to have leaped up and felled Duhshasana to the ground instead of arguing over legal intricacies.

A similar conspiracy of silence diminished the office of the President of India in the summer of 2007. The official candidate for the largely ceremonial office was a woman Congress party leader, Pratibha Patil, against whom there were extensive corruption charges that were widely reported in the press. She had started a cooperative bank in Maharashtra whose licence was cancelled by the Reserve Bank. Her bank had given 'illegal loans' to her relatives that exceeded the bank's share capital. It had also given a loan to her sugar mill which was never repaid. The bank waived these loans, and this drove it into liquidation. The government liquidator of the bank, P.D. Nigam, said, 'The fact that relatives of the founder chairperson (Pratibha Patil) were among those indiscriminately granted loans and that some illegal loan waivers were done has come up in our audit.' Six of the top ten defaulters in Pratibha Patil's bank were linked to her relatives.

In July 2007, the nation had a Bhishma-like person of unquestionable integrity in Prime Minister Manmohan Singh. But he remained largely silent, deferring to his party's choice of the presidential candidate. In passing, he called it 'mudslinging' by the opposition, and the nation believed him. In any case, the Congress had the votes and Pratibha Patil replaced perhaps the most upright and popular president in Indian history. After that, the charges were never investigated

Before the scene ends in the *Sabhaparvan*, Duryodhana sees another opportunity for making trouble—this time to create dissension between the Pandava brothers. He asks Yudhishthira's brothers to tell the assembly whether their brother was in the right to stake them and his wife. This puts the Pandavas in a fix. They can either free Draupadi by declaring that Yudhishthira was wrong—that he spoke falsely in wagering her. Or they can uphold their brother's honour and reputation, and sacrifice Draupadi. Bhima replies that King Yudhishthira is their elder brother, and if he considers that he has been beaten in a fair contest, then all the Pandavas have lost fairly. 'I feel tied by the noose of dharma,' he adds. His brother, Arjuna, however, thinks that the nature of the 'self' might be at stake in Draupadi's question:

> *The king was our master when first he played us . . .*
> *That you should decide, ye Kurus assembled.*[74]

Arjuna's statement has philosophical implications. When Arjuna asks in what sense King Yudhishthira was 'our master' he raises a doubt about the status of the 'consciousness' that gambled and lost. Was it the unreliable, phenomenal 'self' of Yudhishthira who gambled away the kingdom? We can all relate to this capricious consciousness within us that keeps changing from moment to moment like an unreliable movie in our minds. Or was it Yudhishthira's timeless *atman*, unchanging soul? If the 'self' was that of fickle consciousness, then the gambler may well have been a narrative fiction. Perhaps the kingdom is not really lost. 'It is dangerous to claim to be a self.'[75]

This may also be why Yudhishthira remains quiet. Alf Hiltebeitel, the *Mahabharata* scholar, asks: 'Should he claim to be a self who wagered Draupadi first, [then] he [would] simply lie and lose her forever. If he claims to be a self who wagered her after he lost himself, he might keep her [albeit in slavery] ... Indeed, should he claim, like Nala, that in betting and losing his wife "I myself was not its doer", the self he wagered would be counterfeit, making him a more deceiving gambler than Shakuni.'[76] More than Draupadi's humiliation, what Duryodhana cares about is to prove that Yudhishthira is a liar, not the great man of dharma that the world believes him to be. Clearly, Draupadi and the Pandavas have gone and confused the assembly with irrelevant issues about what it means to wager one's soul and about the nature of the self and of truth.[77]

Walter Lippmann, the distinguished American public intellectual, said in a speech in 1941 that people do not become happy by satisfying desires. Happiness comes from upholding a certain balance, by living according to a system of beliefs that restrains them and gives coherence to their desires. 'Above all the other necessities of human nature, above the satisfaction of any other need, above hunger, love, pleasure, fame—even life itself—what a man most needs is the conviction that he is contained within the discipline of an ordered existence.'[78]

Lippmann did not realize it but he was addressing Draupadi's question. He was speaking about dharma, which also means upholding a certain balance. Dharma is precisely this 'discipline of ordered existence', a 'belief system that restrains and gives coherence to desires'. Persistently, the epic keeps asking, how are we to achieve the right balance in our individual and collective lives? Although dramatic, what happened to Draupadi is not unique. Our own public figures constantly challenge this balance of dharma in our 'uneven' world. The transgressions of Duryodhana and the surrounding conspiracies of silence are not dissimilar to the same sickeningly banal acts in our contemporary life.

3

YUDHISHTHIRA'S DUTY

'I act because I must'

*I act because I must. Whether it bears fruits or not, buxom Draupadi,
I do my duty like any householder.*

—Yudhishthira in exile, to Draupadi, *Mahabharata*, III.32.2–4

'Dharma, I find, does not protect you'

As though once were not enough, Yudhishthira goes on to play
a second game of dice with the Kauravas. He loses again and is
banished for thirteen years. In accordance with the terms of the
agreement, the Pandavas must go into exile for twelve years and
spend a thirteenth in disguise in society without being discovered.
If discovered during that thirteenth year, they must repeat the
punishment. After losing, Yudhishthira sets off into the jungles,
accompanied by Draupadi and his brothers.

One day, a few years after the game of dice, the Pandavas are
feeling particularly low in the Dvaita forest. Draupadi is in tears
as she thinks about her royal husband sleeping on the hard earth
when he is accustomed to sheets of silk and pillows of down. He
eats roots from the forest when he ought to be feasting like a
king, served by thousands of retainers. Draupadi laments:

> *I remember your old bed and I pity you, great king, so unworthy*
> *of hardship ... sorrow stifles me ... I saw you bright as a sun,*
> *well oiled with sandal paste, now I see you dirty and muddy ...*
> *I have seen you dressed in bright and expensive silks ... and now*
> *I see you wearing bark!*[1]

She cannot get over the bitter memory of her humiliation in the
assembly, especially since the Kauravas snatched their kingdom
through a rigged game.

> *That crook with his gang has brought this suffering on a man like*
> *you ... You are upright, gentle, bountiful, modest, truthful—how*
> *could the spirit of gambling swoop down on you? My mind has*
> *become utterly bewildered and burns with grief as I see this sorrow*
> *of yours and this great distress.*[2]

She asks Yudhishthira, what is the point of being good when it
only brings grief? What kind of world is it where the bad seem
to be rewarded while the good, who uphold dharma, suffer such
hardship?

> *Dharma is supposed to protect the good king, but I find that it*
> *doesn't protect you. You have never strayed. You have always*
> *treated everyone alike. Even after winning all the earth, your head*
> *did not grow. After losing the crooked game of dice, you remained*
> *faithful to your word.*[3]

Draupadi has raised the classic problem of unmerited suffering:
'Why do bad things happen to good people?' When things were
going so well for Yudhishthira, why did tragedy have to strike?
She cries out in anger:

> *When I see noble, moral and modest persons harassed in this way,*
> *and the evil and ignoble flourishing and happy, I stagger with*
> *wonder. I can only condemn the Placer, who allows such outrage.*[4]

'Why be good?'

Isn't it better, Draupadi tells her husband, to give up this forest living, raise an army, and fight the evil Kauravas for what is rightfully theirs?

> *I think, king of men, it is time to use your authority on the greedy Dhartarashtras, who are always offensive. There is no more time to ply the Kurus with forgiveness: and when the time for authority has come, authority must be employed. The meek are despised, but people shrink from the severe: he is a king who knows both.*[5]

Yudhishthira responds by reminding Draupadi that he has given his word. To fight, he says to her, is easy; to forgive is more difficult. To be patient is not to be weak; to seek peace is always the wiser course. Draupadi, however, wonders why her husband does not feel outrage, like a kshatriya warrior, at the injustice of their situation.

> *Why doesn't your anger blaze? ... Truly, O best of the Bharatas, you have no anger, else why is it that your mind is not moved at the sight of your brothers and me?*[6]

Yudhishthira explains to Draupadi that forbearance is superior to anger.[7] But she feels frustrated, and wonders why her husband has adopted a stubborn pacifism while their enemies exploit his goodness. Power, Draupadi argues, is what really counts in the world. 'Why be good?' she asks her husband. Yudhishthira answers her patiently in a sparkling dialogue in the *Vanaparvan*, which presages much thinking about ethics in the major schools of Western moral philosophy.

Yudhishthira is taken aback by the strength of Draupadi's emotion, and he gently explains to her why he must be good. He says:

> *I do not act for the sake of the fruits of dharma. I act because I must. Whether it bears fruits or not, buxom Draupadi, I do my duty like any householder ... I obey dharma, full-hipped woman,*

not for its rewards ... but by its nature my mind is beholden to dharma.[8]

In a typically modest way, Yudhishthira expresses his instinctive sense of duty: 'I act because I must'. He does not follow dharma because of any hope of reward that might come. He acts from a sense of what he has to do. Dharma or 'what he has to do' is a standard of conduct, and a society needs standards. 'He who doubts dharma finds in nothing else a standard,' Yudhishthira says, 'and ends in setting himself as a standard.'[9] He is saying, in effect, that following dharma is its own reward. When one acts thus, it is motives and not consequences that are important. Krishna will elaborate this idea later—of acting without thinking of the 'fruits' of one's action. I will raise the question if it is possible for ordinary human beings to act in this selfless manner.

I confess that I have not met many individuals who had Yudhishthira's instinctive sense of duty, and who did what they did because they had to. One of the very few was the new and young CEO of a company, whose board I joined in the late 1990s. Seventy per cent of the company's production was sold to a government company that insisted on receiving 2 per cent of the invoice as a kickback in cash. The bribe was shared systematically among a number of employees in the state-owned company. Our new CEO refused to pay the bribe. As a result, our company's bills were unpaid for nine months. He tried everything—cajoling, political influence, cutting off supplies—but nothing worked. As the receivables mounted, we discovered one painful morning that our company was bankrupt and would cease operations in two weeks, and 829 people would lose their jobs.

In an emergency meeting of the board of directors, the CEO wanted the board's advice. It was the first time that the board heard about these improper payments, although they had been going on for decades. My first reaction was to rush for cover. Was I liable as an independent director? Should I resign from the board? Then I thought about the future of our 829 employees. As we dug deeper into this ugly mess, we discovered that our CEO had explored all possible options. It seemed to come to an either/or—either to pay the bribe and save the company or to refuse and close it.

Most board members were of the view that since this was the way that things had always been done, we should pay the bribe and get on with it. They were upset with the CEO for having rocked the boat. A few of us, including the new CEO and I, were opposed and we prevailed in the end. The board decided to close the company's government business and retain only the 30 per cent business with private sector customers. This meant that the company would limp along for a while. The CEO promised to try vigorously to replace the lost business by gaining new customers in the private sector. Sadly, 390 workers lost their jobs. I felt guilty about that, but I think we did the right thing.

I admired the CEO for standing up like Yudhishthira. He claimed that we were unlucky to do business with the government, where kickbacks were standard practice. 'It is somebody's money in the private sector and they won't allow it to be stolen in kickbacks,' he added. I reflected on the initial reaction of most board members and I realized they had been persuaded to change their minds because of the fear of disclosure by the auditors. I wondered if people are only honest because of the fear of punishment. I later asked the CEO why he had decided to blow the whistle and made his own life difficult. He mumbled something about not having had a choice—it was a sense of duty, not a fear of disclosure in his case.

Yudhishthira does not elaborate on his laconic statement, 'I act because I must', and this is why Draupadi remains unconvinced. Immanuel Kant, the eighteenth century German philosopher, in trying to understand this sense of duty, said: 'When moral worth is at issue, what counts is not actions, which one sees, but those inner principles of action that one does not see.'[10] These 'inner principles' led me to think about human motives. I was reminded of a newspaper report about a young man who jumped into the

Arabian Sea on a crowded beach and saved a child from drowning. He instantly became a hero. But he confessed a few days later to the *Times of India* that he might not have jumped if no one had been watching. He did it, he said, to impress his friends on a college trip, and particularly one girl. Yudhishthira (or even the CEO) might have jumped even if no one had been looking. So, motives do matter when it comes to duty.

'But a child was saved in the end,' the young man might have protested. 'So, who cares about my motives?' He would have a point. Consequences of one's acts do matter, but so do motives in trying to understand why we behave morally. Where does our sense of duty come from? David Hume, the Scottish philosopher, argued that our moral sense originated in human sentiments. 'The sentiments, dependent on humanity, are the origin of morals,' he said.[11] Kant also felt that one's sense of duty originates in one's humanity, but he added that the 'noble descent' of duty lies in the 'autonomy of the rational being'. Kant located the origin of dharma in man's ability to reason, and the ability to reason underpins man's autonomy. 'This condition,' Kant wrote, 'requires that a person never be used as a means when it is an end in itself.'[12]

Whereas Kant justified duty based on man's humanity and reason, earlier Western thinkers had appealed to 'natural law'. They claimed that human beings have inside their nature a law or a guide to what is right and wrong. Christian thinkers like Thomas Aquinas offered a brilliant exposition of natural law theory in the Middle Ages. Later, John Locke provided an influential variant of this idea based on 'natural rights'. He argued that human beings had certain rights when they started out in a state of nature, and these rights continued even when that state of nature was over and they became citizens of a civil society.[13] Locke's notion of human rights, as we know, had a deep influence on the making of the American and other constitutions and continues to hold sway in the moral and political debates of today.

Yudhishthira's answer to Draupadi implies that consequences or ends do not justify the means. Although the Pandavas have a perfectly legitimate end in regaining their stolen kingdom, they must recover it only by honest means, without compromising dharma. He says that he gave his word when he lost the dice game and he must now abide by his promise. Mahatma Gandhi's refrain to Indians in the first half of the twentieth century was similar. Although throwing off the foreign yoke was a just cause, he felt that Indians had to adopt the right means in winning freedom of their country.

Draupadi, however, does not believe that this principle works in politics, especially when one's political opponents are ready to employ 'dirty tricks' to gain power. In contemporary democracies politicians may not 'steal' an election through a dice game and they usually do not tell outright lies, but they always use 'spin' in order to 'package' themselves in a way that maintains their popularity. Draupadi is pragmatic and she would favor consequentialist ethics to get the Pandavas to act.

'To save the family, abandon the individual'

Yudhishthira senses that Draupadi is dissatisfied with his duty-based answer to her question, 'Why be good?'. Hence, he takes a different tack, shifting his focus to the consequences and away from intentions: he offers heaven as the reward for being good.

> *He who resolutely follows dharma, O beautiful woman, attains to infinitude hereafter.*[14]

But Draupadi remains unmoved. Yudhishthira then tries another approach. He appeals to her based on the law of karma, which teaches that human deeds will inevitably have consequences. 'Knowing that acts bear [karmic] fruit, the wise man is content even with a little,' he says.[15] The law of karma is rooted deeply in the innate human belief in the efficacy of action. Human beings act on the assumption that their desires, intentions and actions will lead to an intended goal. As Manu, the Indian lawgiver, explains:

> ... *it is impossible to be free from desire* ... *Intention is the root of desire* ... *Nowhere in this world do we see any activity done by a man free from desire; for whatever that a man may do, it is the work of someone who desired it.*[16]

Human desire and intentions work on our innate belief in cause and effect, and this assumption led ancient Indians to postulate a dharma based on the consequences of human action—and, accordingly, a harmonious, cosmic law of karma. This is why Draupadi is outraged when she sees the virtuous Pandavas suffering in the forest. It creates a dilemma in her mind. What keeps the Pandavas going is their belief that virtue will be rewarded eventually. In fact, the sage Markandeya reassures Yudhishthira that actions always bear fruit. Those fruits, according to the law of karma, might emerge in this world, but they might also emerge in another world.[17]

There are others in the epic who also judge the rightness of an action from its results. The respected counsellor Vidura, who is half-brother of King Dhritarashtra, appeals repeatedly to the king to stop his wicked son from proceeding with the dice game. Vidura believes that an act is good only if it promotes good consequences. And an act that promotes the good of many persons is better than one which promotes the good of a few. He is against the dice game not only because of the deception involved, but because it will eventually create strife and harm the interests of the country and the people. As a true 'consequentialist', he says:

> *To save the family, [one must] abandon an individual. To save the village, abandon a family; to save the country, abandon the village.*[18]

Vidura's position is that if an action produces good consequences, then it is good. Yudhishthira might not have abandoned an individual for the sake of the family. His sense of duty to *ahimsa*, non-violence, might not have allowed him to sacrifice even a single human life. He goes further than Kant: he looks upon all sentient beings (not just human beings) as ends in themselves. When one sacrifices an individual for a village then one treats that individual as a means rather than an end.

It is dilemmas such as these—between intentions and consequences, and ends and means—that make dharma subtle, as Bhishma pointed out to Draupadi in the assembly. Perhaps because he feels guilty for not 'saving' Draupadi on that day, Bhishma will return to the difficulty of being good in Book Twelve when it comes to a trade-off between telling the truth and saving a life. He tells Yudhishthira about Kaushika, an ascetic without much learning, who is accosted one day by a group of thieving cut-throats who are seeking the man who had witnessed their crime. Kaushika had seen the witness run into the forest and he knows that if he reveals it, he is issuing a death sentence. He must choose between the dharma of *satya*, telling the truth, or of *ahimsa*, saving a life.

Kaushika chooses the duty of *satya* over *ahimsa*. The robbers catch and kill their prey, and the ascetic ends in a gruesome hell because he failed to understand that dharma in this instance required him to tell a 'white lie' to the villains. Bhishma explains that while 'there is nothing higher than the truth',

> the thing most difficult to understand in the whole world . . . is that truth should not be spoken and that falsehood should be spoken, where falsehood would be truth, or truth falsehood. Someone simple is dumbfounded in that circumstance where truth is not fixed . . . If escape is possible by not singing your song, then you should not let out the smallest note. But if your not singing would arouse suspicion, then you absolutely have to sing away.[19]

In Western literature, the most dramatic example of this trade-off came in a question posed by Fyodor Dostoevsky in *The*

Brothers Karamazov. Ivan asks whether it is justified to torture a child in order to bring incalculable happiness to the rest of humanity?

> Tell me honestly, I challenge you—answer me: imagine that you are charged with building the edifice of human destiny, the ultimate aim of which is to bring people happiness, to give them peace and contentment at last, but that in order to achieve this it is essential and unavoidable to torture just one little speck of creation, that same little child beating her chest with her little fists, and imagine that this edifice has to be erected on her unexpiated tears. Would you agree to be the architect under those conditions? Tell me honestly![20]

Alyosha, his brother, does not have an answer, and Dostoevsky seems to feel that such questions are unsolvable. This is perhaps why dharma is 'subtle'. But Yudhishthira, with his commitment to the absolute principle of *ahimsa*, 'non-violence', would probably have refused to torture the child no matter how benign the consequences. Bhishma and Krishna—like most political leaders who have to run a state—would have chosen the more practical approach of looking at the consequences of an action.[21] The sensible Vidura, who is also close to power, would have argued that by sacrificing one child, he would have been able to save millions of children from suffering in the future—saving them from disease, hunger, violence and other forms of pain. The ethic of absolute standards and perfection appeals more to those who are far removed from public office like Yudhishthira when he is in the forest.

In our present ethical mood, we intensely admire an individual like Yudhishthira. The nineteenth-century public, however, was influenced by Jeremy Bentham, whose Utilitarian philosophy focused on consequences. He judged an act to be 'good' or moral by the net amount of pleasure or happiness it produced. Bentham would answer Draupadi's question like Vidura: what is good is that which promotes the greatest happiness of the greatest number. Bentham too may have sacrificed a family for the sake of a village or tortured one child in order to save all children from suffering. The great divide in ethical thinking is between those who judge an act based on its consequences versus those who judge it based on duty or some rule.

The attraction of Consequentialism is its simplicity. I can quickly tell if I am being good by examining the consequences of my act. Everyone is equal in the equation, whether a servant or a master.[22] My criticism of it is that it ignores the justice or fairness in the distribution of goods. It is indifferent to the needs of the weak and the poor as long as society's overall satisfaction is maximized.[23] Indeed, it is all too easy to ignore the circumstances and the freedom of a minority in maximizing the welfare of society as a whole.[24]

'Dharma is a ship that guides one to the farthest shore'

We return to husband and wife in the Dvaita forest. Yudhishthira can see that his 'beautiful' Draupadi is still not satisfied, and he gropes for another answer to her question, 'Why be good?' He turns to the social benefits of moral action. He compares dharma to a ship that allows human beings to journey through life, just as it allows a merchant to travel to the farthest shores. 'Were dharma to be fruitless,' he says, 'the whole world would sink into a bottomless darkness ... and [people] would live like cattle.'[25] His assumption is that human beings can live together only if they cooperate. If people do not trust each other, the social order will collapse. Our moral rules, such as *ahimsa*, 'not hurting others', or *satya*, 'telling the truth', are, in fact, rules for cooperation, without which we would 'sink into a bottomless darkness', he says.

David Hume also felt that the rules of a society were a social creation. While at the individual's level moral rules may well be inviolate injunctions that a person must follow unquestioningly, at society's level they are justified by social utility. This justification of morality is sometimes called Indirect Utilitarianism. Its attraction lies in its ability to combine both the approaches—one that judges the goodness of an act by looking at its consequences and the other of looking to the intentions behind the act. In the case of Yudhishthira—he can still act based on principle and observe dharma because he regards it a duty. Moral rules, such as *ahimsa*, 'not hurting others', or *satya*, 'telling the truth', are imperative duties for him. The duties themselves, however, are justified separately by their ability to produce positive consequences—i.e. keeping society going or keeping 'the ship afloat', as he puts it. This argument combines, somewhat opportunistically, the best in both the 'consequences' and 'duty' or 'intention'-based moral positions.

Draupadi does not immediately respond to her husband, but I suspect she would have accepted this argument. This is one of the fundamental themes of the epic and it repeats it often in the form of an abstract axiom: 'Where there is dharma, there is victory'.[26] By this, the epic means that dharma yields good fruits not only for the individual but for society as a whole. Indeed, Draupadi's frustration in this case is not with the principle. She is disappointed with her husband for ignoring the social consequences of his actions. In her view, he neglects the dharma of the king and of the ruling kshatriya caste. Because of his bull-headed insistence on remaining in the forest, she feels he lets his people down, and fails to uphold dharma. The king's dharma is to ensure that society functions harmoniously. How can he observe this dharma if he is unwilling to fight, regain his kingdom, and be a dharmic king?

'Why cover yourself in tatters of dharma and throw away *artha* and *kama*?'

Having overheard Draupadi make a heroic but unsuccessful effort to get his older brother Yudhishthira to get up and fight, Bhima joins them now. He confesses that he cannot get over the theft of their kingdom and he exhorts Yudhishthira to get up and fight to recover what is rightfully theirs. He uses a different argument, however, and without realizing it, offers another answer to Draupadi's question, 'Why be good?' By remaining in the forest, he says, the Pandavas are neglecting the three aims of a good and flourishing life. The classical Indian texts enjoin an individual to pursue *kama*, 'pleasure', *artha*, 'material well-being', and dharma, 'righteousness', in order to fulfil life's purpose.

> *Why should we dwell in this austere wilderness and miss out on dharma, artha and kama? . . . Why cover yourself in some tatters of dharma, king, and throw away artha, which is the [material] basis for [the pursuit of] dharma and kama?*[27]

Bhima does not mention the fourth aim, suggesting that, perhaps, the last aim of *moksha*, 'spiritual liberation', may have been added later. He makes the sensible point that it is difficult to be virtuous in conditions of extreme deprivation when one is constantly thinking of the next meal. 'But one who is destitute of wealth cannot practise dharma.'[28] A person needs a minimal level of material security even to practise dharma properly.

Bhima concedes that when the three aims of life come into conflict, dharma trumps the other two. It disciplines the pursuit of pleasure and wealth, and thus provides balance to a good human life. But by remaining in the forest, Yudhishthira neglects the other two aims of life, and thereby fails to fulfil life's purpose. The ancient Greeks reached a similar conclusion. They also believed that human life had a *telos*, 'purpose', and Aristotle felt that the human life had multiple ends, and virtue was one of them.

∽

In this dialogue, the *Mahabharata* has offered a number of answers to Draupadi's question, 'Why be virtuous?' Yudhishthira's first answer is instinctive—he 'acts because he must'. He follows dharma because it is there and he feels it his duty to follow it. Yudhishthira feels an inclination, a *svabhava*, a 'predisposition to act in a certain way'.[29] He upholds the truth and he sticks to his promise because he has an inner disposition to do so. This is an important distinction, one similar to the ancient Greek idea of 'character', and it is a dimension absent from the approaches based on 'duty' and 'consequences'. Whatever the temptations or the advantages of raising an army in order to recover his kingdom, Yudhishthira will not break his vow to King Dhritarashtra.

> ... the promise I made is a true one, remember
> I choose over life and eternity, dharma
> Neither kingdom, nor sons, neither glory nor wealth,
> Can even come up to a fraction of the Truth![30]

Since this answer does not appeal to Draupadi, the epic offers several other arguments based on the consequences of one's behaviour. The first is the standard religious one: a person will go to heaven if she is good. The second is the law of karma. The third is the more general benefit of virtuous behaviour to society. Finally, the epic offers, via Bhima, an answer that students of ethics know as 'virtue ethics'. It connects 'being good' with character and fulfilling the purpose of human life. A good and flourishing life demands that a human being observe dharma.

Yudhishthira did not succeed in convincing Draupadi on that day. The question 'Why be good?' is left hanging in the air and it will hang over the epic till the end, when the Pandavas will still be searching for an answer. Yudhishthira, however, is sad and contrite. He feels that he has let his family down. 'I do not blame you for your bitterness. For my wrong course brought this misery upon you,' he says.[31] Both Draupadi and Bhima try to cheer him up, saying that victory will ultimately follow if they pursue the kshatriya's dharma. But Yudhishthira is unconvinced for dharma to him is a deeply personal matter. Being truthful and non-violent has little to do with being a kshatriya warrior.

To her dismay, Draupadi can sense his real and bull-headed commitment to his sense of duty.[32]

'That is the way it is!'

'It is not the Indian style to send heroes off to the forest and then continue, "After twelve years they came back". The romance of the forest was too gripping and the theme of the prince exiled too popular.'[33] During their wanderings the Pandavas face many hardships, encounter sages and enchanted spirits, and have many adventures. In the thirteenth year, they move to the capital city of the king of Virata. To avoid being discovered, they assume disguises: Yudhishthira becomes a dice master at the royal court; Draupadi, the queen's handmaiden; Bhima, a cook in the royal kitchen; Arjuna dresses like a woman and gets the job of a eunuch to guard the ladies' chambers and to teach the royal women dancing; Nakula becomes a groom in the stables; and Sahadeva looks after the royal cattle. Duryodhana sends spies to find them, but they remain undetected during their year of masquerade.

After thirteen years of exile and adventure, including several attempts on their lives by the Kauravas, the Pandavas return to reclaim their inheritance. They have fulfilled the terms of the agreement and now expect their rightful share of the kingdom. But Duryodhana refuses. Elaborate peace negotiations follow between the two sides. Duryodhana, however, remains adamant. So, war becomes inevitable.

The decision to declare war is an awkward moment for Yudhishthira who is dedicated to preserving dharma. Lamenting the failure of the peace negotiations, Yudhishthira says that 'war is evil in any form'.[34] He goes on to say:

> *The ultimate disaster for which I dwelled in the forest and suffered is upon us in spite of all our striving . . . For how can war be waged with men who we must not kill? How can we win if we must kill our gurus and elders?*[35]

Yudhishthira's brothers try to reassure their elder brother. They remind him of his duty to his family, to his kshatriya heritage and to his people—he is a king, after all. There is much discussion among the mighty warriors about the rightness of war. To stop the endless debate Krishna exclaims impatiently and bluntly, 'That is the way it is!'[36]

The Pandavas' decision to go to war marks a turning point in Yudhishthira's thinking about dharma. Yudhishthira has evolved from a guileless idealist who stands for absolute moral standards into a pragmatist who understands the limitations of those who have to rule a state.[37] Sanjaya, the emissary of the Kauravas in the second peace negotiations, does not realize this change. He suggests to Yudhishthira: 'Do not destroy yourself! If the Kurus will not grant you your share . . . without resorting to war, then in my opinion, a life of begging . . . would be better than winning your kingdom through war.'[38] The earlier Yudhishthira in the forest might have accepted this suggestion to turn the other cheek; now, he finds it preposterous. Sanjaya chides him:

> . . . if you must commit an evil act of such hostility, Parthas, after all this time, why then, Pandavas, did you have to live in the forest for those successive years, in miserable exile, just because it was right? . . . And why have you spent these successive years in the forests if you want to fight now, Pandava, when you have lost so much time? It is a foolish man who fights . . .[39]

Yudhishthira's answer comes as a surprise:

> . . . in times of trouble one's duty alters. When one's livelihood is disrupted and one is totally poverty-stricken, one should wish for other means to carry out one's prescribed duties . . . which means that in dire situations one may perform normally improper acts.[40]

Chastened by thirteen harsh years in exile, Yudhishthira has become pragmatic. As he takes charge of the war effort, and assumes 'complete control of his brothers and his allies',[41] he also recognizes the limits of absolute goodness. He agrees with his ally, Satyaki: 'No law can be found against killing enemies who are plotting to kill us.'[42] He tells Sanjaya, 'I am just as capable of peace as I am of war . . . as I am of gentleness and severity.'[43] His new, down-to-earth view of dharma is grounded in self-interest but without being amoral. His new position avoids both ideological extremes—the Hobbesian amorality of Duryodhana as well as the idealistic super-morality of the earlier Yudhishthira in exile.

I approve of this prudent Yudhishthira. One should be realistic and pursue only what is attainable. Unnecessarily demanding ideals are easily discredited. Although 'prudence' does not have a high moral purchase these days—it suggests a person who is self-interested and expedient—I believe one can be 'prudent' when one's own interest is not involved. A 'prudent' mother is concerned for her child's welfare. A 'prudent' person looks at the future consequences of actions. These do not make them selfish actions. They are compatible with acting considerately and bearing in mind the interest of others. Accordingly, this new Yudhishthira, however different he may appear on the surface, is the Yudhishthira who at the epic's end will hold up the virtues of *ahimsa*, 'non-violence', and *anrishamsya*, 'compassion', as the highest dharma.[44]

Yudhishthira's moral journey from Book Three (*Vanaparvan*) to Book Five (*Udyogaparvan*) of the epic has brought him to a rational and sensible position. Indeed, Machiavelli might have been addressing the earlier Yudhishthira when he wrote, 'a man who wishes to profess goodness at all times will come to ruin among so many who are not so good'.[45] Yudhishthira's new position is more akin to the evolutionary principle of reciprocal altruism: adopt a friendly face to the world but do not allow yourself to be exploited. Recent insights of evolutionary scientists throw some light on this pragmatic middle ground, in terms of both how we live and how we ought to.[46] There is always a risk in deriving moral values from nature's workings; an unwarranted inference from what 'is' to what 'ought to be'—this is what philosophers call the 'naturalistic fallacy'. There is also a risk in over-reading the data of the young discipline of evolutionary biology. Still, I believe that it can illuminate the moral temper of the *Mahabharata*.

To be sure, human beings have evolved through a long struggle in which only the fittest have passed on their genes. But to conclude that life is a tooth-and-claw struggle—or that morality is merely in the interest of the strong, as Duryodhana claims—is a mistake. Nature is full of examples of dharma-like goodness. Dolphins will help lift an injured companion for hours to help it survive. Blackbirds and thrushes give warning calls when they spot a hawk even if it means risking their own lives.

Evolutionary biology assumes that societies have developed moral principles in order to get people to cooperate. Moral rules are grounded in human self-interest but are tempered by our need to live with others—a pragmatic assumption that also runs through the *Mahabharata*. So, where might our dharma-like behaviour originate? In *The Descent of Man*, Charles Darwin speculated that in the course of evolution, if a person helped another, he would also receive help in return. 'From this low motive,' Darwin wrote, 'he might acquire the habit of aiding his fellows; and the habit of performing benevolent actions.'[47] This thought of Darwin's led biologists to hypothesize that 'an individual who maximizes his friendships and minimizes his antagonisms will have an evolutionary advantage, and selection should favour those characters that promote the optimization of personal relationships'.[48] One observes that human beings do tend to behave altruistically towards their relatives and this suggests a link of reciprocity with kin selection in evolution: 'A gene that repaid kindness with kindness could thus have spread through the extended family and by interbreeding to other families.'[49]

To see how such a 'reciprocal altruism' might work in practice, let us look at the famous Prisoner's Dilemma.[50] It might help explain why Yudhishthira changes his moral position in the *Mahabharata*. In this game, the police are trying to get two prisoners to confess to a jointly committed crime. If one of them confesses, he will be let off and the other will spend his life in jail. If neither confesses, both will spend minimal time in jail. If both confess, then both will have to spend seven years in jail. The logical selfish strategy is to confess, betray your partner, and hope that he won't betray you. The 'altruistic' strategy is not to confess, but then you run the risk of spending your life in jail if your partner betrays you. The best strategy is collaborative— neither should confess. In that case, both would be free after spending a minimal time in jail.

The Prisoner's Dilemma teaches us something about how strangers cooperate in society. A round-robin tournament of the Prisoner's Dilemma was held in which contestants played two hundred games with one player and then moved to the next, the objective being to minimize the time in jail. The reason for repeating the games was to simulate real life, in which people meet each other repeatedly in large, anonymous cities. The winner of the game was neither altruistic nor egoistic—but the person who used a strategy called 'tit-for-tat', or what Indians call *'nehle pe dehla'*.[51] 'Tit-for-tat' is in effect 'reciprocal altruism': do not confess on the first move; this sends a signal to your opponent that you are a nice person; from the second move onwards, however, mimic what your opponent does; if he is nice to you, reciprocate by being nice; if he is selfish, punish him in kind. This sends a message to the Duryodhanas of the world that you will retaliate if necessary.

Each time that the tournament was replayed, 'tit-for-tat' or reciprocity won. Those who followed the selfish strategy always lost. Those who tried to be good like the earlier Yudhishthira in the forest also lost. Neither pure meanness nor pure goodness paid off.⁵² I learned from this game that the principle of reciprocity keeps cheats like Duryodhana in check. In contrast Mahatma Gandhi's and Jesus's teaching about turning the other cheek sends them a wrong signal that cheating pays. So, Draupadi does have a point when she tells Yudhishthira to get up and raise an army. What she is saying, in effect, is 'do not be a sucker'— counter meanness with meanness.

However, 'tit-for-tat' should not be confused with an aggressive strategy. It calls for presenting a friendly face to the world—the first move in the game is always to be nice. Yudhishthira presents an affable face during the interminable peace negotiations. And he will make an exceptionally generous offer to Duryodhana, as we shall soon see. The difference is that Yudhishthira is no longer willing to be exploited. It has taken him thirteen long years to realize that Draupadi may have been right.

It does seem extraordinary that evolutionary biology and the Prisoner's Dilemma should be able to shed light on the pragmatic temper of the *Mahabharata*. When Yudhishthira gave the order to start the war—albeit reluctantly—he acted like a reciprocal altruist and became a prudent ruler of the middle path. It is a path somewhere between the 'amoral realism' of Duryodhana and the 'ethical idealism' of the earlier Yudhishthira in the forest. Having said that, we still admire this earlier Yudhishthira who instinctively told Draupadi, 'I act because I must.' Although we cannot be like him, he does appeal to our ideals, and every society needs ideals. As always, Oscar Wilde says it best, 'We are all in the gutter. But some of us are looking at the stars.'

Can dharma be taught?

In goading Yudhishthira to fight for his kingdom, Draupadi showed an admirable bias for action that would make any CEO proud. She elaborated her managerial principle thus: 'One first decides [keeping] one's mind on one's goal, then achieves it with acts . . . an act capably done, well planned by the doer, is clearly distinguished from an incompetent one.'[53] In saying this, Draupadi is gently rebuking her husband. While his *sva-dharma* is clearly that of a kshatriya, a man of action, he behaves too often like a brahmin, a man of contemplation. Draupadi is using the word 'dharma' here in the sense of a 'calling', which is also the connotation that my father had in mind when he would proclaim that 'engineering' was his dharma.

In the same dialogue, Draupadi suggests that those who have a sense of 'dharma as a calling' are fortunate. She says, 'For who knows what his task is, [he] is one in a thousand!'[54] I expect she feels this way because such fortunate persons have an intrinsic motivation for their work. She would have been proud of the primary schoolteacher in Dharmapuri district in Tamil Nadu who I read about in the *Times of India* in May 2005—a man who has bicycled 32 kilometres each day for the past twenty years without missing a single day of school. Because of his commitment, as well his ability to inspire students, a surprising number of his former students went on to become hugely famous. When asked about the roots of his motivation, he answered, 'Teaching is my dharma,' the sort of answer that a professional like Drona, the teacher of the Kauravas and Pandavas, would also have given.

Contrast this with the findings of a study on government primary school teachers in India by Michael Kremer of Harvard University and others (including members of the World Bank) that shocked the Indian nation in 2003. From it we learned that one in four teachers in our government primary schools is absent and one in four, although present, is not teaching. Thus, one in two teachers out of roughly 1.5 million primary school teachers is not doing his/her job. Aside from the institutional aspects of the failure, a teacher who is chronically absent wounds dharma and demeans the teaching profession.

Dharma is not only a matter of personal well being. It is also a matter of social and political health, and the epic is deeply concerned with 'the dharma of the king' and his officials and it will elaborate this further in Book Twelve. Among the officials of the state are schoolteachers in government primary schools in India, who fail dharma when they are absent. The *Mahabharata* has offered a number of reasons to these schoolteachers to be good. First, because it is one's duty; second, good acts produce good consequences; third, the social order would collapse if people did not keep to their commitments; finally, virtue or dharma is necessary for leading a good and flourishing life. The absentee schoolteacher wounds dharma on all counts—he/she fails her duty; he/she fails the consequentialist test, destroying the futures of her students; and he/she neglects his/her own capabilities, failing to achieve life's purpose.

Plato wrote more than two thousand years ago that the reform of schools is everyone's work—the work of every man, woman and child. While school reform—say punishing a teacher for absence—would certainly bring errant teachers back to school, how does one address the moral failure? How does one get a teacher not only to be present but also teach with a sense of calling? Can dharma be taught so that there are more inspiring teachers like the one in Dharmapuri? Both Plato and Aristotle believed that virtue could be taught. A person's character is not something that one is born with. It is constantly evolving through repeated actions, and one can be educated to become more moral. Aristotle gives the example of a musician in the *Nicomachean Ethics*. To become a musician, Aristotle says, requires skill and repetitive practice. In the same way, to become virtuous requires repeating virtuous actions.[55]

I tend to view the old concept of karma in this light. When I repeat certain actions, I accumulate karma of a certain kind, which builds a certain kind of character and predisposes me to act in a certain way. Karma for me is not something supernatural but *svabhava*, 'an inclination to act in a certain way' as a result of my habits, which have been formed as a result of my past actions. So when Yudhishthira tells Draupadi that eventually human acts do bear fruit, even though the fruit is invisible,[56] one might interpret 'fruit' to mean the building of character through repeated actions. Yudhishthira was certainly aware that repeated actions had a way of changing one's inclinations to act in a certain way. That inclination is character.

Ancient Indians shared Aristotle's belief that character could be built. They regarded the *Mahabharata* as a 'dharma text' which could teach dharma. It is plausible to expect that when one hears repeatedly of the unfair suffering of Draupadi or Yudhishthira one becomes gradually more empathetic. Moral experiments show that 'subjects who were urged to relax and use their imaginations when hearing a story of distress reported both greater emotion and a greater willingness to help the victim than did subjects who were urged to remain detached and "objective". It would seem, then, that people who attend to the distress of another in a manner sufficient for compassion have motives to help that person.'[57]

The epic forces us to reflect on our beliefs and our behaviour. It makes us aware about how we deceive ourselves. Even Yudhishthira confesses to Draupadi and Bhima at the end of this scene, saying that he is not the good man that they think him to be. He had accepted the dice game because of a secret hope that he would win and thereby expand his kingdom. Even when he was losing, he knew that the game was crooked, but he could not stop because he was caught in the gambler's frenetic whirl. Thus, Yudhishthira's mask falls off, and with this devastating discovery Draupadi becomes silent. Secretly, perhaps, she may have been pleased to see that her husband is human and vulnerable, like any other person. It could not have been easy to live with such a principled man. Yudhishthira's confession shakes the listeners of the epic as well, making us aware how difficult it is to be good in a world where right and wrong are intricately mixed in a bewildering manner.

The *Mahabharata* could never be a 'how to' book given its ambivalence towards moral truth. Yudhishthira is unable to convince Draupadi about 'why we should be good'. It does suggest, however, that 'being good' is not a one-off event but a continuing attitude to life and other human beings. Although dharma can be learned, it is an inner 'journey of self-discovery, overcoming self-deception'.[58] Mahatma Gandhi tried to cultivate the moral instinct in an unusual way through his famous 'experiments with truth'. He employed fasts as an instrument of moral growth and was courageous in making a 180-degree turn when it was warranted. He said, 'It may entail continuous suffering and the cultivating of endless patience, [but] step by step one makes friends with the entire world.'[59] The pitfall on this journey, he reminds us, is the human tendency for self-deception. No one 'ever understands quite his own artful dodges to escape from the shadow of self-knowledge'.[60]

Being good may come naturally to Yudhishthira and to the CEO who refused to bribe in order to get government business, but to Draupadi and to most of us, it needs effort. Even when one is able to recognize moral behaviour, one is not able to practise it. One tries to project one's good side and hide one's weaknesses. One admires individuals who are ethical, believing that their lives are somehow more integrated. Why is it then so difficult to behave morally? Is it because goodness is not rewarded more tangibly and generously in the world? The virtuous Pandavas endure banishment, deprivation and hardship, while the wicked Kauravas flourish in their palaces. This is why Draupadi is tempted to accept Duryodhana's view that dharma is merely a disguised form of the interest of the stronger—that people are basically selfish and they invoke dharma in order to further their own interests. Hence, she concludes that it is better to be powerful than virtuous.

One has come across people who are less than virtuous but who are successful, wealthy and powerful. They are even admired and sometimes loved. At the same time one also knows 'good' people who end up poor, helpless, and even pitiable. One sympathizes with them for it seems reasonable to want and achieve some degree of success. Is a 'good' person likely to have as much chance of succeeding as a 'bad' person? Draupadi seems inclined to believe that the world is so structured that only the selfish, the powerful and the dishonest will have an edge in life. Yudhishthira, however, shows by his own example that there is another way to live. One need not assume that a competitive, self-centred life dedicated solely to self-advancement is the only way.

The *Mahabharata* reminds us that it is natural and desirable for human beings to want happiness and pleasure as they seek to be good. *Kama* is one of the legitimate goals of human life. The Christian denial of physical pleasure, especially sexual pleasure, is happily absent from the epic and most ancient Indian texts. So is the 'thou shalt not' approach, which makes one feel guilty, and turns one off the moral project. The notion of dharma as it emerges from the *Mahabharata* is a plural one. Being plural makes greater demands on one's reason, for human objectives sometimes conflict with each other, and this forces one to choose. The attraction of a clean ethical theory like Utilitarianism is that it attempts to resolve moral issues on the basis of a single criterion. Pluralism is more complex but no less rational. One needs to order different virtues in a hierarchy in order to help one to choose in the case of a conflict.

Dharma is supposed to uphold a certain cosmic balance and it is expected to help us to balance the plural ends of life—desire, material well being, and righteousness—when they come into conflict. Dharma sets limits on the pursuit of pleasure and wealth. In practice this implies, for example, that one maximizes one's pleasure as long as it does not diminish another's. What we have learnt so far, however, is that dharma does not do a very good job of it.

4

ARJUNA'S DESPAIR

'There are no victors in war'

'I shall not fight,' [and] he fell silent.

—Arjuna to Krishna, Bhagavad Gita II.9

'The magic bow slips from my hand'

Krishna personally leads the final embassy to the court of Hastinapura in a last-ditch effort to persuade the Kauravas to make peace. He hopes that his godly stature and his neutrality (somewhat compromised though it is) will help to reach a settlement between the warring cousins. Although this is the third diplomatic attempt to avert war, the intractable Duryodhana remains unmoved. Eventually, Yudhishthira makes an exceptionally generous offer to Duryodhana. He will forgo his share of the kingdom and accept only five villages—a deal which the hawks in the Pandava camp find appalling.[1] But Duryodhana stubbornly refuses, saying:

I shall not cede Yudhishthira even a pinprick of land.[2]

On his return, Krishna tells the Pandavas, 'War is the only course left.' The mood of the epic changes to dread and foreboding at the approaching horror of the war.[3] Both sides begin to make furious preparations. Yudhishthira assembles seven armies, against eleven of the Kauravas. All the great kingdoms of the time are now allied to one or the other side. As expected, Bhishma is named commander-in-chief of the Kauravas. On the first day of battle:

> *under a clear sky, the kings, at Duryodhana Dhritarashtra's orders, marched against the Pandavas. They had all bathed and purified themselves, wore garlands and white robes, held swords and banners, and had offered into the fire and had the svasti pronounced.*[4]

While describing the battle formations of the troops at the end of *Udyogaparvan*, Book Five, the epic portrays with a touch of irony the mood of the warriors:

> *There were berserk men there, clutching their weapons—twenty thousand standards commanded by champions. There were five thousand elephants ... Behind followed hundreds of thousands and myriads of men, marching and shouting in thousands of formations. And in their thousands and tens of thousands the happy warriors sounded their thousands of drums and tens of thousands of conches.*[5]

'Happy' warriors, indeed—soon, there will be 'no more happy warriors, only resigned ones'.[6]

The world-famous philosophical poem, Bhagavad Gita, now commences in a profound 'moment of stillness before the tempest' in Book Six of the *Mahabharata*.[7] In its opening lines, the Gita announces that this is no ordinary battlefield—it is also a moral field (*dharma-kshetra*). Dhritarashtra, the blind king, turns to Sanjaya, his bard and charioteer:

> *Sanjaya, tell me what my sons*
> *and the sons of Pandu did when they met,*
> *wanting to do battle on the field of Kuru,*
> *on the field of sacred duty?*[8]

Sanjaya, who has received a special boon of distant vision, becomes one of the world's first war correspondents. He describes how the heroes and the troops on both sides are arrayed on the battlefield at Kurukshetra. His focus is on Arjuna, the greatest warrior of his age, who stands at the head of his troops, alongside Krishna, his charioteer:

> *Standing on their great chariot*
> *Yoked with white stallions,*
> *Krishna and Arjuna, Pandu's son*
> *sounded their divine conches.*[9]

As Arjuna sees the enemy troops in formation, with weapons ready to begin, he raises his bow, but stops. He says:

> *Krishna,*
> *halt my chariot*
> *between the armies!*
>
> *Far enough for me to see*
> *these men who lust for war*
> *ready to fight with me*
> *in the strain of battle.*[10]

Krishna halts their splendid chariot between the two armies.

> *Arjuna saw them standing there:*
> *fathers, grandfathers, teachers,*
> *uncles, brothers, sons,*
> *grandsons and friends.*[11]

As he surveys the field full of his kinsmen who want war, Arjuna is filled with a strange pity and he says:

> *My limbs sink,*
> *my mouth is parched,*
> *my body trembles,*
> *the hair bristles on my flesh.*

The magic bow slips
from my hand, my skin burns,
I cannot stand still,
my mind reels.

I see omens of chaos,
Krishna; I see no good
in killing my kinsmen
in battle.[12]

He sees so many on the enemy side who are blameless, for whom he has great affection, with whom he played when he was young. In the ensuing war he will have to kill them. How can it be right to kill the ones you love?

Saying this in the time of war
Arjuna slumped into the chariot
and laid down his bows and arrows,
His mind tormented by grief.[13]

This well-known episode, known as *Arjunavishada*, has become a celebrated protest against war.

'I shall not fight'

Sanjaya continues:

Arjuna sat dejected,
filled with pity,
his sad eyes blurred by tears.

Seeing him thus, with his famous Gandiva bow on the ground, Krishna asks,

Why this cowardice
in time of crisis, Arjuna?
The coward is ignoble, shameful,
Foreign to the ways of heaven.[14]

Arjuna replies,

> *It is better in this world*
> *to beg for scraps of food*
> *than to eat meals smeared with the blood of elders.*

> *'I shall not fight,'*
> *[and] he fell silent.*[15]

It is an extraordinary sight: the greatest hero of his time is suddenly full of uncertainty and indecision just before his supreme test. Arjuna had hitherto been of the 'war party' along with Draupadi, and Krishna is dumbfounded at this sudden development (as indeed, say, General Patton's driver might have been had his boss dithered on the eve of the invasion of Sicily in World War II). Unlike Achilles in the *Iliad*, Arjuna does not refuse to fight because of pride, but because he has grasped the inner meaning of war. And as if to prove it, his courageous sixteen-year-old son, Abhimanyu, will be among the first heroes to fall, and in a most unjust way.

Karl von Clausewitz, the German strategist, set out to explain the 'inner meaning' of war. He wrote, 'War has no limits to violence . . . [The reason is that] each of the adversaries forces the hand of the other, and this results in continuous escalation, in which neither side is guilty even if it acts first, since every act can be called pre-emptive.'[16] Once war begins, it inevitably escalates, without limit. (When Winston Churchill made the decision to fight Adolf Hitler, he did not know that the war would escalate into the fire-bombing of German cities in which thousands of civilians would die.) Great tragedy is inescapable in war.

Arjuna's older brother, Yudhishthira, also understands this. In trying to prevent the war, he had earlier expressed the idea that total annihilation was certain even though the war might be won.

> *The aftermath [of war] is evil, for survivors do survive. The*
> *survivors regain their strength and themselves leave no survivors*
> *but aim at total annihilation to put an end to the feud.*[17]

Later, as if to prove this prescient truth, Ashwatthama, the son of their archery teacher, Drona, will avenge the unjust killing of his father. He will set on fire the entire victorious and sleeping armies of the Pandavas and their allies—a deed as heinous as the dropping of the atomic bomb over Hiroshima in World War II or the burning of Atlanta in the American Civil War. Of the hundreds and thousands of warriors who begin to fight in the war, only eleven are left after eighteen days. Seeing this, Yudhishthira says, 'there are no victors in war', and from here onwards, the mood of the *Mahabharata* also changes.

What should Arjuna do?

Arjuna has no doubt that his cause is just. He is also confident that his side will prevail, in part because of his own considerable skills as an archer, but also because he has Krishna, the God, who is his charioteer as well as the master strategist of the Pandavas. The Kauravas and the Pandavas had both wanted Krishna on their side. Krishna had given them a choice—they could either have him or his armies. Arjuna chose him while Duryodhana took the God's awesome armies. And now, despite having God on his side, Arjuna is dejected. The prospect of killing his loved ones fills him with anguish. He suggests to Krishna that, perhaps, the Pandavas ought to give up their claims to the kingdom as the lesser of the two evils.

Krishna devotes the next '700 fratricidal verses' to persuade Arjuna to fight, and this becomes the Gita.[18] He offers many reasons, some more persuasive than others. One of them is that Arjuna must fight because it is his duty as a warrior.

> *Look to your own duty;*
> *do not tremble before it;*
> *nothing is better for a warrior*
> *than a battle of sacred duty.*[19]

This appears to be similar to Yudhishthira's first and instinctive response to Draupadi's question, 'Why be good?' when they were in exile. It is a superficial resemblance, however, for the meaning of duty is different in the two cases. For Krishna, Arjuna's duty is to fight because he is obliged to do so as a warrior of the kshatriya caste. Yudhishthira's duty was to keep his promise based on the dictates of his conscience. As noted before, the epic distinguishes between the two meanings of dharma—caste duty as *sva-dharma*, which varies from caste to caste; the duty of conscience is *sadharana-dharma*, which is the same for everyone. In this dialogue there exists the same tension because of the two differing senses of dharma. Krishna has in mind dharma as 'caste duty'; Arjuna is dejected because the dharma of his conscience tells him that it is wrong to kill.

In any case, the 'duty' argument of Krishna seems to have little effect; so Krishna sweetens it with an offer of heaven, not unlike Yudhishthira's second response to Draupadi. Krishna adds to it a 'no-lose' temptation:

> *If you are killed, you win heaven;*
> *if you triumph, you enjoy the earth;*
> *therefore, Arjuna, stand up and*
> *resolve to fight the battle.*[20]

Since this does not move Arjuna, Krishna tries a metaphysical approach, arguing that only the body dies, not the soul. In killing his enemies, Arjuna would be destroying only the transient body, not the *atman*, the 'real self', which would continue to exist.

> *He who thinks this self a killer*
> *and he who thinks it killed,*
> *both fail to understand;*
> *it does not kill, nor is it killed.*[21]

> *Arjuna, when a man knows the self*
> *to be indestructible, enduring, unborn,*
> *unchanging, how does he kill*
> *or cause anyone to kill?*[22]

Arjuna, however, is a man of action and appears to be impervious to metaphysics. So, the divine charioteer Krishna resorts next to a truly novel moral argument based on action. When an individual acts for the sake of his work rather than for the personal reward from it, Krishna says, the individual is likely to do the right thing. This moral insight is famously called *nishkama karma* or *nishphala karma*. '*Nish*' means 'without' in Sanskrit; '*kama*' means desire; '*phala*' is fruit; '*karma*' is action—literally, 'disinterested action' or an action performed without thinking of its fruit. Krishna expresses it famously in the Bhagavad Gita's 47th verse of Book II:

> *Be intent on the action,*
> *not on the fruits of action.*[23]

Krishna does not define what the right action is. Any action performed in a selfless spirit is superior. The action in this case is to fight a 'just war' in order to, as Krishna puts it, 'preserve the world'.[24] If he fights disinterestedly without thinking, for example, of 'winning the kingdom' or achieving personal fame, then his action will be 'virtuous' and will not accumulate karma. 'Preserving the world' is, of course, a king's duty—i.e. to act on behalf of his people. But it also entails preserving the natural order of society and its classes. Therefore, Arjuna cannot abandon his social duty as well, his *kshatriya-dharma*.[25] He is a warrior and a warrior's duty is to fight, especially if his cause is just.

Arjuna's moral dilemma is about which duty he should follow. Should he observe Krishna's advice—follow his kshatriya ethic and fight a just war in order to uphold a higher good and preserve a just order? Or should he follow the call of his conscience, which is to be a non-violent human being and not to kill his own family members, elders and teachers?

What should Arjuna do? In a practical sense, putting down his arms will achieve nothing. The war will still go on; there might, in fact, be more killing on his side if he does not fight. Moreover, his just cause would be lost. So he should fight. But this practical sort of reasoning, which rationally weighs the consequences of actions, as well as their costs and benefits, does not really solve his moral dilemma.[26] Arjuna must choose either to be a dutiful kshatriya warrior, fight this *dharma-yuddha*, 'righteous war', and rid the world of truly wicked people; in the process he will, of course, kill his family members, teachers and friends, or he can be a non-violent human being and save the lives of his family and kin; in this case, he will lose the kingdom that rightfully belongs to him and his brothers, and worse, he will allow the forces of evil to prevail. Should he fight when he knows that the war will lead to disaster, like most wars in history, and not benefit anyone? It is a *dharma-sankat*, a 'tragic dilemma'. Both choices involve serious wrongdoing and there seems to be no right answer, as is so often the case in the *Mahabharata*.

Krishna points to Arjuna's duty to fight irrespective of the consequences. It is a just cause, and as a warrior and commander of the Pandava forces, he must obey his kshatriya duty and take up arms. Krishna's advice assumes that moral worth lies in a person's motives rather than in the consequences of the action. Hence, he advocates the single-minded pursuit of duty without any thought to the consequences. Arjuna, on the other hand, thinks of the consequences of war. He has laid down his arms not because he is a pacifist and is upholding a principle of non-violence. He is thinking about the killing of his kin, his friends, his teachers, and of others. There are echoes here of the conflict between Yudhishthira and Draupadi that we have already encountered in the forest.[27]

The difference in their positions comes down to the problem of means and ends. Krishna believes that the end of 'preserving the world' justifies fighting. Arjuna believes that there are limits to what may be done even if the end is worth pursuing, and even when not pursuing that great end may be very costly. He understands that the gains from fighting clearly outweigh the costs, yet he believes that there is something terribly wrong in fighting and killing, especially his kin. The clash between Krishna's and Arjuna's positions is no longer a question about which outcome would be worse. Nor is it about choosing between two different outcomes. It is about choices between alternative paths. One of those paths entails inflicting terrible suffering in a war.

'I am time grown old'

When I asked the question, 'Who is right, Arjuna or Krishna?' to military leaders in both India and the United States, their response was uniformly that Arjuna has a duty to fight and he ought to get on with it without this fuss. 'We don't want officers to agonize self-indulgently; it's harmful and it weakens the resolve of the troops.' The English poet Robert Graves expresses the same thought as follows: 'The way I see it, when you put the uniform on, in effect you sign a contract. And you don't back out of a contract merely because you've changed your mind. You can speak up for your principles, you can argue against the ones you're being made to fight for, but in the end *you do the job*.'[28] This might be the right position for a soldier or an officer, but it is not the right stance for a ruler. It is political leaders who decide to take nations to war. Arjuna is, of course, not merely a commander, he is also a political leader of the Pandavas.

In the Gita, Krishna wins the debate. Not having succeeded in persuading him through argument, Krishna finally reveals his awe-inspiring aspect as God. Sanjaya, the correspondent, describes what Arjuna sees:

> *If the light of a thousand suns*
> *were to rise in the sky at once,*
> *it would be like the light*
> *of that great spirit.*
>
> *Arjuna saw all the universe*
> *in its many ways and parts*

standing as one in the body
of the god of gods.[29]

Arjuna is filled with amazement at this sight and he speaks, his voice stammering with terror:

Seeing the many mouths
and eyes
of your great form,
its many arms,
thighs, feet,
bellies, and fangs
the worlds tremble
and so do I.

Seeing the fangs
protruding
from your mouths
like the fires of time,
I lose my bearings
and I find no refuge . . .[30]

Arjuna begs him, 'Tell me—who are you in this terrible form?' Krishna replies:

I am time grown old,
creating world destruction
set in motion
to annihilate the worlds;
even without you,
all these warriors
arrayed in hostile ranks
will cease to exist.

Therefore, arise
And win glory!
Conquer your foes

And fulfill your kingship!
They are already slain by me.
Be just my instrument,
the archer at my side.[31]

Thus, the divine charioteer reveals his terrifying form as creator and destroyer of the universe. Arjuna sees that he has already destroyed both the armies. Krishna reveals himself as the incarnation of cosmic power that periodically descends to the earth in order to restore order in times of chaos. The sight of Krishna's terrible power is too much for Arjuna, and he begs him to stop and return to his more tranquil human aspect.

The experience makes Arjuna realize that his duty to fight is linked to Krishna's divinity. He begins to feel that his emotions of pity for his kin are, perhaps, really a weakness. His not wanting to kill his relatives is based on worldly, human desire. His true duty lies in making his own actions and his dharma conform to a cosmic dharma. It does not mean that he has to renounce the world—he can do so by acting with 'discipline', without attachment to the fruit of action.

Towards the end of the Gita, Krishna makes an extraordinary proposition to him. He says that now that Arjuna has learned about the truth, he should think about it and do what he thinks fit.

This knowledge I have taught
is more arcane than any mystery—
consider it completely
then act as you choose.[32]

'Act as you choose'—these are remarkable words from the mouth of God! Arjuna agrees to fight. Although he has been persuaded here, his ambivalence to killing those who 'ought not to be killed' will reappear from time to time. At a crucial moment when he has to kill his grandfather, Bhishma, Arjuna is again filled with self-doubt and he wavers.

> *Sovereignty, with hell later, having killed those who ought not to be killed, or the tribulations of forest dwelling—which should I choose?*[33]

Soon, however, he recovers his resolution and tells his frustrated charioteer:

> *Drive the horses to where Bhishma is! I will do your bidding. I will fell that invincible elder, the Grandfather of the Kurus.*[34]

That the greatest fighter of his age should have dithered at his finest hour, and should have considered following the dharma of non-violence, does say something about the Indian epic hero. At that moment of indecision, the invincible, self-assured hero becomes a doubting anti-hero, like his elder brother. That God should have given him a choice—to make a reasoned decision based on what he has learned—says something about the relationship between man and God in classical India.

The Gita has become one of the most influential texts in the history of philosophy. Through the ages, people in India have tended to identify with Krishna's position (not least because he is God). Even Mahatma Gandhi, the great apostle of non-violence in the twentieth century, felt inspired by Krishna's words in the Gita, even though it meant having to acquiesce in the horrendous killings of war. For Gandhi, the Gita was an allegory of the struggle between good and evil within each one of us. The poet T.S. Eliot also seemed to endorse Krishna's high-duty-based position in the *Four Quartets*, when he wrote:

> *And do not think of the fruit of action.*
> *Fare forward . . .*
> *So Krishna, as when he admonished Arjuna*
> *On the field of battle.*
>
> *Not fare well,*
> *But fare forward, voyagers.*[35]

I do not think that Arjuna was ever fully convinced that the great end of preserving the world from evil justified the violent means that he would have had to employ in the war. I can empathize with both Arjuna's and Krishna's positions because as human beings we are susceptible to both types of moral intuition. On some occasions we let 'ends' dictate our behaviour; on other occasions, 'means' seem to matter more. Our make-up also inclines us to one or the other type of intuition. The Gita calls such an inclination *svabhava*, a concept that we have already encountered. It seems to me perfectly possible for an individual to feel strongly the force of both 'means' and 'ends'. When this happens the moral dilemma is acutely painful as both courses of action are repugnant. This is at the heart of Arjuna's tragic dilemma.[36]

Some leaders may have claimed that they were not as bothered by this dilemma. Most famously, President Truman did not think that he had reached those limits of moral pain when he ordered the dropping of an atomic bomb on Hiroshima in World War II. He justified his act, much as Vidura would have done in the *Mahabharata*, that bombing Hiroshima would save more lives in the end (certainly more *American* lives) because the war would have ended earlier.

Some have argued that Arjuna is, in many ways, a better model of ethical deliberation than Krishna, for he takes responsibility for the consequences of his actions. Amartya Sen, the Nobel Prize winner, says that 'Arjuna is bothered not merely by the fact that many will die if war were to take place, but also by the fact that he himself will be killing lots of people and by the further fact that many of the people to be killed are persons for whom he himself has affection . . . Another observer who is uninvolved in these events need not attach any special importance to the fact that Arjuna (not *he*, but *Arjuna*) will be killing people, and that among the dead will be people for whom Arjuna (not he, but Arjuna) feels closeness and affection. Arjuna cannot reasonably take a similarly detached view of the consequences of his choice.'[37] Sen's position of agent-sensitive evaluation is in contrast to the usual Utilitarian formula that the evaluation must be independent of the evaluator; he believes that moral responsibility demands *situated* valuation by agents.

I too applaud Arjuna for being aware that going to war entails moral culpability. A political leader has to be aware that he will have 'dirty hands'. 'The recognition that one may have "dirty hands" is not just self-indulgence: it has significance for future actions . . . It informs the chooser that he may owe reparations to the vanquished . . . When the recognition is public, it constitutes an acknowledgement of moral culpability.'[38] Arjuna's tragic dilemma teaches us that moral choices are not merely private. When it comes to matters of war and public policy, they should be deliberated in public. A political leader should include the moral dimension in making a decision, alongside the economic, strategic and other dimensions. It is not enough to weigh the pros and cons of victory and defeat as King Dhritarashtra does before the war begins:

> *By subtle and clear sighted calculation of the pros and cons with proper judgment, the sagacious and intelligent man, who desired victory for his sons, precisely weighed up the strengths and weaknesses, and then the lord of men began to work out the capabilities of each side.*[39]

The world has too many politicians like Dhritarashtra, who think that 'if they wring their hands enough they can do anything that they like . . . [By raising this question] Arjuna has learned something about the difference between self-interest and moral commitment.'[40] Arjuna's doubts at the beginning of the war, far from betraying cowardice, ought to remind our own leaders that they should think about the violence, cruelty and injustice of wars before they embark on them. They ought to worry far more about the moral consequences of war, and take steps to avoid it as far as possible.

'A hero bound for heaven'

The first ten days of the war have been indecisive. The ancient patriarch of the Bharatas, Bhishma, has successfully led Duryodhana's armies, repelling the Pandavas' attacks. After Bhishma's death Drona becomes leader of the Kauravas. Though a brahmin by birth, Drona has been instructor to both the Pandavas and the Kauravas. Like Bhishma he accepts his post reluctantly because of his affection and respect for the Pandavas, especially for Arjuna. As the fighting gathers pace, Duryodhana is desperate to win and he accuses Drona of partiality towards the Pandavas. Drona replies that only if the great Pandava warrior, Arjuna, is removed from the battlefield will the Kauravas have any chance of success.

Duryodhana also develops a curious idea: if he can capture Yudhishthira alive, he will trap him in another bout of gambling and exile him once again for a dozen years. So, on the twelfth day of the war, he gets his allies, the Samshaptakas, to divert Arjuna to the southern end of the battlefield, leaving Yudhishthira exposed. Drona sets about destroying the army that Arjuna has left behind. He creates an impenetrable military formation, *chakra vyuha*, in the form of a lotus-like circular array. In it, he places the greatest Kaurava warriors, and they begin to advance menacingly towards Yudhishthira.

With Arjuna pinned down in the southern theatre, the only one in the Pandava army who knows how to penetrate the *chakra vyuha* is Abhimanyu, who had learned it in his mother's womb, when Arjuna, his father, was describing it to her. Yudhishthira turns to him, and the young warrior is more than happy to oblige. But before he enters the formation, he warns his uncle, 'My father taught me how to break in not how to come out.'[41] His mother had fallen asleep, it seems, before Arjuna could tell her how to exit the treacherous circular formation. Still, the Pandavas have no choice, and a great and unbearable responsibility falls upon the sixteen-year-old Abhimanyu.

Abhimanyu's arrowhead pierces the *chakra vyuha*, and he smashes his way in 'like a lion's cub assailing a herd of elephants'. Once Abhimanyu is inside, the powerful Jayadratha, ruler of Sindhu, quickly moves his troops and seals the breach. Thus, Bhima and the other Pandavas cannot enter, and Abhimanyu is trapped behind enemy lines. The boy fights valiantly, single-handedly causing so much destruction to the enemy forces that Duryodhana is frightened. It takes the top six Kaurava generals (including Karna, Drona, Kripa and Ashwatthama) to subdue the 'lion's cub', who goes down fighting.

Sanjaya, the ubiquitous war correspondent, announces Abhimanyu's death to King Dhritarashtra, squarely blaming his own side:

> *O my king. So, it was that one died at the hands of many. One warrior who had trampled our whole army as if it were just a lotus beneath his feet but now lay in the splendour of death, a wild elephant killed by his hunters. Your soldiers stood in a circle around him where he fell . . . Six of the fighters from Dhritarashtra's horde, Drona and Karna chief among them, had cut this lone body to the ground in what I would name a sin. Yet how beautiful the rich earth was as it cradled that dead hero.*[42]

Sanjaya then reports the reaction of the Pandavas to this 'sin' of the Kauravas:

> *The Pandus looked upon the broken figure of Abhimanyu who had once been bright as the sun and the moon, and they were struck down with sorrow. Still only a boy and dead before his prime . . . The whole army of the Pandavas rushed to the feet of the righteous king. The matchless Yudhishthira looked upon them and saw how his men suffered at the youth's death and said to them: 'Here is the hero bound for heaven. He was one that would die rather than run. Take heart, do not be downcast. We will win this war and overcome our traitors.'*[43]

As the sun is setting on this unhappy scene, and the enemy warriors, tired and battered, are leaving the battlefield, Sanjaya tells his blind king:

> *We had killed their champion but still we felt the wounds where his arrows had struck us and we returned to the camp at the end of the day soaked in blood. My king, as we made our way back weak with exhaustion, we all gazed out across the battlefield insensate and wordless into a dusk alive with strangeness, an uneasy time disjointed from night and day, all full of the cries of jackals. The sun sank down slowly behind the mountains . . . and heaven melted into earth where the delicate flame in the sky blazed at the horizon.*[44]

When Arjuna hears of his brave son's death, he weeps bitterly. He blames himself: 'I had taught the poor boy how to get in, but I had yet to teach him how to get out.' Seeing Arjuna lamenting his death, the epic mourns the brief careers of young warriors. It will maintain a list of all the children who will die in battle—it is its way, I suppose, of making an anti-war statement.[45] Krishna tries to console him, but Arjuna tells him to go and comfort his wife (and Krishna's sister), Subhadra.

Gradually, Arjuna's sorrow turns into anger. He vows, 'Truly, I swear I shall kill Jayadratha before sunset tomorrow.'[46] If he does not avenge his son's killer, Arjuna declares, he will immolate himself. Krishna censures him for making this rash oath: the Kauravas, he says, will now protect Jayadratha with all their might, and they will eagerly await your 'entry into the fire'. Fearing just such an outcome, many in the Pandava camp do not get any sleep that night.[47]

'Like a fire urged by the wind'

On the following day, it is a different Arjuna. He is ready for revenge. 'Like a fire urged by the wind that consumes a dense forest of trees', he rages over the battlefield inflicting terrible losses on the enemy. The Kauravas have only one objective on that day—to protect Jayadratha—and they keep him behind a fortress of chariots, elephants, horsemen and soldiers. All afternoon Arjuna rushes against time to fulfil his oath.[48] The sun keeps moving relentlessly westward. Just as the sun is going down behind the Asta mountain, Arjuna battles his way through and reaches Jayadratha.

'As the sun is setting', Arjuna shoots down both Jayadratha's standard and his charioteer.[49] But his final assault is too late. Krishna reminds him that he still has to kill six warriors who are protecting Jayadratha, an impossible feat in the seconds remaining. At this moment Krishna has an idea:

I shall employ yoga and cover the sun. Only the king of Sindhu will see it. He will think, 'The sun has set' and he will relax his guard . . . This is when you should strike when he is not paying attention.[50]

Krishna's trick works. Jayadratha thinks that the sun has set and he lets down his guard. In that instant Arjuna pierces him with a fierce arrow.[51] Moreover, he shoots it with such amazing skill that Jayadratha's head does not fall on the ground. Thus, he escapes Jayadratha's father's curse: that the head of anyone who caused his son's head to fall in battle would burst into a thousand pieces. Jayadratha's head lands on the lap of his father, who has been meditating. The father unwittingly drops his son's head and becomes the victim of his own curse as his own head bursts.[52]

In the Greek epics, *aristeia* refers to a warrior's finest moment, usually during an extended battle scene in which the hero exhibits great valour in pursuit of glory. This is Arjuna's *aristeia* as he performs extraordinary feats on the fourteenth day at Kurukshetra, much like Achilles in the *Iliad*.[53] Both heroes are driven to action and revenge after the death of a loved one. Arjuna is roused after Abhimanyu's death; Achilles is awakened from his sulking slumber by Patroklos's killing by Hector.

Just as Achilles is 'the best of the Achaeans', so is Arjuna called the 'best warrior on the earth' by Duryodhana.[54] Both heroes have a single, divine parent from whom they have inherited extraordinary qualities. Arjuna's father Indra, the Vedic god of war and thunder, has given his son powerful weapons. Achilles's mother, Thetis, had dipped her son by the heel into the sacred river Styx in order to make him invulnerable (but his heel, alas, had remained dry and unprotected). Both depend on divine aid to win. Arjuna needed Krishna's help to defeat Jayadratha as Achilles turns to Hephaestus to overcome the wide flowing Skamandros river of Troy. In both epics, the *aristeia* of the hero follows the death of someone very close. Arjuna's rage after Abhimanyu's death sends him on an *aristeia*, driving him to fight with superhuman energy. Achilles avenges himself on Hector, thus turning the tide in the war against the Trojans.

Both heroes face a crisis of conscience but their differing responses teach us something about the two epics. Achilles is full of rage. Not only does he kill Hector but he desecrates his body. He drags it behind his chariot before the walls of Troy, steadfastly refusing to allow him funeral rites. Arjuna also responds with great power on the battlefield to avenge Abhimanyu, but he never quite forgets that he could only vanquish Jayadratha because of Krishna's trickery. He had felt the same sense of guilt when he killed his grandfather through subterfuge. A cloud of moral ambiguity, thus, hangs over him till the end of the war, reminding him of his Pyrrhic victories. He is, after all, the same Arjuna who had put down his arms and refused to fight at the beginning of the war.

The *Iliad* is bloodthirsty, driven by anger and violence. The *Mahabharata* is just as gory, but it questions the violence. The first word in the *Iliad* is *menin*, rage, as Homer asks the Muse to sing about the 'wrath of Achilles'. The Gita's first word is *dharma-kshetre*, 'field of righteousness', signalling that this is no ordinary war enacted on a battlefield; it is also a war of dharma in the conscience of each human being.[55] Achilles, like Arjuna, faces a conflict between the demands of divinity and humanity. After doing wrong, Achilles is able to get on with it. Arjuna, however, never quite forgets that the Pandavas are employing deceit in order to win.

Gradually, Achilles rises above his rage. When Hector's father, the distraught King Priam of Troy, comes secretly to the Greek camp to plead for his son's body, Achilles receives him graciously, and in one of the *Iliad's* most moving scenes, he relents and allows him to take the body away. In this act of kindness, Achilles has identified with Priam's grief and the pain of being a victim. In recognizing his kinship with the dead and the defeated, he has realized that he too might die in battle. When he kills Lykaon in Book XXII, Achilles says, 'Come friend, you too must die.' In that statement is his recognition of the inevitability of death, and his common bond with humanity. During the last few books of the *Iliad*, Achilles becomes more and more like the Pandava hero. Even as he rages against Hector's corpse, he foresees his own death.

The ethical impulses of Achilles and Arjuna are confused, ambiguous, and even pessimistic. The Indian and the Greek epic heroes face the same question: Does the good life consist in dying young in battle, like Abhimanyu, and going to heaven? Or should one pursue another, more humane way of living based on less violent values? Where does true honour lie? The battlefield is indeed a field of dharma in which there are no easy answers.

'Is ours a "just war"?'

The *Mahabharata* calls its war a *dharma-yuddha*, a 'just war'. The epic's language is full of words of moral judgment—aggression, self-defence, appeasement, cruelty, atrocity, massacre. It is profoundly aware that a just war can be fought unjustly, just as an unjust war can be fought in strict accordance with the rules. It examines three aspects of the Kurukshetra War: its causes, its conduct, and its consequences. Medieval scholastics in the Catholic 'just war' tradition called these three *jus ad bellum* (cause), *jus in bello* (conduct) and *jus post bellum* (consequences). Whereas this chapter focuses on the first; Chapter 7 will examine the second; and Chapter 9 will look in on the third.

To determine if the Kurukshetra War is a 'just war', the epic offers a number of perspectives. The first is Duryodhana's, who derides all talk about the 'morality of war'. He believes that might is right and there are no moral rules between states. You cannot trust anyone, least of all your neighbour. You better conquer him before he invades your territory. The only thing that matters is to win, and this means that anything goes. Duryodhana acts on the premise of the ancient text, *Arthashastra*, in which a wise ruler guards against his neighbour. Since a neighbour's neighbour is inevitably a friend, it develops a theory of concentric circles, a sort of 'ready-reckoner' for the ruler to quickly determine his 'natural' friends and enemies and help him make appropriate alliances.

The ancient Athenians shared this ethic. When the Athenian embassy told the people of Melos in 416 BC that it was a natural law for the strong to rule the weak, they were warning them that Melos could not remain neutral in the conflict between Athens and Sparta. Contemporary political leaders of modern states will have no trouble in identifying with Duryodhana's position, as they have been brought up in the '*realpolitik*' school of international diplomacy. Made famous by Prince Metternich, the Austrian statesman at the Congress of Vienna, it set the tone for nineteenth and twentieth century's 'balance of power' diplomacy. Henry Kissinger, the American secretary of state (who taught me a course in college) has been its most articulate proponent in recent times.[56]

This 'realistic' way of thinking insists that war lies beyond moral judgment, expressed in the Latin saying, *Inter arma silent leges*, 'in the time of war the law is silent'. Someone like Kissinger, however, would also argue that there is a deeper morality to this stance—that effective and ruthless balance-of-power management reduces warfare and suffering in the long term. He felt that Jawaharlal Nehru, the first prime minister of India, injected a dangerous note of morality in the Cold War between America and the USSR.

At the other extreme is the idealistic position of the earlier Yudhishthira, who refused to take up arms when he was in exile. Even though his cause is just he will not fight because of his deep commitment to *ahimsa*, non-violence and peace. He is sceptical about the possibility of a 'just war', which is what Draupadi and Bhima had advocated in the Dvaita forest. Yudhishthira's position resonates in our perilous world of nuclear weapons. During the Cold War, especially in the 1960s and 1970s, many young people feared that a conflict between the United States and the Soviet Union might lead to all-out nuclear war. They concluded that contemporary warfare is so destructive that it could never justify going to war. Hence, they turned pacifist and joined the movement for unilateral disarmament.

In India, Yudhishthira's position gained legitimacy and popularity because of Mahatma Gandhi's extraordinary success in winning India's independence by non-violent means. The British rulers did not quite know how to respond to Gandhi, who following Jesus told his followers: 'Do not resist one who is evil. If anyone strikes you on the right cheek, turn the other one.' Although it is not the epic's preferred position, the *Mahabharata* does have sympathy for the pacifist idealism of the earlier Yudhishthira. It also underlines it when Arjuna springs a surprise at the beginning of the war, as we have just seen, refusing to fight. At the end of the war, when everyone is dead, it seems as though this pacifist position has been vindicated. Yudhishthira asks, what was the point of it all?

The *Mahabharata* offers a middle ground between the realism of Duryodhana and the idealism of the younger Yudhishthira.

Bhishma, a statesman used to running public affairs, articulates this position after the war in Book Twelve, and succeeds in reconciling the remorseful Yudhishthira to the throne. Unlike the Realists, he believes that moral principles make a claim on a political leader, but there is a sharp limit to these claims. A wise ruler cannot trust other nations. He must be on guard, and sometimes be willing to take up *danda*, 'arms'. He cannot afford to be pacifist like the inflexible younger Yudhishthira, a position that is sometimes embraced by contemporary liberals of the far left, who fail to realize that the application of morality to wars and foreign policy is complex and difficult. Jawaharlal Nehru, who tended to bring moral discourse in post-war diplomacy, espoused the cause of communist China in the 1950s. Later, to his embarrassment, he had to deal with the Chinese invasion of India. He would have done well to follow Bhishma's advice. In saying that 'dharma is subtle', Bhishma is, in effect, telling Yudhishthira (and Nehru) that no matter how attractive the earlier Yudhishthira's high moral position, it is difficult to be non-violent in a violent world.

As the *Mahabharata* weaves a moral regime in the midst of the war's violence, its sympathies are with the Pandavas. *Dharma-yuddha* can have the following meanings. It can mean a war fought as a duty by a kshatriya; or a war fought according to the rules of war; or a war fought for the right or just reasons. The first meaning is trivial—if it were true, every war fought by a kshatriya would qualify as a 'just war' since it is the kshatriya's duty to fight. As to the second meaning, the Kurukshetra War was fought unfairly—both sides broke the rules governing warfare (as we shall see in Chapter 7).[57] As to the third criterion, Krishna explains why the war is just from the Pandavas' viewpoint, as he catalogues Duryodhana's crimes when the latter is dying:

> I beseeched you, O unwise one, to give the Pandavas their paternal share of half the kingdom. But you were greedy! Under Shakuni's evil influence, you almost poisoned Bhimasena; you tried to burn

the Pandavas with their mother in the house made of lacquer; you had Yajnaseni [Draupadi] pushed into the assembly when she had her period. O evil one, you employed the son of Subala [Shakuni] in a crooked game of dice to defeat someone deceitfully who did not know dice but knew dharma . . . [and finally] you had Abhimanyu, a child who fought against so many, struck down in battle. For all these crimes, you have been killed, O wicked one![58]

Dharma-yuddha has its equivalent in the 'just war' theory of the Roman Catholic Church, which stretches from Augustine in the fifth century through Aquinas in the thirteenth century to the present day. Like Bhishma's doctrine, it is based on the recognition that war is inevitable in human affairs; rather than hope for its abolition the best one can do is to mitigate its effects. Saint Thomas Aquinas gave justum bellum its systematic exposition in his Summa Theologica. He discussed not only the justification for war, but also the kinds of activity that are permissible in war. He enunciated three simple criteria: a war is just when it is a defence against aggression or an attempt to stop atrocities. Second, the values at stake override the presumption against killing—the expected good must outweigh the cost of killing and destruction. Finally, war must be a last resort when all other alternatives are exhausted.[59] Our modern war conventions, such as the Geneva Convention, grew out of the 'just war' tradition of the Catholic Church.[60]

Obviously, the Kurukshetra War was not a war of self-defence; nor was it against aggression or threatened aggression. It was a civil war to reclaim legitimate power. The Pandavas' half of the kingdom was usurped, and they waged the war after the failure of extensive peace negotiations. It would thus seem to meet Aquinas's third criterion of 'just war'—it was waged as a last resort, when all other alternatives had been exhausted. Having said that, bear in mind that the Pandavas' claim to the throne was a dubious one, based on a highly confused genealogy. Moreover, the Pandavas did employ deceit to gain a victory, and for this they were rightly censured. There is, thus, no easy answer to the question if theirs was a 'just war'.

Having considered the pros and cons, I tend to feel that our moral sense would have been offended had the Kauravas won at Kurukshetra. It would have been equivalent to Adolf Hitler winning the Second World War. A Nazi triumph would have been a disaster not only for the conquered nations but also for all of humanity. Most of us would agree that the Allies' cause in World War II was 'just' (which cannot be said of the First World War). Neville Chamberlain, the British prime minister in the 1930s, was just as naïve as the younger Yudhishthira. He adopted a policy of appeasement in order to keep the peace. Just as Yudhishthira failed to read Duryodhana, so did Chamberlain fail to recognize the threat posed by Hitler, believing that the Nazis were merely continuing the policy of the earlier Weimar regime.

One of the important questions of our times is the justice of the wars of humanitarian intervention in order 'to protect the human rights of citizens who are being massacred or enslaved by their government'.[61] This is a painful and complex issue, for no one wants to start a war to end another one. But there is a growing consensus that these are 'just wars' if they are prosecuted under some sort of collective sanction such as that of the United Nations. Despite the consensus, a Rwandan genocide does take place, and so does a slaughter in Darfur. The new consensus has not deterred genocidal groups who hate each other, nor has it stopped bands of guerrillas from committing atrocious and humiliating acts around the world.

The moral reasoning contained in the *Mahabharata* and in the Catholic 'just war' theory would have judged the American intervention in Iraq in 2003 rather badly. Saddam Hussein was as evil as Duryodhana and his record of aggression abroad and brutal repression at home was atrocious. Removing him from Iraq was a benevolent act, but it ought to have been achieved without a full-scale war. It seems to me that some force in Iraq was probably necessary in order to capture Saddam and contain his regime. Enforcing an embargo might have needed force. But it ought to have been far less than was employed. A full-scale assault was certainly not called for, and whatever action had to be taken ought to have had UN support. The best moral position on Iraq, I believe, lay somewhere between the disastrous diplomacy of the Bush administration and the equally obstructive position of the French (who rejected every opportunity to provide an alternative to war).

'To one who is killed, victory and defeat are the same'

Like Tolstoy's *War and Peace,* the *Mahabharata* can see both sides of war. It glories in immortal feats of courage, daring and self-sacrifice like those of Abhimanyu. It looks on with admiration at Arjuna's *aristeia.* The relentless battle scenes of the epic yield 'the finest poetry of the epic'.[62] Yet, the epic is also aware that these valiant acts that it honours are also feats of lunacy. The same *Mahabharata* condemns the approaching war in Book Five in the most savage terms. While lamenting the failure of the peace negotiations, Yudhishthira leaves no doubt about what he thinks will be the consequences. He expresses his feelings so forcefully that one wonders if Krishna might have given his message to the wrong Pandava in the Gita.

> *War is evil in any form . . . To one who is killed, victory and defeat are the same . . . the victor too is surely diminished . . . and behold, when he has lost his strength and no longer sees his sons or brothers a loathing for life will engulf him completely, Krishna. It is the modest warriors, noble and with a sense of compassion, who are killed in war, and the lesser men escape.*[63]

Chastened by thirteen harsh years in exile, Yudhishthira has begun to adopt a more pragmatic view of the world. As we have noted, he has become a prudent ruler of the middle path. His pragmatism should not be confused with an aggressive world view; its default position (in accordance with ideas about reciprocal altruism) is to be friendly and collaborative. Unlike Dhritarashtra, he does not merely weigh amorally the pros and cons of victory and defeat. The considerations of dharma are a part of the deliberations of the prudent ruler of the middle path. He is weighed down with moral concerns during the peace negotiations even as he is more and more resigned to the inevitability of war. He asks Sanjaya:

Why should a man knowingly go to war?
Who cursed by his fate would choose war?
The Parthas who hunger for happiness act
For the fullness of dharma and the common weal.[64]

One wishes there were more statesmen in the world like Arjuna and Yudhishthira, who place the demands of dharma in the same equation as the material pros and cons of going to war. The modern liberal answer to Yudhishthira's and Arjuna's dilemma is to limit the power of democratic leaders in prosecuting war. John Locke and the American founding fathers sought to separate power in different branches of the government by means of the constitution. They accepted the inevitability of war but recognized that the problem lay in the 'undue and unbalanced concentration of it in one person'. Liberal Americans who have lived through the Vietnam and Iraq wars in recent times have felt let down by this 'constitutional system', however. It has been unable to stop the American executive from waging unjust wars. As these wars turned increasingly unpopular, the president tried to exaggerate their importance to the national interest and to hide their full implications. Presidents Johnson, Nixon and Bush in their different ways forgot that one should not wage a war that can only be won at an unacceptable moral and political price.

In his celebrated *Histories*, Herodotus, the great Greek historian, tells us about Xerxes, the great king of Persia, who invaded Greece in 480 BC with an army of two million men. He stopped on the way at Hellespont and he saw, as Arjuna did, his regiments arrayed across the plains. At first this grand sight cheered him. But then he grew dejected like Arjuna, and he began to weep. Although Xerxes's mood and concerns were different, both men were questioning the value of human action. Both were resigned to human imperfectibility and condemned the unbridled pursuit of military power. Had the Buddha been Arjuna's charioteer rather than Krishna, the *Mahabharata* would have gone in a different direction.[65]

5

BHISHMA'S SELFLESSNESS

'Be intent on the act, not on its fruits'

> *Be intent on the action,*
> *not on the fruits of action*
>
> —Krishna to Arjuna,
> Bhagavad Gita II.47

What to do with the 'self'?

My most unusual class during our 'academic holiday' was with the humanist Paul Friedrich, with whom my wife and I read the Gita as a work of literature. Friedrich was the author of some unusual-sounding books: *The Meaning of Aphrodite, Music in Russian Poetry, Bastard Moon* and *Princes of Naranja*. I wondered what he was doing teaching a course on the Gita. He had come to the text, it seems, via two famous American literary figures, Ralph Waldo Emerson and Henry David Thoreau. They had discovered the Gita in the 1840s, and were filled with excitement. Emerson wrote in his journal, 'I owed—my friend and I owed— a magnificent day to the Bhagawat Geeta. It was the first of books; it was as if an empire spoke to us, nothing small or unworthy, but large, serene, consistent, the voice of an old intelligence which in another age and climate had pondered and

117

thus disposed of the same questions which exercise us.' Thoreau said, 'I remember the book as an hour before sunrise' and as a result, 'Farthest India is nearer to me than Concord or Lexington.'[1]

Friedrich knew a little Sanskrit but he was not an Indologist. Like me, he had studied it briefly with Daniel Ingalls, but he made up for his lack of expertise with an abundance of wisdom and self-effacing charm. He was the son of the political scientist Carl Friedrich, who had been professor at Harvard when I was there. His family had fled Nazi Germany. On arrival in America, the immigration officer had demanded to know their religion. Without batting an eyelid, Friedrich senior had replied, 'Homeric.'

There were seven of us in Paul Friedrich's class, and we came from various disciplines—philosophy, religion, anthropology and literature. On Friday mornings between nine and noon, we could be found in Harper Hall reading the ancient text line by line. When we had read a verse or two, we would pause and discuss. There was a timeless quality about our Socratic dialogues, in which 'truth, goodness and beauty' seemed alone to matter. Sometimes we might spend an hour over a single verse. Our ponderings inevitably turned to why Arjuna must fight. Of all the reasons, I was most attracted to Krishna's notion of performing one's duty for its own sake without thinking about 'what's in it for me'. I felt that an action performed with this attitude must take on a new meaning. This moral insight, as we have seen, is called *nishkama karma*. In perhaps the most quoted and the least observed verse in contemporary India, Krishna says:

> Be intent on the action,
> not on the fruits of action.[2]

Knowing the Indian tendency to renounce the world, Krishna makes it clear that acting in this selfless spirit of detachment should not result in non-action. Both Krishna and Draupadi reflect a healthy bias for action in the *Mahabharata*.

Perform necessary action;
it is more powerful than inaction;
without action you even fail
to sustain your own body.[3]

In other words, do not renounce the world and become a hermit. Instead, learn to change your attitude while living and working in the world. Do something 'because it must be done'. If you succeed in changing your attitude, then it will not feel like work. It is as though you are doing 'nothing at all'. Nor will you 'incur guilt'. You will be

Content with whatever comes by chance
beyond dualities, free from envy.[4]

You will feel 'unattached and free'. To learn how to change your attitude and act in a selfless way you must learn to cultivate discipline:

Perform actions, firm in discipline,
relinquishing attachment;
be impartial to failure and success—
this equanimity is called yoga.[5]

This disciplined attitude of *karma yoga* will make you less selfish, more tranquil. Self-control will also lead to greater skill in performing the action.

... so arm yourself for discipline—
yoga is skill in actions.[6]

In the spirit of Indian pluralism, Krishna offers Arjuna three paths to liberation from human bondage. These are the paths of knowledge, action and love. My father's chief interest in the Gita lay in the third way of love. He was quite mesmerized by *bhakti yoga*, which seeks freedom from the law of karma through a deep and passionate love of God.[7] On the other hand, I am mainly interested in the possibilities of the second path of *karma yoga,* the way of action. So was Emerson, and he wrote that he was 'chiefly interested in Krishna's teaching that works must be done without thought of reward and a person may have a tranquil mind even in activity'.[8]

Nevertheless, I was sceptical. As I thought about my own dharma journey, I asked myself if it was possible to actually live in this way. I wondered if I could shrink my ego that far in order to live and work in the way that Krishna had suggested. It seemed to me a nice ideal that human beings ought to strive for, but I felt that *karma yoga* may well be as hopelessly idealistic as Rousseau's or Marx's goal of equality.

A pillow for a hero

On the tenth day of the war, Sanjaya, the bard, bluntly announces to the blind Dhritarashtra that their commander-in-chief, Bhishma, has fallen in battle. At this moment, the *Mahabharata* presses the reverse button. We are suddenly back in time and the war at Kurukshetra is about to begin. The slaying of Bhishma is still on our minds when Arjuna suddenly feels confused and dejected, and as we have seen in the Gita, he puts down his weapons, and shrinks from killing his kinsmen.[9] Krishna consoles him, and tries to assuage his guilt over the imminent killings of war.

I asked myself what the *Mahabharata* is telling us in placing Krishna's message of self-forgetting immediately after Bhishma's death. Is it holding Bhishma up as an exemplary human being? Is the patriarch of the Bharatas an example of someone who is 'intent on the act and not its fruits'? Is he revered in the epic because he is Krishna's model of a selfless person who acts with detachment from a sense of duty?

When Yudhishthira returns after thirteen years in exile, the first person he enquires after is Bhishma. He asks Sanjaya:

> *How is our venerable, wise grandfather, who is so intelligent and endowed with every virtue? Is Kauravya Bhishma in good health, young man? Is his character still the same?*[10]

The 'character' that Yudhishthira is referring to is Bhishma's uncommon selflessness. Aside from Krishna, the *Mahabharata* does not say if any of the other characters possesses the virtue of *nishkama karma*; nor does it call anyone a *karma yogi*; but if anyone in the epic does deserve this designation, it is Bhishma.

Devavrata Bhishma was the eldest son of Shantanu, the Bharata king and the ancestor of the Pandavas and Kauravas. Bhishma would have become king had his father not fallen in love with Satyavati, the daughter of the chief of a tribe of fishermen. As a condition of their marriage, the bride's father was adamant that the kingship should descend on Satyavati's children. To make his father happy, Bhishma renounced his right to the kingdom and vowed to remain celibate in order to avoid potential disputes in succeeding generations. It was such a terrifying and awesome act of self-sacrifice that flowers rained from the sky when Devavrata took this oath. Voices were heard, 'Bhishma! Bhishma!' This is how he got his name Bhishma, 'the awesome one'.[11]

Bhishma keeps his promise and remains celibate all his life. His stepmother, Satyavati, has two children from his father and he brings them up lovingly like his own brothers. When they are young, he rules the kingdom dutifully in their name as a guardian and regent. When they grow up, he arranges their marriages. They die early, however, without producing any heirs, and Satyavati beseeches Bhishma to sire children on her widowed daughters-in-law. But he refuses, saying that he cannot possibly go back on his word.

With the royal succession at risk, Queen Satyavati, as we know, summons her illegitimate son, Vyasa, to impregnate the widows. Vyasa thus fathers Dhritarashtra by the elder widow, Pandu by the younger one, and Vidura by a maid. Since Dhritarashtra is disqualified from the succession because of blindness, Pandu becomes king. He has five sons through divine intervention. The eldest, Yudhishthira, is born just before Dhritarashtra's own son, Duryodhana. Soon, Pandu renounces the throne and retires to the forest, where his children, the Pandavas, grow up. Blind Dhritarashtra, whose name means 'he who holds the kingdom', assumes the regency. While he believes that Yudhishthira has first claim to the realm, he has a weakness for his eldest son, Duryodhana, whom he promotes secretly, and who becomes the de facto ruler of Hastinapura.

All this time Bhishma continues to administer the realm. He is guardian for another generation until Dhritarashtra and Pandu come of age. He performs his role with detachment, serving the kingdom selflessly and acting from a sense of duty rather than personal interest. When Duryodhana begins to rule Hastinapura, Bhishma is in semi-retirement—he is a grandfatherly presence whose advice is sometimes sought and often ignored.[12]

With the coming of the war, Bhishma is torn. His sympathies are with the Pandavas but his duty is to the throne. Duryodhana elevates him to supreme commander of the Kaurava troops, a role that he fulfils valiantly and wisely. He successfully leads the Kaurava army in repelling the Pandavas. Like a 'fire blazing in the forest', the patriarch of the Bharatas slaughters thousands of warriors during the first ten days of the war. Yudhishthira, seeing his troops decimated, realizes that their 'grandfather' has to be eliminated if they are going to win.

On the evening of the ninth day, Yudhishthira tells his brothers about an eerie pledge that Bhishma had made to him. Although he had agreed to fight on behalf of the Kauravas, Bhishma had said openly that he would give the Pandavas counsel since he was their 'grandfather'. Late that night the Pandavas and Krishna visit Bhishma's camp, and Yudhishthira asks, 'Tell us, O lord, the means of your own death.'

Bhishma tells the Pandavas that he is invincible in battle; he can only be defeated when he lays down his bow and weapons. He tells them about a vow he made long ago that he would never hurt a woman—or someone who had once been a woman. Bhishma suggests that they have such a person in their midst, who is their ally. The mighty Panchala prince, Shikhandi, was born a woman, but later changed her sex. If Shikhandi were to appear before him, Bhishma tells them, he would have to not attack him/her. At that moment, Arjuna could kill him. 'I do not see anyone in the three worlds who can kill me [otherwise].'

The following day the war is especially bloody and Bhishma slays ten thousand warriors. The Pandavas despair. Finally, on Krishna's goading, Arjuna places Shikhandi in front of him and moves resolutely towards Bhishma. Seeing the feminine in Shikhandi, Bhishma holds himself back because of his vow, and Arjuna, seeing this, draws his Gandiva bow and pierces him with twenty-five arrows. Bhishma falls from his chariot, not on the ground but on a bed of arrows. Seeing this sight, the warriors are awestruck. As the patriarch lies dying at sunset, the warriors on both sides lay down their weapons, forgetting briefly that they are enemies, and pay homage to this selfless 'renouncer', who has become the first major victim of the war.

Arjuna notices that Bhishma's head is hanging down, and he shoots three arrows into the ground and lifts his grandfather's head tenderly and places it onto a 'hero's pillow'. Realizing that Bhishma is thirsty, Arjuna gets up on his chariot, circumambulates the fallen commander, and fires an effulgent Parjanya arrow into the earth. Out gushes a pure jet of cool water, which quenches his grandfather's thirst. Because of his remarkable vow of celibacy, Bhishma had received a gift—of being able to choose his time of death. So, although he has fallen, he does not die. He lies upon the battlefield through the end of the war and far past it, having chosen the moment of the winter solstice to pass away.

What does one make of this extraordinary figure who lived his life for the sake of others? He certainly managed to create a huge problem of succession. His vow of celibacy turned out to be a curse on the Bharata dynasty that led eventually to a horrendous war of succession. Is the *Mahabharata* telling us that even selflessness has its limitations? Bhishma sacrificed his own happiness for the father's sake. He did not marry; he did not become king; he administered the realm disinterestedly for two generations. Yet, if he had acceded to Satyavati's request, he might have continued the royal line of the Bharatas, lived a peaceful, domestic, *grihastha* life of the second stage, and spared the world mass destruction. (In that case, we might not have had the *Mahabharata* either, whose legendary author, the sage Vyasa, was Satyavati's illegitimate son and father of the flawed Dhritarashtra and Pandu.)

It is difficult to understand why this selfless hero did not get up in the assembly on that fateful day of the dice game to stop the public humiliation of Draupadi. Vidura tried, at least. Bhishma must have known that more than anyone else in the assembly, he could have saved Draupadi. 'He had the authority to stop the shameful spectacle. Instead, he sat there futilely discussing what was dharma and what was not dharma.'[13] One expected him to strike Duhshasana to the ground when he tried to pull off Draupadi's garment. It has been suggested that Bhishma 'had eaten Duryodhana's salt' and was thus forced to support him. This is obviously not a morally sound argument. Patronage does make a claim on one's loyalty, but the claim stops before one's conscience. I find it difficult to believe that courageous Bhishma would have turned coward or become afraid of Duryodhana at the end of his life, especially when he had lived the rest of his life selflessly on behalf of others. The fact remains that when it came to Draupadi's question in the assembly, he failed.

When Bhishma says to Draupadi, 'dharma is subtle', his mind appears to be in genuine conflict. He is aware that Yudhisthira is also profoundly guilty for having wagered and lost his wife. As a statesman, he has a legal mind and he cannot find a lawful reason to declare the last wager void. He also views dharma from the viewpoint of state policy and his concern is to strengthen the interests of the Hastinapura state and preserve the Bharata line. He worries about Hastinapura's alliance with the Gandhara and the political implications of alienating Duryodhana's uncle, Shakuni's, powerful military state in the northwest.[14] Whatever the reason, moral courage did desert him on that day and he did not stop the disrobing of Queen Draupadi when he could have.

Does this mean that the ethic of selfless detachment failed on that day? Has Bhishma's whole life been a fruitless sacrifice as Irawati Karve suggests? I do not think so. The Mahabharata has presented us with another moral dilemma to which there are no easy answers—reminding us once again about the difficulty of being good. As I mentioned in the Prelude, it is a human tendency to deceive oneself, to rationalize one's actions, and find fault in others while remaining blind to the same fault in oneself. The epic is wary of all absolutes—there are even limitations to Krishna's idea of *nishkama karma*. Perhaps, Draupadi's question did not have an answer. Hence, I disagree with Irawati Karve's pessimistic lesson from the Mahabharata that 'All human effort is fruitless, all human life ends in frustration'.[15]

The difficult art of self-forgetting

Bhishma's story made me think about what it means to act selflessly, without vanity. Quite apart from Bhishma's failures, it made me question what Krishna has in mind when he advises Arjuna to be 'intent on the act and not its fruits'. Is a person capable of acting in this disinterested way? Krishna is exhorting me, perhaps, to transfer my attention away from myself to something outside, for example, to my work or to others. He is asking me not to act from personal ambition but, perhaps, for ambition for the work or for performing the work well. I wondered what sort of action it would be where I could forget my ego or myself.

Human beings appear to be essentially self-interested. I have been brought up on a steady diet of modernism, which claims that to be self-interested is to be 'rational' and 'prudent'. Adam Smith taught me: 'It is not from the benevolence of the butcher, the brewer, or the baker that we expect our dinner, but from their regard to their own interest. We address ourselves not to their humanity but their self love.'[16] It is not only economists who believe this but all social scientists accept it as dogma.[17] Hence, I found it difficult to accept Krishna's premise and I just did not believe that one could act selflessly, not for any length of time at least.

Nevertheless, I did not dismiss the Gita's insistent idea even though at times it seemed to me hopelessly idealistic. I continued to wrestle with it. I observed that we do, in fact, act disinterestedly *sometimes*. We do show a concern for others; we do cooperate even when it does not serve our narrow interest; we express a sense of solidarity; and we are public-spirited for reasons that go beyond 'prudence'. Hence, 'self-interest' does not fully explain our behaviour.[18] Even Adam Smith in his *Theory of Moral Sentiments* admits that people commonly feel other emotions which are contrary to their narrow self-interest. They feel, for example, the disinterested emotion of sympathy for the misery of others.[19] Jean Jacques Rousseau says that a person feels pity when he sees a child in danger of being clawed by a wild beast.[20]

If sentiments like 'sympathy' and 'pity' exist, social scientists may have gone too far in claiming that self-interest is the only motive of human actions. I also recalled that there are times when my 'self' seems to disappear. When I am deeply absorbed in a book, for example, I tend to forget myself. I can lose myself for hours, and when I become aware, I find myself saying, 'Is it already six o'clock?' I had forgotten my 'self' during this period. During this 'lost time', perhaps I had been acting for its own sake. I was not aware of my personal ambition during this time. Was Krishna, then, urging me to learn this attitude of 'self-forgetting' in his concept of *nishkama karma*? Is this what athletes call 'being in the zone'?[21]

Yet, I could not fully shake off my modernist bias, believing that self-interest is the primary motive driving human beings, especially in economic and political life. I asked myself, could I act without desire? I did not think I would wake up in the morning if I had no desire. So, I did not think *nishkama karma* meant desirelessness in that sense. Could being 'intent on the act' mean that I ought to perform an activity for the sake of the 'excellence' of the activity? Stated thus, it sounded almost Aristotelian. One afternoon, I stumbled on to what Harry Truman, the former American president, had said: 'Your work will succeed as long as you don't care who gets the credit.' In his folksy American way he seemed to be saying something that seemed suspiciously similar to *nishkama karma*. Was it then a universal idea? Some Western psychologists had also observed this quality in human behaviour, I noted.[22]

'I see the bird, but I don't see the tree or you'

The Upanishads are amongst the earliest philosophical speculations of human beings and they had foreseen the downside of human vanity. Composed in a period of intellectual ferment—roughly 800–400 BC, a time which also produced the Buddha and Mahavira in India, Socrates in Greece and Confucius in China—the Upanishads realized that the 'self' is the source of many of our day-to-day troubles. It produces harmful thoughts of 'me and mine', selfish desires, cravings, attachments, hatred, ill-will, conceit, pride and egotism, and even wars between nations. The Upanishads trace these problems of the self to our sense of 'I-ness' or *ahamkara* (literally 'I-maker') which is our subjective sense of identity and which has its origin in our consciousness (*aham*). In classical Sankhya philosophy, the empirical world of the senses and the mind emerges from the evolution of the *aham*, and liberation from this empirical existence requires the negation of *ahamkara*.

The *Mahabharata* is aware of the 'I-maker' and how the 'self' comes in the way of performance. Arjuna, the greatest archer in the *Mahabharata*, demonstrates to his admiring teacher, Drona, that he stops thinking and forgets himself and everything else at the moment of shooting an arrow. He only sees the target.

> *The left-handed archer stretched the bow until it stood in a circle and kept aiming at the target as his guru had ordered. After a while Drona said to him ... 'Do you see this bird sitting there? And the tree? And me?' 'I see the bird,' Arjuna replied, 'but I don't see the tree or you' ... 'If you see the bird describe it to me?' 'I see its head, not its body.'*[23]

Buddhists have always had an interest in 'self-forgetting', especially in Dhyana Buddhism or what the Japanese call Zen. An aspiring student makes the same point as Arjuna: 'Man may be a "thinking person" but his great works are done when he is not calculating and thinking ... In the case of archery, the hitter and the hit are no longer two opposing objects, but are one reality. The archer ceases to be conscious of himself as the one who is engaged in hitting the bull's eye which confronts him. This state of unconsciousness is realized only when [one is] rid of the self.'[24] Baso (or Ma-tsu), who died in 788, claims that one needs to restore the 'everyday mind', which means 'sleeping when tired, eating when hungry'. When a person reflects, deliberates and conceptualizes, the original unconsciousness is lost and thought interferes.

The *Mahabharata* teaches one to grin at human vanity, and I have found plenty to smile at in my own life. As I reflected on 'self-forgetting', I found that distractions of the ego often came in the way of performance in my working day. Instead of focusing on the job, I brooded, and mostly about myself. 'Why did I get a smaller raise than he?' Not only did this sort of thing generate negative energy, it also led to boredom at work. It was my 'big fat ego', as Iris Murdoch calls it, that was making me want to be more important than others. What was often an exciting job became 'work' and an unsatisfactory life.

Although my father was not without vanity, he was not driven by it. Shy and self-effacing, he preferred to listen rather than to hold forth. If someone asked him a personal question, he would gently change the subject and preferred to talk about the other. He was an engineer, and he said that his job was his dharma, and he 'had to do it because it was there'. He also seemed less affected by the behaviour of others around him and less bothered by what others thought of him. As a result, he was free from the worry of measuring up to their expectations. He had a rare inner confidence which is absent in many of us who care about the attentions of the world. People liked him because he was not thinking about himself all the time.

John Stuart Mill would have preferred my father to me. Mill says, 'selfishness [is] the principal cause which makes life unsatisfactory'.[25] He had learned from Auguste Comte that the opposite of selfishness is altruism, which he felt was at the heart of moral virtue. Comte and his followers were so taken up by this idea that they overreacted by suggesting that all our actions should benefit others. They made altruism an obligation. But I think that is going too far. (I shall return to this idea in Chapter 10 in connection with Yudhishthira's compassion.) I do not believe that Krishna's notion of 'being intent on the action and not on its fruits' leads one only to altruism. Self-forgetting ought to make one less selfish, which is not the same thing as saying 'all our actions should be designed to benefit others'.

Writers always seem to have more than the usual problems with vanity, and it is perhaps because of it that T.S. Eliot, E.M. Forster and others have been attracted to the Gita. Forster, writing in the aftermath of World War I, was hugely enthusiastic about *nishkama karma*. He saw in it the possibility of conquering not only human vanity but fear as well. It could lead one to the divine, which, of course, is one of Krishna's central purposes in conceiving of the idea:

The man of discipline has joy,
delight, and light within;

becoming the infinite spirit
he finds the pure calm of infinity.[26]

After summarizing Krishna's three reasons for fighting, E.M. Forster goes on to say: 'The saint may renounce action, but the soldier, the citizen, the practical man generally—they should renounce, not action, but its fruits. It is wrong for them to be idle; it is equally wrong to desire a reward for industry. It is wrong to shirk destroying civilization and one's kindred and friends, equally wrong to hope for dominion afterwards. When all such hopes and desires are dead fear dies also, and freed from all attachments the "dweller in the body" will remain calm while the body performs its daily duty.'[27] Fear dies, Forster says, when one is freed from the attachments of one's ego. I think my father's attitude illustrates this point. Being happy to get on with his work, and not being too concerned with the opinion of others, he did not fear people in the upper hierarchy at his office. He seemed to be 'inner-directed' rather than 'outer-directed' and this allowed him to stand up to his boss on several occasions.[28]

I was nine when my mother came home one day looking very agitated. We were living at the time on the site of the Bhakra Dam in the Punjab in north-west India. My father was working with hundreds of engineers in building the dam. That morning he had committed the great sin of hierarchy—he had disagreed with his boss in public about the width of one of the load-bearing walls. It ought to be much wider, he had said, or it would collapse. He had expressed these views in a meeting where his boss's boss was also present, and his boss had lost face.

The news of my father's 'defiance' spread quickly in the engineers' colony. My mother heard about it in the market from one of the other wives. My mother was worried because my father's boss had the reputation for being vindictive. He was full of himself, and wanted his ego massaged by his juniors, and my father had not joined his coterie of sycophants. She must have transmitted her fears to me for I have never been able to forget this incident. It was my first schooling in the morality of hierarchy.

I was formally introduced to the principles of this corporate morality in my first job in Bombay. At twenty-one I was a trainee at Richardson Hindustan Ltd, a company that was later acquired by Procter & Gamble. Every company in those days seemed to have a south Indian accountant, and ours was no different. One day the accountant took me to a south Indian café near Flora Fountain. Over a lunch of idli and dosa he gave me advice on how to gain influence within the company. 'What is right is what the boss wants,' he said. 'Senior managers need to feel comfortable, and the job of a junior manager is to put him at ease. Otherwise, a junior will not be trusted and will end up leading a troubled and anxious life.' He taught me that a subordinate owes fealty principally to his immediate boss: 'Keep your boss from making mistakes. If he is error prone, there is temptation to let him make a fool of himself, but others will be suspicious of you if you don't protect him. Never, I repeat, never contradict your boss in public. To violate this rule is a death wish. Don't speak out of turn at meetings and make an effort to laugh at your boss's jokes.'

My father had broken these rules on that morning, and our family had many anxious months over the 'load-bearing wall'. He was removed from his job, designing the powerhouse, and reassigned. He was told that he 'could not be trusted', and his life became unpleasant. His colleagues were afraid to talk to him. My mother found all this very distressing but my father bore it well. He plunged enthusiastically into his new, inconsequential job, and improved performance there so dramatically that his boss was even more infuriated. Gradually, he realized that my father did not respond to the usual incentives, and since he needed him, he quietly brought my father back to his original position. One of his colleagues' wives said to my mother, 'Sister, your husband is a *karma yogi*!' It was my first encounter with the

Gita's concept of *nishkama karma*. Indeed, my father did seem 'to be intent on the act, not its fruit'.

This is the point that E.M. Forster was also trying to make in his essay. He said that a person who is freed from attachment to rewards and who remains calm doing his daily duty 'will be unstained by sin, as is the lotus leaf by the water of the tank. It will attain to the eternal peace that is offered to the practical man as well as to the devotee. It will have abjured the wages of action, which are spiritual death, and gained in their place a vision of the Divine.'[29] I do not know if my father attained the divine vision, however.

The hero as renouncer

Indians have always been fascinated by the *sanyasi*, 'renouncer'. He stands tall and splendid, 'a theatrical figure in ochre robes'.[30] In a famous essay Louis Dumont wrote, 'the secret of Hinduism may be found in the dialogue between the renouncer and the *grihastha*, "man-in-the-world".' The renunciatory ideal took a mesmerizing hold on the ordinary householder even before the advent of ascetic religions like Buddhism and Jainism. Hinduism's flexible nature allowed dissent in post-Vedic society, as dissenting renouncers chose direct knowledge of liberation through perception and meditation over the rituals of the brahmins, thus challenging brahmin monopoly over salvation.[31]

The departure of great men (and women) into the jungles created its own problems for society. Asceticism became a major issue, and the classic text of laws, the *Manusmriti*, had to forbid men from becoming renouncers until they had successfully fulfilled the previous three stages of life and discharged their debt to secular society. To those who were torn between the two ways of life, Krishna's advice of *nishkama karma* offered a way out: they could now live in the world but with the attitude of the renouncer; they could live authentically if they remained detached and self-possessed in the midst of worldly activity, avoiding the extremes of indulgence and asceticism through self-discipline.[32]

Nishkama karma thus gave new meaning to the day-to-day life of the ordinary householder, who had to make a living, look after his family, live as a citizen in society, be a good friend and neighbour, discharge his responsibilities and prepare for the next stage of his life. To him the Gita offered the solution of living life based on self-control. By making the householder take charge of his life, the Gita devalued both the attractions of the rituals of the brahmins and of the ascetic life of renunciation. It offered the ideal of a 'secular ascetic'.

In the *Mahabharata* Bhishma comes closest to the ideal of a 'secular ascetic'. His life was motivated by duty to the state and characterized by detachment from personal reward. His vow of celibacy did not make him a 'secular ascetic'. Indeed, the *Mahabharata* is ambivalent about his celibacy, which turned into a curse for the Bharata dynasty. The Gita does not expect householders to be celibate either. (Celibacy is a virtue at the previous *brahmacharya* stage of studentship but not of the *grihastha*, the householder.) The Gita focuses on the positive results that come from becoming less self-centred and among these is an escape from karma.

> . . . *be without personal aspirations or concern for possessions, and fight unconcernedly. They who follow this view of mine, believing it without disputing it, are freed from their karman.*[33]

The *Mahabharata*, and Indian tradition in general, regards karma as bondage. Actions, both good and bad, bind one to an unhappy cycle of birth and rebirth due to the relentless moral accounting enforced by the law of karma. The purpose of life is liberation from the phenomenal world, which is a 'prison of karma'. Detaching one's actions from personal reward changes the quality of one's actions, according to the Gita. As one becomes less self-centred, karma does not stick to one's actions. By acting in a selfless way one also achieves liberation from the consequences of one's actions.

The generation that struggled for India's freedom from Britain recognized the power of *nishkama karma*. The novelist Bankimchandra Chattopadhyay introduced this concept in nationalist discourse in the late nineteenth century in Bengal.[34] Bal Gangadhar Tilak, the firebrand from Maharashtra, examined it in depth in his commentary on the Gita, giving it a socially activist interpretation in the early twentieth century. Mahatma Gandhi then followed in the 1920s with even greater success, rallying people on the path of non-violent resistance to colonial rule. For Gandhi, the hand spinning of cloth became a symbolic assertion of the ideal of *karma yoga*—action performed without regard for its 'fruits'—as millions of men and women began to spin khadi cloth. Indian philosophers have been trying to interpret *nishkama karma* as a spiritual ideal for centuries.[35]

But what is my duty?

G.W.F. Hegel, the great German philosopher, had much difficulty with Krishna's notion of acting selflessly from a sense of duty, and some of these difficulties were similar to the objections he had to Kant's notion of duty. Hegel wrote a long review in 1827 of Wilhelm von Humboldt's lectures on the Gita in Berlin, and he specifically focused on *nishkama karma*. Humboldt regarded this as a personal attack on himself and he never spoke to Hegel for years.[36]

While Hegel recognized the moral attractiveness of 'doing one's duty only for duty's sake', and agreed that this was a great moral intention, the practical problem lay in knowing what one's duty is. Krishna does specify moral duties in the Gita, but the moral law of acting disinterestedly does not necessarily lead one to virtuous acts. It might lead one to kill kinsmen in a bloody war, which is Arjuna's dilemma. Hegel concluded that *nishkama karma* does not 'lead to anything, and from itself there cannot result any moral duties'.[37] Hegel's words were prophetic, for 125 years later, many Nazis did, in fact, justify their evil acts against the Jews at the Nuremberg trials on the grounds that they were not acting for selfish ends: they were doing their duty to their country.[38]

In her account of the trial of Adolf Eichmann, Hannah Arendt raises the same question. Eichmann was a senior Nazi SS officer and considered by many to be the 'architect of the Holocaust'. Thanks to his considerable organizational talents and ideological reliability, he was charged with the task of deporting Jews to ghettos and exterminating them in Nazi-occupied Eastern Europe. After the war, Eichmann travelled to Argentina using a fraudulently obtained *laissez-passer* issued by the International Red Cross and lived there under a false identity working for Mercedes-Benz until the 1960s. He was captured by Israeli Mossad agents in Argentina and tried in an Israeli court on fifteen criminal charges, including crimes against humanity and war crimes. He was convicted and hanged in 1962.

During the trial, Eichmann confessed that of the millions of cases that passed through his hands, he allowed sympathy for the Jews to sway him from the path of duty on only two occasions. He implied that he generally felt sympathy for the Jews he was sending to the gas chambers. However, he steadfastly stuck to his job because he believed one should do one's duty unaffected by sympathy.[39] Other Nazis spoke the same language. As Arendt recounted: 'In a speech to the SS Einsatzgruppen, special squads appointed to carry out the killing of groups of Jews, Heinrich Himmler told his troops that they were called upon to fulfil a "repulsive duty" and that he would not like it if they did such a thing gladly. He had recently witnessed the machine-gunning of about a hundred Jews and he had, he said, "been aroused to the depths of my soul" by what he had seen; but he was obeying the highest law by doing his duty.'[40]

In recounting these cases of Nazi officers, I am not suggesting that *nishkama karma* sanctions or justifies mass murder. Rather, the idea that we should act selflessly for the sake of acting or do our duty for duty's sake without asking for further justification can be dangerous. This is Hegel's point as well. Both Krishna and Immanuel Kant were understandably reacting against a traditional view of reward and punishment, but their alternative approach—following duty with little thought to the consequences—brings problems of its own.

The basic problem, then, with basing one's actions on 'duty' is the question, 'What is my duty?' What I think is my duty might be very different from another person's notion of his duty. Krishna thinks Arjuna's duty is to fight because he is a warrior. Arjuna thinks his duty is not to kill others. Both make an appeal, in a sense, to their 'conscience'. What if what is inside my conscience or my 'nature' turns out to be wrong, however? One person's conscience might tell him/her to do something quite unsavoury. It is not easy to be good.

'Karma yogi was my father, Dhirubhai Ambani'

In December 2004, Anil Ambani—whom we met in Chapter 1— employed Krishna's idea of *nishkama karma* as a strategic weapon in his war against his elder brother Mukesh. In the thick of the struggle, Anil Ambani wrote a curious article on *nishkama karma* in the *Times of India* on 4 December 2004 in a space called 'The Speaking Tree'.

In it, Ambani wrote, 'Karma yogi was my father Dhirubhai Ambani's other name. He was a man of action. But as a true follower of the Bhagavad Gita, he acted not for himself, but for humanity. In the true spirit of nishkam-karma, he remained free from attachment to the fruits of his action . . . Ego is the source of all our troubles. It is as the divine text puts it, the feeling of separateness, the sense of duality, the idea of being distinct and different from others. It is an arrogant and obsessive sense of ownership . . . that has lost touch with dharma. Humility then is neither a sign of human weakness nor just another polite virtue. It is the essential foundation for building everything that is just, lasting and permanent. This was the abiding truth which guided the life of Dhirubhai. He never saw himself as an owner ... I have often asked myself if humility and trust are matters of individual temperament—an aspect of our samskar and karma—or, in today's parlance, genetic coding. And, every time, I have come to the contrary conclusion. It's not easy, I admit, but we can all learn to be humble and trustful, as long as we have the ability to love all beings as one's own self. That is the quintessential first step in a long journey of individual, social and spiritual evolution.'

This article was clearly the work of a highly intelligent man who had wrestled with the moral issues raised by the Gita's message. Nevertheless, it was also self-serving, which is ironical since it extolled the virtues of selflessness and humility. It did not fool anyone. Most people said at the time that Anil Ambani had written it to win public sympathy in his epic battle against his brother. One reader's shocked reaction was: 'I thought only Gurus write such things. Never knew billionaires do it ... If he is so motivated by the Gita (and not money)—I have a simple solution. Give up everything and go to the Himalayas.'[41] The reader had, in fact, got Krishna's message completely wrong—*nishkama karma*, as we have seen, is not about going to the Himalayas but about living self-effacingly in the world like Bhishma.

If Anil Ambani is to be believed, his and his father's ambition was for the success of their enterprises and not personal reward. Even if one accepts this self-serving characterization on Anil's part, it does point to the same weakness in the concept of *nishkama karma* that Hegel had pointed out. One can 'be intent on the act, not its fruit' and still destroy competitors, break laws, bribe people as the Ambanis had done. Selflessness does not necessarily make one a moral person.

'Sonia Gandhi, a karma yogi'

Human beings admire selflessness. We are taught to respect those who are selfless in their actions, and as we grow up we equate selflessness with being moral. In India, selflessness has an exceptional status partly because of Krishna's counsel in the Gita. Mahatma Gandhi was commonly referred to as a *karma yogi* during India's struggle for independence in the first half of the twentieth century. Mother Teresa is revered for the same reason. When Sonia Gandhi refused to become prime minister after the Congress party triumphed in the elections in May 2004, her supporters also likened her to a *'karma yogi'*.

Is 'selflessness' a practical ideal in public life? Like most young persons in the mid-twentieth century, I was a socialist in my youth and I admired the selfless ways of many socialists. I was in particular awe of my Marxist uncle, Sat Pal Dang, and his Kashmiri wife, Vimla, who had sacrificed material comfort and dedicated their lives to bringing justice to exploited workers in industrial Amritsar in north-west India. Some of my professors were Marxists and they inspired their students to selflessly go and change the world. A few of my friends did become socialist activists.

My own love affair with socialism ended when I discovered that a poor nation like India could not become prosperous via the selfless ideals of Marxism. I concluded that its ideal of equality was unattainable because of *ahamkara*, 'the I-maker'. The ego will not diminish to the extent that Marxism demands. My readings in economic history had taught me that in 1750 the per capita income of all nations was by and large the same—everyone was poor. Then the industrial revolution came in the West and brought unprecedented prosperity. The same thing happened in the Far East between 1960 and 1990. And this transformation is now going on in China and India at the beginning of the twenty-first century. Nations have gradually conquered poverty and turned middle class, not through selflessness but through the 'self-interest' of individuals in the marketplace. Nations have grown prosperous because they depended on institutions that allowed them to unleash the power of modern technology. Among these institutions were law and order, stable governance and property rights—all of which encouraged the growth of trade, markets and entrepreneurs. These liberal institutions presume that the citizen will act on the basis of self-interest rather than through selfless acts of heroism.

In the twentieth century, the world has had to learn this lesson painfully after Stalin and Mao inflicted monumental grief on their people. Aristotle had warned us of this danger more than two thousand years ago. He had objected to Plato's ideal of common ownership of property because some people would resent those who 'labour little and receive or consume much'. He had thought private property was natural and legitimate, for 'the love of the self is a feeling implanted by nature and not given in vain, although selfishness is rightly censured; this, however, is not the mere love of self, the love of self in excess, like the miser's love of money . . .'[42] Aristotle makes the same sensible distinction (as Adam Smith and others) between rational self-interest and selfishness. One should not make the common mistake in believing that the opposite of selflessness is selfishness. There is a liberal middle ground of 'self-interest', which drives ordinary human beings. This is what successful liberal institutions depend upon.

We must also admire the benevolent acts of many philanthropists, social activists and environmentalists to even out the excesses of capitalism. Kindness and compassion are virtues and one cannot imagine a decent civilized life without them. These are, however, moral *ideals* rather than moral *rules* for society. Enlightened philanthropy can make a difference, but in the end, liberal institutions will do far more in lifting people out of poverty and oppression. Liberal, lightly regulated institutions depend on the natural 'self-interest' of ordinary persons rather than on selfless acts of heroic leaders.

Although I admire Krishna's message of *nishkama karma*, I believe it is unattainable for the ordinary human being. Even Bhishma's selfless vow got him into trouble when it came to doing the right thing over the succession to the Hastinapura throne. Nor did it save Draupadi in the assembly. Unattainable ideals often seem to give someone a stick to beat others into submission. They give the likes of Stalin and Mao a pretext for resorting to strong-arm tactics to make up for the deficit in human selflessness.[43] Hence, 'rational self-interest' is the correct basis on which to design public institutions, especially when they involve large numbers of people who do not have day-to-day contact with each other. These are the institutions of democratic capitalism.

Nevertheless, I believe the ideal of *nishkama karma* does have a place in our lives. Modern social science has gone too far in relying exclusively on self-interest to explain human behaviour. Reading the Gita turned out to be a nice corrective in my dharma education for it reminded me of the ideal of selfless action. Game theorists, as we saw in the Prisoner's Dilemma, have observed that if individuals only pursue self-interest, defined narrowly, they actually undermine the collective good and harm themselves. So, one must take into account both selfish and unselfish motivations of human beings. If one adopts the 'cautious strategy' and designs institutions based *only* on selfish motives, one might erode whatever public spirit that might otherwise exist. If one assumes too high a level of public spirit, one runs the opposite risk.[44]

'Let no man do to another that which is repugnant to himself'

I have been fascinated with *nishkama karma* ever since I encountered it and wondered how it might influence my day-to-day life. I have a humbling awareness that I am interrogating the Gita from 'the outside'. If I believed in Krishna as God, I would instinctively accept that my duty lies in following Krishna's command. I would then become 'an insider'. I would try to renounce the fruits of my actions in God's favour and move along a more traditional, religious path. But in interrogating the text from 'the outside', I have to be extra careful and not try to impose a modern, secular sensibility on to an ancient religious text. The Gita is still the most popular religious authority in India, partly because it addresses the universal problem of how to live one's life. It offers the devotee a seductive way to be *in* the world and yet not be *of* the world by renouncing the ego. I did not wish to 'wound' this world view of the believer.

Krishna obviously hopes that ordinary human beings will be able to diminish their 'big fat egos'. On the face of it, this is not an outrageous expectation, since we do observe ego-less acts in our daily life. We also experience 'self-forgetting' from time to time, especially when we are engaged in doing something that we like. Arjuna 'lets himself go' as soon as he picks up his Gandiva bow. The challenge is to be able to do it *all* the time.

What intrigues me is the relationship between *nishkama karma* and being a 'good' human being. Does being 'intent on the act, not its fruits' lead to being more moral? It would certainly make for an attractive world if there were fewer selfish Duryodhanas, crusted over with pride and self-importance like the Ambani brothers, whose sibling rivalries threaten the well-being of millions. We could do with more self-effacing Bhishmas who lead their lives without expecting applause.

I am not sure if there is a direct connection between selflessness and 'general benevolence'. While it is reasonable to expect a person who acts disinterestedly to also adopt the 'impartial perspective' and empathize with strangers, it does not necessarily follow.[45] Certainly, it did not happen in the case of Rudolf Hoess, the commandant at Auschwitz, who systematically murdered 2.9 million Jews. He wrote in his autobiography that he suffered great emotional pain, but he did his job disinterestedly as a duty to national socialism.[46] The moral perspective is arrived at when one is able to think beyond oneself, beyond one's family and friends, and put oneself in the shoes of another. The *Mahabharata* endorses this idea. It says famously:

Let no man do to another that which is repugnant to himself.

How does one learn to do that? How does one awaken the 'impartial spectator' within oneself? A good way to begin might be to read a text like the *Mahabharata*. Children in Java who had been exposed to the *Mahabharata* seemed to be more tolerant, according to the British historian Benedict Anderson.[47] Claude Helvetius, the Enlightenment thinker, recommended that to make a child 'humane and compassionate',[48] one had to 'habituate him from a tender age to put himself in the place of the miserable'. Psychologists' studies show how our moral attitudes and dispositions are formed in infancy. Psychologists tell us that an infant is 'omnipotent' or 'pure ego' as it emerges from the womb, and slowly begins to distinguish the difference between itself and external objects. It is curious about the world. It explores faces and begins to delight with the world. Thus, it forms attachments to others beyond itself. And as the child extends its 'circle of concern' beyond itself to others, it learns to become more compassionate and ethical. Indeed, this is how Jean Jacques Rousseau expected Emile to learn compassion. Emile's teacher taught him to focus on the common vulnerability of human beings. As Rousseau puts it, our fragile happiness is born from our weakness.[49]

Nishkama karma is valuable if only to remind one that a person without vanity is an appealing human being, who is lucky to be freed from the unhappy bondage of the human ego. It may be one of the reasons that so many literary figures have been attracted to the Gita. T.S. Eliot compared the Gita to Dante's *Divine Comedy* in its greatness as a philosophical poem. He spoke about love beyond desire, and felt that *nishkama karma* could liberate one from the future and from the past:

This is the use of memory:
For liberation—not less of love but expanding
Of love beyond desire, and so liberation
From the future as well as the past.[50]

Eliot seemed to find here the answer to the riddle of life and of death and time. He agrees with Krishna that striving after the 'fruits' of an illusory future is futile and even destructive. One must learn to live in the present moment like a *karma yogi*, an attitude that is consistent with the existential ethic popular in Eliot's time after the collapse of the Enlightenment project and the despair brought on by the futile World War I. Hence, he advises one to act with the mind fixed, not on the fruits (future) but on the pleasure one gets in performing the activity, in being alive and vital in the present. He imagines Krishna telling Arjuna:

At the moment which is not of action or inaction
You can receive this: 'on whatever sphere of being
The mind of a man may be intent
At the time of death'—that is the one action
(And the time of death is every moment)
Which shall fructify the lives of others:
And do not think of the fruit of action.[51]

P.S.: 'One bird eats the fruit while the other watches'

If I was going to learn to diminish my 'self' as a part of my *nishkama karma* project, I felt I needed to learn something about my 'self'. Since this search is not central to my quest for dharma, I have added it here as an optional postscript for the reader who might be interested in the nature of human consciousness.

My father held the traditional Hindu view that the real 'self' is an immortal soul or spirit, *atman*, and is not to be confused with the phenomenal self of my subjective feeling of 'I-ness', which he believed to be illusory. My own starting point, however, was this illusory sense of 'I-ness'. Indians have long been fascinated by the nature of the 'self'. They observed in the Upanishads that the sense-of-'I' was present in every human activity. It persisted whether a person was awake, dreaming, or asleep. Even after waking from the deepest slumber, one recognized that it was the same 'I' that had been dreaming. However, one could not identify the 'I' with the human body or any of the individual's senses. Nor could one say that the human mind was the real 'self', for all mental states had something constant other than the mind as their referent. Through a process of elimination, the Upanishads concluded that the real self must transcend the material world. Through a further process of inference, they arrived at an even bolder and more startling conclusion—this *atman*, which is present in all living beings, is identical with the ultimate principle of the universe, *brahman*. They famously stated this identity as *aham brahma asmi*.

Because humans have an impressive capacity for thinking, imagining and acting to shape our world, the Upanishads felt there must be a link between the energy of human beings and that of the universe; behind our world of distinct and separate objects, there must be a fundamental unity. My father believed that the purpose of life is to achieve and experience this identity and liberate oneself from our fragmented, finite and suffering existence. The Gita offers multiple paths by which one can fulfil this purpose of life—through meditation or knowledge, or selfless action (about which we have just been speaking), or devotion and love.

In pursuit of this aim, Indians began to elaborate early on mental exercises or meditative disciplines, which became known by the generic term 'yoga'. The earliest references to yoga are found in the Upanishads, but over time many different kinds of yoga developed. The word 'yoga' comes from the Sanskrit root *yuj*, 'to yoke'—in the sense of yoking one thing to another—the point being to merge or unite the *atman*, the 'soul', with the *brahman*, 'universal essence'. Although the ontology varies from system to system, the common starting point is that ordinary daily life is characterized by 'being led astray' by our phenomenal 'self' (our sense of I-ness, *ahamkara*) and the distracting busy-ness of one's mind and everyday activity. Patanjali stated the purpose of yoga concisely in the first sentence of his classic *Yoga Sutras*: *chitta-vritti-nirodha*, 'calm the ceaseless activity of the mind'. Through mental steadiness, right breathing and benevolence towards others, one's mind becomes 'one-pointed' and prepares to distance itself from the deluded sense of I-ness, recognizing the true 'self'.[52]

The Buddha, in the sixth century BC, challenged the very existence of the immutable 'self' (*atman*). One is conscious, he said, of countless and changing sensations and thoughts, and one mistakenly assumes there is a permanent entity that is 'the thinker of thoughts, feeler of sensations'. But this 'idea of the self is an imaginary, a false belief' which has no corresponding reality.[53] The Buddhist doctrine that denies a permanent 'self' or soul is called 'not-self' (*anatman* in Sanskrit, *anatta* in Pali). If the 'self' does not exist, then one is not distracted by the need to 'save' or liberate it. One can focus on being good in the world, an idea that fits in nicely with the overall Buddhist goal of compassion. (Buddhist scholars have long wrestled with the dilemma that if there is no 'self', then the standard arguments for moral responsibility fall apart as well.)[54]

In the West, David Hume embarked on a similar search in 1739. He wrote: 'When I enter most intimately into what I call myself, I always stumble on some particular perception or other, of heat or cold, light or shade, love or hatred, pain or pleasure. I never can catch myself.'[55] Hume did not find his 'self', but Descartes, the seventeenth century French philosopher, did. He concluded his 'self' was not his brain, but it did exist, nevertheless, because 'I think, therefore I am'. He convinced me that the mind and body are two distinct entities, and ever since, I have pictured the 'self' as a sort of ghost sitting behind my eyes which owns and controls my body just as I control my car.[56]

Contemporary thinkers in the West have mostly rejected Descartes's 'dualism' of mind and body in favour of 'materialism' of the body alone. Gilbert Ryle's *The Concept of the Mind* deeply influenced their thinking when it first came out in 1949, persuading them that the mind is also purely physical—it is just the brain. It is like the computer's central operating system, organizing and directing the rest of the body's functions. There is no ghost, no soul, no spirit; dualism is a fallacy. Neo-Darwinian evolutionary theory, and the writings of Richard Dawkins and others in the 1970s and 1980s, further reinforced scientific materialism. However, the question remains: no matter how the mind and body interact, how did this operating system develop the sense of the 'self'?

Contemporary consciousness theorists in the West follow a similar line of thinking. Daniel Dennet, the American philosopher turned cognitive scientist, believes that the 'self' is not a real entity in the universe, something which particle physics or neuroscientists can identify. It is a mistake to start looking for it in the brain: there is no thinker behind our thoughts. All that one is aware of is a stream of thoughts and feelings. Virginia Woolf, the writer, made a similar observation:

Examine for a moment an ordinary mind on an ordinary day. The mind receives myriad impressions—trivial, fantastic, evanescent, or engraved with the sharpness of steel. From all sides they come, an incessant shower of innumerable atoms; and as they fall, as they shape themselves into the life of Monday or Tuesday the accent falls differently from of old; the moment of importance came not here but there; so that if a writer were a free man and not a slave, if he could write what he chose, not what he must, if he could base his work upon his own feeling and not upon convention, there would be no plot, no comedy, no tragedy, no love interest or catastrophe in the accepted style, and perhaps not a single button sewn on as the Bond Street tailors would have it. Life is not a series of gig lamps symmetrically arranged; but a luminous halo, a semi-transparent envelope surrounding us from the beginning of consciousness to the end.[57]

Dennet goes on to explain that the self is somewhat like the narrator in fiction.[58] He argues that man acquired consciousness because he happened to have a brain that was larger than what he needed purely for evolutionary purposes. He speculates that before human beings learned to speak, our primitive ancestors 'just blurted things out' unconsciously. 'Then one day one of our ancestors asked a question in what was apparently an inappropriate circumstance: there was nobody around to be the audience. Strangely enough, he heard his own question, and this stimulated him cooperatively to think of an answer, and sure enough the answer came to him. One component of the mind had confronted a problem that another component could solve. Sometimes talking and listening to oneself can have wonderful effects.'

The *Mahabharata* is aware of this primordial dialogue between our two selves. The Mundaka Upanishad gives the example of two plumed birds in a peepul tree. One eats the fruit, while the other, eating nothing, looks on intently:

> *Two birds, twin images*
> *in plumage,*
> *friends, ever inseparable,*
> *cling to a tree.*
>
> *One eats the fruit,*
> *eats of the sweet and eats*
> *of the bitter,*
> *while the other watches,*
> *watches without eating.*

Buried in the bole
of the self-same tree
one suffers, engulfed
in his impotence.

Yet as he watches the watching
bird, the adorable one, and sees
the sweet bitter glory
as His alone,
he rises, free
from grief.[59]

We are two selves inside, one that is doing and acting and another that is watching the one who is doing. The Upanishad goes further and suggests that in this duality is an intimation of the idea of the human and the divine: the bird who eats the fruit is the human self, while the witness is the spirit or the principle of the divine.

Contemporary thinkers increasingly liken consciousness to literature. The self's interaction with an object, says Antonio Tomasio, is a 'simple narrative without words. It [has] characters. It unfolds in time. And it has a beginning, middle and an end.'[60] However, not all of these theorists dismiss the 'autobiographical self' as an illusion. They are content to leave it as 'an inner sense'.[61] The 'I-maker' seems like a literary narrator because literature is so good at capturing what cognitive theorists call *qualia* or the sensory content of subjective experience, the 'raw feeling'.[62] It is the 'painfulness of pain, the scent of sandalwood, the taste of Bourbon-Vanilla or the extraordinary sound quality in the tone of a cello.'[63]

The problem of consciousness comes down to the problem of how to give an objective, third person account of what is essentially a subjective, first person phenomenon. In a famous essay called 'What is it Like to be a Bat?', Thomas Nagel concludes that the only way to experience what a bat experiences is to be a bat.[64] Indeed, according to the distinguished neuroscientist, V.S. Ramachandran, the 'need to reconcile the first person and third person accounts of the universe . . . is the single most important problem in science.'[65] This goes back to the question that Descartes puzzled over: how can consciousness arise in a purely physical universe? Today, the problem of consciousness—perhaps together with the question of the origin of the universe—marks the very limit of human striving for understanding. It is the 'the last great puzzle', says Thomas Metzinger.[66]

Religions have always been suspicious of the 'self'. Hindus think of the 'I-maker' *(ahamkara)* as the source of all human problems. Christianity exhorts people to suppress the sinful 'self', and be selfless and humble. In the Middle Ages, the Catholic Church tried to restrain human desire on the premise that the individual was wayward and dangerously unstable; thus, he had to submit to authority. The Renaissance, however, challenged this premise, and a new awareness of the self began to emerge, which represented a major break in Western thought. Jacob Burckhardt provides the classic account of how a radical new consciousness was born. He writes, 'In the Middle Ages . . . man was conscious of himself only as a member of a race, people, party, family, or corporation—only some general category . . . [In Renaissance Italy] man became an individual, and recognized himself as such. This thought led to the humanist movement, which encouraged people to be more self-confident, and, in fact, take a delight in being human.'[67]

Although Shakespeare's Hamlet is not inclined to feel this delight, he is a good example of the birth of the subject and an autonomous self in Renaissance literature. When he says, 'To be, or not to be',[68] he is not merely expressing self-doubt or weariness with the world. When he adds a little later, 'conscience does make cowards of us all',[69] he is not just displaying anger or uncertainty or moral upheaval. He is making us aware of a rich interior self, confident in its desire to fashion itself—an impulse that came into being in the Renaissance.[70]

By the early seventeenth century a new subjectivity had emerged in the West, what we today call 'liberal', 'humanist' or 'bourgeois'. Hegel captured this positive new individuality. The growth of rationalism in the eighteenth century culminated in Descartes's 'I think, therefore I am'. The Cartesian cogito fostered a conscious, self-determining individual as the one certainty in the universe. By the mid-nineteenth century this humanist affirmation of the individual had become 'self-reliance' in the America of Ralph Waldo Emerson. A positive sense of self also infected educated persons in India during the British Raj, and this led to the 'Bengal Renaissance' in the nineteenth century and the movement for independence in the twentieth century. In the same way it has influenced almost all cultures around the globe in the making of the modern world.

Nishkama karma forced me to think about the nature of the self. I have concluded that I am comfortably ensconced in the broad humanistic tradition of John Locke, Immanuel Kant and William James, although I do not agree with everything they say. I am attracted to the concept of the self as a unique, autonomous, morally responsible human being whose inner life can be known through introspection. For this, I do not have to believe in the existence of an immortal soul *(atman)*, nor worry if the mind and the body are separate. Unlike Dennet or Buddhist monks, I do not feel the need to call the 'self' an illusion. I do not mind using the words 'soul' or 'spirit' to signify some uniquely valuable quality in human awareness. I am content to admit modestly that 'something like the sense of self does exist in the human mind as we go about knowing things'. And if the 'self' turns out to be a fiction, then 'it may perhaps be the supreme fiction, the greatest achievement of human consciousness, the one that makes us human'.[71]

6

KARNA'S STATUS ANXIETY

How could a doe give birth to a tiger?

How could a doe give birth to a tiger who resembles the sun, with his earrings and armour and celestial birthmarks? This lordly man deserves to rule the world!

> —Duryodhana, leaping up like 'a rutting elephant from a lotus pond', *Mahabharata*, I.127.15[1]

'No more fiendish punishment could be devised than that one should be turned loose in society and remain absolutely unnoticed . . . If no one turned around when we entered, answered when we spoke, or minded what we did, but if every person we met "cut us dead" and acted as if we were non-existent things, a kind of rage and impotent despair would well up in us.'[2] So wrote the American philosopher William James about the common human anxiety over status. His observation is an apt description of Karna's worry over his social position in the *Mahabharata*. Karna is the most exciting figure in the epic, and his tragic struggle over his identity made me think beyond questions of status to our common notions of inequality, caste, fidelity, and even generosity. My own moral journey in search of dharma was considerably enriched by Karna's tragic story.

151

'Whatever you have done, I shall do better'

When the sons of Pandu and Dhritarashtra were young, they were trained in the martial arts by the brahmin Drona. One day the king, on the advice of their teacher, decides to hold a tournament to display their skills in a public assembly.[3] Invitations are sent far and wide. On the chosen day, princes, nobles and common people gather. The crowds 'like an ocean, rippling in waves' fill the stands to observe the great spectacle. In the royal stand, 'decked with gold leaf and screened off by pearl-studded lattice', sit King Dhritarashtra, Queen Gandhari and Kunti, the mother of the Pandavas. Watching 'the powerful bulls of the Bharatas descend with their bows, armour, and belts tightened,' the spectators are 'wonderstruck'. Arjuna, in particular, appears 'like a rain cloud ... aglow with lightning' and he wins the crowd's heart.

> *When the rising theatre had somehow calmed, the Terrifier [Arjuna] began to exhibit his different weapons. With the agneya he created fire, with the varuna water, with the vayavya wind, with the paranjaya rain; with the bhauma he entered the earth; with the parvata he brought forth mountains. With a disappearing weapon, he made it all vanish. One instant he stood tall, the next squat; he was up in front of the chariot, the next instant he jumped to the ground.*[4]

The people cry, 'he is the greatest in arms, the upholder of dharma'.

When the tournament is almost over, the crowd has thinned, and the music stopped, there comes from the area of the gate the sound of arms being slapped, like the crash of a thunderbolt.

> *All the spectators looked towards the gate ... and Karna ... entered the arena, wearing his inborn armour, his face lit by earrings. Carrying his bow and sword ... was this magnificent son of the Sun.*[5]

By birth, Karna is the son of Surya, the sun god, and Kunti, the Pandava queen. When she was a young girl, Kunti had looked after the ill-tempered sage Durvasa with extraordinary hospitality. Durvasa rewarded her with a boon—a mantra by which she could invoke any god and have a child by him. After she married Pandu and discovered he could not have children, Kunti used this boon to obtain three sons—Yudhishthira, Bhima and Arjuna—from the gods Dharma, Vayu and Indra respectively. Long before her marriage, however, she had accidentally invoked Surya, and discovered too late that the boon worked. She found herself with an unwanted child, Karna, who was born wearing a protective armour and earrings of immortality, which made his ears shine with splendour.[6]

Ashamed of the baby and desperate to hide her affair with the sun god, Kunti sets the infant afloat on the river and prays for his safety. The baby is picked up by Adhiratha, a charioteer, who takes it home to his childless wife, Radha. They bring up the child with warmth and affection. Even as he grows up as a charioteer's son, this prince by birth manages to acquire extraordinary martial skills and yearns to be a champion warrior.

> *The strong-armed champion glanced about the circle of stands,*
> *[and] with none too great courtesy, bowed to Drona and Kripa.*
> *The entire crowd was hushed and stared at him, and a shudder*
> *went through the people as they wondered who this stranger was.*
> *With a voice rumbling like a thunderhead, the son of the Sun,*
> *spoke to his unrecognized brother: 'Partha [Arjuna]! Whatever*
> *you have done, I shall do better!'*[7]

To everyone's amazement the stranger fulfils his promise.[8] Next, Karna challenges Arjuna to a duel. As the two heroes get ready and the spectators begin to take sides, Kunti, who knows the stranger's identity, faints. Vidura, ever solicitous, splashes her 'with water in which sandalwood had been sprinkled', and she revives. She stares in grief at her two sons.

As the two fighters raise their bows, the match referee, Kripa, announces that the rules require Karna to make his identity known. 'This is the youngest son of Pandu, born from Pritha, a scion of Kuru, who will engage you in a duel, sir. You too must identify yourself. Tell us the name of your mother, your father, and your kshatriya lineage. Only then may Partha [Arjuna] fight with you.' When he hears this, Karna's face fades 'like a lotus that has been showered by the rain'.[9]

Duryodhana seizes the moment. Realizing that this warrior might come in handy one day in his fight against the Pandavas, he comes to Karna's rescue.[10] 'According to the rules,' he announces, 'there are three ways to become a king: to be born one, to become a hero, or to lead an army.[11] If Arjuna is not permitted to duel with one who is not a king, I shall anoint him king of Anga.'

Thus Karna is consecrated on the field by the Vedic rites, and when the cheers subside an old man enters the scene 'sweating and trembling ... swaying on his feet, held up by a stick'.

> *When Karna saw [Adhiratha] he let go of his bow and moved by reverence for his father, he greeted him with his head, which was still wet with water from his consecration. Nervously, the chariot driver covered his feet with the end of his dhoti, and said to the crowned Karna, 'Ah, my son!'*[12]

Overhearing this exchange, Bhima realizes that Karna is a mere charioteer's son, and he bursts out laughing. 'Son of a charioteer, you don't have the right to die in a fight with Arjuna! Better stick to the whip which suits your family,' he jeers.[13] At these words, there is a slight tremor on Karna's lower lip. But Duryodhana again comes to his rescue. He declares that the greatest warriors do not think of origins. Besides, Karna, he adds, appears to be a hero:

> *How could a doe give birth to a tiger that shines like the sun?*[14]

At this moment the sun goes down and the tournament comes to a close. Kunti is filled with pleasure, having found her lost son.[15] Duryodhana is happy to have discovered a great warrior, someone who can match Arjuna. Yudhishthira's fear, however, begins to grow. So, the scene ends.

'I do not choose a charioteer!'

Human beings tend to view each other in accordance with their place in the world. Unlike Bhima, however, most of us do a better job of hiding our feelings. Some societies are more hierarchical than others, and it is difficult to escape one's origins. The *Mahabharata* is set in such a social order. Karna is slighted constantly and the epithet *sutaputra*, 'charioteer's son', dogs him all his life.

What hurts most is the power of the snub, especially when a beautiful woman delivers it. Karna discovers this to his humiliation when he goes to the court of Drupada, the Panchala king, to vie for his daughter's hand. It is the occasion of her *swayamvara*, 'bride choice', when the princess Draupadi will choose a husband. Young, ambitious noblemen are gathered from near and far. To help her select the best man she poses a test—the winner must string an extremely stiff bow and with it hit a golden target suspended in the sky. All the princes fail, except Karna, in a variant reading of the text. But the beautiful, haughty princess rejects the unwanted suitor because of his low birth. She says:

I do not choose a charioteer![16]

Arjuna, on the other hand, succeeds in winning her hand. Karna leaves dejectedly, but the undercurrent of sexual desire for Draupadi does not go away. We are reminded how difficult it is to escape one's origins in pre-modern societies.

Like most people, Karna wants to be 'somebody'. It must have hurt to sit in the stands at the tournament, ignored, as Arjuna enjoyed the admiration of the world. Later, when his own skill is discovered and he is praised by the crowd, Karna begins to feel worthy. Anxiety about one's place in the world tends to distort one's character. It makes Karna excessively proud. Like Achilles in the *Iliad*, he refuses to fight at the beginning of the war because he has been slighted by Bhishma.[17]

Status anxiety also makes him boastful and self-promoting, something that does not go down well with the noblemen of the old school. Bhishma chides him, 'Although [Karna] always boasts, saying "I shall slay the Pandavas", he doesn't possess even a small part of the Pandavas' great soul.'[18] Kripa, the instructor of martial arts, finds him exasperating, 'Son of a charioteer, you growl like an autumn cloud that is without water!'[19] To which Karna replies good-naturedly, 'Heroes always thunder like storm clouds in the monsoon, but like a seed dropped to the earth in the [rainy] season they quickly bear fruit.'[20]

Boasting is, of course, a critical part of heroic poetry. A noble hero is expected to show pride and disdain in order to evoke the heroic *rasa*, 'mood'.[21] But Karna also boasts in order to 'to be observed, to be attended to, to be taken notice of with sympathy, complacency and approbation'.[22] The attention of other people matters because human beings are uncertain of their own worth.

The writer Alain de Botton explains that our sense of identity is held hostage to the opinion of others: 'We may not admit it, but the truth is that we all seek to be loved by the world. When we are babies, we are loved whether we burp or scream or break our toys. But as we grow up, we are suddenly thrown into a world where people judge us by our achievements or our status (rather than as our mothers did). Hence our anxiety about how we are perceived. No human being is immune from this weakness.'[23] The ego (*ahamkara*, 'the 'I-maker') is a 'leaky balloon, forever requiring helium of external love to remain inflated, and ever vulnerable to the smallest pinpricks of neglect. There is something at once sobering and absurd in the extent to which we are lifted by the attentions of others and sunk by their disregard.'[24] Even great heroes like Yudhishthira and Arjuna are guilty of this sort of vanity.

We all want to be 'somebody'

In feudal societies, people worried less about their social position. Status was determined at birth and there was little hope for moving upwards. Indeed, if Karna had not possessed outstanding talent and a burning ambition, he might have led a reasonably well-adjusted life as a charioteer's son. But he was a kshatriya warrior who, the epic tells us, had an inborn *svabhava*, 'natural inclination', for a heroic life. He wanted to learn the use of the Brahmastra, the highest martial art. Even when Drona told him that only a brahmin or a kshatriya was permitted to learn it, Karna did not give up. He was driven to realize his natural potential.

Alexis de Tocqueville, the famous French traveller, observed far greater status anxiety in nineteenth century America (the first truly modern society) than in feudal Europe, where there was much less social mobility. In India too, there has been a growth in unease about one's status with the rise of democracy over the past sixty years. Lower caste persons can now aspire to higher status, and this causes unease among high-caste Indians who worry about their own position. This anxiety has intensified after the 1991 reforms, when India embraced the market and affirmative action for the 'other backward castes'. The rapid growth in the middle class has resulted in upward mobility—and with it insecurity about one's position.

The modern Indian middle class originated with the coming of the new professions in the nineteenth century. The British needed educated Indians to collect revenue, man the railways, guard the forests, and argue in the courts—in short, to run the country. My grandfather was one of these men. He was largely self-made. He came from a village and found success as a lawyer in the provincial town of Lyallpur in the old undivided Punjab. The memory of village poverty was never far from his mind, and he transmitted it to his children. Should his legal practice fail, the family faced the catastrophe of returning to a life of poverty in the village. This powerful association in his mind between low rank and catastrophe denied his offspring the emotional security to go out into the world with confidence about their own value. And these fears, I think, flowed down the generations to me through the insecurities of my mother.

My grandfather's status rose when he married his daughters to Class I officials of the colonial bureaucracy. The eldest married an official in the Indian Railways, who impressed us because he travelled in a luxurious saloon-on-wheels. The second married a professor of English in the anglicized Government College at Lahore. He was an accomplished tennis and bridge player and this gave him an entry into a social world denied to the rest of the family. When he came to visit us in Lyallpur, he did not fail to casually drop important names in his conversation. The third, my mother, married a civil engineer in the Punjab government's department of irrigation; and the fourth, an officer in the Indian army. By marrying his daughters sensibly to high-ranking professionals, my grandfather bought social status and security for his family. We rose from the middle to the upper middle class in two generations.

I remember vividly my own anxieties about our family's status when I was a schoolboy in Simla, soon after Independence. My father was a shy mid-level government official, a man content with his own company. But my mother wanted 'to see and to be seen'; she wanted to mix with the elite of Simla; she wanted to be a 'somebody'—and she lived in fear that her own world was insignificant compared to the grand world beyond. The natural solution was to join 'the club', the ADC. Although it had begun as an Amateur Dramatics Club, a sort of extension to the Gaiety Theatre during the British days, it was now mainly a social club and, more importantly, the meeting place of the fashionable in Simla. Unfortunately, with three children in private school, my mother couldn't afford it.

I must have been ten years old when a bachelor friend of our family's saw me one day outside the ADC, peering in with yearning curiosity. He put his arm around me. 'Come, my boy, let's go into the Green Room for a cup of tea,' he said. We were greeted by the hall porter and we walked past smoke-filled card rooms to another room full of young people and laughter. I looked around me with awe. Bearers in starched white uniforms with green cummerbunds and sashes and tassels were gliding between the tables. 'So, this is where the smart people of Simla meet,' I thought. As my host hailed a group of young people to join us, I was intoxicated by my first encounter with an inaccessible and forbidden world—the glamour, the clothes, the sophistication of language and manners. I imagined these people dwelling in big houses, with tall hedges and high gates, leading a life quite unlike my own.

Among them I recognized a girl from my school. She was stylishly dressed and looked beautiful. I kept looking at her, hoping she would recognize me. But she looked through me. Even when I smiled at her she ignored me. I couldn't sleep for weeks thinking of her. I have known many snobs in my life, but no one quite matched her in my memory. I got to know her better later in life but she had not changed. Like all snobs, she continued to see the world in hierarchical terms. Her life was dedicated to flattering the influential and ignoring the humble. She had only one yardstick—she judged people by their position in the world.

This was the first of many painful episodes in my anxiety-ridden adolescence. Although I have grown more confident with age, status anxiety continues to plague me. I feel the need to impress strangers—to tell them I am a 'somebody'. Recently, at the hospital in Delhi where I had gone for a check-up, I found the duty nurse leafing absently through the *Times of India*. I urged her to turn to page 14. She looked puzzled, but then she found my column with my picture next to it. She smiled and I was relieved that she knew I was not a 'nobody'. It was pathetic! Why should the opinion of the duty nurse, whom I might never see again, matter to me? The truth is that one's ego is a 'leaky balloon' that needs constantly to be refilled through the praise and attention of others.[25] In my years in the corporate world, I discovered the truth of the saying, 'A man will not sell his life to you, but will give it to you for a piece of ribbon.' Good managers are aware of this human desire for recognition, and they are able to motivate their employees by praising them liberally, thus getting the best out of them.

'Brahma emitted brahmins from his mouth'

People everywhere want to feel superior to others. Hence, status anxiety is a universal problem. But only in India has hierarchy been rigidly institutionalized and sanctioned by tradition. India's caste system separated the social classes and did not tolerate marriages between them; it did not allow them to sit and eat together; and it restricted their occupations. No wonder Karna's story resonates in this India.

Although there is no definitive theory about the origin of the Indian caste system, J.H. Hutton, a respected British census commissioner, offered a plausible account. He described the Indian subcontinent as 'a deep net' into which various races and peoples of Asia drifted over time and were caught.[26] The tall Himalayas in the north and the sea in the west, east and south isolated this net from the rest of the world, which led to the development of a unique, plural society, in which diverse peoples of different colours, languages and customs have lived together in reasonable stability. According to this theory, the caste system made it possible for people of great diversity to live together in a single social system over thousands of years. Caste was thus a natural response to historic migrations and folk wanderings of many peoples and tribes who came to India over thousands of years and made it their home. Every time a new intruder arrived, it was absorbed by begetting a new *jati*, 'sub-caste'.

In the classic four-caste hierarchy, the brahmin, 'priest, teacher', is at the top, followed by the kshatriya, variously 'landholder, warrior, ruler'. The vaishya, 'businessman', comes third, and the shudra, 'labourer', is last. Below the four are casteless 'untouchables' or Dalits and tribal people. In the *Mahabharata*, King Shalya reminds us of the origin of this four-caste hierarchy:

Brahma emitted brahmins from his mouth and kshatriyas from his arms. He emitted vaishyas from his thighs and shudras from his feet. This is sacred learning! And from them then came the special social classes—those born against the grain and those with the grain—because of the intermixture of the four social classes with one another, Bharata. Kshatriyas are traditionally regarded as protectors, gatherers of wealth and benefactors. Learned brahmins were deposited on earth in order to assist people by offering sacrifices, teaching and accepting pure gifts. According to the law, vaishyas have agriculture, animal husbandry and giving. And shudras have been decreed as the servants of brahmins, kshatriyas and vaishyas. Charioteers have been decreed as the servants of brahmins and kshatriyas. In no way should a kshatriya listen to anything from charioteers![27]

The three upper castes constitute roughly 15 per cent of today's India but they have ruled the country for millennia. About half of India is shudra, divided among hundreds of sub-castes. Some are occupational—cobblers and carpenters, for example; others are geographic. About 20 per cent of Indians are 'untouchable' Dalits. (The remaining 15 per cent Indians belong to other religions—12 per cent Muslim; the rest Sikh, Christian, Parsi etc.) The common mistake is to confuse the four classic castes (*varnas*) of the *Mahabharata* and the Sanskrit texts with the thousands of local sub-castes or *jatis*, which really matter in people's day-to-day lives. There are about 3,000 such *jatis*, and their members broadly identify themselves with the four historical *varnas*. Some are social in origin; others are occupational; some are territorial. People of one *jati* often share a vocation, and will not marry or dine outside the *jati*. As they become prosperous, *jatis* tend to rise in the social scale from one *varna* to another. For example, oil pressers in Bengal upgraded themselves from shudra to vaishya several generations ago.

Once India became politically free in 1947, its liberal-minded leaders lost no time in abolishing 'untouchability', and making its practice a criminal offence. Wide-ranging affirmative action programmes were launched and roughly 22 per cent of seats were reserved in colleges, universities and jobs in the government. In this manner, the new nation attempted to atone for centuries of injustice. But if the original aim was to lift the most backward people, the initiative gradually became a tool to demand a share of patronage. There has been continuous clamour in India for more quotas. The Congress-led coalition government that came to power in 2004 tried to extend quotas to Other Backward Castes in all institutions of higher learning to 49.5 per cent, thus effectively reducing seats available on merit to half. It justified this step on moral grounds, but it was obvious to everyone that it was a vote-getting ploy.

One cannot legislate away thousands of years of bad behaviour. Prejudice persists in contemporary India although the old untouchability is gradually disappearing in the modern urban economy. A Dalit middle class has emerged thanks to affirmative action programmes. Although caste barriers are rapidly fading in the cities, competitive politics have created 'vote banks' in the rural areas and strengthened the consciousness of caste. I wonder, along with many Indians, if the nation has gone too far. Something is wrong, I feel, when half the government jobs and seats in colleges may not go to the most talented.

There are, however, strong arguments for affirmative action, which have been made both by the US and the Indian Supreme Courts. While American courts have always opposed quotas or reservations (on grounds of reverse discrimination and unequal treatment for equals), they have enthusiastically supported vigorous efforts to raise the status of blacks and women on grounds of diversity and integration. Even in the two famous judgments in the case of the University of Michigan in June 2003, Justice O'Connor wrote glowingly about the benefits of a diverse student body. But the morally stronger reason for preferences, which she did not emphasize enough, is that a university's role is to develop leaders for a nation in all fields and from all communities. If India's future leaders in commerce, arts and the professions come only from the 15 per cent upper castes, the losers would not be the low castes alone, but also the Indian people, who would have failed to create a healthy civil society. In the same way, it would be a diminished United States if all its leaders were white.[28] The recent election of Barack Obama in the US and Mayawati in India makes the point.

The poet Rabindranath Tagore made out a case based on the restitution of historical wrongs in one of his songs: 'O my unfortunate country/Those whom you humiliated,/In humiliation you will have to be/Equal to all of them.'[29] But there is an obvious problem in trying to correct historical wrongs. Those who did the wrongs are long dead; so are the victims. Why should a young white male in the US today have to pay for the wrongs done to the blacks by his ancestors? Or why should the upper caste candidate in India today lose his place in the university for the sake of discrimination practised by upper castes for thousands of years?

There are three objections to affirmative action: it is inefficient, it is unfair, and it damages self-esteem.[30] Those better qualified will perform better as doctors, engineers or electricians, and society will have to bear the cost of this inefficiency when you have preferential admissions—this is the argument for efficiency. The unfairness argument is that you treat equals as unequal or you engage in reverse discrimination when you practise affirmative action, and this subverts the ideal of equality under the law. Finally, you damage the self-esteem of the beneficiaries (even those who would have got in regardless) who must live with the stigma for life. These are all strong arguments for not having preferences, and I agree with him. But they do not outweigh the need for 'exceptional measures to remove the stubborn residues of racial caste'. Hence, I go along with affirmative action, but do not favour numerical quotas. I also believe that affirmative action must be a temporary step and not remain for perpetuity.

When the Indian cabinet met in May 2006 to consider the proposal for raising caste reservations in institutions of higher learning from 22.5 per cent to 49.5 per cent it ought to have played the following thought game. It should have imagined that it is the admissions committee of one of India's top colleges. It has to choose whether to admit the son of a backward-caste but wealthy businessman from a posh South Delhi address who received low marks or the son of a poor brahmin schoolteacher from a village in Orissa who scored much higher marks. Under the cabinet's proposal, it would be forced to admit the privileged, lower-scoring son of the lower caste businessman and reject the higher-scoring son of the poor, high-caste schoolteacher.

There are a number of lessons to be learned from this thought game. First, our innate sense of fairness seems to accept more easily affirmative action on behalf of the poor rather than the low caste. Second, lowering admission standards for one group appears to be unfair because it treats equals unequally and offends our idea of a just, merit-based society. Third, it is especially unjust when beneficiaries of reservations are prosperous low caste persons, whom the Indian Supreme Court calls the 'creamy layer'.

Is there a better way to lift the low caste persons than through quotas in higher education and in jobs? The answer, I believe, is through scholarships paid by the state, beginning in kindergarten, and continued through high school and up to college. The scholarship programme ought to be based on economic criteria rather than caste. (The poor are likely to be of low caste, but at least this preserves the idea that one is not building a divisive, 'casteist' society.)

In the year-long national debate in 2006 on extending quotas to the 'other backward castes', there was much talk about compromising merit. During the debate I found that people used the word 'merit' as though it were a fixed and absolute thing. But I find that merit in one society may not be the same as in another. It depends on the way a society defines it.[31] When Arjuna pierced the target, he performed an act of merit and was suitably rewarded with Draupadi's hand. In the contemporary Indian society, Draupadi would be more likely to choose a high performer in the competitive exam for admission into one of the Indian Institutes of Technology. A well-functioning society rewards talented persons whose actions further their idea of a good society.

In the private sector it is easier to spot merit and reward it. If one's actions consistently increase the company's profit, one gets promoted and one's fellow employees think it fair. In the public sphere, citizens of a nation would like to reward those who promote the common good. The quota debate has forced Indians to think about *their* idea of the common good. For the philosopher John Rawls, a good action is related in some way to lifting the worst off in society, as we have seen. For Amartya Sen, it would lessen inequality, and hence he has consistently supported reservations for Dalits. As a libertarian, I would not go that far. The key point is that there is no natural order of 'merit' that is independent of one's value system.

On the face of it, rewarding those who combine intelligence with effort and score high marks, which gets them into good colleges, does not seem unfair. These are probably the individuals who will go on to build competitive companies, and these in turn will create thousands of jobs and help the nation compete in the global economy. But Lani Guinier, law professor at Harvard, questions if these exams are, in fact, the best selectors of talent. If she is correct, then we ought to re-look at our selection exams and ensure that they not only remove a bias against the low castes but are good predictors of future performance.

'Draupadi will, in time, approach you'

Karna struck a great blow against the Indian caste system when he refused to switch sides. Krishna, the master strategist of the Pandavas, realized that victory was going to be difficult with Karna on the opposite side. After the failure of his final peace mission at the Kaurava court, he takes Karna aside and makes a desperate bid to win him over. He reveals to him the secret of his royal birth. As Kunti's son, Krishna tells him, Karna is the eldest Pandava. If he crosses over, he will be king. Yudhishthira, the crown prince, will stand behind him holding the royal fan; Bhima will hold his 'great white umbrella'; all the Pandava allies, kings and their noble sons, will pay tribute and touch his feet.[32] Listing the long pageant that will follow his train, Krishna proclaims:

> Let the Pandavas sound out Karna's triumph!
> Surrounded by princes, you will be the moon with its stations.[33]

It is a tempting offer. Although Duryodhana had crowned Karna king of Anga, he had in reality remained Duryodhana's retainer; he was never treated as a kshatriya, nor allowed to marry one. Knowing Karna's weakness for Draupadi, Krishna lures him also with the prospect of enjoying Draupadi—he will share her as a wife with his brothers.

> Draupadi will, in time, approach you.[34]

But Karna, to his great credit, refuses to switch sides. (Some Indians do not give him credit for his nobility of character, but see in this act Karna's stubborn refusal to acknowledge Krishna's divinity.) Karna tells Krishna that his loyalty is to Duryodhana, who was there when he needed him. And it is not just a matter of loyalty—it is a question of his word, which he has given publicly. It would be a breach of dharma if he now joined the other camp. 'I cannot act in an untruthful way against the wise son of Dhritarashtra's,' he says.[35] Karna goes on to explain that Kunti, his natural mother, abandoned him as though he were inauspicious, while Radha, the charioteer's wife, brought him up. Hence, Radha is his true mother and Adhiratha his true father: true parentage comes from affection and not from birth.[36] In parting, Karna asks Krishna to keep his identity a secret from the Pandavas. If a principled man, like Yudhishthira, were to find out, he would immediately surrender the realm to his older brother. And he, Karna, in turn, would be forced to pass it on to Duryodhana. Therefore, 'Let conscientious Yudhishthira be king forever,' he tells Krishna.[37]

Kunti now tries to get her son to cross over. She goes to look for Karna and finds him praying on the banks of the Ganges. As she waits in the shadow of his tall frame, he opens his eyes and greets her with folded hands. 'I am Karna, the son of Radha and Adhiratha,' he says. She tells him, no—he is her son, who came into the world 'as a divine child surrounded by beauty, with earrings and armour'.[38] He should return to his real family and join his brothers.

If you and Arjuna are united nothing would be impossible in the world.[39]

The Kauravas would be defeated, the realm that has been expanded with Arjuna's valour would be regained and Karna would gain for himself the splendour that was Yudhishthira's, Kunti says. But the way she puts it, particularly in the importance she gives to Arjuna's role in expanding the kingdom and to Yudhishthira's status as its sovereign, reveals her unconscious mind. Karna feels that she still places Yudhishthira and Arjuna above him. Suffering from anxiety about his status and thus sensitive to these nuances, he finds Kunti's desire to get him back functionally motivated and not driven by affection. Even an appeal from his father, the sun god Surya, who instructs him to 'obey his mother's wishes', does not make him waver.[40]

In reply, Karna addresses Kunti, not as 'mother', but formally as 'kshatriya lady', a deliberate gesture on his part to make a point about his low status. He tells her bluntly that he was abandoned by her; so how could he be expected to have sympathy for her as a mother? Worse, being abandoned meant that he was denied fame and glory. Bitterly, he adds:

> I was born a kshatriya, but never received what was due to a kshatriya
> What enemy would do anything so evil![41]

He cannot cross over now, he says politely. It would imply that he had joined Arjuna and Krishna out of fear. If he deserts his friends and allies, they would not think of him as a 'genuine kshatriya'.[42] Besides, he says, true dharma consists in respecting the bonds with those who care and nurture you rather than mere bonds of blood. In a parting gesture, he promises Kunti with bitter graciousness that he will not slay any of the Pandava brothers except Arjuna. She will thus always have her five sons. If he falls there will be Arjuna, and if Arjuna falls he will be there.[43] Thus mother and son part, with Kunti trembling with grief. The next time she sees her son, Karna is lying dead on the battlefield at Kurukshetra.

When Karna told his mother that his 'real parents' were the low caste family who had brought him up and not his royal family to which he had been born, he was in effect rejecting the claim that status arises from birth. In the feudal culture of the

Mahabharata this must have taken great courage. Moreover, to stand up to his mother and resist her entreaties was also a daring act in a society where one's parents' wishes are almost sacred. Even more admirable, Karna showed a commitment to his word and to Duryodhana. In the end, principle triumphed over his hunger for status. In making this unselfish choice he holds up to the audience an admirable sense of dharma. A grand moment, indeed, in my journey in search of dharma!

Karna's search for his identity reminds one of the terrible mistake that society makes in forcing individuals to privilege one identity over all the others. Karna has many identities: he is a caring son, an outstanding warrior, a father, a husband, an extremely generous person, a loyal friend of Duryodhana's. Why must his father's background trump his many rich—perhaps, far richer—identities and become the sole basis of his status in society?

'Give me your right thumb'

Karna's problems with identity have been eclipsed in contemporary India by another young man from the *Mahabharata*. Today, Ekalavya is the symbol of Dalit revolt and Dalit and tribal rights. In Book One, the epic narrates the tale of Ekalavya, the son of a Nishada chieftain, who comes to Drona with a request to learn the martial arts.[44] Nishadas were tribals who hunted and were on the fringe of Hindu society. The brahmin archery teacher refuses to accept the casteless pupil. The disappointed Ekalavya touches his head to Drona's feet and leaves for the jungle. There he makes a clay image of Drona, and before it he practices daily with great intensity and dedication, while paying respect to his absent teacher. Soon he becomes a great archer.

One day the Pandavas are out hunting, and their dog wanders off and comes upon Ekalavya. The dog starts barking and to shut him up Ekalavya shoots seven arrows around his mouth and zips it up. The dog is not hurt and returns whimpering to the Pandavas. They are amazed at this extraordinary feat. Ekalavya informs them innocently that he is Drona's pupil. Arjuna, Drona's star student, is shocked to hear that his teacher has a secret pupil, who might pose a challenge to him.

Drona is just as puzzled when he hears this and goes to see the Nishada prince, who is honoured and delighted to see his teacher.

'If you are my pupil, then you will have to pay me my teacher's fee,' says Drona.

'Command me, my guru,' says Ekalavya. 'There is nothing I shall not give my guru.'

'Give me your right thumb,' commands Drona.

Ekalavya keeps his promise, cuts off his thumb and gives it to his supposed teacher. Arjuna is relieved. This cruel and sad story from the *Mahabharata* illustrates social change during the long period of the epic's composition. The caste system was beginning to form: *jatis*, 'castes', were coalescing around clans and occupations. New invaders from central Asia, Shakas and Kushanas, were being assimilated into Hindu society by forming sub-castes within the fourfold *varna* system.[45] But there remained aboriginal people who lived in tribes, as they do today. They were not accommodated within the four-fold caste system and continued to be casteless and 'untouchable'.

This unhappy tale has become a political rallying point for Dalits today. A literature of protest has arisen, and a contemporary poet has this to say about Ekalavya:

If you had kept your thumb
History would have happened
somewhat differently.
But ... you gave your thumb
and history also
became theirs.
Ekalavya,

since that day they
have not even given you a glance.
Forgive me, Ekalavya, I won't be fooled now
by their sweet words.
My thumb
will never be broken.[46]

This Ekalavya is different. His is a cry for social reform. The epic's Ekalavya did not revolt against the caste system. While the *Mahabharata* understands why Drona could not teach a person who was outside the society of its time, it also makes Ekalavya a charismatic figure. We are horrified at Drona's command, which the epic calls *daruna*, 'terrible', and it tarnishes the ruthless teacher forever in our eyes. The more sensitive Arjuna does not come out well either. When the dusky hunter cuts off his thumb, the *Mahabharata* reveals Ekalavya's humanity, and in doing so it honours the lowest of the low born, who live in tribes in the jungles outside the pale. It teaches us that they too are human beings who are owed dignity and respect.

Ekalavya did not face the moral dilemma of Karna, who had to choose between the life of a high-born kshatriya and a low-born charioteer's son. However, the Ekalavyas of today do have to come to terms with the predicaments of affirmative action. Indian newspapers prominently carried a report in June 2005 about an outstanding Dalit doctor who resigned his position from a well-known hospital in Delhi because he was constantly humiliated by his patients and the hospital staff. He said he was 'sick and tired' of being dubbed a 'quota' doctor. I could empathize with his loss of self-esteem, and this is one of the reasons why I do not favour quotas.

'I fear not death as I fear a lie'

Since Ekalavya was not a 'would-be' kshatriya, he did not experience some of Karna's worries over status. The problem with status anxiety is that it distorts one's natural behaviour. Not only does it make Karna boastful, but he is also generous to a fault. His generosity, especially to brahmins, is legendary in the epic and, possibly, compensates for his low status. Connected to his liberality is undoubtedly a hunger for fame, a quality not unusual among epic heroes. Like Achilles, Karna prefers death with glory to a safer, longer life.

One night, his father, the sun god Surya, appears to him in a dream and warns him that Indra, the king of gods and Arjuna's father, will come to him disguised as a brahmin in order to deceive him.

> . . . *listen to my words, son . . . All the world knows [of your vow] that you will not refuse what a brahmin asks of you . . . don't give [Indra] your earrings and armour when he begs you. Appease him as far as you can . . . Try to satisfy him . . . with gems, women, pleasures, riches of many kinds. Karna, if you give away your beautiful inborn earrings you forfeit your life . . .*[47]

This does put Karna in a dilemma. If he refuses, he would be guilty of breaking his celebrated vow. 'The divine armour is meant to protect your life,' Surya reminds him insistently. But Karna finds it irresistible that a great deity should place himself in the position of a supplicant and want something that only he can provide. Clearly, our hero fears death far less than either the infamy of breaking his word or the possibility of earning incalculable fame from such a munificent, albeit suicidal, act.[48] He does not pay heed to his father's counsel, who had reminded him before leaving that there are other things in life that matter more than fame—such as the 'human duties of the living'. He had added, 'What use is fame to a dead man? . . . [It] is like a garland on a corpse'.[49]

Indra does appear, as expected. He comes at noon disguised as a brahmin. For one who has effectively decided to die, Karna is relaxed and speaks to the king of gods in a light-hearted, almost bantering way. Before making his demand, Indra wants to know if Karna is the 'one whose vow is true'.[50] Karna replies that he knows the identity of the brahmin standing before him. Indra ignores this remark and gets to the point—he begs Karna for his earrings and breastplate. Karna reminds him laughingly that if he were to do what Indra asks, then he would become vulnerable.

If I would give you, O deity, both my ear-rings and breastplate,
I would give myself a death sentence . . .[51]

And that would reflect rather badly on the 'lord of the gods'. In fact, wouldn't it be more appropriate for a god to give a gift to a mortal than the other way around? But Indra is adamant. Karna then proceeds to cut off his divine protection bloodily with a knife. There is a roar in the sky as the other deities and celestial creatures are appalled at this self-sacrificing, suicidal deed.[52] As he hands over the breastplate 'wet with blood' to Indra, the epic proclaims that 'Karna achieves glory in the world'.[53] By giving away his celestial earrings, Karna has given away his 'self', his identity (one of the meanings of 'Karna' is 'the eared').[54]

When it is time for the final duel with Arjuna, Karna is without the protection of his armour, earrings and weapons. Although the Pandavas instigated this perfidy, Indra was quite capable of thinking up this deceit on his own. But when they did find out they were not ashamed. They rejoiced. Not surprisingly, Krishna, the devious strategist, had a hand in the deceit. And when he learned that Karna was no longer invincible, he danced with delight and became 'overjoyed'.

Why did Karna make this extraordinarily generous sacrifice? Why did he let Arjuna's father, Indra, take away his divine gifts and invite death? Perhaps it is his leitmotif—his lack of restraint. But I do not think this episode is merely about a hero who is prepared to exchange death in return for extraordinary heroic fame.[55] What I learned for my own dharma education is the importance of commitment. Karna makes this gesture because he has to live up to a promise. Rightly or wrongly, he has made a vow—he cannot refuse what a brahmin asks of him. Hence, he is forced to ignore his divine father's advice and the tragedy follows. He tells Surya, 'I fear not death as I fear a lie.'[56] How refreshingly tall he stands, I felt, beside a god who is ever ready to receive a bribe, especially if the prize is a woman!

'I tried my best to follow dharma, but dharma did not protect me'

Karna did not fight during the first ten days of the war because he resented Bhishma's attitude towards him.[57] After Bhishma fell, Karna entered the fray under Drona's leadership, and the level of violence rose dramatically. So did the casualties on the Pandava side. Book Seven, *Dronaparvan*, culminates in Drona's perfidious death, and this is where we pick up the story. The Kaurava armies are depressed at their leader's death. Seeing his forces in gloom, Duryodhana tries to rally them: 'Victory or death is the lot of all warriors ... Let us resume the fight, encouraged by the sight of lofty-minded Karna.'[58] Thus, the Kauravas install Karna on the sixteenth day of the war as their commander-in-chief, bathing him according to the rites with golden and earthen pitchers of holy water. Talent conquers caste; the son of a charioteer has become the leader of kings on the field of Kurukshetra. (The irony, however, does not escape the audience which is aware that Karna is in reality a kshatriya nobleman.)

On the dawn of the seventeenth day, Karna meets Duryodhana to discuss strategy and asks for the skilful Shalya, king of the Madras, to be made his charioteer. Duryodhana knows that Arjuna has an advantage with the incomparable Krishna as his charioteer. In an effort to neutralize it, he agrees to Karna's request. But King Shalya feels outraged at having to serve the son of a charioteer.

I am a king! I was anointed on the head and born in a family of
royal sages. I am celebrated as a great warrior. I should be served
and praised by bards! I can't now become the chariot-driver for a
charioteer's son! You have insulted me.[59]

Duryodhana tries to win him over patiently, alternately flattering
him and praising Karna.[60] Just as Karna is superior to Arjuna, he
says, so is Shalya better at handling horses than Krishna. After
listing Karna's many achievements, Duryodhana concludes, 'Thus,
I don't think Karna was born into a family of drivers.'[61] Shalya is
won over.

As Karna and Shalya ascend their chariot the following day,
their horses stumble in a humorous but threatening warning.
Karna begins the warrior's ritual boast of his upcoming victory
over Arjuna.[62] He compares himself to Indra in valour. Suddenly,
Shalya tells him to quit bragging. As they engage in battle,
Shalya begins to praise Arjuna while disparaging Karna. Karna
doesn't know quite what to make of this, and he returns the
abuse in kind. It turns farcical as the pseudo-charioteer and the
pseudo-charioteer's son try to outdo each other in name-calling.
Finally, Karna angrily calls Shalya 'an enemy with the face of a
friend'.[63]

Although the morning's fighting goes well for the Kauravas,
and Karna betters Yudhishthira twice, the tide begins to turn by
mid-day. The fighting gets bloodier in the afternoon and there
are huge losses on both sides. Finally, the great moment arrives
that the epic has been waiting for. It is almost sundown and the
epic's two greatest heroes are going to engage in battle. There is
great excitement among the gods as well. The celestials take
sides. Those who will cheer for Karna are headed by Surya, the
sun god, while those who support Arjuna are headed by the rain
god, Indra.[64] As the gods debate the qualities of the two heroes,
they implore Brahma to keep the universe intact during the
period of the contest.

When the battle begins, Karna asks Shalya to drive his chariot towards Arjuna's and he shoots a dazzling fiery arrow called the Serpent.[65] The arrow, spitting fire, searches for Arjuna's head, but in the nick of time, Krishna presses down Arjuna's chariot and sinks it five fingers deep into the ground. The arrow misses Arjuna, but knocks off his crown. Arjuna is red with anger, and he in turn fixes an arrow to finish off his opponent. At this moment, the left wheel of Karna's chariot gets stuck in the bloody mire of the ground.[66] As he descends to lift it out of the rut, Karna grows downhearted. He rails against dharma:

Those who know dharma say that it always protects the righteous. Although I tried my best to follow dharma, I find that dharma does not protect me.[67]

While he is on the ground, he is hit repeatedly by Arjuna's arrows, and the impact begins to take its toll. Karna seizes his sunken wheel with his two arms and tries to lift it up, but the earth rises to a breadth of four fingers. Seeing his wheel swallowed, he is in tears of anger, and beholding Arjuna, he says,

... wait a moment, till I lift this sunken wheel ... Brave heroes observe the laws of dharma and do not strike [at the helpless].[68]

Krishna hears this appeal and he answers: 'It is all very well to remember dharma when one is in distress. Where was your dharma when Draupadi, clad in a single garment, was dragged and disgraced before the assembly? Or when the rigged game of dice was played in order to usurp the Pandavas' kingdom? Or just four days ago, when the Kaurava warriors encircled Arjuna's young son, Abhimanyu, and killed the defenceless boy?'

Karna hangs his head in shame and does not reply. Arjuna, not wanting to take advantage of this moment when Karna is in distress, hesitates. But Krishna urges, 'Waste no more time, go on, shoot ...' So Arjuna raises his Gandiva bow and sends a razor-headed arrow at Karna's standard. With it falls 'glory, dharma, and victory, and all dear things'.[69]

Finally, Arjuna lets loose his Anjalika weapon at the helpless Karna and strikes 'the beautiful head, with a face that resembled a lotus of a thousand petals'.[70]

From the body of the felled Karna
Splendour blazed in the sky.[71]

Thus dies 'a wronged hero, wronged by teachers, brothers and mother, more wronged and more heroic than other wronged heroes'.[72] After the war, when Yudhishthira is told about Karna's identity, he realizes how deeply wronged his half-brother was:

Because of the curse of the exalted brahmin Rama, because he
granted Kunti's wish, because of Indra's magic, because of
Bhishma's contempt . . . because Shalya snuffed out his inner fire,
and because of Krishna's tricks, Karna Vaikartana, whose brilliance
was equal to that of the Sun, was killed in battle . . .[73]

Karna's story is a tale of 'double standards, conniving divinities, and vengeful brahmins [who] stand out in sharp contrast to Karna's displays of generosity to brahmins, his remarkable physical ability and immense resilience and courage . . . Therefore it is of little surprise that Karna is writ large in the central *Mahabharata* trope of the great battle as the great sacrifice,' says the Sanskrit scholar Adam Bowles.[74]

'Enemy with the face of a friend'

The last thing Karna needed on his final, fateful day was a treacherous charioteer. The *Mahabharata* explains how this came to pass. After the peace negotiations had failed and when both sides were gathering allies, the Pandavas and the Kauravas tried to woo the accomplished King Shalya. Since he was their uncle through Pandu's second wife, Madri, he naturally chose to side with the Pandavas. When he set out to join his nephews, Duryodhana thought up a clever scheme to arrange temporary, luxurious guest houses along the journey. There he was honoured and flattered by Duryodhana's officials. Thinking that it was Yudhishthira's uncommon generosity, Shalya offered a boon to his benefactor. When he discovered his mistake, it was too late. Thus, he was forced to join the Kauravas and become Duryodhana's ally.

Arriving at the Pandavas' headquarters in Upaplavya, Shalya felt ashamed and helpless. In order to salvage something from this disastrous reverse, Yudhishthira conspired with his uncle to demoralize Karna and diminish his *tejas*, 'fiery energy', during the battle.[75] Ever since Karna had appeared on the scene, Yudhishthira had built up an obsessive fear of him.[76] Shalya's long tirade about Karna's low status was, thus, a hypocritical sham, a part of strategy.

The *Mahabharata* uses Shalya's betrayal to reflect on the moral character of human beings. Both Yudhishthira and Duryodhana exploit Shalya's vanity. Shalya feels flattered when they compare his skills with Krishna's. Karna too is vain—he boasts and promotes himself.[77] But the lesson I learned in my dharma education is about human friendship and its limitations. Karna proves time and again to be a remarkably loyal friend of Duryodhana's. After Duryodhana came to his rescue during the tournament of the princes, he tells his benefactor that what he values most is 'your friendship!'[78] But his overwhelming sense of obligation turns to excess. He is unable to see Duryodhana's flaws. Always eager to impress his feudal lord, Karna is 'more royal than the king'. An innocent friendship turns into *bhakti*, 'devotional surrender'—what one usually reserves for a deity.[79]

Karna comes out particularly badly in the gambling match. He is visibly happy when Duhshasana drags Draupadi into the assembly. He calls her *bandhaki*, 'harlot'—because she has many husbands—and *dasi*, 'slave'. He is the one who commands that she be disrobed.[80] The Pandavas will never forget these insults and Draupadi, in particular, takes them to heart. 'My pain will not go away—for Karna ridiculed me!'[81]Yudhishthira remembers how deeply those words had wounded Arjuna.[82] So, when Krishna finds Arjuna wavering at the sight of the vulnerable Karna trying to dig out his chariot wheel, he reminds him about this affront and it has the desired effect.

Despite these excesses, Karna is remembered for his friendship and loyalty and Shalya is remembered as 'the enemy with the face of a friend'.[83] When it is Shalya's turn to be named commander, there is more than a hint of irony as Duryodhana says, 'The time has come, O you who are devoted to friends, when among friends wise men examine carefully for friendship or enmity.'[84] As for Shalya's end, when Gandhari surveys the corpses on the Kurukshetra battlefield at the end of the war, Shalya's tongue is being eaten by birds.[85]

'How could a doe give birth to a tiger?'

Karna's is a universal problem of all mankind. All of us like to feel important. We are concerned about our value in the eyes of the world. We want to be cared for, flattered, and deferred to. No one wants to be neglected. Few of us may admit it, but all of us worry about it, and some even kill to get attention. The *Indian Express* reported on its front page on 26 April 2006 that Pravin Mahajan, brother of the powerful Bharatiya Janata Party politician Pramod Mahajan, confessed to the investigating officer in Mumbai that he had shot his brother 'because he ignored me'. He added, 'When I stepped out of the lift and entered my brother's house he was reading the newspaper. He looked up, saw me, and continued to read the paper ... When I asked why he was ignoring me, he said that he had mistaken me for a newspaper delivery boy. This turned out to be the last straw. He had not taken my phone calls and had been humiliating me for days.'

All of us feel diminished at times by the success of our friends and relatives. Most people do a reasonable job of hiding it. It does not become a constant obsession as in Karna's case. Nor does it take the form of Duryodhana's hugely destructive envy for everything that the Pandavas possess. At the root of status anxiety is an excessive concern about what others think of us. Hence, we might consider following the sensible advice of the aunt of my friend who lives in America. She used to tell him when he was growing up: 'You'll waste a lot less time worrying about what others think of you if only you realized how seldom they do.' To this we might add Albert Camus' wise words: 'To be happy one must not be too concerned with the opinion of others. One should pursue one's goals single-mindedly, with a quiet confidence, without thinking of others.'

Karna, like the other heroes in the *Mahabharata*, forces us to look at ourselves and at our frailties. When Karna is not allowed to train in weaponry because he is a *suta*, it makes one ask, 'What if my child had been denied entry into college because of her birth?' Karna had to pose as a brahmin to get in. When he was discovered, his teacher cursed him—he would forget all he had learned at the moment that he needed it most. We don't want our children growing up dogged by epithets like 'charioteer's son'. We want them to feel secure and confident about their position. We want them to be treated with respect as equals.

The *Mahabharata* is not content simply to point out the weaknesses of human beings. It criticizes society's flaws. It raises the question whether a person's social position should be defined by birth or by some other criterion, such as accomplishment of some sort. Karna does pose a challenge to India's caste system, although one cannot forget the irony: he is not what he seems. It isn't surprising that traditionalists find this 'would-be kshatriya' a subversive character. He challenges their traditional understanding of dharma—as inherited status—and offers a new notion of dharma as deserved status.

Karna did become king of Anga through his accomplishments. It was not a token gesture of Duryodhana's. Anga is a large territory in the north-east of India corresponding to today's south-east Bihar. However, 'Duryodhana's liberal attitude to social classes is, in the eyes of the epic poets, a marker of his essential corruption and one of the principal motivations given for the necessity of his demise. His attitude is representative of the breakdown of social order and customary behaviour that occurs when class divisions are not properly maintained.'[86] Indeed, when Duryodhana states, 'How could a doe give birth to a tiger?', he is veritably setting a cat among the pigeons (to mix the metaphor). In traditional eyes he is raising the prospect of the mixing of castes, a great sin according to the Code of Manu, the authoritative textbook on caste dharma.

Despite being crowned king, Karna could not shake off his lowly origins. He kept feeling slighted both by the Pandavas and the Kauravas. This is not an uncommon experience among Dalits in India and blacks in America. Despite becoming middle class, and despite great achievement in many cases, they continue to experience social prejudice. When they rise through affirmative action, they are not allowed to forget 'society's favours'. Political intervention cannot easily erase the human tendency to discriminate. K.R. Narayanan, the former President of India and a Dalit, once confessed in an unguarded moment that he was not allowed to forget his origins even in his home, Rashtrapati Bhavan. I don't know if there is a satisfactory political answer to social discrimination.

I sometimes wonder if Karna had not strived to be a hero, he might have lived a quiet and contented life as a charioteer's son, amidst the warmth and affection of his adopted family. But with his great talent bursting to get out, I don't think he would have been satisfied with a comfortable life. He had to challenge the boundaries of the social order and suffer the pain in doing so. He had to be 'the wrong person in the wrong place'—this is what Karna symbolizes to many minds today. Atal Bihari Vajpayee, the recent prime minister of India, was once called 'Karna' for being the 'right man in the wrong party'.

Life may have been unfair to Karna but he rises above pity.

Despite his flaws we admire him. Despite enormous temptation, he did not switch sides. At a stroke he could have had all that he wanted, but he stood up courageously to Krishna and to his mother and remained faithful to his lowly foster parents who had raised him. Thus, he rejected society's claim that status arises from birth. By rejecting the royal status of his birth, he showed true nobility. Even though it meant ending up on the losing side, he remained loyal to Duryodhana. If Shalya is remembered for betrayal, Karna is remembered for friendship and loyalty.[87]

In contrast to Duryodhana's life of envy and resentment, Karna's heroic life shines because he remained true to his word. When he tells Krishna to keep the circumstances of his birth secret, he is concerned that the Pandavas, particularly Yudhishthira, should not get excessively demoralized. His life once again reminds the audience that true dharma is not the *sva-dharma* of caste, but the *sadharana-dharma* of truth, commitment, generosity and friendship. Thus, it does not come as a surprise to hear him acknowledge that fame, victory, and other heroic goals can only be achieved through dharma. When he says 'where there is dharma, there is victory', he is not being hypocritical. He is being true to himself.[88] When Karna falls, we cherish his many wonderful qualities, and how he turned out to be greater than his cruel circumstances. Status anxiety may have contributed to his many flaws—especially his lack of restraint—but this only heightens his tragedy. We are moved by Yudhishthira's lament when he discovers too late about his brother's identity. This is why Karna is 'the most lamented hero of the war' and his tale is still sung in villages across India.[89]

7

KRISHNA'S GUILE

'That is the way it is!'

Aren't you ashamed ... of striking me down so unfairly?

—Duryodhana, as he lies dying
at Kurukshetra, *Mahabharata*, IX.60.27[1]

'Aren't you ashamed of striking me down so unfairly?'

After Karna's death, the war comes to a quick close. Almost all
the great warriors on the Kaurava side are gone. In despair,
Duryodhana flees from the battlefield to a lake nearby. Using
maya, 'magic', he solidifies its waters and enters into it, resolving
to rest there in suspended animation. The Pandavas manage to
find him, however, and so the stage is set for the war's last
duel—between Bhima and Duryodhana. As it begins, Krishna
doubts if Bhima will be able to defeat Duryodhana in a fair
fight—he will need some sort of dodge. Arjuna gets the point,
and he slaps his left thigh, signalling to Bhima to strike a blow
below the navel. Bhima hurls his mace unfairly at Duryodhana's
thigh, smashing it, and wins. Thus, the war ends.

As he lies dying on the battlefield late in the afternoon of the
eighteenth day, Duryodhana enumerates Krishna's many

misdeeds during the war. He accuses him of perfidy in the way
he had all the top Kaurava commanders killed:

> *Aren't you ashamed, O heir of Kamsa's servant, for having me*
> *struck down so unfairly! When Bhima and I were fighting with*
> *clubs, you told Arjuna to remind Bhima to break my thighs.*
> *Aren't you ashamed that you have had so many kings who were*
> *fighting fairly and valiantly in battle killed by crooked means?*
> *You killed our grandfather by placing Shikhandi before [Arjuna].*
> *You behaved viciously in having the elephant of the same name as*
> *Ashwatthama killed; when our teacher cast down his armour, you*
> *did not stop the hateful Dhrishtadyumna from killing him …*
> *And you had Karna, the best of men, struck when he was in*
> *difficulty, trying to pull out the sunken wheel of his chariot. Had*
> *you fought fairly with Karna, Bhishma, Drona and me, you would*
> *certainly not have won.*[2]

It is not unusual for an epic hero to win through cunning. The
Greeks did it all the time. The *Odyssey* glorifies that master
trickster, Odysseus. It recounts the great deception of the Trojan
horse. The *Iliad* reveals the duplicity of Athena, who posed as
Hector's brother, Deiphobos, to put him off his guard in his final
battle. The difference between the Greek and the Indian epic is
that the action stops in the *Mahabharata* when the hero does
something wrong. Dubious acts are placed under the lens of
dharma, and are examined from different angles before being
finally condemned. 'The *Iliad*, on the other hand, mentions them
and gets on with it without remorse.'[3]

Duryodhana's condemnation of Krishna's deceits belongs to
this tradition. Kunti, the Pandavas' mother, had earlier warned
Krishna:

> *Do whatever is good for them in whatever way you see fit, without*
> *hurting dharma, and without deception, enemy-tamer.*

Krishna, however, instead of safeguarding dharma, instructs the Pandavas to do precisely the opposite in the name of 'strategy'.

Casting aside virtue, ye sons of Pandu, adopt now some contrivance for gaining the victory.[4]

Some acts in war are always more dishonourable than others. It is these considerations of honour which led these ancient warriors to define a set of mutually agreed rules of combat. The rules became part of the *kshatriya dharma*, a 'warrior's code of conduct', defining meticulously what is right and wrong conduct in the course of war. In the language of Western medieval scholastics, this is called *jus in bello*, 'justice in the conduct of war'. Chapter 4 on Arjuna addressed *jus ad bellum*, 'the just reasons for going to war'. Chapter 9, 'Yudhishthira's Remorse', will deal with *jus post bellum*, 'justice of the consequences of war'. The epic seems resigned to the inevitability of war and seeks ways to inject some fairness. It elaborates the rules of fighting, and reminds the combatants what these rules are and then condemns those who break them.

Duryodhana may have had good reasons to denounce Krishna, but Krishna believes that Duryodhana is really the guilty one. He blames him for the failure of the peace talks. Rolling his eyes in anger, Krishna replies to Duryodhana:

When you burned with envy for the wealth of the Pandavas . . . you plotted that evil, heinous dice game. What sort of a man are you who would molest the wife of a kinsman? You had Draupadi brought into the hall and spoke to her as you did! You manhandled the queen . . .[5]

Krishna firmly believes that once you make the fateful decision to go to war then you must win at any cost. As he sees it, the Pandavas' cause is just, and once the war begins the only thing that matters is victory. The *Mahabharata* is not so sure that 'anything goes' in war.

'War is hell'

General Sherman made a similar point in the American Civil War. He believed that once leaders start a war, soldiers have to win it at any cost. He expressed this doctrine in the phrase 'war is hell'. It is a common mistake, perpetrated by Hollywood movies, to think that this is a description of war. It is a doctrine. 'It is a moral argument, an attempt at self-justification. Sherman was claiming to be innocent of his many questionable acts: the bombardment of Atlanta, the forced evacuation of its inhabitants, the burning of the city, and the march through Georgia.'[6] Sherman's doctrine is that war has its own logic and momentum once it begins. It inevitably escalates, and you cannot blame soldiers or generals for the killing. You can only blame those who start the war.

When he heard about Sherman's plan to burn Atlanta, General Hood, the shocked Confederate commander, wrote to stop him. Sherman replied that war was indeed dark. 'War is cruelty and you cannot refine it.' Therefore, 'those who brought war into our country deserve all the curses and maledictions a people can pour out.'[7] He himself was, he said, only an innocent soldier who was doing his job. 'War is hell' is the moral position of those who have to fight and win wars which they did not start. The Pandavas, of course, do not have the luxury of falling back on General Sherman's defence for they *were* the leaders. And indeed, as victors, they feel enormous guilt and remorse for their wrong acts during and after Kurukshetra.

The Allies behaved no better than Krishna in the terror bombing of Dresden, Hamburg and other German cities in World War II. They had a clear intention of killing German civilians in order to destroy Nazi morale, hoping that this would lead Nazi Germany to surrender. In doing so, they clearly violated the 'just war' doctrine. Yet they were not hauled up before any Nuremburg court, which judged Nazi war criminals after the war. This is because the Allies were victors and only losers are tried for war crimes.

The *Mahabharata* faces this dilemma squarely. What if good persons, who have excellent reasons to wage a war, can only win it by unfair means? In that case, how can one think of them as 'good persons'?

'Untruth may be better than truth'

Once the peace negotiations fail and preparations for the war begin, the epic lays down elaborate rules of warfare in *Bhishmaparvan*. Lest anyone forget, it repeats them several times.

> *A person who fights with speech should only be opposed with speech during battle. One doesn't kill a person who has left the battlefield. A charioteer should only fight a charioteer; an elephant rider by [one who rides an] elephant; a horseman against a cavalryman; and an infantryman by [one in the] infantry . . . One is allowed to strike another according to usage, heroism, power and age, by [first] calling out, [but] not at one who is unwary, or in trouble, or fighting another, or is looking the other way, or without armour or whose weapons are exhausted. One does not hit [those who provide services, such as] charioteers, weapon-helpers, those who blow conches and beat drums . . .*[8]

Sanjaya, who is narrating the action of the war to the blind Dhritarashtra, begins to rebuke those who break the rules. In this way the war correspondent becomes the epic's conscience. He reproaches Arjuna for killing the otherwise invincible Bhishma unfairly by breaking the cardinal rule that one 'doesn't strike an enemy who is already engaged in fighting another'. As we know, Arjuna struck Bhishma when the old man was engaged by Shikhandi. The patriarch was particularly vulnerable because he was meticulously observing another rule of war—not to strike a woman or someone who was once a woman as in Shikhandi's case.[9]

After Bhishma's death, Krishna incites the killing of Drona, the next Kaurava commander-in-chief, in a most deceitful manner. Like Bhishma, Drona had also told Yudhishthira how he might be killed:

I really don't see [anyone in] the enemy who is capable of killing me in battle. The one exception is, O king, [when I have] . . . cast down my weapons after hearing bad news from a man of integrity.[10]

Learning of this, Krishna confers with Arjuna and suggests that the only option is to employ 'strategy'. He says: 'Cast aside virtue . . . let a device be adopted for victory.'[11] Arjuna does not approve of this but everyone else does. Yudhishthira accepts the advice 'with difficulty'.[12] So, Bhima kills an elephant named Ashwatthama, which is the name also of Drona's beloved son, and spreads the news. Since Drona knows that Ashwatthama is invincible, he ignores the rumour and continues to inflict great damage upon the Pandava armies. Later in the day when he sees Yudhishthira on the battlefield, he asks gloomily if Ashwatthama is dead.

According to Sanjaya, 'Drona firmly believed that Yudhishthira would not speak an untruth, even for the sake of the sovereignty of the three worlds.'[13] Yudhishthira confirms that Ashwatthama is indeed dead, muttering '*iti gaja*' (it's an elephant) under his breath. The grief-stricken father lays down his arms. Dhrishtadyumna, Draupadi's brother, seizes the defenceless general by his hair and severs his head. The epic punishes Yudhishthira instantly. Sanjaya tells us that Yudhishthira's chariot, which had always travelled slightly above the ground, now sinks to the earth.[14] Arjuna, who had earlier been horrified at Krishna's scheme, is now filled with remorse. When Kripa, the other teacher of the Kuru princes, recounts the scene to Ashwatthama, he says that Arjuna had wanted his teacher to be taken alive, and he regrets that he did not intervene.[15] Drona, of course, had trusted Yudhishthira implicitly thinking that 'this Pandava is endowed so completely with dharma, and he is my pupil'.[16]

The *Mahabharata* has a problem on its hands when the greatest upholder of dharma achieves success by telling a lie. Krishna tells Yudhishthira that a lie is permissible when it is for a greater good.

Untruth may be better than truth. By telling an untruth for the saving of life, untruth does not touch one.[17]

Yudhishthira must have found this Utilitarian advice very disturbing, especially as it came from God. The epic describes Yudhishthira as being torn. He is 'sunk in the fear of untruth but [yet] clinging to victory'.[18] Arjuna, whose dharmic antenna is always acute, is even more upset, and he accuses his brother of deceit:

Our guru depended on you ... For someone who is conversant with dharma, you performed a very great adharma ... [Moreover] you spoke untruth in the garb of truth ... We harmed our old guru, our benefactor, dishonourably for the sake of sovereignty.[19]

Arjuna's verdict is clear—a crime has been committed, the murder of an innocent and unarmed man. The motive was base self-interest, the method was underhand, and the opportunity came when Drona was disarmed.

Karna becomes the next commander of the Kauravas after Drona, and the next victim of Krishna's deceit. When asking Arjuna to wait until he has finished lifting the sunken wheel of his chariot, Karna reminds Arjuna of the rules:

Arjuna, the brave don't hit those who turn away their face, whose hair is undone, who are brahmins, who seek protection, who put down their weapons, who are in difficulty, who are without arrows or armour, or whose weapon is broken ... Since you are brave, O son of Kunti, have patience.[20]

Arjuna, as we know, wavers when he hears this but Krishna tells the dithering warrior, 'Strike now ... Here is your chance!'

Given all this treachery, Duryodhana is, perhaps, right to accuse Krishna—the war could not have been won without his manipulations. All the great commanders of the Kaurava armies—Bhishma, Drona, Karna and Duryodhana—were killed unfairly, under instructions from the master trickster. Although he did not shoot a single arrow, Krishna won the war for the Pandavas through cheating. He, of course, calls it 'superior strategy', but the text is clear that he violated the dharma of war in doing so. Indeed, Krishna had acquired a reputation for deception very early in the war so that when Arjuna unlawfully cuts off Bhurishrava's arm, the latter exclaims:

Who, indeed, could commit such a crime who was not a friend of Krishna's?[21]

V.S. Sukthankar, editor of the Pune Critical Edition of the *Mahabharata*, called Krishna a 'cynic, who preaches the highest morality and stoops to practice the lowest tricks ... An opportunist who teaches a god fearing man to tell a lie, the only lie he told in all his life! [He is a] charlatan who ... advises a hesitating archer to strike down a foe who is defenceless and crying for mercy.'[22]

Nevertheless, the epic's sympathies are clearly with the Pandavas. Sanjaya frequently reminds the audience that the Pandavas follow dharma while the Kauravas are evil.[23] On a number of occasions he catalogues their wicked deeds. They tried to burn the Pandavas in the house made of lacquer, usurp the Pandavas' kingdom through a crooked game of dice, and tried shamefully to disrobe Draupadi. Krishna's defence is that the only way to defeat evil is with evil. The Kauravas are the stronger side—they have more divisions and greater warriors. The threat of their victory looms over the epic and there is a danger that evil might triumph. Hence, the Pandavas must match their might with 'strategy'. But the *Mahabharata* does not buy his logic. It makes sure that everyone is aware, including the

Pandavas, of the immorality of these acts. After Drona is killed, Arjuna is disconsolate and Bhima has to remind the unhappy warrior to stop harping on dharma:

> *You are right in what you say, O son of Prtha! You have spoken of dharma as though you were a sage who had retired to a forest. But you are a warrior, whose duty is to protect living creatures from harm ... It doesn't do you honour or your family to speak thus like a fool.*[24]

'Moreover,' Bhima reminds his brother, 'wasn't the kingdom of one devoted to dharma [Yudhishthira] carried off immorally?'[25]

As the war progresses, and as their brilliant commanders fall one by one, we begin to sympathize with the Kauravas. As victims of Krishna's deceitful tricks, they even begin to appear as underdogs. Some of the Kauravas did behave in an exemplary manner. Duryodhana's unusual brother, Vikarna, as we know, did get up to defend Draupadi after the game of dice—the only member in the august assembly to do so.[26] Even the villainous Duryodhana demonstrates some virtues,[27] and the text refers to him in Book Fifteen as a good king,[28] who invited great loyalty from Karna and Ashwatthama. Bhishma also admits that Duryodhana has always been called a hero.[29] In humanizing the Kauravas, the *Mahabharata* reminded me again of an important lesson: on my dharma journey when one begins to see the 'other' as a human being with empathy, as someone like oneself, that is the moment when the moral sentiment is born in the human heart.[30]

The *Mahabharata* is sometimes called a tale of deceit and illusion, and Yudhishthira's lie is a prime example of this. This illusory nature of the epic led an early German scholar of the *Mahabharata* to propose the thesis that in the 'original' epic the Kauravas were the heroes, which also explains why Duryodhana is often referred to in the epic as Suyodhana.[31] False words mask or they manipulate. In lying, one conceals oneself and enmeshes the other person in an illusion of one's making.[32] By deceiving Drona, Yudhishthira corrupts his teacher's relationship with the world. So do we every time we lie—we corrupt the 'other' in the same way. The epic is aware of this and of Yudhishthira's terrible deed as it reminds us:

> *There is no higher morality than truth, nor a greater sin than falsehood. Truth is the foundation of morality; therefore, one should not suppress truth.*[33]

When Drona's son Ashwatthama hears of the ignoble deed, he denounces Yudhishthira, accusing the *dharmaputra*, 'son of virtue', of becoming an 'impersonator of virtue'. But Vyasa, the legendary author of the epic, explains to Ashwatthama that the whole battle and everything in it might have been an illusion. Krishna was merely fighting one illusion with another illusion. It was not a simple battle of good versus evil, with God on one side and the evil Kauravas on the other. The two sides may not have been fighting each other. They were battling the common enemy of illusion, whose most insidious form is lying—concealing the self and ensnaring the other in an illusion of one's own making. This is perhaps why in real life dharma is 'subtle' and the *Mahabharata* is an allegory of the elusiveness of dharma.

Who is Krishna, man or God?

The problem, of course, is that Krishna is not merely the master-strategist of the Pandavas, he is also a god. He is not simply *a* god, but he is 'the God' (with a capital G). The epic thus has a difficult task in defending his dirty tricks. It tells us early in Book One that the war of the *Mahabharata* was needed because demons had begun to oppress the world. The earth had appealed to Brahma, who had asked the other gods for help. Thus, some gods assumed human form. One of them was Krishna—an incarnation of the great god Vishnu.

We first meet Krishna at Draupadi's *swayamvara*, where she is to choose her husband from among competing princes. Krishna appears to be dark and handsome, a nice enough young man of the Yadava clan. He is not a suitor but he recognizes the disguised Pandavas in the assembly and prevents a fight from escalating between them and other royal suitors. Later, as he is leaving for Dwarka with his brother Balaram, he salutes his aunt Kunti, but like a good diplomat he avoids the subject that is on everyone's mind—the extraordinary situation that Draupadi has got into by marrying all the five Pandava brothers. Next, we run into Krishna at Prabhasa, a pilgrimage spot, where he has become, as the epic says, 'Arjuna's dearest friend'.[34] Soon they become related as Krishna contrives to have his sister abducted by and married to Arjuna. The abduction is typical of the daring adventures of the two young men.

Early on, Krishna shows a penchant for cunning and mischief. He devises a deceitful strategy to overcome the menacing ogre King Jarasandha, who has terrified and repeatedly attacked the innocent Yadavas. As a result, Krishna's kinsmen have had to flee for safety from Mathura to Dwarka, on the western coast of India. Krishna gets Arjuna and Bhima to join him, and the three disguise themselves as brahmin novitiates. They provoke Jarasandha, spurn his offerings, break his kettledrums, and snatch garlands from his shops, before finally killing the wicked king. Jarasandha's end could have been achieved more easily without all the drama, but that would have been too easy for a mischievous god who loves tricks, not unlike the Greek hero Odysseus.

In the *Udyogaparvan*, as we know, Krishna works hard to bring about a truce and prevent war.[35] This Krishna is bright, keen-witted, enterprising and eloquent. He is also a crafty negotiator. That he does not succeed is not his fault, but that of Duryodhana, who is 'a large tree full of anger', and who refuses to part even with five villages for the Pandavas.[36] But his finest hour comes in the Gita as the godly charioteer of Arjuna. He stands confident and debonair, ready to do battle, amidst the arrayed forces and the tumult of the conches. Just as war is about to begin, his commander swoons. He does not have much success in persuading Arjuna until he resorts to his authority as God. As we have seen, Arjuna sees the most amazing sights—all created animals on the earth enter Krishna's mouth, 'driven powerfully and inevitably, like all rivers merging into the ocean and disappearing like insects plunging into the fire only to die'. Krishna says, 'I am Time, and as Time, I destroy the world.' The awestruck Pandava can only say, 'I salute you. I salute you in front and from behind and on all sides.'[37]

Once the battle begins, Arjuna and the Pandavas forget Krishna's divinity. The epic vacillates—sometimes Krishna is human, at other times he is God. He plays innocent pranks, he frets over the outcome of battles. As a war counsellor, he advises the Pandavas to perform dirty tricks. Until the end they are never quite sure of winning—even with God on their side—and there is real suspense over the outcome of the war. After Duryodhana's fall, Krishna tells Yudhishthira, 'It is lucky that you won!'

These are not the sentiments of an omnipotent God. So, who is Krishna, man or God? There are many opinions. Some scholars believe he was a *kuladevata*, an ethnic and family god of a confederation of Rajput clans. He was also probably a 'patron god of the Pandavas'.[38] Others believe that Krishna was not a god in the 'original' *Mahabharata* or in the parts generally thought to be its earliest versions: his godly aspects are later interpolations with the rise of the devotional worship of Krishna. Sukthankar thought that 'there is no cogent reason to separate Sri Krishna from the other chief actors in this drama . . . just as the latter are uniformly treated as incarnations of the minor gods and the anti-gods of the Indian pantheon, so Sri Krishna is also consistently treated as the incarnation of the Supreme Being.'[39]

The nineteenth-century Bengali writer Bankimchandra felt that

Krishna was not God but an ideal human being. Given Krishna's ambiguous deeds, this seems to be an extraordinary conclusion, especially since the epic makes Krishna's divinity quite clear.[40] Peter Brook, the director of the well-known production of the *Mahabharata*, sensibly ducked the issue of whether Krishna was man or God. He said, 'It is obviously not up to us to decide. Any historical or theological truth, controversial by its very nature, is closed to us—our aim is a certain dramatic truth. This is why we have chosen to keep the two faces of Krishna that are in the original poem, and to emphasize their opposite and paradoxical nature.'[41]

It seems to me the question—man or God—is posed incorrectly. One must accept Krishna as he appears in the epic. The epic is clear that Krishna is God, Vishnu's incarnation. The historical or theological truth matters less than the dramatic truth *within* the epic. One must accept both sides of Krishna, no matter how paradoxical or contrary. Despite his faults, the characters in the epic admire him. For two thousand years Indians have known of these contradictions and have continued to worship him. If anything, his popularity has grown. I must confess I am drawn to the Krishna who gets thirsty and hungry; who gets tired and old with time; who is surprised and upset when Arjuna will not shoot at Bhishma; and who is not sure quite how the war will end. This is the same Krishna who is accidentally killed by a hunter in the forest at the end of the epic. It seems to me that it is impossible to separate this human and 'original' Krishna from the impressive legends that were later built around him. The other Krishna is, of course, the superhero, who makes Draupadi's sari go on and on indefinitely; who creates an illusion that made his enemy think that the sun had set; and who shows Arjuna his divine form at the beginning of the war.

My father used to believe that the *Mahabharata*'s purpose was to advocate *bhakti*, 'devotion', to Krishna. According to him, Krishna teaches that an action which is free from selfish desires, and is performed in the name of God, is true moral action. Hence, the epic's morality is subordinate to Krishna the God. Krishna's ambiguous nature says something about the *Mahabharata*'s and the 'Hindu' conception of the divine, which is so different from the one in Christianity and Islam. Although this Krishna is able to pull a few strings, he is obviously not able to bring easy victory to the Pandavas.

Another way to think about Krishna's mystery is to imagine that it illustrates the elusive nature of the divine presence in human life. Human beings seem to require a divine actor to resolve the dilemmas of day-to-day life and to give their lives coherence. Krishna, in this sense, is not a mystery to be solved. One of the *Mahabharata*'s objectives is to represent the divine mystery in narrative form. The epic's search for dharma is grounded in Krishna's divine presence and Krishna's complexity lies in the human struggle to ask many different things of God. His mystery is thus a commentary on the human condition.[42]

Krishna tries to negotiate a peace

During the wedding celebrations of Abhimanyu, Arjuna's son— soon after the Pandavas had completed their thirteen-year exile— Krishna proposes to the gathered Pandavas that they send an ambassador to the Kaurava court to demand the former kingdom of the Pandavas. Thus, a respected priest from Draupadi's father's court is dispatched to Hastinapura to ask for the return of the Pandavas' share of the kingdom. But he achieves nothing except to frighten Dhritarashtra about the Pandavas' growing strength. Dhritarashtra in turn sends Sanjaya to pacify Yudhishthira and the Pandavas. Since Sanjaya is not authorized to make an offer, his embassy doesn't go anywhere either. What it does do, however, is to sharpen the positions of some of the key actors with regard to war and peace, depending on their different conceptions of dharma.

Yudhishthira's position, as we have seen, changed during

these negotiations, and Krishna was primarily responsible for the conversion. Early in his exile in the forest, Yudhishthira believed intensely in *ahimsa*, 'non-violence'. To him war was an unmitigated evil, leading to the slaughter of human life, a sin under any circumstance.[43] There could not be peace unless one side was totally annihilated. So, he wanted to give up the kshatriya world of violence and live a peaceful life in the forest.

Krishna disagrees. He reminds Yudhishthira that a king has a duty to his family, his kingship and his subjects, as well as a duty to the society that has nurtured him. It is improper and cowardly to lead the life of non-activity in order to escape the destructive path of war. One has to act in the world; nothing in the world would exist without action—even the gods have to engage in work. There will always be evil individuals like Duryodhana, who will disturb the balance of order in society and nature. The only course is to destroy them.[44]

Yudhishthira is forced to concede that Krishna's is the more practical position, but being the sort of person he is, he desperately tries to avoid war and makes a huge concession. As Sanjaya is leaving, Yudhishthira says that the Pandavas will be content with only a province or just five villages, instead of their half of the kingdom.[45] But Yudhishthira's generous concession has no effect on Duryodhana, who is unmoved. He is only interested to know from Sanjaya about the Pandavas' military strength. He interprets Yudhishthira's forbearance as fear.

Krishna, however, decides to make one last try at a settlement. He goes personally to the Kaurava court, where he employs every possible means in the ancient art of diplomatic negotiation.[46] His first strategy is reconciliation, and he tries to arouse brotherly affection in the Kauravas. When this fails, he uses the tactic of fear—he tries to frighten them by recounting his own and the Pandavas' exploits. This too fails. Next, he employs the policy of dissension. Since Karna could make the difference between success and failure in the war, Krishna tries to make him switch sides.

Finally, when Karna refuses his offer, he attempts a policy of generosity—he repeats Yudhishthira's offer to renounce his kingdom if the Pandavas can have the five villages. He is rebuffed on each occasion. In the end, the peace negotiations having failed, the only recourse is force. Yudhishthira, with a heavy heart, takes the decision to go to war. Krishna's misdeeds have to be seen in the context of one who tried very hard to prevent a war between the Pandavas and the Kauravas.

'Methinks that time is out of joint'

After the disastrous game of dice, Draupadi had said:

> Methinks that time is out of joint . . . This ancient eternal dharma
> is lost among the Kauravas.[47]

The Pandava queen may also have dropped a hint about why God plays dirty tricks during the Kurukshetra War. The game of dice is a signal that things are not quite what they appear. This game was meant to be a ritual, as we noted in Chapter 1, a part of the celebrations to confirm Yudhishthira's supremacy.[48] Instead, in this charade, Yudhishthira is doomed from the beginning. If dharma had been functioning properly, a younger brother or cousin would never have challenged an older one. The queen would not have been left 'unprotected amidst her protectors'.[49]

What Draupadi means in saying that 'time is out of joint' is that the *Mahabharata* is being enacted in our imperfect age of *Kali Yuga*, 'the age of Kali', when it is common for brothers and families to fight.[50] During this age it is hard to know right from wrong. This is why Bhishma answers Draupadi helplessly, 'Dharma is subtle, my dear. I fail to resolve your dilemma in the proper way.'[51]

In the classical Indian sense of time, dharma has been declining in the universe. The *Mahabharata* explains that in the first *yuga*, 'age', human beings were perfect and lived in a golden age. They have since worsened morally by a quarter in each subsequent *yuga*. The epic tells us:

> *Dharma was four-footed [whole] and complete ... in [an earlier golden age] Krita Yuga ... After that dharma declined by one foot [in each subsequent age] and adharma increased, with theft, untruth, and illusion.*[52]

The game of dice, which led to the exile of the Pandavas and the Kurukshetra War, reflects the decline of dharma. The Kurukshetra War was, thus, inevitable. It was meant to lead to *pralaya*, 'end of the world', after which would emerge a new golden age, the *Krita Yuga*, another throw of the dice, under the rule of the good king, Yudhishthira. Krishna, too, defends his questionable acts on this basis. He says:

> *Know that the Kali Yuga has arrived and the promise of the Pandava [has been fulfilled]. Let the Pandava be considered to have made good his hostility and his promise.*[53]

By this he is saying, in effect, that he, Krishna, had to resort to trickery in order to even the playing field in an age where dharma had declined. In order to preserve dharma in this imperfect world of *Kali Yuga*, he had to commit 'smaller wrongs' for the sake of a 'bigger right'.

Indians have always found this a perfectly acceptable explanation. They continue to invoke *Kali Yuga* to explain incomprehensible adversities or the corrupt ways of their wayward politicians. The myth helps them to be reconciled to an imperfect world in which it is so difficult to be good.

The world is Krishna's *lila*

There is, of course, the traditional believer's straightforward explanation for Krishna's moral lapses. When I asked my father about Krishna's dubious acts, he replied that Krishna is God and

200 / *The Difficulty of Being Good*

the world is a stage on which he enacts his play. We are his *maya*, 'illusion', and our lives are a part of his *lila*, 'play', including the war at Kurukshetra. I found echoes of this in Draupadi's complaint, who referred to human beings as 'toys of God', who treated us as a puppeteer treats his puppets. From this perspective, Krishna's tricks are merely God's moves on the stage to make sure that the righteous win in the end. The Pandava victory is Krishna's *prasada*, 'grace'—his way to ensure dharma's victory in the *Kali Yuga*. Vaishnav devotees of Krishna, in fact, do not say 'where dharma is, there is victory'; they chant:

> *Where Krishna is, there is dharma; where dharma is there is victory.*[54]

Kali Yuga, my father explained, is the flawed age in which we live. This is why we can identify so easily with the blemished, human characters of the *Mahabharata*. Krishna too must have his flaws when he becomes human, an actor on the epic's stage like other actors. But since he is also divine, he is able to step aside, and become the instrument for fulfilling the divine prophecy at Draupadi's birth:

> *Superb among women, the Dark Woman [Draupadi] shall lead the [kshatriyas] to their doom.*[55]

It is Krishna's will, accordingly, that the entire kshatriya class should perish in atonement for their overweening pride and relieve the earth of the excessive burden of an overpopulated world. In order that this may come about, hostility must be sown between the hundred sons of Dhritarashtra and the five sons of Pandu. 'Since all warriors have to die, in any case, in this murky age,' said my father, 'does it matter if Krishna plays a few tricks and enjoys himself along the way?'

The *Mahabharata* was composed during the long period of transition from the Vedic gods of nature (like Indra, who represented thunder) to the sectarian gods of Hinduism. Just as

Rama becomes the great god of the *Ramayana*, so does Krishna in the *Mahabharata*. Also called Vasudeva, Krishna is an incarnation of Vishnu. There is a reference to one Krishna, the son of Devaki, during the Vedic period, where he is merely a wise, enquiring man seeking for the highest truth.[56] Panini, in the fifth century BC, mentions a *bhakta*, 'devotee' of the god, Vasudeva. Thus, Krishna the sage and Vasudeva the god may originally have been different but only later became the same deity through syncretism.[57] The Bhagavata sects also began in this period with the worship of Bhagavan, the Lord, a name for Vishnu. Gradually the Vedic gods faded as Vishnu and Shiva became the most popular great deities. In the *Mahabharata*, people specifically mention that they worship a god of their sect.[58] Gradually, the way of *bhakti*, 'devotion', caught the people's imagination, and it spread across India via the medieval *bhakti* saints, who 'bhagavatized' the country. Krishna's narration on *bhakti* in the Gita in the *Mahabharata* is a peak moment in this process.

The gods thus evolved over time, and the Krishna of the later period of the *Puranas* is even more playful than in the *Mahabharata*. This Krishna steals butter as a child; he plays pranks all the time; he grows up to be the divine lover not only of his beloved Radha, but also of a thousand cowgirls in the Vrindavana forest. He entices the women with his flute and his romantic melodies.[59] Tricks are a part of Krishna's character, and his 'trickery implies an open defiance of traditional morality, which is of major significance for the total meaning of the work: even as it recapitulates the human condition ... it is also the sign of Krishna's transcendence.'[60]

It is extraordinary, I find, how the epic manages to balance the worldly and the divine identities of Krishna. It does not gloss over his contradictions, nor does it try to idealize him—his flaws are there for all to see.

'Let us go home and rest'

Cheerful throughout the epic, Krishna becomes grave after Duryodhana's death and he gives a sobering message to the victors:

> Listen Pandavas, the Kauravas were great warriors and you could not have defeated them in a fair fight. So, I had to use deceit, trickery, and magic on your behalf ... To defeat Duryodhana fairly was even beyond the messengers of death. So, let's not [get carried away] by Bhima's heroics. We have succeeded, it is evening now—let us go home and rest.[61]

Instead of celebrating his side's triumph, Krishna becomes subdued. After the war Queen Gandhari, the mother of the Kauravas, reproaches him for being indifferent to the terrible carnage of battle when he could have prevented the war in the first place. She curses him to die like a common beast in the wilderness for having caused the death of all her sons, her kinsmen and her friends.

The *Mahabharata* is clearly uncomfortable with Krishna's conduct during the war. This explains, in part, why the mood of the epic now swings downward. There may have been good reasons why Krishna had to do what he did to win—the good had to defeat evil; the world had to be brought to an end before a new age could be ushered in—but the epic does not believe that the ends justify the means. It does not approve of the breaking of the rules of warfare. It does not believe a *dharmayuddha*, 'just war', can be fought unjustly. It is resigned to the fact that war cannot be abolished; hence, the rules of war are a way to make it tolerable.

The *Mahabharata* shares this concern with the Catholic Church, whose 'just war' tradition also defines the rules of war (*jus in bello*). The latter defines them under two broad principles: the principle of discrimination specifies legitimate targets that a soldier can hit in a war and the principle of proportionality is concerned with how much force is morally right in a given moment. The first principle in this Western tradition exhorts soldiers to discriminate between combatants and non-combatants to prevent unnecessary bloodshed. When a soldier joins the army he is prepared to become a target and loses the immunity due to civilians. Still, sometimes the killing of civilians is unavoidable. Bombing a munitions factory in a residential area does not violate the first principle even if it is clear that some civilians will be killed. This is what American military jargon calls 'collateral damage'. The second principle of just conduct holds that the force employed against the enemy should be proportionate to the desired objective. Again, the purpose is to temper war's violence and minimize suffering.

Jus in bello requires that soldiers be held responsible for their actions. Saint Augustine opposed the prevailing belief of the soldier 'who is but the sword in the hand of him who uses it, is not himself responsible for the death he deals'. When soldiers start killing non-combatants, or pursue their enemy beyond a reasonable limit, they are no longer committing legitimate acts of war but acts of murder. This principle also raises the question if obeying orders that one knows to be wrong or claiming ignorance of the effects of one's actions is immoral. The rules that shape our military conduct comprise the 'war convention'. It tells soldiers not to use poison gas, for example. Although it has been expounded, debated and revised over many centuries, 'it remains one of the more imperfect of human artefacts'.[62]

I believe that the Second World War was an example of a 'just war', and I expect most people would agree. A world dominated by a victorious Nazi Germany would have been even more intolerable than the one ruled by Duryodhana. In that war the victorious Allies did some nasty things. In the last five months of World War II in the Pacific theatre, American 'fire bombing' raids killed more than 900,000 Japanese civilians—and this happened before they dropped the atomic bomb on Hiroshima and Nagasaki. In the European theatre, the British killed more civilians with their bombing of German cities than were killed by Germany's blitz on Britain.[63] The Pandavas' acts seem like indiscretions in comparison.

Many believe that the Allied bombing of Germany was vindictive and broke the rules of war, and that Churchill stuck to it perversely, even after the cost to both the bombers and the bombed had escalated and had become increasingly awful. The irony is that the bombing did not achieve its objective. At the time, of course, the Allies did not know they would win. Even after Stalin's gigantic army began to march against Hitler, the Nazi propaganda machine was announcing to the world that it possessed secret weapons that would alter the war's course. This was a lie, of course, but how were the Allies to know it? When they were fighting the only thing that mattered was to defeat Hitler, and as quickly as possible.

Ever since the Nuremberg trials, interest in the moral conduct of war has grown around the world. We are better informed about wartime offences thanks to the media and human rights groups. Despite frequent lapses, the world does seem to have made some progress. The doctrine of 'just war' and the rules of the Geneva Convention appear increasingly to influence the behaviour of governments and individual leaders. It is sobering to remember though that the *Mahabharata* had been expressing these concerns more than two thousand years ago.

The epic is ambivalent about Krishna's pragmatic defence. It refuses to accept the idea that good consequences outweigh evil methods. Ultimately, there seems to be an austere and unforgiving streak of dharma which appears to run through the epic. If good persons are not allowed to win by any means, and if they must fight justly, then one must be prepared to face the fact that they might lose. There is no guarantee that truth and goodness will prevail in human history. The Pandavas must accept this and wait, perhaps, for another day. The important thing is that they fight fairly. Since they did not, they failed in their dharma. Therefore, they have to be judged and punished. Accordingly, the Pandavas are not allowed to 'live happily ever after'.

The war convention

The detailed code of warfare elaborated in the epic places the men of the *Mahabharata* closer to the chivalric knights of the Western middle ages. They were aristocratic warriors, who had a sense of themselves as men of a certain kind, engaged in an activity that was of moral value. They were noble kshatriyas, not mere mercenaries, ruffians and bandits. They were also different from soldiers in modern national armies who fight and die in anonymity. Yet their concerns about the just war convention are the same as ours.

Shakespeare's much-admired hero Henry V faced a similar problem as the Pandavas, although he seems to have had fewer moral qualms. Like Yudhishthira, Henry had to decide whether to go to war with France in order to enforce his claim to the throne. In the first scene of Act IV, Henry warns the French governor of Harfleur that if the city does not surrender, he will not be able to restrain his soldiers, who will rape virgins and impale infants upon their pikes. The guilt for this, he suggests, will be on the head of the governor for not surrendering. The audience finds this disturbing for it is clearly wrong that soldiers should *inevitably* kill innocent women and children. Yet, Shakespeare seems to think otherwise, for he regards Henry a noble and just king in his play. He assumes (probably rightly) that war will bring rape and murder of the innocent. It does not occur to him that these are crimes *even* in war. Like most of us, he did not have a high opinion of the efficacy of war conventions.

Henry's argument sounds similar to those of modern leaders, who also do not give much thought to their responsibility for the deaths of civilians in the wars that they prosecute. When George W. Bush launched the American attack on Iraq in 2003, he must have known that many innocent Iraqis would be killed by American bombs. But he does not appear to have given it much attention. Thousands of civilians had died from American bombardments and from the civil strife that followed. President Bush did not intend to kill Iraqi civilians, but this does not absolve him of responsibility for their deaths.

When Amnesty International claimed in 2005 that the United States had been complicit in the torture and detention of the suspects of terrorism in secret locations around the world, there was outrage in America and abroad. Amnesty claimed that Yemeni men had been tortured in Jordan, and then kept for eighteen months in secret detention. The *Washington Post* ran a detailed account of the violent and protracted interrogation— ending in death—of a former Iraqi general. When the US collected prisoners in Afghanistan and Iraq, it did have a choice to treat them as criminals, which means they had a right to be represented and to face a court, or to treat them as prisoners of war. America set up military tribunals, but many Americans were suspicious about this move for those courts did not provide enough protection to prisoners. Some felt that civilian courts should have been used for these trials.[64]

Critics, however, countered that some prisoners released from Guantanamo Bay may have ended up as insurgents in Iraq. True, but in a decent judicial system some guilty people will always be acquitted. This does not mean that they should have been held incommunicado and treated as people without rights. If the war on terror 'takes on the aspect of a real war, then you fight it within the rules of the Geneva Convention. If it is police work, then you do it subject to the laws of a constitutional democracy.'[65]

My favourite general, Erwin Rommel, illustrates how an unjust war can be fought justly. Rommel was one of Hitler's famous commanders during World War II who seems to have escaped the moral infamy of the Nazis. His biographers tell us that he was an honourable man. 'While many of his colleagues and peers in the German army surrendered their honour by colluding with the iniquities of Nazism, Rommel was never defiled.'[66] He confined himself to the soldier's professional task and when he fought he followed the rules of war. 'It was Rommel who burned the Commando Order issued by Hitler on 28 October 1942, which laid down that all enemy soldiers encountered behind the German line were to be killed at once.'[67] He did not shoot prisoners. Rommel was a servant, not a ruler, of the German state; he did not choose the wars that he fought but like Prince Andrey in Tolstoy's *War and Peace*, he served his 'Tsar and country'.

The *Mahabharata* understands that war is terrible. Hence, it lays down elaborate rules of fighting. It reminds warriors that fighting should be broken off at sunset; one does not strike the enemy from behind; one does not engage in ambush or surprise attacks. The epic creates limits on the intensity and duration of the combat or the suffering of soldiers. Yet, it is also cynical about these restraints. It doubts if these rules will be observed. It has the same mocking attitude that we have towards the defective Geneva Convention. When the best of men, the Pandavas, break those rules, then what about ordinary persons? It is not easy to be good.

The problem of evil

Uttanka, the hermit, did not know that the war at Kurukshetra had taken place. Krishna told him about it when they chanced to meet in the desert sands of Rajasthan. Uttanka got angry with Krishna when he heard about this and he accused him of not having prevented the brutal killing of war. Krishna replied that he was helpless. The hermit was, indeed, surprised to hear God claiming helplessness. Krishna explained that the process leading to the war had begun much earlier, and by the time he had got involved there was already too much hate and hostility on both sides. War had become inevitable. Moreover, he told the hermit that when he, Krishna, assumed the *avatar*, the 'form', of a human being, he had to act as one. He did try to negotiate a peace but the Kauravas did not listen to him. All he could do was to try and see that justice was done in the end, and the kingdom restored to the Pandavas.[68]

Uttanka's innocent question reminded me of the classic 'problem of evil' in Christian theology: how can God, who is supposed to be perfect, allow evil to exist? Epicurus, one of the first to raise this question, asks: 'Either God wants to abolish evil, and cannot; or he can, but does not want to . . . If he wants to, but cannot, he is impotent. If he can, but does not want to, he is wicked . . . If, as they say, God can abolish evil, and God really wants to do it, why is there evil in the world?'[69]

Put another way: If God is good, why is his world so bad? Why is there so much unmerited suffering of the sort that Draupadi spoke about in Chapter 3? Epicurus concluded that the existence of suffering is incompatible with the existence of God. When Draupadi was in exile with the Pandavas, she 'staggers with wonder' and 'condemns the Placer' for the unmerited suffering experienced by her family.[70] When everything was going so well for the Pandavas, why did the tragedy of the dice game and their consequent exile have to strike her family? Epicurus's simple answer would have been that since there is evil in the world, God does not exist.

I believe that the problem of evil exists only if one believes that God is all-powerful and benign. This may not hold true in the *Mahabharata*. Krishna seems to be suggesting that all of life is subject to the law of karma. A person is free to act, but once the deed is done, no one can stop its relentless consequences. Even God cannot interfere. The law of karma is relentless and it trumps even God. 'The Hindu conception of God does not include the attribute of omnipotence', and this is in striking contrast to Judeo–Christian theology.[71] To a Hindu, it makes sense for Krishna to tell Yudhishthira at the end of the war that the Pandavas won partly through 'luck'.[72] The Indian medieval philosopher Shankara explained this in his commentary on the *Brahma Sutras*. He said that one merely reaps the results of one's moral actions sown in the past. One's karma decides if one will experience pleasure or pain, and this is decided by one's previous actions. God does not want to come in the way of this cosmic justice. Hence, God is not unjust.[73] Accordingly, the problem of explaining unmerited suffering does not arise, and the problem of evil is a problem of ignorance. Karma explains it all.

But this intellectual interpretation leaves the average person dissatisfied. Clearly there is unjust suffering. Draupadi did suffer in the jungles. The Pandavas grieved mightily over the death of the young Abhimanyu, Arjuna's son, whose unjust killing hangs over the 'battle books' of the *Mahabharata*. Even though one may believe in karma, one feels the psychological need to be comforted. One feels anxiety and guilt over one's bad deeds and this leads to a feeling of helplessness. This is where the benign and loving God of *bhakti*, 'devotion', comes in. It was, in part, on this very human need for faith in God's grace that Ramanuja built his *bhakti* philosophy in the eleventh century in south India. Hence, many Vaishnav devotees of Krishna (as 'God' with a capital G) believe that He can 'override' karma. And this contradictory idea sits side by side with a belief in the 'unyielding power' of karma. Karma has its optimistic side in a human being's ability to act with freedom, and be responsible for this act. Its pessimistic side is a feeling that we cannot escape from our past.

An influential defence of God in the West argues that human free will is something of value. God cannot eliminate evil and suffering in the world without also eliminating the free will of human beings to do evil and good things. If God allows people to be free, they need to have the capacity to commit crimes and to be immoral as well. You cannot blame or praise people unless they have a certain amount of freedom to act.[74]

But why would God risk populating the world with free

creatures if he knew that they would mess it up with wrongdoing? The neat answer to that is although free will makes evil possible, it is also responsible for love and goodness and human joy. Giving a human being free will is worth the risk.[75] Some of the evil in the world, however, is not the result of the free choices of people but arises from natural disasters, such as an earthquake, which takes innocent lives unexplainably. The 'free will defence' cannot explain why God allows such 'natural evil' to exist. The usual Jewish and Christian response to this challenge is to say that God allowed natural evil to enter the world as part of Adam and Eve's punishment for their sin in the Garden of Eden.

'The meanest death in history'

When Queen Gandhari curses Krishna for not preventing the war, he replies:

Lady, I shall destroy the Yadava clan, which I had planned [to do, in any case]. You have just reminded me of what I have to do.[76]

Hearing this, the Pandavas become 'afraid and worried', and they realize that the killing in the war was only a part of the divine plan of a broader destruction, in which Krishna's own Yadava clan would also be finished. They are reminded with terror of the Krishna who has shown Arjuna his form of Time, the destroyer. Krishna remains true to his word.

Years go by, and one day when the sun is eclipsed in the sky above Dwarka, members of Krishna's Yadava and Vrishni clans are drunk and noisy after much festivity. During the revelry, the few survivors of the Kurukshetra War are reminded of those terrible events. Satyaki accuses Kritavarma: 'Can anyone be more cruel than you who killed the ones who were asleep?'[77] Kritavarma remembers the ghastly nocturnal slaughter by the three Kauravas (which we shall encounter in the following chapter). He retorts angrily by listing how the Pandavas brought down all the great Kaurava generals through deceit. The wrangling gets more and more bitter between the two survivors of the great war. Ancient wounds are reopened, and soon Satyaki draws his sword and kills Kritavarma. Instantly, others join the fray, and Satyaki and Pradyumna, Krishna's son, are killed. During this terrible fight, Krishna remains a silent spectator. Finally, he stirs and picks up a blade of *isika* grass. In his hands the blade of grass turns into a weapon, and within minutes he has wreaked devastation. The entire clans of the Yadava and the Vrishni vanish as the sea crosses its shore and engulfs Dwarka. Krishna is calm, unmoved and relentless.

A few days later as Krishna lies resting in the forest, an ordinary hunter mistakes him for an animal, and pierces the sole of his foot with an arrow. It kills him. He does not die the noble death of the warriors of the *Mahabharata*. Flowers do not fall from above as they did at Karna's or Duryodhana's deaths. He dies like any creature in the forest. It is 'the meanest death in history'.[78] While recognizing his divinity, I believe it is the epic's way of showing disapproval of Krishna's misdeeds.

Krishna's role in the epic forces one to confront a moral dilemma. How does one explain that 'good' persons, who had strong and persuasive reasons to make war, could win only by unfair means? How can one think of them as 'good' if they can succeed only by fighting in unfair ways? How, then, does one distinguish between the 'wicked Kauravas' and the 'good Pandavas', and indeed, between good and evil? The Pandavas, along with Krishna, were supposed to be 'the good guys'; yet they managed to kill every Kaurava commander—Bhishma, Drona, Karna and Duryodhana—by foul means. On the other hand, the Kaurava heroes—supposedly 'the bad guys'—fought honestly and heroically, especially Duryodhana and Karna.

These are genuine dilemmas, and the text does not offer easy answers. If the *Mahabharata*'s editors had to defend themselves, they might have said something like this: like all human beings, the epic's characters are an 'ineradicable mixture of good and evil'.[79] It is a mistake to slot them into compartments labelled 'good' and 'evil'. 'Both sides engage in good and bad deeds, and there is greatness on both sides.'[80] It would have been easy to make Krishna a perfect god, who always upholds dharma. However, the point of the *Mahabharata* is that dharma is *sukshma*, 'subtle', and it is often difficult to tell right from wrong. Since Krishna's deceptions take place on the human stage, they are an expression of our ambiguous human condition. To have done otherwise would have been to miss the point.

8

ASHWATTHAMA'S REVENGE

'Now I feel the whirligig of Time'

Where is sleep for the man who is suffering?
... How in this world can a man express the grief
Remembrance of his father's murder brings?
My heart burns day and night but never burns it out.

—Ashwatthama to Kripa, *Mahabharata* X.4.21, 23[1]

'This owl has tutored me'

Sauptikaparvan, the slim Book Ten of the *Mahabharata,* opens on the fateful night of the eighteenth day of battle.[2] The Pandavas are victorious after destroying the Kaurava armies. All the sons of Dhritarashtra are dead. Duryodhana lies on the ground, his thighs broken. Among the Kaurava warriors, only Drona's son, Ashwatthama, his uncle Kripa, and Kritavarma remain. Seeing his commander felled unfairly by Bhima, Ashwatthama is filled with rage. As the dying Duryodhana anoints him the last commander of the Kauravas, he vows revenge.

Fleeing from the jubilant Pandavas, the three warriors take refuge in a forest. They spot a banyan tree and descend from their chariots. They untie their horses and perform their

213

evening prayers under the tree. Their limbs dragged down by sleep, Kripa and Kritavarma fall asleep.

> *But Drona's son ... overpowered*
> *By shame and wrath, could not sleep and lay there ...*
> *Peering at one particular, teeming spot,*
> *The warrior saw a banyan tree covered in crows ...*

> *But as those oblivious, trusting crows slept on*
> *Ashwatthama beheld a terrible owl ...*

> *It stooped as swift as Garuda, screeching loud,*
> *Unnaturally taloned, freakishly beaked.*

> *Then uttering soft deceitful cries, like any bird*
> *Come down to roost, it fell upon the tree—*
> *Stooped on a branch, and slaughtered countless sleeping crows ...*
> *Slicing the wings of some, beheading the rest ...*

> *Then, Drona's son, a witness to that guileful deed*
> *Accomplished by the owl at night, resolved*
> *To do a similar deed himself, reflecting:*
> *'This owl has tutored me in war. My thoughts*
> *Are locked on my enemies' death, and*
> *Now the time has come ...'*[3]

Learning from the owl, Ashwatthama resolves to massacre the enemy forces when they are asleep. He reasons that the three Kauravas are too weak to take on the skilled and powerful Pandava army and their Panchala allies. But they might succeed through deceit. So, he awakens his companions and tells them of his decision. He knows that what he intends to do is 'corrupted', but he cannot help it, he says.

> *And now I feel the whirligig of Time:*
> *For in reality this has fallen out*
> *Just as it had to; whatever the effort—*
> *However exceptional—the result would have*
> *Been precisely the same.*[4]

Kripa recoils from the foul proposal and tries to dissuade him from this terrible, immoral enterprise. Kripa says,

Rest tonight, sleep tonight, dear lord—you have the strength
To rise to this, but you have been awake too long.[5]

His nephew, however, cannot forget the murder of his father by the Pandavas.

Where is sleep for the man who is suffering?
. . . How in this world can a man express the grief
Remembrance of his father's murder brings?
My heart burns night and day, but never burns it out.
That special way in which my sire was slain
By evil men—you saw it all. And it is that which
Rips my vitals now.[6]

Ashwatthama recalls that barely three days ago, his father, Drona, the commander of the Kaurava forces, was destroying everything in sight. The Pandavas, as we saw in the last chapter, decided to play a trick: kill the elephant named Ashwatthama and shout, 'Ashwatthama is dead'. Drona did not believe his son was dead until Yudhishthira, as tutored by Krishna, confirmed that Ashwatthama (and he said 'elephant' under his breath) was indeed dead. We know the rest—Drona laid down his weapons, assumed a yogic posture, and Dhrishtadyumna, the Panchala prince, cut off his head.

The blind Dhritarashtra had predicted that this would be a turning point in the war: 'I lost all hope for victory, O Sanjaya, when I heard that the teacher, Drona, was slaughtered by Dhrishtadyumna. Dharma was, thus, violated for Drona at that time was sitting in his chariot unarmed.'[7]

Ashwatthama is in a rage as he remembers the dark moment.

Life is unbearable until I've killed
Dhrishtadyumna in battle. He murdered
My father, and so he must be killed by me,
Along with all his Panchala allies

So the question of my holding back now doesn't
Arise. No man in this world can deflect me
From this, my duty. My mind is made up . . .[8]

Kripa tries to dissuade his nephew, reminding him that such a heinous act of revenge will violate dharma, which is, after all, one of the three ends of life. He warns him that his false sense of duty will land him in hell.

In this world, the slaughter of the sleeping
Is not respected as conforming to dharma.
The same applies to those whose arms have been laid down,
To those whose fighting chariots have been unyoked . . .

Tonight, my lord, the Panchalas will sleep,
Their armour unbuckled, unconscious as the dead,
All unsuspecting through the dark till dawn
The wicked man who seeks to harm them in that state,
Without a doubt, would dive into a raftless,
Fathomless, shoreless hell.

. . . in you an unworthy action would inspire
Revulsion—like blood splattered on a white tunic,
So it seems to me.[9]

But Ashwatthama is unmoved. He is intent on revenge even though he is aware of its terrible karmic consequences.

Truly, if killing my father's murderers,
The Panchalas, as they sleep in the night, means
Rebirth for me as a worm or a moth, I shall
Suffer it gladly.[10]

With these words, Ashwatthama yokes his horses, mounts his chariot, and sets out, followed by his uncle and Kritavarma. At the threshold of the enemy camp,

. . . his hair rose on his scalp, for he saw
Guarding the gate, a great bodied spirit, bright as

The sun and moon combined.
It was draped in a tiger's skin soaked in blood,
Its upper garment, black antelope skin.
Its sacred thread a snake.
... Its gaping jaws and their jutting tusks spoke terror—
Brilliant eyes in their thousands stared from its face.
... From every orifice—from its mouth, its nostrils,
Its ears, from those thousands of eyes—there licked high flames.[11]

Ashwatthama attacks the horrific spirit with arrows, a javelin, his golden sword and a blazing club, but the spirit devours them all. Disarmed and in great distress, Ashwatthama thinks that this is his punishment for wanting 'to kill those who should not be killed'. Yet he cannot turn back for that would be cowardly. Perhaps fate, in the form of this towering spirit, has overtaken him.

Surely this terrible being that comes
To obstruct me is the fruit of my impure
Intention, produced with no regard for dharma.

And he concludes:

So my turning back from battle has been
Determined by fate: fate alone can check me here.[12]

Ashwatthama bows his head and invokes the god Shiva's aid to help him destroy this 'terrible instrument of fate'. He offers himself as a sacrifice and enters the flames of the sacrificial altar. Shiva is moved. The god explains that he has been protecting the Panchalas so far, but their time has obviously run out. He gives Ashwatthama a sword and enters his body.

'The Night of Time'

Ashwatthama advances towards the enemy camp, while Kripa and Kritavarma wait unseen by the gate. He spots the tent of his father's killer and enters stealthily.

So entering Dhrishtadyumna's tent, Ashwatthama
Saw the prince of the Panchalas sleeping
On a bed close by—
On a great bed covered with a priceless quilt
Of spotless linen, fragrant with powder
And incense, and hung with beautiful garlands.
Then with a kick Ashwatthama awoke
High-souled Dhrishtadyumna, sleeping in his bed,
Secure and trusting.

. . . as he rose from bed, mighty
Ashwatthama seized his hair in both his hands and
Ground him into the earth.
Crushed by that force and his own fear, the Panchala
Prince was trapped half out of sleep, quite paralyzed.
So one foot on his chest, the other on his throat,
Ashwatthama prepared to kill him, groaning
And quivering like a sacrificial beast.
Then Dhrishtadyumna, tearing with his nails
At Drona's son, cried in a muffled way:

'Son of the teacher, best of men, kill me
With a weapon. Quickly! Strike! So by your hand
I may reach the worlds of those whose deeds were good.'

Hearing those garbled words, Drona's son spat back:
'There are no worlds for those who kill their teachers,
Defiler of your race. And that is why,
. . . you do not merit death by arms.'

So speaking, enraged Ashwatthama drummed
Violently on that hero's vitals with his heels,
Like a lion mauling an elephant in rut.[13]

Then, with his sword like a sacrificial knife, Ashwatthama crashes through the camp, slaying the sleeping victorious armies of the Pandavas, Panchalas, and their allies. It is an orgy of slaughter.

Like Death himself let loose by Time, his limbs
Painted with their blood, he cut down with his
Mighty sword, warriors, elephants, and steeds.
So as they struggled, and as he plunged and raised
And stabbed convulsively, Ashwatthama
Was triple-dyed in blood.

And excellent, valiant men, who had risen
From their beds and rushed to meet him, he killed
From afar, and offered them to the Night of Time.[14]

After avenging his father's death on Draupadi's brother Dhrishtadyumna, Ashwatthama goes on a killing spree, felling indiscriminately Pandava officers, including the five children of Draupadi. Meanwhile, Kripa and Kritavarma set the camp on fire. Everyone perishes, except the five Pandava brothers and Draupadi, who were away from the military camp that night. They were with Krishna. Satyaki and Dhrishtadyumna's chariot driver also survived.

The devastated Pandavas asked Krishna the following day: How was it possible for three men to destroy the entire victorious army of the Pandavas? Krishna explained that the great Lord Shiva, who is not easily offended but is easily pleased, had aided them.

'An epic of revenge'

What explains this terrible deed of Ashwatthama's? The night-time massacre of the sleeping armies was a deed of such repulsive proportions that it turned the mood of the epic from heroic triumph to one of dark, stoic resignation.[15] Yet, by all accounts, Ashwatthama was a fine young man—confident, modest and fair-minded. The son of the great martial arts teacher Drona, he grew up in a privileged environment, in the company of princes. His father taught him archery and other skills along with the Pandavas and Kauravas, and Ashwatthama always dealt with both sets of cousins correctly and impartially. Although a brahmin, he acquired from birth the broad-chested ethic of the kshatriya warrior and looked upon glory in battle as his life's goal. He believed unquestioningly in what Duryodhana said to Kripa in the *Shalyaparvan*, 'Fame is all that one should acquire here [on the earth]. That fame can be obtained in battle, and by no other means.'[16]

When war is declared, Ashwatthama finds himself on the wrong side, not unlike other honourable men—Bhishma, Drona and Vidura. Like them, he acts with integrity and fights with honour till the end. However, his sense of justice is wounded early by Duryodhana's sham game of dice. Hence, he draws a line during the cattle raid on Virata; he tells Duryodhana to ask the cheat, Shakuni, to go and fight the Pandavas as he had done so deceitfully well at dice.[17]

Ashwatthama is not afraid to speak his mind. When Duryodhana chides him for his sympathy for the Pandavas, he erupts. 'You are right, my father and I are naturally fond of the Pandavas. But our friendship has nothing to do with our actions on the battlefield.' He adds, 'We are striving to do our best to win this war for you, ready to shed our blood if needed . . . It is you who are greedy, self-centred, and treacherous; in fact, it is your suspicious character that is the problem.'[18]

Ashwatthama's personality begins to change when his father is slain deceitfully. He is filled with pity as he recalls how Bhima killed his leader, Duryodhana, unfairly with a treacherous blow to the thighs.

> . . . *whose heart is so pitiless*
> *It would not burn to have heard, as I have,*
> *Wailing of the king whose thigh's been shattered?*[19]

He remembers the other misdeeds of the Pandavas—how Karna, Bhishma and Bhurishrava were killed on the battlefield. Thus, his mind turns to revenge and the terrible massacre at night is the result.

The *Mahabharata* has been called 'an epic of revenge' and Ashwatthama happens to have been at the wrong place at the wrong time. From this perspective, the Kurukshetra War was the Pandavas' vengeance against their humiliation at the game of dice. When Draupadi was dragged into the assembly of men, wearing only a single piece of clothing stained with her menstrual blood, and when Duryodhana invited her to sit on his thigh, Bhima vowed to break those thighs in revenge. And so he did. 'The narrative fabric of the epic is ... a network of tales of vengeance, and ... avenging Draupadi is Bhima's speciality.'[20] Ashwatthama's revenge was the next escalating act in this cycle of vengeance.

Crime and punishment

If a good person suffers, then the bad person should suffer even more: this is an idea that seems embedded in the human psyche. Consciously one denies it, of course, and proclaims piously, 'I'm not the sort of person who holds grudges.' Yet one unconsciously applauds when the villain 'gets what he deserves'. Wanting to punish a villain or seeing him punished is ubiquitous in literature, movies and politics. From the rage of Achilles in the *Iliad*, to the bloodbaths of Renaissance tragedies, to the calculated revenge of Roger Chillingworth in Hawthorne's *The Scarlet Letter*, to popular Hollywood films, human beings want to get even. The desire for retribution, to right the catastrophic wrongs done to American slaves and Indian 'untouchables' drives the politics of Afro-Americans in the US and of Dalits in India respectively.

'Vengeance has the power of an instinct. The "lust of vengeance" and the "thirst of revenge" are so powerful that they rival all other human needs.'[21] Contemporary thinking about revenge and other emotions has been influenced by advances in psychology. Some think that revenge is neurotic and aberrant— 'vindictiveness damages the core of the whole being'.[22] Others argue that vindictive emotions like anger, resentment and the desire for revenge actually deserve a more legitimate place in our emotional, social and legal lives.[23]

I am inclined to believe that revenge fulfils a legitimate human need. I think retribution is useful because it brings a 'profound sense of moral equilibrium impelling us to demand that people pay for the harm they have done to others'.[24] Punishment is thus a form of revenge by society, fulfilling both a human need for a moral equilibrium and the need to demonstrate to offenders that some behaviours are unacceptable. The US Supreme Court employed this logic in legitimizing the death penalty in 1976. Some crimes are so terrible, it felt, that capital punishment is the only adequate penalty.

Human beings have long wrestled with establishing the right relationship between a crime and its punishment. This is also the central issue in Ashwatthama's story. What, if anything, ought Ashwatthama to have done after his father's killing? How should he be punished after his heinous revenge? When human beings lived in tribes, revenge was a matter of clan's vendetta in the form of 'blood money'. As they moved into civil society, they developed the legal doctrine of 'pollution' for serious crimes. Most ancient societies—including Greek, Hebrew and Indian—regarded a crime such as murder an offence against society, and only allowed the state to revenge it. Punishment under the law, executed by officers of the state, is thus a human institution, not a natural fact. Indeed, Bhishma instructs Yudhishthira (after he becomes king after the war) that punishment must follow a proper judicial process:

> Listen, scion of Kuru, to what the rod of punishment is and how it is judicially prescribed: for the rod of punishment is the one thing in this world upon which everything depends. Great king, judicial process is regarded to be a name of Law. The very proceeding of judicial process is directed to this end.[25]

Thinkers from Plato onwards have believed in the legitimacy of retributive justice. Even an absolute moralist like Kant felt that imposing a just punishment showed respect for the criminal's human autonomy. I happen to agree with forward-looking 'consequentialists' who justify punishment on the grounds of social control: it provides an incentive for a normal person to comply with laws, helps reduce crime and thus maximizes human welfare.[26] Backward-looking 'retributivists', on the other hand, believe that the guilty *deserve* to be punished.[27] Punishment, in their view, is supposed to correct an injustice, protect the individual rights of the innocent, and restore moral equality between the offender and victim. To fail to impose a penalty is as much an injustice since it makes the offender superior to the victim; hence, perpetrators must be punished to reaffirm human equality. According to the political philosopher Jean Hampton, the aim of punishment is not to avenge wrongdoing or to inflict pain and injury on the offender but 'to annul the offender's claim of superiority'.[28] In both cases, private revenge is pre-empted, as the ordinary citizen of a well-functioning modern state is confident that offenders will be arrested and convicted.

During the past fifty years, public opinion around the world, including in America and India, has shifted from efforts to reform and rehabilitate offenders to retribution and incarceration. Sociologists and criminologists became disillusioned in the 1960s with the rehabilitation programmes in prisons in America.[29] The debate today is about ensuring that the sentence is fair, deserved and proportional to the crime, which is also the key issue in Ashwatthama's revenge. This doctrine of proportionality is consistent with human intuition, as these dramatic lines from Exodus 21:22–25 demonstrate: 'If men strive, and hurt a woman with child, so that her fruit depart from her . . . and he shall pay as the judges determine . . . thou shalt give life for life, eye for eye, tooth for tooth, hand for hand, foot for foot, burning for burning, wound for wound, stripe for stripe.'[30]

Proportionality in punishment is also what Bhishma counsels Yudhishthira when he becomes king after the war.

> *The rod of punishment is to be applied differentially and according to Law, not haphazardly: Punishment may be censure, imprisonment, gold, expulsion, severing a limb from the body, or execution. Banishment, death, and the various corporal afflictions should not be imposed for any trivial reason.*[31]

Yet one is painfully aware of how difficult it is to achieve proportionality in practice. There are wide variations in prison sentences handed out for the same crime even in the same country, and capital punishment continues to be controversial. Ashwatthama's example shows that 'inflicting punishment is an unparalleled opportunity for the abuse of power'.[32] Both Nietzsche and Foucault believed that human beings seem to 'get intrinsic even if disguised satisfactions out of inflicting authorized harm on others'. A self-appointed judge like Ashwatthama illustrates Nietzsche's point. Hence, contemporary liberal democracies have arrived at a more modest solution. It is what John Rawls called 'pure procedural justice', which means that punishment is authorized under a fair penalty schedule. 'No other conception of deserved punishment can be defended' even though one is aware in the end that punishment has a largely symbolic rather than an intrinsic value.[33]

'For three thousand years you will wander this earth'

In the end Ashwatthama is, indeed, punished for his heinous deed. Was his punishment just? Did it meet the test of proportionality? I now turn to these questions.

When Draupadi hears of Ashwatthama's awful deed and of the death of all her children, she cries out for revenge.

> *O Partha, ever since I heard that they were*
> *Slaughtered in their sleep by Drona's wicked son,*
> *Grief burns me up, like fire running through a house.*
> *If the life of this evil's author, Drona's son,*
> *And the lives of his followers are not rubbed out*

By you today in combat, on this very spot
I shall fast to death.
Don't doubt it, Pandavas—if Drona's son does not
Reap the fruit of his evil deed, I shall do this.[34]

Bhima and the other Pandavas set out in pursuit and encounter Ashwatthama on the bank of the Ganges. Cornered, Ashwatthama makes an arrow from a blade of grass, charges it with *brahmashiras*, and hurls it at the Pandavas. Arjuna then releases an equally powerful weapon in order to neutralize Ashwatthama's. Together, these two dreadful weapons threaten universal destruction, a sort of nuclear nightmare. Realizing this, Arjuna withdraws his weapon, but Ashwatthama cannot. He diverts it into the wombs of the Pandava women, making them barren. This would have ended the Pandava dynasty, but Krishna managed to revive the foetus of Abhimanyu's widow, Uttara, who bore him a son, Parikshit, and he went on to rule the Kurus for sixty years.[35]

Krishna then turns to Ashwatthama and says:

But as for you, the wise shall know you as a
Murderer of children and a coward,
Whose evil deeds are beyond all tally.
And so you must harvest those evil deeds;
For three thousand years you shall wander this earth,
Alone, and totally incommunicado.
You shall stray companionless in desert wastes,
For Villain, you have no place among men.
Stinking of blood and pus, driven to the
Inaccessible wilderness, you shall wander,
Subject to every plague that blows, you black-souled wretch![36]

What is one to make of Krishna's punishment of Ashwatthama? I asked this question to a class of fourteen-year-olds in a middle class school in South Delhi in March 2005. They were satisfied on the whole that the punishment met the test of proportionality. They said that Ashwatthama's crime was of such a monstrous nature that it deserved an equally horrific retribution. Many felt that a death sentence would have been too kind under the circumstances for he would not have suffered the consequences of his terrible deed. There was no mention of rehabilitative justice. One child argued that since Krishna is a loving god, it would have been more appropriate if he had forgiven Ashwatthama. She was shouted down by her classmates.

'Forgiveness is the strength of the virtuous'

The opposite of revenge is, of course, forgiveness. Draupadi wanted revenge against the Kauravas for stealing the Pandavas' kingdom. But the idealistic Yudhishthira calmed her down in the forest, saying 'forgiveness is the strength of the virtuous'.[37] In that poignant scene he said, 'To fight is easy, but to forgive is difficult. To be patient is not to be weak; to seek peace is always the wiser course.' Forbearance, he added, is superior to anger.[38] In taking revenge, a man is but even with his enemy; in passing it over, he is superior. That which is past is gone, irrevocable, and the wise have enough to do with present matters.

Draupadi wondered why her husband did not feel anger and resentment, emotions that are normal in a victim. She asked how it could be virtuous to forgive Duryodhana, who had stolen their kingdom and humiliated her. She feared that Yudhishthira's 'forgiveness' glossed over the seriousness of Duryodhana's crime. The overwhelming tradition of retributive justice is, of course, on Draupadi's side. It is grounded in the belief that victims also deserve respect. Draupadi's resentment is a 'natural instinct', and to acknowledge that resentment is to respect Draupadi as an individual.[39] Hence, only sincere and sustained repentance by the wrongdoer can make forgiveness acceptable. Otherwise, the propensity to forgive is a moral defect.[40]

The profound grief that Yudhishthira experiences at the end of the war is an example of such a repentance when forgiveness is justified. It made me rethink my position on retributive justice and look upon forgiveness more sympathetically. There are a number of reasons why I felt that revenge and retributive justice are wrong: it employs the suffering of another human being to satisfy oneself; it is connected with obsession, rage, escalating violence—all of which are morally objectionable; those against whom we take revenge are unlikely to concur with our perceptions of the wrong; finally, revenge goes against our obligation to respect human beings and to limit their suffering.[41] Thus, I sympathized with the earlier Yudhishthira, and I began to believe that the capacity to overcome anger and resentment amounts to a virtue. I realized that forgiveness allows the victim to see the wrongdoer also in a different light. It is not merely passive. By changing the way one perceives the other person, forgiveness makes one want to act rather than merely feel.[42]

Yet, I felt that there are strict limits to forgiveness. It took Yudhishthira thirteen harsh years in exile to realize this. The first sign of this change came, as we have seen, on the day after Abhimanyu's wedding, when Satyaki proclaims in Virata's court, 'No law can be found against killing enemies who are plotting to kill us.'[43] As he took charge of the peace negotiations, Yudhishthira is aware that he might have to go to war. His new pragmatic, down-to-earth view of dharma recognizes the limits of goodness. It is grounded in human self-interest, but without being amoral. Retributive justice avoids both extremes—the amorality of Duryodhana and the idealistic super-morality of the earlier Yudhishthira.

Ultimately, Yudhishthira accepts that there will always be wrongdoing in the world, and if necessary, a king must go to war to protect the innocent. And he does. After the war, Bhishma instructs him on the dharma of a good king and teaches him that retributive justice protects his kingdom and indeed *danda*, 'the rod' or retributive justice, is the source of civilized behaviour:

If the rod of force did not exist in this world, beings would be nasty and brutish to each other. Because they fear punishment,

beings do not kill each other, Yudhishthira. As they are preserved
by the rod of force day after day, king, his subjects make the king
grow greater; therefore the rod of force is what is most important.
It puts this world into a stable order quickly, king.[44]

Yudhishthira in the end agrees.

O lord, the rod of punishment that reaches everywhere with its
tremendous fiery energy is the best thing for all living beings.[45]

It is difficult to say what Yudhishthira would have advised
Ashwatthama in order to cope with his grief. The horror of the
war will tempt him to renounce his throne and adopt the
peaceful, non-violent paths of Buddha and Mahavira. This is
when one begins to understand that the theme of the *Mahabharata*
is not revenge but peace and reconciliation. We get an intimation
of this change on the following day when Yudhishthira learns
about Ashwatthama's night-time massacre of his sleeping armies.
He cries out:

We who were their conquerors have at last
been conquered by the foe . . .
How can we call it victory when we are the
Vanquished . . .[46]

Forgiveness and reconciliation

The only one who rejoices at Ashwatthama's heinous deed is
Dhritarashtra. Instead of horror, the blind king expresses regret
that Ashwatthama's revenge came too late. He asks Sanjaya, the
narrator:

Why is it this mighty warrior, Drona's son,
Could not achieve this feat before . . .
And why is it only
When the warrior Duryodhana is dead,
Has the great archer committed
This action? Tell me that![47]

Sanjaya replies baldly that it had happened because the soldiers were asleep; moreover, Krishna and the Pandava brothers were absent.

Later that day the Pandavas come to console the blind king and Gandhari over the death of their children. Dhritarashtra is still burning for revenge, especially against Bhima, who had killed Duryodhana. He rises to embrace Bhima, but Krishna, sensing devious thoughts in the old man, instantly substitutes an iron image of Bhima. The powerfully built king embraces the statue with all his desperate strength, and crushes it to pieces. His anger is thus cooled, and the last act of revenge in the epic is aborted.[48]

Despite the enmity, Yudhishthira behaves magnanimously with Dhritarashtra after the war. At his coronation, he declares:

Our father, the great king Dhritarashtra, is our highest God, and those who wish to please me must obey his commands and heed his preferences. It is because of him that I am still alive after my vast slaughter of my kinsmen. I will always obey him unflaggingly. If you would be kind to me then please comport toward Dhritarashtra as you did before. He is the lord of the universe for you as he is for me.[49]

Yudhishthira does not pursue the path of retributive justice but of forgiveness. Even though he knows that Dhritarashtra's unwillingness to control his son, Duryodhana, had been the cause of the war, he does not hold trials of war criminals. Yudhishthira must have realized that punishing his uncle would not have healed the Pandavas' wounds nor helped to restore political community. He uses the word *kshama*, 'forgiveness', several times, just as he had used it earlier in an attempt to cool down Draupadi's anger in the forest. *Kshama* has connotations of forbearance as well as forgiveness.

While forgiveness suggests a degree of 'self-righteousness', forbearance points one in the direction of the classical virtue of magnanimity. The magnanimous person is forward-looking and does not suffer from the 'victimization' complex of the forgiving person.[50] In the *Nicomachean Ethics*, Aristotle extolled this big-hearted 'virtue of a great man'. Seventeenth-century painters celebrated Alexander the Great's magnanimity after defeating the courageous Indian king Puru (Porus) of the Punjab. The magnanimity of the victor towards the defeated has also been codified in the Geneva Convention. Yudhishthira demonstrates this virtue after the war and thus makes it easier for the political reconstruction of the fractured community of Hastinapura.

Many liberals today, however, would be sceptical of Yudhishthira's policy of reconciliation.[51] They would argue that reconciliation in a political community comes through political participation, which is supposed to heal relationships and restore communal solidarity. Excessive emphasis on social harmony and communal solidarity might actually compromise the legitimate rights of individuals, such as the right to reparations.[52] They believe that social and political harmony results from certain constitutional procedures. When citizens freely and openly confront conflicting interests and values they help to restore a fractured, polarized society far more effectively.[53] Hence, former American Secretary of State Madeleine Albright frequently stressed 'first justice, then peace' during the war in Yugoslavia. She believed that retribution had to precede healing, and legal accountability for the past regime's offences was necessary for restoring communal trust.[54]

The problem with the modern liberal position is that it works well only in a stable and peaceful constitutional environment. After a civil war, if one focuses on punishing offenders of the past regime, one often neglects to rehabilitate the victims. Moreover, it is difficult to pinpoint culpability even in a brutal dictatorial government which has engaged in ethnic cleansing or genocide. This was the case after the downfall of vicious regimes in Cambodia, Chile, Liberia and Rwanda. Because evidence of criminal wrongdoing was more easily available for lower officials, senior political leaders escaped. Even in the *Mahabharata*'s civil war—forgetting for a moment that almost everyone died—it would have been difficult to prosecute offenders because the claims to the throne were ambiguous.

The story of Argentina in the 1980s illustrates why Yudhishthira's reconciliatory approach may be better than the pursuit of punishment. The democratic government that came to power in Argentina after the atrocious 1975–79 'dirty war' chose to prosecute and punish senior state officials who were guilty of human rights violations. Instead of restoring a sense of community, the trials polarized society, 'us versus them', and weakened institutions. They led to the illusion that only a small group of military and police officials were guilty.[55]

The opposite example is South Africa's oft-quoted success with reconciliation. It shows that the 'extension of forgiveness, repentance, and reconciliation to whole nations is one of the great innovations in statecraft of our time'.[56] The South African judge Richard Goldstone, who served as prosecutor for the International War Crimes Tribunal in The Hague, observed that truth-telling is more important than trials in healing and restoring political community. Desmond Tutu, chairperson of South Africa's Truth and Reconciliation Commission, adds, 'There is no future without forgiveness.' Pope John Paul II echoed the same sentiment. 'Indeed, if strict justice is viewed as a precondition for peace, then the quest for national unity and peace may be doomed to failure.'[57]

More recently in India, Professor J.S. Bandukwalla asked Muslims to forgive the 2002 killings in Gujarat. On India's west coast, Gujarat is one of India's most prosperous states, but it allowed genocide to happen in broad daylight. In 2002, around 1,500 Muslims were killed in retaliation for the alleged murder of Hindu pilgrims who were torched in a train near the city of Godhra. Those who presided over the killings of the Muslims were elected to power and their complicity was confirmed on camera by an exposé in *Tehelka* magazine in 2007. But Bandukwalla argued, 'Forgiveness will release Muslims from the trauma of the past. It may also touch the conscience of Hindus, since the crimes were committed by a few fanatics in the name of Ram. Most important, it may give Gujarat a chance to close the tragic chapter of 2002 and move on.'

My first reaction to his proposal was: 'No, the guilty must be punished.' But after the chief minister Narendra Modi was re-elected with a thumping majority, I wondered if it was not a great opportunity for him to make a magnanimous gesture to heal the state's wounds and lay to rest the ghosts of 2002. I felt that forgiveness might actually work better than retributive justice. I suggested, therefore, in my Sunday column in the *Times of India* that it was worth trying Professor Bandukwalla's idea.

I got a lot of hate mail from both sides after my column appeared. Those who believed in legal accountability disagreed vehemently, arguing that healing and communal trust would only be restored in Gujarat once the guilty were punished and the victims' right to reparations fulfilled. Hindus, on the other hand, were outraged; they felt that it was they who should be doing the forgiving for the torching of the train in Godhra. Nevertheless, I followed up my article with a suggestion that the hugely popular chief minister, with a big electoral majority, would gain a great deal of goodwill if he set up a 'truth and reconciliation commission' (as Nelson Mandela and Desmond Tutu had done in South Africa) and followed it up with a plan to rehabilitate victims on both sides. This might bring to an end a tragic chapter.

In the post-9/11 world, I find that revenge is increasingly associated in the world's eyes with Islam. My friend Murad Ali Baig explains that revenge was an old Arab custom that unfortunately got mixed up in Muslim tradition. A survival from the precarious life in the desert, the certainty of vengeance acted as a deterrent against oppressors; this is how small tribes of Arab Bedouins protected themselves against bigger tribes. But revenge also became intertwined with early Islamic politics. The early khalifs, Umar and Uthman, and the Prophet's son-in-law Ali were all assassinated. The Bedouin Kharajites, unhappy that Ali did not avenge Uthman's assassination, caused a split between the Sunni and Shia sects, and this brought its own bloodshed. The Kharajite view of the world has been passed on through the Wahhabis to today's Taliban.

'The word jehad,' according to Baig, 'is rarely found in the Qur'an but is referred to 199 times in the Hadith, which was written two centuries after the death of the Prophet. The Wahhabis interpreted jehad to mean a holy war, even though it had actually meant 'striving'; a Mujahideen was originally not a holy warrior but only one who strives. For Muhammad there were two jehads and the greater one meant a struggle against one's own weakness while a lesser jehad was to fight against injustice.'[58] Baig goes on to explain that the Qur'an clearly forbade killing in the name of Islam. It is clear to me that unless today's Muslim clerics disavow revenge and the extreme views of Wahhabis and others, Islam and Muslims will continue to be viewed with suspicion around the world.

9

YUDHISHTHIRA'S REMORSE

'This victory feels more like defeat to me'

> *If someone is victorious but grieves like a poor afflicted imbecile, how can he think of that as victory? In fact, his enemies have defeated him ...*

—Yudhishthira, after winning the war
at Kuruskshetra, *Mahabharata* X.10.13[1]

'This grief holds me in check'

As soon as the war is over, Yudhishthira's first thought is to the Kauravas' mother, Gandhari. He goes to her and begs her for forgiveness. He does not make excuses, nor does he remind her how his demand for just five villages could have avoided the war. He simply says:

> *I, Yudhishthira, am the cruel killer of your sons, great lady. Curse me!*[2]

It is time for the *Mahabharata* now to begin to pick up the pieces of the legacy of the war—the relentless bloodshed, the revenge and violence against all human feelings, which it has described in great poetry in the battle books. It seeks reconciliation in Books Eleven and Twelve to heal the wounds of a shattered polity.[3]

There is a great build-up of *shoka,* 'burning grief'.[4] The morning after the war, the women of Hastinapura gather on the Kurukshetra battlefield to find their men.

The clamour of the afflicted women bewailing the destruction of the Kurus became tremendous and shook the worlds. They were like beings on fire when the end of an age has arrived . . .[5]

When the women reach the field of battle, they see

their sons, brothers, fathers and husbands who had been killed there being eaten by all the flesh-eaters—jackals, jungle crows, goblins, Pishachas, and night prowling Rakshasas . . . Some stumbled about amidst the bodies and others dropped to the ground. [They] were in shock and helpless and they lost their wits.[6]

On the field is Queen Gandhari, the mother of Duryodhana, who says:

The earth is so muddy with flesh and blood [that] one can scarcely move upon it.[7]

Seeing the women 'sink into misery as they drop to the earth littered with brothers, fathers and sons', Gandhari observes the newly-married Uttara holding in her arms the body of her husband, the dazzling hero Abhimanyu, the son of Arjuna. The pregnant bride caresses her dead husband. Slowly she undoes his guilded armour and passionately embraces the wounded, blood-soaked body of one who was merely a boy.[8]

Cradling his head in her lap as if he were still alive, pushing aside his blood-matted hair with her hands, she asks, 'How could those great warriors kill you when you stood in the middle of the battle? . . . Did [they] have any heart . . . when they closed around you and strove to kill you, one boy alone?'[9]

Imagining her husband to be asleep, Uttara keeps talking to him. Soon she begins to picture him in heaven and torments herself, thinking that he is being entertained by celestial beauties.

Abhimanyu's death (as we saw in Chapter 4) is one of the epic's great moments. Yudhishthira blames himself now—he shouldn't have allowed the boy to enter the treacherous military formation alone. His grief becomes uncontrollable when he learns the secret of Karna's birth. 'With Karna and Arjuna beside me I could have conquered even Indra's heaven.'[10] He recalls that he had always felt a certain tenderness each time he saw Karna's feet. Now he understands why—they resembled his mother's. Ever since Duryodhana and Karna came together at the tournament of the princes, a great fear overtook Yudhishthira. He was filled with anxiety.[11] He spent sleepless nights thinking about how Karna stood in the way of recovering his kingdom.[12] This is what led him to hatch the unholy conspiracy with Shalya to destroy Karna's morale before his battle with Arjuna. When the wheel of Karna's chariot got stuck in the mud, Karna had appealed, 'You can see that the earth has swallowed my left wheel . . . don't kill me while you stand in your chariot and I'm on the ground . . . Recall dharma and wait for a moment!'[13] But the Pandavas had not heeded dharma.

Thinking of Karna, Yudhishthira's eyes fill up with tears and he speaks sadly to his mother, 'Ah woman, you have slain us by keeping this secret . . . There is nothing that we could not have won! Not even what is in heaven. This grotesque butchery that has finished the Kauravas would not have happened.'[14] In torment, he curses all women: 'They will not keep secrets!'[15]

A month thus goes by in mourning for the dead warriors on the banks of the Ganges. It is now time for the king to enter the city victoriously and assume the throne. Yudhishthira's sense of guilt and shame, however, show no signs of abating. Full of remorse, he laments:

To get a piece of the earth we totally abandoned men who were equal to the earth, men whom we should never have killed. And now we live with our kinsmen dead and our wealth exhausted . . . like dogs we greedily went after a piece of meat! Now our piece of meat is gone, and so are those who would have eaten it.[16]

He tells Arjuna:

The heroes are dead. The evil is done. Our kingdom has been laid waste. Having killed them, our rage is gone. Now this grief holds me in check![17]

Famous words, indeed—*shoko mam rundhayaty ayam!*—'this grief holds me in check'. But they provoke a crisis for the state. Yudhishthira declares:

I am going to say good-bye to all of you and go to the forest . . . You rule this wide earth which is now at rest; the thorn has been removed from it.[18]

He tells Arjuna that he plans to live the life of a wandering ascetic.

You will not get me back on that road the rich travel. No way! I am going to leave behind the pleasures of society and go. The road one travels all by oneself is peaceful . . .[19]

And he offers a compelling, lyrical picture of another kind of life:

. . . ridiculing no one, frowning at nothing, my face always cheery, all my faculties thoroughly restrained, questioning no one about the road, travelling by any way whatsoever, not seeking to go in any particular direction, nor to any particular place, paying no heed to my going, not looking back, straight and steady as I go, but careful to avoid [hurting] creatures moving and still—so will I be.[20]

Arjuna is stunned. Normally correct and respectful towards his elder brother, he attacks him now with uncharacteristic fierceness:

What heights of sissy feebleness . . . how can you renounce everything now that your enemies are slain, unless you are daft. How can a eunuch be a king? Or one who shilly-shallies?[21]

His 'beautiful, long-eyed Draupadi' is even more incredulous. 'Usually haughty towards Yudhishthira', she looks him in the eye and reminds him of all the suffering they have undergone for the sake of this prize.

The [Pandavas] have striven hard, and success has come to them, but now that you've got the entire earth, you are turning success into disaster all by yourself . . . After being abused like that by our enemies, I want to live now![22]

She berates him for abandoning his *kshatriya-dharma*. To this, Yudhishthira retorts with such passion against the 'big-chested' ethic of the kshatriya warriors that she is taken aback.

Damn the kshatra way! Damn the power of the mighty chest! Damn the unforgiving stubbornness that brought us to this disaster . . . Because of our greed and our confusion, we . . . have been brought to this condition for the sake of a trifling kingdom. Now that we see our kinsmen lying dead upon the ground, no one can rejoice at being king.[23]

Draupadi turns conciliatory and reminds her husband affectionately of his duty, foremost of which is to accept the throne and give up all thoughts of renunciation:

Most excellent of kings, friendliness towards all creatures, generous giving, study, asceticism—all this may be the dharma of the brahmin, but it is not for a king. Restraining the wicked and protecting the pious, and not fleeing in a war—this is the highest dharma of kings.[24]

'One who gains victory also suffers loss'

Yudhishthira's grief is all the greater because he had foreseen the hollowness of victory. During the peace negotiations, he had told Krishna that he wanted to avoid war because:

> *Victory and defeat, O Krishna, are the same to one who is killed.*
> *Defeat is not very much better than death, I think; but he whose*
> *side gains victory also suffers loss.*[25]

What he had predicted has come to pass. It was he who gave the fateful order to begin the war, and he considers himself 'a sinful wrongdoer' who has caused the deaths of 'people who should not be slain'.[26] Painful memories keep nagging at him. He remembers the fall of Bhishma:

> *I used to roll around playing on his lap ... and when I saw him*
> *fallen upon the earth, drenched in blood, a racking fever entered*
> *into me. He who nurtured and watched over us as children, I*
> *brought his killing to pass [since I was] lusting to rule the*
> *kingdom ... I am responsible.*[27]

He recalls how 'wickedly I lied to [Drona] about his son when he approached me during the battle' by putting a 'little jacket on the truth':

> *... the teacher said to me, 'Your words, king, are true. Tell me if*
> *my son is alive.' ... I acted falsely by saying 'elephant' under my*
> *breath ... I put a little jacket on the truth and told my teacher*
> *'Ashwatthama has been killed' when it was only an elephant that*
> *had been killed. What heavenly worlds will I go to now that I have*
> *done this dreadful deed?*[28]

He identifies with the pain of Hastinapura's women who have become widows. In empathizing with the undeserved misfortune of others, Yudhishthira has embarked on a moral journey that will lead him to the core of dharma. His brothers may feel regret, but he feels remorse. He speaks of his victory in the war 'as a great sorrow that is constantly in my heart'.[29]

∾

Remorse is different from regret. A remorseful person feels 'radically singular', and hence remorse is a kind 'of dying to the world'.[30] Remorse 'sticks with us in a way radically different from other forms of suffering. Someone who is true to their remorse will always reject, as inappropriate, consolation which is based on their recognition of the guilt of others. Any other kind of suffering . . . may be consoled by being seen in the light of the suffering of others.'[31] Because remorse is isolating and difficult to console, the Pandavas feel frustrated. Draupadi finds Yudhishthira completely unresponsive. He craves solitude in his guilt, and he is unable to relate to others.

Another king who felt remorse was Oedipus. Sophocles's tragedy, *Oedipus Rex*, describes how Oedipus unknowingly killed his father and married his mother in fulfilment of a divine prophecy. When he realized what he had done, he blinded himself, saying that he was unfit to face the children of his incestuous union. Remorse can exact a terrible price. Yudhishthira, like Oedipus, feels guilty that a great tragedy has befallen and it was his fault. He was responsible for the deaths of his teacher Drona, his brother Karna, his nephew Abhimanyu, and many others. Like Oedipus, he believes he is unworthy to rule and he atones by renouncing his crown. Both kings are acutely aware of the humanity of their victims, which is the hallmark of remorse. 'In remorse we respond to what it means to wrong another . . . Far from being intrinsically self-indulgent, lucid remorse makes one's victim vividly real.'[32]

Remorse is a more intense emotion than regret. When a child is accidentally hit by a car, an onlooker may feel regret, but the driver feels remorse even if it was not his fault. The regretful person says 'too bad, it happened'; a remorseful person is scarred, sometimes for life.[33] By recognizing the reality of the other person, both Yudhishthira and Oedipus have gone beyond regret. They have rendered themselves vulnerable to the other person who is capable of causing unfathomable grief. Both have a shocked and bewildered realization of what it means to wrong another.

The problem with remorse is that it can easily degenerate into self-pity. Indeed, some Indians find Yudhishthira self-indulgent. Spinoza, the philosopher, was also suspicious of remorse—he thought it was a 'species of sadness' and hence 'injurious and evil'. He felt that one 'comes to the right path more through reason and love of truth than through Remorse and Repentance.'[34] Aldous Huxley dismisses remorse as well: 'On no account brood over your wrongdoing. Rolling in the muck is not the best way of getting clean.'[35] Bernard Williams, the English philosopher, objects to remorse because it turns the focus on oneself rather than on the one who is injured. A remorseful person is more concerned with preserving his 'own integrity or purity or virtue at others' expense'.[36]

I disagree. I do not think it is self-absorption. The self-absorbed person is focused on himself whereas the genuinely remorseful person cares for the other person who has been wronged. A moral sentiment like remorse is valuable for it offers a psychological basis for the moral life. When we look upon the misfortune of worthy persons like Yudhishthira and Oedipus with sympathy, even though they are characters in a narrative, it becomes a powerful training ground for learning about compassion. These reverses could happen to us as well.[37] Empathy for Yudhishthira's remorse at the end of the Kurukshetra War was invaluable in my dharma journey. It opened up a new understanding of dharma and taught me how to cultivate the moral life.

From *shoka* to *shanti*

A curious sight this: a victorious king refuses to ascend the throne because he is convinced that the demands of kingship and dharma are inconsistent.[38] Yudhishthira's grief creates a crisis for the state. The violent deeds of the war torment him. His *shoka*, 'burning grief', endangers the Pandavas' victory. His is a tragic dilemma of a good man who had to engage in violence in the performance of duty, and who now hesitates to ascend the throne because of the violence inherent in the king's role. It is an existential crisis of a good human being who is unable to cope with the violence inherent in the imperfect human condition.[39]

Yudhishthira's *shoka* has to be cooled and converted to *shanti*, 'peace'. The classic strategy in yoga for doing that is to still the mind, reduce the human impulse to react, and bring about a state of inner calm.[40] The epic now recalls his grandfather in order to 'cool the king' and make him fit to rule. We had left Bhishma in Chapter 5, resting his head on a hero's pillow of arrows. Now he is brought from his deathbed to the hugely embarrassed Yudhishthira to teach him that violence, power and war are integral to kingship.[41] The purpose of *Shantiparvan*, Book Twelve of the *Mahabharata*, is to calm Yudhishthira's remorse by instructing him about the nature of the dharma of the king.[42]

Bhishma teaches Yudhishthira that kingship and dharma are not contradictory. The king has to wield the *danda*, 'the rod', but he must do it justly under the constraints of the law. Conceding that the ethical value of *ahimsa*, 'non-violence', is highly desirable, Bhishma says that the king can promote it in society by ruling justly. 'Ruling justly' may require the king to use violence at times; this violence, however, must be grounded in laws and principles:

> ... *the king exists for dharma, not for doing what gives him pleasure. The king is protector of the world ... People depend upon dharma and dharma depends upon the king.*[43]

It is, then, dharma which sanctions the use of violence by the king in order to curb unsocial behaviour. And if a king is too idealistic in pursuit of the moral and abandons the rod, the results may be catastrophic.

Bhishma's point about the need for sovereign power is not unlike the conclusion which Thomas Hobbes reached in mid-seventeenth century England. Writing after the English Civil War and the overthrow of the Stuart monarchs, who had claimed to rule by divine right, Hobbes explained that peace could only prevail in society if there was a sovereign power to punish those who misbehave. Hobbes wrote in 1651 in *Leviathan* that mankind has 'a perpetual and restless desire of power, that ceaseth only in death'.[44] For this reason, in the natural condition of mankind all human beings would live in a state of war 'where every man is Enemy to every man . . . And the life of man, [is] solitary poor nasty brutish, and short.'[45] Although Bhishma does not elaborate on the state of nature or share Hobbes's pessimistic view of human beings, his prescription is just as blunt. Indeed, if there is one thing that the horrific Kurukshetra War teaches, it is that there will always be human beings like Duryodhana who are driven by the will to power. Society needs an executive to curb this drive with legitimate and superior authority, maintaining peace by punishing those who breach it.

Yudhishthira and Ashoka

How does a king protect his subjects from external or internal attacks if he gives up arms? How does he keep peace in society by non-violent means? This is the question raised by Yudhishthira who bears an uncanny resemblance to Emperor Ashoka of the great Mauryan empire, which ruled over India from 317 BC to 180 BC. Ashoka too was caught between the demands of kingship and his conscience after a bloody war in eastern India. His famous thirteenth rock edict says: 'On conquering Kalinga, the Beloved of the Gods felt remorse, for when an independent country is conquered the slaughter, death and deportation of the people is extremely grievous to the Beloved of the Gods and weighs heavily on his mind.'[46] Ashoka converted to Buddhism, renounced war and devoted the rest of his reign to teaching non-violent dharma to his subjects.[47] He was a hugely charismatic and influential personality, and it is hard to imagine that the *Mahabharata* escaped his influence. Scholars have speculated that the epic had to counter the impact of Ashoka's ideal of *ahimsa*, which was spreading across the subcontinent, as a result of his Buddhist 'Dharma campaign'.[48]

Although the earliest compositions of the *Mahabharata* may date back to around 400 BC, it was not written down until around the first century BC. Society evolved during this long period and many of the changes are reflected in the epic. During the early part of this period, Aryan tribes in north India settled down and integrated with the indigenous people. They became urbanized and gradually formed monarchical states. New ideas appeared, which challenged the old Vedic ideals and the religion of the Aryans. Young men began to question the old order. They were drawn in particular to the ideal of renunciation, which challenged the orthodox life of the ordinary householder and the pre-eminent place of the brahmin.

New sects appeared. The Buddhists, the Jains and the Ajivikas were the most strident in rejecting the old orthodoxy. They criticized brahmins, dismissed the Vedas, and condemned animal sacrifices as violent, cruel and immoral. They adopted the idea of *ahimsa*, 'non-harming', in part as a reaction to the Vedic *yajnas*. These social and philosophical changes are reflected in the *Mahabharata*, which appropriated the exciting new ideas of Sankhya, Yoga and *bhakti* even though it did not abandon the old Vedic way of life. It retained contempt for those who deny the Vedas and calls them *nastikas*, 'atheists'.

Ashoka came to power around 265 BC and became the most famous Buddhist king in history.[49] He was the grandson of

Chandragupta Maurya, who founded the dynasty in 320 BC, soon after Alexander the Great's invasion in 326 BC. Like Yudhishthira, Ashoka was obsessed with dharma. He had 'dharma edicts', expressing ethical, religious tolerance, and social and ecological concern, erected in stone throughout his vast empire.[50] His twelfth major rock edict states: 'This inscription of *Dhamma* has been engraved so that any sons or great grandsons that I may have should not think of gaining new conquests, and in whatever victories they may gain should be satisfied with patience and light punishment. They should only consider conquest by *Dhamma* to be a true conquest, and delight in *Dhamma* should be their whole delight, for this is of value in both this world and the next.'[51]

Ashoka's edicts also celebrate his vision of a plural, multi-faith society, a message that is especially relevant for our intolerant, fundamentalist times. Those who disparage other faiths, he says, demean and harm their own: 'Again, whosoever honours his own sect or disparages that of another man, wholly out of devotion to his own, with a view to showing it in a favourable light, harms his own sect even more seriously. Therefore, concord is to be commended, so that men may hear one another's principles and obey them.'[52]

The Mauryan empire posed a clear challenge to the brahmins. To their relief, however, the Mauryas were overthrown by a brahmin general, Pushyamitra Shunga, around 185 BC.[53] In this way the Hindu orthodoxy reasserted itself. But the traditional values had changed in the meantime, and this in turn must have influenced the evolution of Yudhishthira's character.[54] The epic could not remain immune to two centuries of Mauryan history. The new values of Buddhism were clearly attractive. Thus, Yudhishthira probably evolved into a Hindu answer to the Buddhist Ashoka, seeking to overcome the contradiction between Ashoka's vigorous policy of *ahimsa* and having to employ state-sanctioned violence as a ruler.[55] Thus, the character of

Yudhishthira is ambivalent—sometimes, he is attracted to the new, gentler values of *ahimsa* and compassion; at other times, he realizes their limitations, such as the moment when he makes the decision to go to war. He is attracted to *nivritti*, 'the contemplative life', but he is reminded of his kshatriya duty to live 'the active life' of *pravritti*. The two sets of values coexist within his tormented character, and this coexistence is a major source of the epic's narrative tension.[56]

'A twig is borne along in a stream'

Eventually Yudhishthira's *shoka* is calmed. He reconciles to the demands of kingship. As he listens to Bhishma's pacifying instructions, he becomes resigned to the tragedy of war and the imperfect human condition.[57] He realizes that renouncing the throne is an escape, not a solution. He must learn to live in the world and become a principled king who will have to employ violence when necessary. Occasionally he expresses disaffection, but his stoic sense of duty to the throne remains strong.[58] Thus, the epic affirms a middle path, a narrow spectrum of moral possibilities that human beings have to learn to live within in order to function in the imperfect age of *Kali Yuga*. One cannot escape the world's suffering, but the values of dharma, especially *ahimsa*, can inform one's life.

Early on, the epic had established the theme of *ahimsa* when it recounted the story of Prince Ruru, who was so furious when a snake bit and killed his bride-to-be, Pramadvara, just before their wedding, that he vowed to kill all snakes that came across his path. One day a non-poisonous snake-lizard crossed his path. As he was about to strike it, the lizard said, '*ahimsa paramo dharma*', 'non-violence is the highest dharma'.[59] More than two thousand years later, Mohandas Karamchand Gandhi made his wife, Kasturba, copy out these three words of the lizard in an exercise book when she was learning the alphabet. The words, *ahimsa paramo dharma* became Gandhi's rallying cry during India's non-violent struggle for freedom from Britain in the first half of the twentieth century. The cry was heard around the world, and was adopted by Martin Luther King during America's civil rights movement.

Since Yudhishthira had wanted to renounce kingship for the life of a wandering hermit, Bhishma addresses this problem—he extols the virtue of *ahimsa*, both as a principle of social behaviour as well as an ascetic ideal.[60] As a part of the instruction of the future dharmic king, Yudhishthira is told a remarkable story. A brahmin named Jajali acquires enormous powers by performing fearsome penance in the forest. He boasts, 'There is none like me in this world ... who can travel through the air.'[61] Jajali is told about a trader of spices in Varanasi, Tuladhara, who is indeed superior to him and who can teach him something about dharma. Hearing this, Jajali goes to Varanasi and finds Tuladhara. He observes that the shopkeeper's merchandise consists of spices and juices, which he weighs and measures with equanimity. Tuladhara treats all his customers alike and works diligently without a concern for blame and praise, without allowing his ego to come in the way of his work.[62]

Jajali is intrigued by Tuladhara and he asks the merchant about his views on dharma. Tuladhara says that 'everyone is confused about dharma'. Right dharma is not just a code of conduct; it is an attitude. He offers the analogy of a twig that moves randomly in a stream:

> As ... a piece of wood is borne along in a stream, and may randomly join up with some other pieces of wood, [and as] other logs join with them from here and there, with straw, wood and refuse, from time to time, senselessly, so it is with behaviour ... as it arises from one source or another.

> O Jajali, in this world there is no dharma, however subtle, [which is] unmotivated: human formulations of dharma are made with past and future interests in mind. Because of its subtleness, the

deeply obscured [true dharma] cannot be identified; only through grasping other [kinds of] conduct [can] it be conceived. For [this] reason one should seek [true] dharma, not follow the ways of the world.

If one man were to injure me and another praise me—listen, O Jajali, in such circumstances [my reaction would be equal].[63]

There is an ironic twist here—a petty trader is teaching a high caste brahmin how to live. The worldly merchant, who presumably ought to covet wealth, is being held up as a model of detachment for a forest-dwelling ascetic. Jajali is told to observe Tuladhara's attitude of disinterested equanimity. Tuladhara is happy to go with the flow like a twig in the river that moves randomly with the current and joins up with flotsam. In the same manner, Yudhishthira is taught that a good king ought to dispense justice with detachment for the good of his people, unlike the usual ego-filled conquerors who want to stamp their mark on history through violence and conquest. It is similar to the message of detached action that Krishna gave to Arjuna on the battlefield—if one acts for the sake of the action and not for the personal reward, then one is liberated from the bonds of karma.

What Yudhishthira learns from Tuladhara's example is that the search for wealth and social standing is an impermanent pursuit. It is wiser to have the attitude of a randomly floating twig in the river. It is not necessary to renounce kingship and become a hermit like Jajali in order to be virtuous. One should live in the world with Tuladhara's attitude. A person who is distrustful of worldly achievement is less likely to step on the toes of others. Such a person is on the way to acquire the virtue of *ahimsa*. Leo Tolstoy came to the same conclusion. Classical liberals of the eighteenth century also viewed the trader sympathetically, although their message was different from Tuladhara's. Adam Smith in *The Wealth of Nations* observed that a typical merchant had to deal with suppliers and customers and was thus at the mercy of an 'invisible hand' of the market, which determined his prices and profits. If the market is competitive, one can see that a trader's position is a bit like Tuladhara's twig being randomly swept along the flow.[64]

'Ahimsa paramo dharma'

The *Mahabharata* calls *ahimsa* the 'heart of dharma' and in its last book reiterates what the snake-lizard had said: *'ahimsa* is the highest dharma.'[65] *Ahimsa* is a foundational concept in classical Indian culture, and like dharma, it is not easy to translate. It is the opposite of the Sanskrit *himsa*, 'harm' or 'violence'; hence, *ahimsa* is 'not doing harm'. The *Mahabharata* uses it to mean 'not taking life'; 'not causing pain'; 'not causing injury'. In the Laws of Manu, *ahimsa* connotes 'not having an aggressive attitude', while in Patanjali's text on yoga, it means 'not having a stilled spirit'—something that might interfere with meditation.[66] Thus, *ahimsa* affects both the object ('non-injury') and the subject ('non-injuriousness').[67] Hence, 'harmlessness' may be the most appropriate way to translate *ahimsa* into English because it suggests both 'non-injury' and 'non-injuriousness'. I find, however, that 'harmlessness' is a weak word with negative connotations. I prefer to stick to the old-fashioned 'non-violence' of Mahatma Gandhi.

Gandhi taught the world that *ahimsa* is not pacifism. Non-violence does not come from weakness but from strength, and only the strong and disciplined can hope to practise it. Gandhi combined *ahimsa* with another virtue in the dharma lexicon, *satya*, 'truth'. He joined the latter with *'agraha'* or a 'holding on to' with force if necessary. Thus, *satyagraha* is 'truth force'. When one's cause is truthful, Gandhi said, holding on to it non-violently can be immensely powerful. Whereas pacifism is passive and harmless, non-violence is active and even dangerous, as the British discovered to their discomfort during India's freedom struggle. 'Non-violence, like violence, is a means of persuasion.'[68] Gandhi's non-violent action was a technique by which 'people who reject passivity and submission and who see struggle as essential, can wage it without violence. Non-violent action is not an attempt to avoid or ignore conflict. It is one response to the problem of how to effect change in politics, especially how to wield power effectively.'[69]

But *ahimsa* has its limitations. Gandhi was fortunate in having as his adversary the British liberal establishment, which was, by and large, open to reason. I have sometimes wondered how Gandhi might have fared against a fanatic, a terrorist, or a dictator bent on genocide. It is very well to be non-violent to non-poisonous lizards but one must defend oneself against poisonous snakes. George Orwell, in his famous essay 'Reflections on Gandhi', wrote that 'it is difficult to see how Gandhi's methods could be applied in a country where opponents of the regime disappear in the middle of the night and are never heard from again'.[70] Liddell Hart echoed this view: 'It is very doubtful whether non-violent resistance would have availed against a Tartar conqueror . . . or a Stalin . . . The only impression it seems to have made on Hitler was to trample on what, to his mind, was contemptible weakness.'

Gandhi would have replied that it is better to resist and die than to give your consent to violent death. 'You will have my body but not my will.' Most Jews in Germany went to their death without resisting. They were, as Lloyd Rudolph argues, 'complicit in their death'. Had the Jews resisted the 'storm troopers' of the Nazi party, who attacked their shops and homes, they might have aroused the conscience of middle class Germans. The attitude of assimilated, educated professional Jews was one of denial and an avoidance of disorder. Unlike Nazi Germany, non-violent resistance was tried with considerable success in the countries of Soviet-occupied Eastern Europe, particularly in Poland and Czechoslovakia.[71]

Bhishma and Krishna—men who had to rule a kingdom, unlike Gandhi—recognize the limits of *ahimsa*. There are times when even a *dharmaraja*, 'good king', must go to war. That is why there is such a thing as *dharma-yuddha*, 'a just war'. Even Yudhishthira was forced to recognize that a policy of *ahimsa* would not work against Duryodhana, and he had no choice in the end but to fight. It seems to me that a policy of *ahimsa* would not be able to usher in an era of peace in the world. Non-violent defence would have to permit an invading army to occupy one's homeland, and I don't think any government would allow it. Nor are there any cases, as far as I know, in which 'civilian defence has caused an invader to withdraw'.[72] Non-violent resistance succeeded in hastening Britain's departure from India because the British believed in restraint and in a moral code.

Peace, not war

When the Kurukshetra War comes to an end, it becomes clear that the theme of the *Mahabharata* is not war but peace. We have been so mesmerized by the heroic and valorous deeds at Kurukshetra, recounted in the battle books of the epic, that it is only during the sorrowful 'bath of tears' of the widows of Hastinapura that we begin to confront the other side of war.[73] Yudhishthira is left with a hollow sense of victory. It is for this reason that Anandavardhana, the ninth century Kashmiri commentator, concluded that the aesthetic mood evoked by the *Mahabharata* is not 'heroic', as one would expect from a war epic, but one of *shanta*—calm resignation, leading to *nirveda*, the end of desire.[74]

Revolted by the violence against all human feeling, remorseful Yudhishthira becomes a disillusioned pessimist. The same thing happened to the proud Athenian, Thucydides. Looking back on the Peloponnesian War which brought Athens—with all its incomparable achievements in philosophy, architecture and literature—to its knees, Thucydides wrote, 'It was love of power operating through greed and personal ambition which was the cause of all these evils.' The story that Thucydides tells in his great *History of the Peloponnesian War* is of a war between Athens and Sparta and their respective allies, which lasted from 431 BC to 404 BC. Just as the continuous Greek wars left Athens defeated, permanently weakened and in moral decay, so did the war at Kurukshetra usher in *Kali Yuga*, an age of deep moral decline.

The kshatriya commanders at Kurukshetra, like their counterparts in Greece, killed most of the men of military age. They were tough-minded and cruel in the cold execution of their soldierly duty. Yudhishthira concludes that there is something terribly wrong with this kshatriya duty, and expresses deep loathing for the warrior ethic of heroism. Once that ethic is stripped of its romance and the embellishments of the *sutas*, 'bards', human nakedness is revealed in all its fearful and murderous selfishness. Draupadi and his Pandava brothers may be able to shrug their shoulders and hide behind the thought that 'after all, this is what war is like', but Yudhishthira cannot excuse the slaughter at Kurukshetra as a 'necessity of war'.[75]

Thucydides did not believe that the Athenian generals were depraved when they gave their murderous orders. In the massacre at Melos in 416 BC, as we have noted in Chapters 1 and 4, the generals must have felt guilty for they tried to defend their actions. They said, like Duryodhana, that if they had not done it, their enemies would have construed their lenient behaviour as an 'argument of our weakness'. Furthermore, the generals said, 'that you likewise, and others that should have the same power which we have, would do the same.' Not true. The Athenians were cruel to the people of Melos because they punished not only the authors of the rebellion but others as well, especially the women and children. Thucydides tells us that in a comparable situation with the Mytilenes a few years earlier, the citizens of Athens 'felt a kind of repentance'. They debated the issues of collective guilt, retributive justice and the deterrent effects of capital punishment, and concluded that their generals had been cruel in their treatment of the conquered people.[76]

Yudhishthira also expresses remorse and he too repents. The irony is that many Indians have a low opinion of him. 'Dharmaputra Yudhishthira' is a derogatory epithet in Bengal. While Arjuna is a brave and valiant warrior, remorseful Yudhishthira is considered weak and indecisive.[77] The contempt for Yudhishthira tells us something about our contemporary society. What we need is more remorse, not less, but it is somehow considered unmanly in most modern societies.

Yudhishthira's remorse and his hypnotic attraction for *ahimsa* posed uncomfortable questions for my dharma education. It made me stop and look at myself. From the earliest moment when I began to think for myself, I realized that I had made choices that have determined the sort of person I have become. Like most people, I failed to choose and allowed myself to be swept along in a direction that others decided. For the rest of my life I have had to deal with the consequences of those decisions. Even in later life I did not reflect on my choices and I continued to be led. In a few unusual situations, I did indeed pause and I asked, 'Who am I?', but even then I was reluctant to make genuinely free moral choices that would have led me to become an authentic human being like Yudhishthira.

Yudhishthira *does* reflect. Unlike most of us, he makes a deliberate choice between following his own interest unthinkingly—his *kshatriya-dharma*—or doing something more difficult, which might even involve some inconvenience, but which is the right thing to do from the larger perspective of a universal *sadharana-dharma* of his conscience. He *decides*, whereas most of us are content to stumble along unthinkingly, succumbing to self-deception and compromise.

On two recent occasions I felt remorse was appropriate in our public life but it was not expressed. When Benazir Bhutto, Pakistan's candidate for prime minister, was assassinated in

December 2007, what struck me most was the singular lack of remorse in that country. There was plenty of grief, even some regret, but no remorse. When I raised the question of Pakistan's lack of remorse in my Sunday column in the *Times of India*, Rahul Gandhi (Rajiv's son and Indira's grandson) sent me an e-mail, which I think is worth quoting, for he connects remorse with democracy. 'Remorse comes when you are able to feel the suffering of fellow human beings to an extent where the suffering becomes your own. To feel deeply human suffering you have to internally accept that all humans are equal and see them as humans and not as a particular group. Once you make this leap, democracy is the only system you can believe in. [India's] leaders in the freedom struggle were able to look beyond divisions and see the human being (including the British). Because of this, they were able to feel the pain of people. The outcome was democracy and remorse for your fellow human being. Pakistan's founders (probably as a result of their fears) were unable to see beyond divisions, and hence, the outcome was an unstable, undemocratic, remorseless system.'

Rahul Gandhi believes that remorse is more likely to be expressed in democratic societies. But I find that even in democracies it is usually absent. It is extraordinary that there was no remorse among the investment bankers on Wall Street after their moral failings had tipped the global economy into a recession in 2008. They were not contrite that their actions had resulted in millions of job losses around the world. They still expected bonuses to be paid, whether their company had lost or made money. It is as though they felt they had a God-given right to earn more than ordinary human beings. One does not object to paying bonuses to outstanding performers, but one does to mediocrities or to executives of companies whose profits decline. To be fair, a few investment banks like Goldman Sachs did show restraint, but the majority behaved like the French aristocracy just before the French Revolution. The *Economist*, a consistent supporter of the free market, asked, 'What will it take for bankers to show a little remorse?'[78]

The *Mahabharata* believes that *purushakara*, 'human initiative', matters. Despite the many occasions when its characters feel frustrated before the weight of circumstances, and despite blaming their feeling of impotence on *daiva*, 'fate', moral autonomy shines through in the epic. Because they have some freedom to choose they can be praised when they pursue dharma or blamed when they follow *adharma*. Yudhishthira in the end *chooses* not to become a 'non-violent' hermit like Jajali. He *elects* to become a just king, who he knows will have to resort to non-violent *danda*, 'punishment', in the pursuit of justice. When the epic's characters make free choices, they become responsible for their decisions. At the moment of making a decision they become conscious of their freedom, and it is this perception of autonomy that gives them the ability to lead authentic moral lives.[79]

Yudhishthira reflected and he showed the courage to choose between two kinds of lives. He made this choice identifying with all human beings, and this led him to the heart of dharma. He would have agreed with Alexander Solzhenitsyn who said, 'let the lie come into the world, even dominate the world, but not through me'.[80]

10

MAHABHARATA'S DHARMA

'Great king, you weep with all creatures'

One should never do to another what one regards as injurious to oneself. This, in brief, is the law of dharma.

—*Mahabharata* XVIII.113.8

'This dog is devoted to me'

Yudhishthira went on to rule justly for thirty-six years. But he found no pleasure in sovereignty because he could not forget the terrible slaughter of his kinsmen.[1] The Pandavas felt a lingering sadness in having to live on without their loved ones. Kunti, Dhritarashtra and Gandhari, who had gone to spend their last days in the forest, died in a forest fire. When Yudhishthira heard of their death, he lamented: 'We who are still alive are in fact dead.'[2]

The last three books of the epic, Books Sixteen to Eighteen, depict a time of twilight for our heroes. As the years go by there is a growing sense of weariness with life. Krishna, as we know, dies a banal and unremarkable death. As he lies resting on the banks of a river, a hunter mistakes his foot for a bird, shoots an arrow and kills him. After Krishna's death, the Pandavas find even less meaning in life. Arjuna, in particular, is sad and exhausted. His powers begin to wane. His bodily strength leaves him and his magical weapons no longer obey him.[3]

Eventually the disillusioned Pandavas decide it is time to leave the world.[4] Yudhishthira reminds Arjuna: 'Time cooks every creature in its cauldron.' They crown Abhimanyu's son Parikshit, Arjuna's grandson, who continues the dynasty at Hastinapura. (It is to Parikshit's son, Janamejaya, that the story of the *Mahabharata* is told at the beginning of Book One.) The Pandavas set out on foot towards the east, in the direction of the Himalayas.[5] On the way, Draupadi and Yudhishthira's brothers fall one by one. Yudhishthira trudges on alone, 'never looking down'. A stray dog follows him. As he nears heaven, Indra, king of the gods, approaches him in his celestial chariot.

'Get in,' says Indra, welcoming him to heaven.

'But this dog, O lord of the past and the future, is devoted to me. Let him come with me,' pleads Yudhishthira.

'You have become immortal like me,' says Indra. 'Leave the dog. There is nothing cruel in that. There is no place for dogs in heaven.'

'But people say that abandoning someone devoted to you', replies Yudhishthira, 'is a bottomless evil, equal—according to the general opinion—to killing a brahmin. And I think so too.'[6]

The god, Dharma, who has been present all along in the guise of the stray dog, transforms himself into his own form and speaks to Yudhishthira, offering affection and gentle words of praise:

> *Great king, you weep with all creatures. Because you turned down the celestial chariot, by insisting, 'This dog is devoted to me,' there is no one your equal in heaven. You have won the highest goal of going to heaven with your own body.*[7]

It had been a trial all along. Yudhishthira's father, Dharma, had been testing him. Recall, Kunti could not have children from Pandu. So, she employed a boon that she had received from a holy man. Thus, she had the gods sire her children. Yudhishthira was born from the god Dharma. The epic often refers to Yudhishthira as dharmaputra, Dharma's son, but he now meets his real father formally. Dharma is happy that his son has passed the test.

'Compassion is the highest dharma'

This was not his first trial, however. Dharma reminds him of their earlier meeting during a test in the Dvaita forest when the Pandavas were in exile.

Once upon a time, my son, I tested you in the Dvaita forest. Your brothers had died from thirst. [Given a chance of reviving only one of them] you abandoned Bhima and Arjuna, your own brothers, and chose to save the life of [your stepbrother] Nakula, because you wanted to deal equally with their two mothers [leaving each with a surviving son].[8]

The incident in question occurred towards the end of the Pandavas' exile, in their twelfth year in the wilderness, before they went into hiding and disguise at the court of Virata.[9] In their final days in the forest, a deer ran off with fire sticks which a brahmin was using in a holy sacrifice. In horror, the brahmin went to Yudhishthira for help to recover them from the deer's antlers, and the Pandavas set off in pursuit. The deer, however, eluded them. At the end of the day, exhausted and suffering from extreme thirst and hunger, they stopped below 'the cool shade of a banyan tree'.

Nakula expresses their accumulated frustration of the past twelve years in exile.

In our house dharma never sets,
Nor does our purpose fail because of idleness,
Then why do we, so superior to all creatures,
Suffer such difficulty, King?[10]

In short, 'why did this have to happen?' The past comes rushing back to the brothers. Bhima looks back and wishes that he had killed the man who had dragged Draupadi into the assembly; Arjuna blames himself for not killing the charioteer's son, Karna, after he had insulted Draupadi; Sahadeva regrets he did not slay Shakuni during the rigged game of dice.

Nakula then climbs on a tree to look for water. When he reaches the top, he hears the screeching of cranes, and thinking there must be water nearby he rushes off. He finds a pond but as he approaches it, a voice calls out to him: 'Do not act rashly; I have a prior claim. You may drink only after answering my questions.'[11] He pays the voice no heed, drinks the water, and falls down dead. One by one, the other brothers go to the pond and suffer the same fate. Finally, Yudhishthira arrives to find the bodies of his brothers along with a strange, one-eyed, fiery creature in the shape of a *baka*, heron, standing beside the water. The creature identifies itself as a Yaksha, a tree spirit, and demands answers to its questions. Unlike his brothers, Yudhishthira accepts the demand.

The Yaksha's questions are about the meaning of life but they are in the form of a verbal puzzle. Known as *prashnas*, these riddles are connected to an ancient speculative tradition going back to the Upanishads. Philosophical, sometimes metaphysical, the questions are formulaic, brief, and appear to be unanswerable.[12] Yudhishthira's life hangs on every answer. Dying of thirst and surrounded by his dead brothers, he is a tormented and embattled figure, something out of a Greek tragedy rather than out of a pastoral Upanishadic dialogue. In this chilling, surreal setting survival is at stake, not merely wisdom.[13]

The Yaksha asks a series of three one-line questions to which Yudhishthira provides three one-line answers. Many questions deal with the moral life—for example, what is happiness? Yudhishthira must have been thinking of his lonely exile when he answers this as follows: '[A person] who cooks vegetables in his own home, who has no debts and who is not in exile, [he] is truly happy.'[14]

The Yaksha next asks the baffling question, 'What is extraordinary?' Considering that a single error could mean his death, Yudhishthira's reply is cool, ironic and elegant: 'What is extraordinary is that one sees people dying every day, and one thinks that one will live forever. What could be more extraordinary!' The Yaksha then returns to the subject of human mortality as he asks the question, 'What is the news?' Yudhishthira replies baldly, 'Time cooks beings—that is the news.'[15] Thus, Yudhishthira replies satisfactorily to each of the Yaksha's questions. Finally, the Yaksha asks his most significant question: 'What is the highest dharma in the world?' Yudhishthira replies: 'Compassion is the highest dharma.'[16]

Yudhishthira uses an unusual Sanskrit word *anrishamsya* (pronounced as a-nri-shumsya) for 'compassion' rather than the more usual *karuna*.[17] It is the same word that the epic employs towards the end in describing Yudhishthira's virtuous attitude towards the stray dog.[18] Literally, it means possessing an attitude of non-*nri-shamsya*, which means one who does not injure; who is not mischievous, not-noxious, not-cruel, not-malicious.[19] It is a double negative, like *ahimsa*, and hence weak, but 'the word has more than a negative connotation; it signifies good-will, a fellow feeling, a deep sense of the other. [It is close to] *anukrosha*, to cry with another, to feel another's pain.'[20] When Indra praises Yudhishthira in the same episode above—'Great king, you weep with all creatures'—he employs *anukrosha*, which is also sometimes translated as 'compassion'. In any case, Yudhishthira's insistence on taking the stray dog into heaven certainly goes beyond 'uncruelty' or 'non-injury' and is closer to 'compassion' in English.[21]

The Yaksha is satisfied, and rewards Yudhishthira by agreeing to resurrect one of his fallen brothers. Faced with this painful and impossible choice, Yudhishthira does not hesitate. He selects

Nakula. Strange choice! Why not one of his real brothers, Arjuna or Bhima, born from his own mother? Yudhishthira explains that his father had two wives, whom he, Yudhishthira, regards as equal. He believes that each mother deserves to be left with a surviving son.

In making this choice, Yudhishthira demonstrates through his actions the significance of 'the highest truth of dharma': *anrishamsya*. This is no longer an academic discussion. Yudhishthira has 'put his money where his mouth is' as the Americans would say. The Yaksha appreciates his extraordinary choice, so much so that he rewards him by reviving all his dead brothers.

Yudhishthira's earlier answer to the Yaksha's question—what is man?—begins now to also make sense. He had answered the Yaksha by saying, 'The repute of a good deed touches heaven and earth; one is called a man as long as his repute lasts.'[22] In other words, a man is only as good as his deeds. And Yudhishthira has proven his own worth by choosing Nakula.

'Of what use is heaven to me?'

The reason that the father has now reminded his son of their earlier encounter in the forest also becomes clear. The virtue that Yudhishthira had displayed by choosing Nakula is the same as he has shown in his behaviour towards the stray dog. On passing his second test, Yudhishthira enters the triple-tiered heaven. The epic suggests that because Yudhishthira is 'bestowed with *a-nri-shamsya*', he has been given the rare honour of entering heaven with his body.[23]

In heaven, the first person Yudhishthira sees is Duryodhana 'luxuriating in glory, shining like the sun'.[24] He frowns at this but is told that Duryodhana is in heaven because he is a kshatriya hero who happened to die in battle. Yudhishthira cannot bear this injustice, and he turns away in disgust. He is reminded of his own brothers and of Draupadi. He looks around but he does not see them anywhere. Indra says, 'Even today the human state touches you, O king. [But] this is heaven.'[25]

'Best of the gods, of what use is heaven to me if I don't have my brothers ... this is no heaven in my opinion,' says Yudhishthira in bewilderment.[26]

A messenger of the gods then takes Yudhishthira on a journey to look for his brothers and Draupadi. On the way, he finds that the path is

covered with darkness, horrible, with hair for its moss and grass, full of the smells of evil-doers, with flesh and blood for its mud; covered with flies and mosquitoes, and with crickets with uprisings of biting insects, surrounded on all sides with corpses on this side and that; strewn with bones and hair, full of worms and maggots, surrounded on all sides by blazing fire; overrun with crows and vultures with iron beaks, and covered with ghosts the size of Vindhya mountains but with mouths like needles; with severed arms, thighs, and hands that are covered in fat and blood, and severed stomachs and feet scattered here and there; hair-raising with a bad smell of corpses.[27]

Revolted by what he has seen, Yudhishthira asks the messenger, 'How long do we have to go on this road?'[28]

The messenger replies, 'If you are tired, lord of the kings, let us go back.'[29]

Feeling depressed and faint, Yudhishthira is thinking of turning back when he suddenly hears the sad voices of his brothers, 'Royal sage, born of dharma, stop ... when you are nearby, a cool breeze blows which brings relief to us ... don't go away.'[30]

Draupadi and all of Yudhishthira's brothers, including Karna, are in hell. Yudhishthira wonders why. Did someone make a mistake? Or 'am I asleep?' He remembers Duryodhana luxuriating in heaven, and gets angry again. Overwhelmed by grief, he curses the gods, including Dharma, and tells the messenger to go back. 'I am staying,' he says with finality.

As he utters these words, the hellish vision disappears. Dharma appears and says, 'I tested you before by taking on the form of a dog, and now this was another test, and you chose to stay in hell for the sake of your brothers.' Indra explains:

> *Great armed, Yudhishthira, don't be angry ... All kings have to see hell ... There are two piles—one of good and another of evil. He who first enjoys his good deeds must afterwards go to hell. And he who experiences hell must go to heaven. Those with the majority of bad karma come first to heaven. You had to see a vision of hell because you deceived Drona on the battlefield on that day about his son's death ... [But] come, come now, and let this fire in your mind disappear.*[31]

At this, the Pandava heroes and the Kaurava anti-heroes lose their human condition.[32] They are transformed into the divine state from which they had emerged and go on to worlds 'beyond which there is nothing'.[33] Thus, the *Mahabharata* ends.

A pair of sparrows nest on Jajali's head

As Yudhishthira was trying to cope with dashed heroic expectations, I was reminded of my own quest to understand dharma, which too was nearing its end. In 'weeping with all the creatures', Yudhishthira taught me that moral integrity begins with the awareness of other human beings. The reality of others looms large in Yudhishthira's consciousness—it is the shining feature of his personality, which leads him to 'the highest dharma'. In the last chapter, I had gone along with him when he was reeling under the impact of the war. I had concurred with his formulation that *ahimsa* (non-violence) was the highest virtue. Now I felt that his behaviour during his three tests—first, in reviving Nakula rather than his blood brothers, second, in insisting on taking a stray dog into heaven, and finally, in preferring to stay with his brothers and his wife in hell rather than return to heaven—entailed something other than *ahimsa*, 'not harming others'. It was a stronger, more positive attitude, exhibiting *maitri*, 'benevolence', which is entailed in acting 'for the sake of others', and this is ultimately 'the highest dharma'.

Jajali had learned the same lesson. We had left Jajali in the previous chapter when he was attracted to self-effacing Tuladhara, who believed in living his life like a twig randomly borne along in a stream. Jajali returned to the forest filled with a desire to become selfless and detached like him.[34] I too was struck by Tuladhara's attitude. He does not seek praise and leads his life avoiding harm to others; he does not cut trees to construct his house; he sells only legal merchandise and he weighs it honestly and gives proper change to customers. Tuladhara seems to be happy to go along with life's flow without trying to impose his ego.[35] Yet something in Tuladhara's detached and passive attitude left me uneasy. It was similar to the discomfort I had felt in Chapters 4 and 5 with regard to Krishna's advice to Arjuna about *nishkama karma* as the war was about to begin. My unease with Tuladhara gradually led to admiration for the new Jajali after he returned to the jungle.

Late in Book Twelve, Yudhishthira asks Bhishma, 'What are the meritorious works Jajali performed by which he achieved this great success?'[36] Bhishma takes up the thread of Jajali's life:

> At one time the great ascetic, fasting, subsisting on air, stood as steady as a piece of wood, never moving at all. As he stood motionless like a tree trunk, O Bharata, a pair of sparrows made their nest on his head. The wise seer compassionately disregarded that couple as they made their nest in his hair with the straws of grass. As the great ascetic, acting as a tree trunk, never made the slightest movement, the pair happily dwelt there [on his head] in complete confidence.[37]

Bhishma describes to Yudhishthira how the birds slowly gained confidence from their intimacy and became infatuated with love. When the monsoon season had passed and autumn came, the birds married 'according to the dowry-less rite' and laid eggs on Jajali's head. 'In the fullness of time, [baby] birds were born; and the ascetic became aware of those little birds [who had now] sprouted wings.' Jajali might have shooed the birds away, but he did not. As a result, he changed from a self-absorbed person who cared only for his own achievements to someone who cared for others. From a self-centred person he became altruistic. Tuladhara, observing what has happened, says to Jajali, 'The birds, cherished by you, cherish [you as their] father; and assuredly you are their father. Call them [your] children, Jajali.'³⁸ Tuladhara likens Jajali's altruism to the natural sentiments of parents for their children. Just as Jajali cherished the birds, so will they esteem him. 'In this story, Jajali's kindness is never repaid—and indeed, like a parent's, it never can be fully repaid.'³⁹

The birds remind Jajali that the obstacle in the way of achieving this new dharma is Jajali's earlier competitive egoism (*spardha*), which is not only harmful to his personality but also diminishes his karma:

> *Thereupon Jajali summoned the birds, [and] verily at the behest of dharma, they sang with wonderful voices, [saying:] 'Competitiveness destroys in this world and the next the merit generated by harmlessness and the like, O Brahman. If [competitiveness] is not destroyed, it destroys the person [who is so afflicted]. We have alighted together [on you] out of a sense of dharma, wishing to put you to the test. Strike down [your] competitiveness.*⁴⁰

The birds suggest that there exists an order in the universe which is based on karma and dharma. Good behaviour grounded in dharma earns good karma. The birds warn Jajali that his accumulation of *ahimsa*-generated merit will be dissipated by *spardha*, 'excessive competitiveness'.⁴¹

Tuladhara and Jajali's story reminded me again of the limitations of selflessness. Tuladhara upholds the ideal of equanimity—of going through life disinterestedly like a piece of wood flowing randomly in the river without seeking the approval or applause of society. While such a person is attractive and superior to the earlier Jajali, who was filled with competitive egoism, his detached and disinterested attitude also runs the risk of becoming uncaring and uninvolved. It is not natural for birds to nest on human heads. But if one has dusty and matted hair and stands stationary in the forest for a long time, then birds will be tempted. In providing a resting place for the sparrows, Jajali expressed the sort of affectionate behaviour that human beings save for their children. It becomes altruism when such concern is expressed towards strangers. The later Jajali's positive feeling of compassion and benevolence towards the birds does seem to express a superior dharma.

The heart of moral virtue

What is one to make of Yudhishthira's insistence in taking a stray dog into heaven? His blunt explanation to Indra is that the dog is a *bhakta*—he is 'devoted' to him. Indra's negative response is also predictable within a tradition that considers a dog *asprishya*, 'unclean'. The loyal nature of the dog, however, trumps traditional prejudice. Because Yudhishthira 'weeps with all creatures', humans and animals alike, he is rewarded with the unique distinction of being allowed to take his own body into heaven. (Other humans who qualify for heaven are merely given a new 'heavenly' body.) The other striking thing about this episode is that the god, Dharma, incarnates himself as an animal, and an unclean one. 'It is as if the God of the Hebrew Bible became incarnate in a pig.'[42] The epic has thus made another ethical point. Compassion, godliness and heaven must extend to all creatures.

At the centre of Yudhishthira's *anrishamsya* is the empathetic question: how would I feel if it was I who was suffering? I would be more inclined to feel compassion towards the other person's suffering if I realized that I am equally vulnerable and the suffering could be mine. This empathetic thought helps to remove barriers with other persons, especially barriers created by class and caste. Yudhishthira's empathy extends all the way to a stray dog. The 'thought of similarity is not absolutely necessary as a conceptual condition: we can in principle feel compassion for others without seeing their predicament as like one that we could experience. Our compassion for the sufferings of animals is a fine example: we are indeed similar to animals in many ways, but we don't need that thought in order to see that what they suffer is bad, and in order to have compassion for them.'[43]

Yudhishthira's *anrishamsya* is a form of altruism, and it is at the heart of moral virtue. It was the French philosopher Auguste Comte who first used the word *'altruisme'*. It came into the English language through Comte's translators in mid-nineteenth century England, where it created something of a sensation in the Victorian Age.[44] Comte taught that 'the grand duty of life [is to] . . . strengthen the social affections by constant habit and by referring all our actions to them' and 'moral discipline should have but one object, to make altruism . . . predominate over egoism'. The Victorians were obsessed with selflessness and were quick to observe a conflict between altruistic duty and selfish inclination. The characters in Victorian novels judge each other constantly, especially when it comes to vanity and selfishness. They weave their narratives between the poles of egoism and altruism. George Eliot, in particular, shows a very deep concern with altruism. But even she does not adopt Comte's extreme position, which makes it an obligation for *all* our actions to benefit others. Neither does the pragmatic *Mahabharata* go that far.

Today, when ordinary people use the word 'altruism', they invariably think of noble acts of self-sacrifice. This places altruism on a pedestal and beyond the reach of the common person. I favour a more modest understanding of the word, one that has to do with limiting one's interests by a constant awareness of others' interests. The *Mahabharata* does not clarify what it means by *anrishamsya*. But in preferring to give up heaven for the sake of a stray dog or choosing to revive his stepbrother before his own, Yudhishthira did reinforce the self-sacrificing connotation of the word.

Our contemporary usage of altruism has been deeply influenced by the Christian idea of charity. It influenced the eighteenth-century philosopher Francis Hutcheson, for example, who believed that a man's duty is 'calm universal benevolence', a virtue that requires one to further the good of others. His contemporary David Hume, however, did not think that one's love of mankind could stretch that far.[45] He conceded that human beings did have 'benevolent dispositions', such as sympathy for other individuals. When one sees a person in trouble, one feels sympathy and this makes one want to help her or him. Obviously, one's sympathy is greater for one's family and friends, but it also extends to strangers.[46] But this is a far cry from 'calm, universal benevolence' or Comte's idea that all our actions should benefit others.

In Chapter 5, I drew a distinction between two types of self-directed acts. The first benefits the agent but it might also harm others, and one calls it 'selfish'. The second type of action simply furthers the agent's interest without harming others, such as waking up in the morning or carrying an umbrella when it rains. In the same way, one can make a distinction between acts that take the interests of others into account versus those actions that are positively intended to benefit others. We commonly use the word 'altruism' to refer to the latter, and this is also the sense in which the *Mahabharata* uses *anrishamsya*. Comte fully expects that when one thinks of the beneficiaries of one's actions, it ought to be humanity as a whole and not merely family, neighbours, or even one's fellow countrymen. Limiting compassion to the latter would mean being 'partial' or 'selfish' towards a particular group.

Comte deeply influenced the English thinker John Stuart Mill, who wrote famously that 'selfishness [is] the principal cause which makes life unsatisfactory'. He hoped that the advance of civilization would lead to 'a fellow-feeling with the collective interests of mankind'.[47] He was enthusiastic about Comte's 'Religion of Humanity', and thought it superior to traditional religion. He disliked Christianity because it appealed to man's selfish motives in pursuit of salvation and heaven. Later Utilitarians thought that the duty of benevolence was excessive and argued that, 'I have a duty to help others but without hurting myself.' If I hurt myself then total utility in the world would diminish.

One cannot escape the considerable irony in the Victorian rhetoric of furthering the interests of humanity at the height of Britain's empire in the late nineteenth and the early twentieth centuries. This is, perhaps, the reason that Victorians went to considerable lengths to reassure themselves that colonial conquests were part of a 'civilizing mission'. To move from one's duties to all human beings towards those especially beneath one's social scale was merely a logical step taken by the socialists and Labour Party intellectuals in England. 'It was during the middle decades of the nineteenth century that in England the impulse of self-subordinating service was transferred, consciously and overtly, from God to man.'[48] The *Mahabharata*'s dharma of *anrishamsya* is strikingly similar. It too 'subordinates' the self for the sake of others; its focus is on man rather than God. The quest for 'dharma' is more important than the quest for 'God' in the epic, something quite remarkable in a semi-religious text.

How would I feel if it was I who was suffering?

It is all very well to conclude, as the *Mahabharata* does, that *anrishamsya* is the highest dharma, but can the ordinary person, in fact, behave altruistically and do so consistently? Most people that I know are usually considerate to their family and friends, but it is rare to find someone who consistently acts keeping others' interests in mind. Hence the question: can the interest of others motivate human beings in significant numbers?

What is there in human nature that would make one want to further other people's well being or happiness? One can answer this question by posing another one: 'How would you feel if someone did that to you?'[49] One usually thinks of the latter in a context when one is a victim or when one does not want to be hurt. But it might also help explain benevolent behaviour. When one puts oneself in the shoes of another person, even in a hypothetical situation, it forces one to acknowledge the reality of others. Exchanging places with another makes one realize something about oneself. This self-discovery about one's attitude to one's own needs comes with the awareness that these are 'simply *someone's* needs, desires, and interests rather than [mine]'.[50] The reason to help another person is simply that *someone* is in need of help. In admitting that one does not like to be harmed, one is making a rational judgement. One realizes that altruism is not only possible, it is the sensible and rational way to behave.

For rare individuals—Yudhishthira, Mahatma Gandhi, Jesus Christ—the other person was very real in their imaginations. They did not have to play this thought game. For most of us, however, the 'other' is remote, and it is useful to try to put ourselves in their place. It leads us to 'an objective element in the concern we feel for ourselves, and generalizing from that'.[51]

A tough-minded egoist like Duryodhana will reject a sentiment like *anrishamsya*, dismissing it as typically weak behaviour on the part of a weak individual like Yudhishthira. He firmly believes that one acts only to further one's interest. If someone needed his help, Duryodhana would probably reply, 'what's in it for me?' The answer to Duryodhana's question is the opposite one: what if you were in extreme distress which could easily be relieved by another person, would you want that person to ask, 'What's in it for me'?

What if you had a gouty toe and it was under Bhima's heel? 'The pain which gives him a reason to remove his gouty toes from under another person's heel does not in itself give the other [person a] reason to remove the heel, since it is not his pain. Anyone who thinks he is an egoist should imagine himself in either role in such a situation. Can he truly affirm that the owner of the heel has no reason whatever to remove it from the gouty toes? Particularly if one owns the toes, it shows a rare detachment not to regard the pain as simply in itself a bad thing, which there is reason for anyone to avert,' says Thomas Nagel.[52] If Duryodhana were to try to imagine that he was the victim of pain and Bhima could relieve it, he would then expect Bhima to act compassionately. It would be the rational course of action as the position of the victim and the oppressor could be reversed. Thus, Duryodhana is not able to sustain his position of ethical egoism.

Immanuel Kant also believed that the duty of altruism flows from human reason. It is irrational not to help others knowing that one may need their help one day.[53] The question—how would you like it if someone did that to you?—appeals to human reason as well as the human ability to empathize with others. Hence, 'the force of altruism springs from our common humanity'.[54]

Even though I think that altruism is rational and sensible, I do not feel capable of acting like Yudhishthira. As I approached the end of the *Mahabharata*, I felt torn between an ideal and a practical way to live. While I admired Yudhishthira's ideal of *anrishamsya*, I did not think it could serve as a moral rule for ordinary people. As we were walking one day in Lodhi Gardens near my house, my philosopher friend Vineet Haksar reminded me of the difference between moral rules and moral ideals.[55] One ought to punish a person for being unjust but one can only dislike or despise him for not being compassionate.[56] Christians will recognize this distinction—the Ten Commandments are moral rules which inform us of our duties. The Sermon on the

Mount offers us moral ideals. Moral rules are the minimum demands of behaviour that a civilized society expects from its members. We do not expect our friends to be saints or heroes, but we expect them to be 'second best' and obey the rules. John Stuart Mill made a similar distinction between a *perfect* obligation to obey moral duties and an *imperfect* obligation to obey moral ideals.

A society without saints and heroes would be impoverished, however. Moral rules and moral ideals have different functions.[57] Having followed Yudhishthira on his dharma journey, I can only say that a moral ideal like *anrishamsya* has an awesome quality. Even though it is seemingly unattainable, it is inspiring and capable of stirring us to action. When Mahatma Gandhi turned the other cheek to the British colonial rulers, he was holding up an ideal of moral perfection. The ideals of dharma, by inspiring us, can give significance to a life that might otherwise be adrift.

The making of an 'un-hero'

Yudhishthira must have wondered after his third and final test, how long is this testing business to go on? When he came down into hell from heaven, he cried in anguish:

> *Did someone make a mistake? Am I asleep? I am in pain and my mind is disoriented.*[58]

Since he did not receive a satisfactory answer, he cursed the gods. For someone who has just been praised so lavishly by the gods—'great king, there is no one your equal in heaven'—it did seem a tad ungracious to reciprocate a compliment with a curse.

Yet, as I think about it, there is only so much that a man can take. The 'mistake' that the tormented Yudhishthira mentions seems to have been made a long time ago. Otherwise, why would he, at the very moment of his greatest triumph—after being consecrated 'king of kings'—have had to play and lose in a rigged game of dice? And his queen, Draupadi—why did she have to be humiliated before an assembly of nobles? Because of the same 'mistake', he and the Pandavas had to suffer thirteen years in exile. After they came back from exile, Duryodhana did not return their kingdom, and he had to fight a war when he would have been happy to live peacefully with his brothers in five villages. Even after he did win the bloody war, it turned out to be a hollow victory as he had to rule over an empty kingdom. If this was not enough, Yudhishthira is rewarded in the end with a series of tests. Talk about mistakes—life has been a non-stop blunder as far as he is concerned. Dharma has been failing him continuously since the beginning.

There is, of course, the possibility that Yudhishthira's problem may have something to do with the fact that the world itself lacks balance—the epic calls it an 'uneven' world.[59] The human condition might be defective. 'Dharma is opaque because our experience is opaque.'[60] Like every human being Yudhishthira yearns for an 'even', predictable world in which the good are rewarded and the bad are punished. But in a world where the rules of the game are determined by a loaded game of dice, enigma and opacity are man's destiny. Draupadi's question in the forest did go to the heart of the matter. She had asked, 'What kind of a world is it where the good suffer and the wicked prosper?' He has never truly owned up to the possibility that our world may be at odds with dharma. Suffering and happiness may be irrelevant to dharma. This world does not care for *my* suffering. So, why be good?

It is not that we were not warned. Perhaps, we did not pick up the signals. Did Krishna not tell Gandhari, who was grieving for her sons at the end of the war, that the *Mahabharata* was divinely pre-planned in order to rid the earth of kshatriyas?[61] This is the epic's way of reminding us that human lives are vulnerable—there is much in this world that we do not control. The *Mahabharata* calls this uncontrollable sphere *daiva*, 'fate'. Yudhishthira recognizes his vulnerability, but being the sort of person he is, he also realizes that his defencelessness is the same as that of the next person. From this thought empathy is born. For him the suffering of a hungry peasant matters, unlike most of us who see the peasant as a distant object. Yudhishthira is able to bring the peasant into his circle of concern and this leads him to the 'highest dharma' of *anrishamsya*.[62]

We begin to understand our hero. Yudhishthira's anguished curse at the end of the *Mahabharata* is an existential protest against the unsatisfactory human condition. It is a cry of frustration against at least two injustices—of having to live in a world where goodness is not necessarily met with goodness; and having to die suddenly without any explanation from anyone. His angry cry at the end is a reaction to 'the central condition of the world of the epic, where action is contingent, where right and wrong behaviour exist but there is no overarching morality, no super-potent or binding system of rules . . . The *Mahabharata*'s time is one in which the end is always imminent [just as] death hangs over every warrior in the battle.'[63] This reluctant kshatriya conducts a war in this opaque world, but he is able to learn something from it, and it leads him to *ahimsa*. Despite his own painful experiences in the uneven world, he is able to think of the other person's suffering, and it leads him to *anrishamsya*. Hence, he offers refuge to a stray dog before going into heaven. While in heaven, he thinks only of the distress of his brothers and of Draupadi, and chooses to go to hell to be with them.

I had earlier compared Yudhishthira's situation to that of Sisyphus. Recall, Sisyphus was condemned by the gods to push a rock up a hill. Just as the rock reaches the top it comes rolling down, and he must begin his futile labour all over again. The look on Sisyphus's face at seeing the rock go down is similar to Yudhishthira's during his third and final test in hell. On the faces of both men is written the absurd, vulnerable human condition in which the only certainty is that 'time cooks all beings'.[64]

It is Yudhishthira's destiny to keep on searching for the dharma

that 'is hidden in a cave'. Having rejected the comfortable,
kshatriya *sva-dharma* of his family and society, he is an *anayaka*,
'un-hero', who treads the lonely path in search of a different
dharma—one that lies within his own conscience. By being true
to this different dharma of goodness, he creates his own meaning
in an inscrutable world. This is how he defies the 'time cooker'.[65]

By choosing to live in a certain way, Yudhishthira creates
moral value, and this serves as a shield against human
vulnerability. Despite repeated references to *daiva*, 'fate', what
shines through is the value of human effort in the *Mahabharata*.
Plato and Aristotle tried to cope with human defencelessness by
demonstrating the power of human reason, which could help
make human beings more self-sufficient.[66] Immanuel Kant
believed that the moral value of the human being's 'good will'
helped to protect a person from uncertainty. In the same way
Yudhishthira has snatched victory in dharma from the tragedy
of a dark war, 'which so disillusioned both sides that everyone
was plunged into confusion and despair in the end'.[67]

Conclusion

The difficulty of being good

With uplifted arms I cry, but no one heeds;
from dharma flow wealth and pleasure.
Then why is dharma not pursued?

—*Mahabharata* XVIII.5.49

It was my grandmother who first introduced me to the *Mahabharata*. When I was four, and India was still undivided, she would take me along on her social rounds in Lyallpur. She would be dressed in a starched white sari and we would set off at eleven in the morning in our horse-drawn carriage, sometimes to mourn a death and at other times to celebrate a birth or even an engagement. On the way home she would take a longer route and reward me with a story from the epic. I would listen with fear and pity to these stories of her great heroes.[1]

My grandmother had no doubt that the events actually happened. They had taken place before our degraded times when the gods mingled with men, and human beings were more inclined to adhere to dharma. She had a sense of cosmic time and she believed that the epic was a true account of the deeds of her righteous ancestors in the Punjab, who with the aid of God, Sri Krishna, defeated unrighteous foes. She had faith in the continuity of our tradition and regarded the epics as *itihasa*, 'history'.[2] She also felt that the *Mahabharata* was a divine work

276

and, hence, she would have found my attempts at grasping the epic's dharma in ironic, human terms as mildly distasteful.[3]

When I went to school, I forgot the *Mahabharata*. Ever since India became a secular republic in 1947, our educational establishment has been somewhat shy about teaching the epic in our schools in the mistaken belief that it is a 'religious' text. I returned to it only after I took early retirement from my business career, in response to my 'third stage melancholy'. I discovered that like any great work, one can read the *Mahabharata* at many levels. It is a cosmic allegory of the eternal struggle between good and evil on one plane. At another level, it is about an all-too-human fight between the cousins of a royal family, which leads to a war and ends tragically in the death of almost everyone. At a third level—and this is primarily the subject of my book—it is about the crisis of conscience of some of its characters.

After spending six years continuously with the epic, I have learned that the *Mahabharata* is about the way we deceive ourselves, how we are false to others, how we oppress fellow human beings, and how deeply unjust we are in our day-to-day lives. But is this moral blindness an intractable human condition, or can we change it? Some of our misery is the result of the way the state also treats us, and can we redesign our institutions to have a more sympathetic government? I have sought answers to these questions in the epic's elusive concept of dharma, and my own search for how we ought to live has been this book's motivating force.

Anrishamsya: the answer to my third stage melancholy

During my business career I worked in a number of countries, and I found everywhere that middle-class parents wanted their children to grow up to be more like Arjuna and less like Yudhishthira. They wanted them to be talented and successful, and become winners in life's rat race. Indeed, the pursuit of competitive success and status seems to be hard-wired in human genes. Sometimes, however, this ideal gets shaken, as it did in 2009 by the Satyam scandal, whose reverberations were felt around the world. In the Prelude, I asked if the *Mahabharata* might offer some insight into why B. Ramalinga Raju, the founder of the highly successful software company Satyam, committed one of the great corporate frauds of all time. He had everything going for him—success, money, fame and power. He had created an outstanding world class company; why did a person of such extraordinary achievement turn to crime?

Even as the story was unfolding, it seemed clear to me that the moral failing was not greed as everyone thought. Nor was it a Duryodhana-like *hubris*, which made Raju believe, like investment bankers on Wall Street, that he was 'master of the universe'. Was it, perhaps, that Raju's stake in Satyam had dwindled to 8.6 per cent, and the company was in danger of slipping out of the family's control? Raju has two sons and a sense of filial duty drove him, perhaps, to create companies in real estate and infrastructure, two sectors of the Indian economy that had not been reformed, and where politicians insisted on bribes to be paid upfront for favours delivered. Since revenues from the new companies were far away, Raju dipped into Satyam to pay the politicians. It might have worked if the price of real estate had continued to rise. But no one counted on a downturn and a liquidity crisis. Desperately, Raju tried to restore the stolen assets to Satyam by merging it with his son's companies but that did not work.

Raju was ruined by his Dhritarashtra-like weakness for his sons. The *Mahabharata* seems to be saying that one ought to nurture one's children, but one does not have to indulge them like Duryodhana, nor leave them a company each, and certainly not by crossing the line of dharma. It takes moral courage to resist the sentiment of partiality towards one's family. Yudhishthira, as we have seen, challenges the old *sva-dharma* of family and caste in the epic, preferring instead the newer, universal *sadharana-dharma*, which teaches one to behave with impartiality towards everyone.

Ramalinga Raju's story caused much discomfort in the Indian middle class because it challenged its unexamined definition of success. It forced them to ask if there is another way to live. Yudhishthira also challenged the kshatriya concept of success in the *Mahabharata*, reminding us to give equal status to persons who are kind, considerate, and who are guided by *ahimsa* and *anrishamsya*.[4] Soon after I took early retirement at age fifty, I met a fourteen-year-old low-caste boy named Raju in a village in Tamil Nadu. His ambition was to grow up to run a computer company and become 'the richest man in the world like Bill Gates'. I applauded this boy for thinking big because he reflected the spirit of a new, self-confident, decolonized India.[5] A dozen years later I find myself holding up to this younger Raju the cautionary tale of the other Raju of Satyam. There is a fine line between healthy ambition and selfish greed, but it is very real.

Yudhishthira's insistence on taking a stray dog into heaven was the defining moment of my own dharma journey. His defiance of the conventional life helped to shake me out of my third stage melancholy. Even though at times the world appeared to be a rigged game of dice and the prize seemed to go to wicked Duryodhana, Yudhishthira remained firm like tormented Dido in the *Aeneid* who said, 'Not inexperienced in suffering, I learn how to bring aid to the wretched.' He went on to become a dharmic king who identified with the suffering of his subjects— not only human subjects, but all sentient beings, including stray dogs. In this way he gave meaning to a life without intrinsic meaning, one in which the only certainty, he keeps reminding us, is that 'time cooks all beings'.[6]

In Chapter 3, I raised the question about the nature of the good life. Is it to die young in battle and go to heaven? Or should one live a long, peaceful, and probably unremarkable dharmic life of non-violence and compassion? Where does true honour lie? This question certainly was the driving force behind the Pandavas' search for the meaning of dharma, but I also felt that it was relevant to my own search for meaning. I had felt the emptiness of conventional success. When Yudhishthira says after the war, 'This victory seems like defeat', it was as though he was expressing my feelings at the height of my corporate career.

After emerging victorious from the Kurukshetra War, Yudhishthira feels responsible for the suffering of so many and is filled with remorse. From remorse is born his commitment to *ahimsa*, 'non-violence'. When the epic says, 'Great king, you weep with all creatures', it announces the next step in Yudhishthira's moral journey. When the feeling of having wronged a specific individual is transformed to a general feeling of *anrishamsya*, 'compassion for others', one has made the leap. One learns to identify not only with their suffering, but also their happiness. One begins to 'rejoice with those who rejoice'. This leads to acts of benevolence. Both *ahimsa* and *anrishamsya* are double negatives, but obviously they do not have a weak connotation in Sanskrit as double negatives do in English. They require the acknowledging of the other person as the *Mahabharata* reminds us:

Who has in his heart always the well-being of others, and is wholly given, in acts, thoughts, and in speech, to the good of others, he alone knows what dharma is.[7]

Yudhishthira has come to understand the right way to engage with the world.

What comes in the way of engaging correctly with the world is human vanity, whose many faces the *Mahabharata* displays in abundance. Vanity in the form of mischievous *ahamkara*, 'the I-maker', enslaves human beings, and is sometimes expressed as Duryodhana's envy, or Dhritarashtra's hypocrisy, or Karna's status anxiety, or Ashwatthama's revengeful emotions. Vanity is an irresistible aspect of the human condition and it invariably spoils our engagement with the world.[8] It is so powerful and persistent that if all the gods died vanity would still survive. Sometimes it comes from our attachment to the pride and prestige of our family's past, but much of it is of our own making. Hence, the famous Vedic invocation to Varuna: 'Lord, release us from the deceits of our ancestors and from those that we have perpetrated ourselves.'

When Yudhishthira rejects the kshatriya tradition of dharma, he teaches us to question society's values rather than lead an unquestioning life. This is what, I suppose, Socrates also meant when he asserted that the 'unexamined life is not worth living'.[9] I had never quite reflected on my life in this deliberate way. I had just assumed that one really did not have a choice in these matters. When Kripa tried to restrain Ashwatthama from committing his heinous act of revenge, he told him the story of two farmers. One works hard, ploughs his field and when it rains, he reaps a fine harvest. The other idles, wastes his time in drink. One cannot ensure that it will rain but one does have a choice in tilling one's field. One does not control the outcome of one's acts, but one can *choose* to work or not.[10] The *Mahabharata*'s position is quite clear—human initiative does matter even though there is much beyond one's control. Kant believed that it is at 'the moment of choosing' that one truly experiences one's autonomy. Yudhishthira shows the way. After losing the rigged game of dice, he confronts the arbitrariness of the world by choosing to live a certain kind of life despite the protests of his family. He *decides* to stick to his word and stay true to his conscience.[11]

On more than one occasion, I wondered why the climactic scene in a heroic epic has a stray dog following an indecisive, non-competitive 'un-hero', who is bent on questioning dharma when he ought to be upholding it. The *Mahabharata* ought to have concluded in a glorious, martial panorama featuring the magnificent Arjuna—'the Indian Achilles'.[12] It might even have closed with Duryodhana dying on the battlefield. Instead the epic goes on to recount the inglorious and melancholic old age of its heroes, expressing profound disappointment with heroic expectations. There is sadness and profound awareness of mortality at the sunset of its heroes' lives. This mood finally precipitates the Pandavas' decision to retire from the world and enter *sanyasa*, the fourth stage of life.[13]

If Yudhishthira had abdicated his throne in Arjuna's favour and gone off to the forest to pursue an ascetic life, it would have confirmed my initial, uninformed prejudice against Hindu ethics. From my stray readings of historians, I had acquired the notion that traditional Indian dharma was passive and quietist. I believed that Indian tradition valued above all else not harming others, not speaking harshly or dishonestly, keeping one's anger in check, and tolerating insults without retaliation. In short, the emphasis was on negative virtues—*not* doing wrong, *not* injuring—rather than on positively striving to help others and doing good.

I began to question this unthinking assumption towards the end of the Pandavas' exile in Book Three, when Yudhishthira chose to revive his stepbrother, Nakula, rather than one of his real brothers. The *Mahabharata* reinforces the value of compassion in another tale in Book Thirteen, in which a parrot who lives in a tree remains loyal. After the tree is struck by a hunter's poisoned arrow, it begins to wither. The other birds abandon it, but the parrot remains loyal and stays on. Indra is so delighted with the parrot's altruistic act that he revives the tree.[14] This is merely a preview to the grand acts of altruism that Yudhishthira displays at the end—insisting on taking a stray dog into heaven and preferring to stay in hell to comfort his family rather than go to heaven.

Both ethical tendencies sit side by side in the *Mahabharata* (and in the broad Indian tradition, I imagine), highlighting the need for both Jajali's positive and Tuladhara's negative virtues. Goodness entails actively helping those in need as well as passively not harming others and being fair and just in one's judgements. Mahatma Gandhi tried to combine the two. He fought for a nation's freedom in the public space, but challenged himself constantly in the private space with regard to the negative virtues. His political philosophy of non-cooperation and passive resistance combined the two virtues. Gandhi believed, like Seneca, that 'what we achieve inwardly will change outer reality'. If this is too ambitious for ordinary persons, and if they cannot change the external environment, they can at least try and transform themselves.

How does one learn *anrishamsya*? Listening to or reading the *Mahabharata*'s moral tale is a good place to start. Like all good literature, it is a conduit for expanding the mind and cultivating a moral sensibility. Yudhishthira teaches by example and not by 'ethical prophecy'.[15] It is not easy to become virtuous; it requires a leap from thought to action, and it takes painstaking effort to learn to identify with people whom one dislikes or to whom one is indifferent.[16] It is best to begin by trying to empathize with *one* individual.[17]

When turning the other cheek sends a wrong signal

When Yudhishthira made the reluctant decision to go to war, he was following a more practical and achievable dharma. In making this decision he was aware that while *ahimsa*, non-violence, is the ideal way to act, violence is inevitable when one is up against a certain kind of adversary. He was acting according to a middle path which is the foundation of justice in society and the basis of moral rules. It is situated somewhere between the unacceptable amoralist position of Duryodhana and the guileless 'super-morality' of the earlier Yudhishthira in Book Three and embraces the moral ideals of *ahimsa* and *anrishamsya*, which the later

Yudhishthira tries to live up to after he is chastened by the Kurukshetra War.

The *Mahabharata*'s middle path is grounded in enlightened self-interest, which pragmatic, upright statesmen like Bhishma and Krishna, who have the responsibility of running a state, must try to follow. In a world of power politics, the dharma of the leader cannot be moral perfection. It is closer to Edmund Burke's 'prudence', which he called a 'god of this lower world'. The political ideology of the *Mahabharata* rejects both the amorality of Duryodhana as well as the idealistic position of the earlier Yudhishthira in exile. It is akin to the evolutionary principle of reciprocal altruism, which socio-biologists have made popular in recent decades: adopt a friendly face to the world but do not allow yourself to be exploited. This down-to-earth approach is based on the assumption that there will always be cheats in the world like Duryodhana and they must be kept in check. Turning the other cheek sends them a wrong signal that cheating pays.

Prudence does not mean that one merely weighs the pros and cons of going to war as King Dhritarashtra does.[18] The claims of dharma are part of the deliberations of the prudent ruler of the middle path, as Yudhishthira shows. He is weighed down with moral concerns during the peace negotiations even as he is more and more resigned to the inevitability of war:

Why should a man knowingly go to war?
Who cursed by his fate would choose war?
The Parthas who hunger for happiness act
For the fullness of dharma and the common weal.[19]

To make sure his moral conflicts are not misunderstood for weakness, he reminds Sanjaya: 'I am just as capable of peace as I am of war . . . as I am of gentleness and severity.'[20]

Nevertheless, Yudhishthira is profoundly embarrassed after the war and like the Buddhist emperor Ashoka, he feels ashamed and guilty for 'having killed those who ought not to be killed'.

He begins to see an inherent contradiction between ruling a state and being good. He wants to renounce the world and become a hermit. To avert a crisis of the throne the dying Bhishma instructs him in Book Twelve. Yudhishthira learns that a human being also has the responsibility to fulfil the 'worldly' goals of life. To try to escape from the world of action means that one loses something valuable. The *Mahabharata*, thus, asserts the realm of politics against the contemplative path of 'the renouncer', which had taken such a mesmerizing hold on young people of its time. The duty of the king, moreover, is to enforce *danda*, the rod of force, which is embodied in the laws of justice. A just ruler must employ the police and the army in order to protect the innocent. As Bhishma puts it: 'If the rod of force did not exist in this world, beings would be nasty and brutish ... because they fear punishment, beings do not kill each other.'[21]

In the end, Yudhishthira is persuaded of the necessity of *via active*, 'the life of action'. He assumes the throne, albeit reluctantly, and goes on to become a great and just king, making his kingdom fertile, prosperous and secure. He eschews the 'ethic of ultimate ends', accepting Bhishma's advice that an 'ethic of responsibility' is more appropriate to political life and not the purity of one's soul.[22] When dharmic goodness and ideology become the driving force of politics then room for negotiation and compromise is significantly diminished and this makes for a dangerous world. He has understood that societies are held together by 'laws, customs and moral habits', and it is these that make up dharma, whose rules are meant to get citizens to collaborate rather than to fight.[23]

The moral temper of the *Mahabharata* is, thus, pragmatic.[24] Its ideal is a world of sociable human beings who find reward in the nobility of character. What that 'nobility' consists of is contentious and is the source of tension right to the end of the epic. It has a place in it both for *danda*, 'retributive justice', and benevolence. Machiavelli had offered the same advice as Bhishma to his own prince when he said, 'a man who wishes to profess goodness at all times will come to ruin among so many who are not so good. Hence it is necessary for a prince who wishes to maintain his position to learn how not to be good, and to use this knowledge ... according to necessity.'[25] Bhishma and Machiavelli are telling us that society exists because it is in everyone's interest to have peace, and peace can only prevail if there is a sovereign authority to punish those who breach it.

A tale for a time of crisis

The *Mahabharata* is a tale for a time of crisis and it is relevant to the economic upheaval that gripped the world in 2008. The epic had a problem with the self-destructive kshatriya institutions of its time, and there are parallels between the *Mahabharata*'s lament and the things that we might say or ought to say about our own crisis. The person who lost her job in the economic calamity would have asked the same question as Draupadi when the Pandavas were in exile. When everything was going so well and Yudhishthira had been consecrated 'universal sovereign', why did this tragedy have to strike? Why was our kingdom stolen in a rigged game of dice?

The person rendered unemployed because of troubles that began on Wall Street, asked insistently, 'Why me? What did I do to deserve this?' When confronted with a similar question, Draupadi had 'staggered with wonder' and 'condemned the Placer'.[26] Later, Uttanka, the hermit, had put Krishna, the God, on the mat for not preventing the war at Kurukshetra. He had accused him for allowing so many to suffer through no fault of theirs.[27] When they were in exile, Draupadi, with her bias for action, had exhorted her husband to go off, raise an army, and win back their kingdom. But Yudhishthira had reminded her that he had given his word. Draupadi countered, what is the point of being good in a world where there is unmerited suffering? Isn't it better to be powerful and rich than to be good? To which

Yudhishthira replied in the only way that he knew, 'I act because I must'. It was the uncompromising, compelling voice of dharma. This is an answer that the investment bankers, who tipped the world into this crisis of capitalism, might ponder over.

The most damaging fallout from the economic crisis may well have been a loss of trust in the democratic capitalist system, especially if those who were unemployed and suffering, began to believe that 'anything goes' in an unfair world. The actors in the financial crisis would have done well to also consider the other reasons that Yudhishthira gave in Chapter 3 for being good. Aside from the fact that it is one's duty to be good, he told Draupadi that good acts produce good consequences. If people do not keep their commitments, the social order will collapse. Finally, virtue or dharma is necessary for leading a good and flourishing life.[28]

'Oh, so you are one of *them*!' is how someone greeted my nephew, who was embarrassed to tell people that he was one of those investment bankers. 'I'd rather say that I run a brothel,' he said. 'At least, that's a business people understand.' Bankers, having brought the world economy to its knees, became pariahs overnight and a target of people's rage. The International Labour Organization reported in early 2009 that global unemployment would hit a staggering 50 million. A typical knee-jerk reaction pointed a finger and called it 'greed'. But that was not very helpful, for we have always known that if envy is a sin of socialism, greed is the failing of capitalism (as we noted in Chapter 1).

There were many dharma failures in this drama in which all actors seemed to behave rationally. When US house prices were rising and interest rates were low, even the poor got a chance to get a mortgage and a home. Who could oppose that! Banks combined these mortgages into a collateral debt obligation (CDO), got it rated, and sold it to institutions, that also gained through better returns. When the housing market turned downwards, the

CDOs became toxic. Who was at fault? In a sense all were guilty. There is a fine line between rational self-interest and selfishness, and the balance of dharma tipped the wrong way. The undeserving recipient of the loan lied about his ability to repay; the banker, moved by short-term reward, promoted the 'sub-prime' mortgage; the rating agency was dishonest in colluding with the bank; the institution that bought the risky CDO failed in its duty to protect its shareholders.

The calamity might have been contained if Lehman Brothers had been bailed out on 14 September 2008. The old rivalry between Dick Fuld, the CEO of Lehman Brothers, and Hank Paulson, the former CEO of Goldman Sachs, may have come in the way. The bluebloods at Goldman Sachs had long harboured a deep prejudice against the upstarts at Lehman. Fuld was arrogant and had always managed to steal the limelight. But Paulson, who was US Treasury Secretary when the world economy went into recession, possibly unconsciously, allowed personal prejudice to influence his thinking when he refused to save Lehman. When Lehman collapsed, so did confidence and bank liquidity, and this was the tipping point of the global collapse.

President Barack Obama castigated Wall Street for paying bonuses to executives at a time when they had been bailed out by the American taxpayer. Particularly embarrassing was the disclosure about John Thain, chairman of Merrill Lynch, who had spent $1.2 million to do up his office, which included a $1400 waste paper basket and a $35,000 commode in the bathroom. He paid $4 billion in bonuses to executives when Merrill Lynch had declared a loss of $15 billion in the fourth quarter of 2008. When he said that the bonuses were needed 'to retain the best people', someone asked him, 'What *best* people? They just lost you $15 billion!'

'Resign or commit suicide' was the honourable choice that the Republican senator Charles Grassley offered to executives at

American International Group (AIG) who had received $220 million in bonuses after the insurance giant was bailed out. When senators begin advising executives to kill themselves, something had gone terribly wrong with the nation's dharma. President Barack Obama sought a legal way to claw back the bonuses and democratic leaders in the Congress suggested an extortionate tax. To want to punish someone in this crisis was understandable but it was a dangerous path. What the world needed instead was the calm and principled voice of a Yudhishthira. In Obama's place he would have appealed for a 'voluntary' return of bonuses while explaining to the American people that Wall Street had been bailed out to save Main Street's pain and honouring bonus contracts was necessary to the rule of law.

It was a lesson for the millions in China and India, who had just risen into the middle class. Successes of capitalism over time produce enervating influences when a generation committed to saving is replaced by one devoted to spending. The ferocious competition 'of interests and passions' that Duryodhana exemplifies is a feature of the free market and it can be corrosive. There is another way to live—like Tuladhara's, the trader of spices, who prefers to float calmly like a twig in the river and does not feel the need to dominate his neighbour. But competition is also an economic stimulant that promotes human welfare, as my father used to say. The choice is not between the free market and central planning but in getting the right mix of regulation. No one wants state ownership of production where the absence of competition corrodes the character even more. The answer is not to seek moral perfection which inevitably leads to theocracy and dictatorship. Since it is in man's nature to want more, one learns to live with human imperfection, and one seeks regulation that not only tames Duryodhanas but also rewards dharma-like behaviour in the market.

For those who had lost their jobs through no fault of their own it was easy to become cynical and amoral. It was tempting to believe that life is unfair, and so anything goes. It is to them that the *Mahabharata* holds up Yudhishthira's inspiring words—'I act because I must'. The epic's message for our leaders in these morally difficult times is to restore trust in the idea of a free society of laws where anything does *not* go. The task of an inspiring leader in *Kali Yuga* is not just to think about the difficulty of being good but how to confront that difficulty—and to place that thinking in the great textual confrontations of the past.

'A series of precisely stated problems imprecisely resolved'

I find that I have been guilty in seeking a singular, coherent dharma in the epic. When I ask, 'What is the epic trying to say?' I seem to be suggesting that the meaning of a work of art is unified and whole for all time. But, of course, this is not true. Even in concluding that the *Mahabharata*'s political ideology is a pragmatic middle path, I may have been culpable of expecting too much logical coherence in the epic when its real position may well be agnostic—that the nature of political power is unsolvable. Consider a traditional reading of the Karna episode in Book Five. When a devotee of Krishna reads the epic he sees the hero as cursed by *daiva*, 'fate', which leads him to ignore God's wise counsel to switch sides. Karna's refusal to heed God leads him to his foolish and blind end. A perfectly legitimate way to read the epic and one which is very different from mine. The epic seems to be saying a multiplicity of things to different readers at different moments in history. Hence, my quest for the meaning of dharma in the early twenty-first century is as legitimate as a second century Vaishnavite devotee of Krishna's.[29]

It is rich irony that the Pandavas waged a war reluctantly in support of a dubious claim, and then employed deceit to gain a victory for which they were rightly censured. The genealogy of both sets of cousins is confused. Karna is the true claimant to the throne and he turns out to be fighting on the wrong side. The Pandavas are warned that Draupadi was born out of a powerful sacrifice in order to wipe out their Kuru race, but they go ahead and marry her anyway. Vidura cautions Yudhishthira not to engage in the game of dice but he does so, and with disastrous consequences.

All this leaves one in a state of moral confusion.[30] I find it difficult to slot the characters into neat compartments labelled 'good' and 'bad'. Even the great war at Kurukshetra may not have been a fight between good and evil as the epic would sometimes have us believe. Although it claims that the war is a *dharma-yuddha*, a 'just war', the fact is that dharma, the measure by which we judge good and evil, is itself contested, ambiguous and subtle. Both sides did plenty of good and bad deeds. Hence, it might be better to call the Pandavas the 'preferred' side and not the 'good' side.[31]

The epic judges its heroes harshly and packs them off to hell, albeit briefly. Both Yudhishthira and Arjuna face genuine dilemmas, get confused, and are reluctant to act. Each time Krishna has to step in and goad them on. When they do act they tend to make a mess. Krishna reasons with Yudhishthira that lying to save one's life is allowed by dharma. The alternative is far worse—losing his kingdom. Either way, he would be wounding a principle of dharma. Telling a lie would compromise *satya* or truth. Losing the war would wound both distributive and retributive justice. Duryodhana would usurp the Pandavas' share of the kingdom and escape punishment for his many wicked acts (including the disrobing of Draupadi). 'Had Duryodhana won the war, it would have wounded our sense of dharma far more.'[32] In the end Yudhishthira tells half a lie to Drona, and his chariot hits the ground. He pays for it by going to hell (from where he rescues his wife and his brothers).

Arjuna's dilemma is to choose between his duty as a soldier and a duty not to kill. He can either be true to his kshatriya ethic and fight a 'just war', or he can observe the dharma of his conscience and eschew the violence of war. As we know, he accepts Krishna's advice and decides to fight. Although the Pandavas win the war, it is a hollow victory. Almost everyone dies and the Pandavas are condemned in having to rule over an empty kingdom, filled with feelings of guilt, shame and remorse for violating the moral principles of *satya* and *ahimsa*. Arjuna pays an additional price of facing the humiliation of the loss of his great heroic powers at the end of the epic. He cannot even protect the few Yadava women of Krishna's tribe who had been left in his care from an attack by ordinary robbers.

Try as it might to justify these ambiguities, the epic leaves one in a vague, hesitating and pessimistic mood with regard to dharma. True, there are mitigating circumstances. A rich network of curses and oaths have predetermined the outcome and diminished human culpability to that extent. True also, dharma has been in a state of decline—it has been declining by one-fourth in each age beginning with the 'golden age'. Only one-fourth is left by the time the *Mahabharata* unfolds on the eve of *Kali Yuga*.[33] But the ethical impulses that drive individuals are seldom straightforward. A person resolves a moral dilemma in one way at one time and in another way on another occasion. Although the two acts may be similar, a person does not follow the same moral standard in judging them. Actions that might be considered selfish in a member of the family may well be acceptable in the larger context of the state, as the good Vidura explains. One might think a friend inconsiderate, but tolerate him as a national leader for 'reasons of state'. Regrettably, it does seem to matter whether the victim is a friend or a foe. The *Mahabharata* does not shy from this incoherence. Neither should we in our lives. 'We are citizens who have a feeling for justice in public affairs, only because we have faction-ridden souls, ambivalent desires and the experience of contrary impulses . . . and we are persons who are normally in dispute with ourselves.'[34]

Certainty is not a virtue, and human goals, heroes and virtues come in many shapes and sizes, as the epic tells us:

Heroes of many kinds . . . hear from me, then, their goals. Rewards are assigned to the families of heroes and to the hero himself. Heroes of sacrifice, heroes of self-control; others who are heroes of truth; heroes of battle are also proclaimed, and men who are heroes of giving. Others are heroes of intellect, and heroes of patience are others; and also heroes of honesty, and men who live in tranquillity. But there are many other heroes by various disciplines. There are heroes of Vedic study, and heroes who delight in teaching. There are heroes in obedience to teachers and others in obedience to fathers. There are heroes in obedience to mothers, and others are heroes in alms. And many are heroes of samkhya, and others are heroes of yoga. There are forest-dwelling heroes, and householder heroes, and heroes in the honouring of guests. All go to heavens won as fruit of their own acts.[35]

Since there are many ways to be a hero, a good society must accept different pulls and pressures. Most of the characters in the *Mahabharata* tend to be more concerned with the group's survival and identity. They value cohesion above other virtues, and we would call them 'conservatives' today. Yudhishthira (and Arjuna occasionally) is keener to protect the individual, and we would call him a liberal. The *Mahabharata* is willing to accommodate both points of view. It does not reject the old morality of the Vedas, nor the growing unequal social order, and allows it to flourish side by side with the individualistic search of Yudhishthira for a more just society.

The *Mahabharata* could never be a 'how to' book since it offers more questions than answers. My friend A.K. Ramanujan says, 'It is not dharma or right conduct that the *Mahabharata* seems to teach, but the "subtle" nature of dharma—its infinite subtlety, its incalculable calculus of consequences, its endless delicacy.'[36] Hence, the epic is deeply concerned with dharma understood as 'law', and legal discussions play an important role: What is the legal position of five brothers marrying a woman? What are Karna's rights after he is crowned king of Anga? Was the game of dice legal and was Draupadi legally wagered? This is the context in which one must judge Bhishma's frustrating and deplorable non-answer to Draupadi's question.

For these and other reasons my search for dharma has been ambiguous, uncertain and frustrating. Not that I was not warned. The *Mahabharata* itself had issued an alert:

> *Because of its subtleness, the deeply hidden [true dharma] cannot be discerned ... At first sight [dharma] appears in the form of a fairyland city, but when scrutinized by the wise it dissolves again into invisibility ... Because people are inclined to abide by the principle of political [advantage], no kind of generally-beneficial behaviour presents itself, [for indeed the behaviour] by which one person profits, grieves another. Modes of behaviour are universally characterized by diversity ... For [this] reason one should seek [true] dharma and not follow the ways of the world.[37]*

Hence, the epic is a 'series of precisely stated problems imprecisely and therefore inconclusively resolved, with every resolution raising a new problem, until the very end, when the question remains: whose heaven and whose hell?'[38]

'I see it now: this world is swiftly passing'

When Draupadi challenged the nobles in the assembly at Hastinapura, insistently demanding to know the nature of dharma, no one turned to God for an answer. We saw in Chapter 2 that Bhishma and Vidura wrestled with the problem, but there was no appeal to a higher authority. Draupadi also appealed to the moral conscience of the assembly rather than to God, and Bhishma's conclusion—'dharma is subtle'—was an admission of intellectual defeat, implying thereby that his powers of reason were unable to come up with an answer. The entire ineffectual interchange on that fateful day was based on the assumption that dharma has a rational foundation rather than being based on faith. The very act of questioning implied that human beings had the freedom to act and were responsible for their actions.

Ultimately, it is left to individuals to decide how best to order their lives, and Indians seem to have come up with two broad approaches to the problem of living. The first we might call Draupadi's way (known in tradition as *pravritti*), which affirms the world and believes that by observing one's social duties (such as the warrior duties of a kshatriya) one attains *swarga-loka*, 'the heaven of the gods'. The second is Yudhishthira's way (called *nivritti*), which is a tendency to deny this impermanent world and its worldly duties and seek liberation from its bondage via an ascetic life of meditation.[39]

Whichever way one chooses, there is the familiar pain of being human, being alive, and not knowing when one is going to die. Karna expresses his sense of mortality thus:

I see it now: this world is swiftly passing.[40]

Whereas Yudhishthira thinks of mortality as 'time cooking us', Karna regards it as unyielding duration. This is the ultimate human dilemma. 'Never very distant is the elegiac regret that no other way seems possible, that the relentless passage of time carries all before it, that the alternatives to this inescapable cycle can only be dimly sensed, like memories from a fading dream.'[41] What is 'dimly sensed', it seems to me, is the very modern possibility that an act of goodness might actually triumph over one's mortality, and this could also give meaning to one's life. To a person who may or may not find ultimate meaning in God, the *Mahabharata* offers an alternative life dedicated to dharma.

Since my father believed firmly that life had a divine purpose, he would not have agreed with my interpretation of the *Mahabharata*. He would have pointed to passages in the epic where the goal of dharma is subservient to the higher goal of *moksha*, 'liberation from human bondage'. While he might have conceded that acts of goodness make for a better world, he would have insisted that the greater advantage in practising dharma lies in improving one's karma and one's ability to achieve spiritual progress. Although not a Vaishnavite, he was drawn to *bhakti* and the devotional life. The epic itself is so vast and voluminous that it lends itself to differing interpretations.

I once remarked to my father, somewhat whimsically, 'Is there any point to our life beyond the fact that we should make it to the station on time?' We had arrived late at the railway station in Beas, barely in time to catch the Frontier Mail to Delhi. I don't remember what my father said in reply but he was not amused. He did not say that 'the purpose of life is to serve God', however. This is the sort of thing a Christian might have said. Nor would my father have thought that 'obedience to God's command is a way to avoid damnation'. He would have spoken about *moksha*. The Bhagavad Gita and the 'Sanatsujatiya' were his favourite parts of the epic. The Gita is, of course, world famous, but the 'Sanatsujatiya', while less well known, has a minor reputation as a philosophical classic. It is from the late Upanishadic period, and the great philosopher Shankara also wrote a famous commentary on it in the early ninth century.[42] The standard Indian response to the *Mahabharata*'s repeated intimations of mortality is to quote from these two texts, saying that *atman*, 'the human soul', is immortal and does not die when the body dies. Krishna offered this consolation to Arjuna just before the war, as did Vidura to the troubled and insomniac Dhritarashtra when he recounted the tale of the ancient and eternal youth Sanatsujata.[43]

The average person continues to link morality with religion, and this makes the *Mahabharata*'s rational deliberations on dharma seem modern and even revolutionary. The three great Semitic religions promise heaven for being good. Christians, Jews and Muslims turn to God to discover their duties.[44] Buddhists are atheists but they too think of goodness within the context of the 'Buddhist faith'. Religion, of course, does not create moral ideas, but as Plato explained in the *Euthyphro*, it gives authority to moral rules that are already present. The West began to separate religion and morality in the eighteenth century as a part of its modernity project. Western thinkers in the nineteenth century were passionately secular: Hegel asserted that reason was superior to belief; Feuerbach said that God diminished man's sublimity; Marx called religion an 'opiate of the masses'; and Freud thought of it as 'an illusion'. Finally, Nietzsche came and declared that 'God is dead'. Despite this intellectual history, the ordinary person in the West connects being moral with being religious.

My own search for dharma has led me to the conclusion that morality is natural to the way human beings have evolved as social, intelligent and enduring mammals. One can be sceptical about the existence of God, but one can still believe in being good and live a deeply moral life.[45] The values of the *Mahabharata*'s heroes may not always be mine but I can grasp what it would be like to live by them. Reading the *Mahabharata* has made me shed my earlier arid scepticism and relativism. It seems to me impossible to counter moral scepticism. No form of scepticism, whether epistemological or moral, can be shown to be impossible. The best one can do is to 'raise its cost, by showing how deep and pervasive are the disturbances of thought which it involves'.[46] One has to imagine oneself being beaten to death as a slave in order to realize that it is almost impossible to support slavery. Even Duryodhana would shed his scepticism if he were to imagine Bhima's heavy foot weighing down on his gouty toe. He would want Bhima to behave morally towards him. 'What if I were the victim?' is the question that helps to shed moral scepticism.

Commentators through the ages have wrestled with the overall meaning of the *Mahabharata*. Among the most celebrated was Anandavardhana, who lived in Kashmir in the ninth century AD.

Towards the end of his *Dhvanyaloka*, he suggests that the protagonist of the epic might not be Yudhishthira but Krishna—and that the epic's world-weary message is that we should cease to desire and seek liberation from the worldly life. 'Although the *Mahabharata* contains much beauty, it is a didactic work. The miserable end of the Vrishnis and the Pandavas suggests that the great sage who was its author meant to convey a disappointing conclusion within a poetic mood of peace. The aim of this work is to produce disillusionment with life and point us towards the human aim of liberation from the worldly life.'[47] My father would have agreed.

My reading of the *Mahabharata*, however, suggests that the epic favours dharma as an end in itself and not subservient to spiritual *moksha*. Yudhishthira does not act compassionately in order to achieve a higher, 'religious' goal. Although the *Mahabharata* gives us a longish lecture on world-weary *moksha*, Yudhishthira seems to act for the sake of moral rectitude—from a struggle in his soul to do the right thing. The epic delights in all manner of altruistic acts—actions done for their own sake. The continuous tension between the ends of dharma and *moksha* reflects a crisis in the *Mahabharata*'s society, especially its kshatriya institutions. Stubborn and perverse Duryodhana represents much that is wrong with these institutions, and his violation of the menstruating Draupadi is the driving force of the narrative.[48] To give people a way out from the failing kshatriya morality of the times, Vaishnav redactors of the epic raised Krishna's stature, converting *a* god into *the* God. It was a comforting idea. Confronted by so much bad behaviour, especially in the ruling class, people began to take refuge in the otherworldly ideal of *moksha*. Thus, *moksha* trumped dharma in the later classics of India. The hero became the 'renouncer', who surrendered his will to the love (*bhakti*) of God, and was thus freed from the bondage of karma.

The *Nasadiya* temper

The tentativeness of the *Mahabharata*'s dharma reflects a sceptical streak both in the epic and in the Indian tradition. It goes back 3,500 years to its very first text, the Rig Veda, and it may well have originated in the charming humility of its '*Nasadiya*' verse, which meditates on the creation of the universe:[49]

> *There was neither non-existence nor existence then ... There was neither death nor immortality then. There was no distinguishing sign of night nor of day ... Who really knows? ... The gods came afterwards, with the creation of this universe. Who then knows whence it has arisen?*[50]

The verse ends with a doubt if even the gods know how the universe was born. This questioning attitude is quite unlike the mindset of the Christian, Jewish or Islamic traditions which proclaim an omniscient and omnipotent God. It might also have led to the invention of a Hindu creator, whose name is the interrogative pronoun *ka* (cognate with the Latin *quis*, French *qui*): 'The creator once asked Indra: "Who am I?" Indra replied, "Just what you said: Who." And this is how the creator got the name, Ka or Who.'[51]

Yet the Vedic ancients also believed that the very substance of the universe is divine. Each god has a secondary or illusory status compared to the divine substance, but it is a powerful symbol nevertheless, and it can help to guide the seeker to the divine. Many gods coexist comfortably in this non-hierarchic pantheon in which no god can afford to be jealous. And one ought to expect the devotee of many non-hierarchical gods to more likely see the many sides of truth—and accordingly be more tolerant.

In early 2006, when the controversy over Islamic cartoons was testing the boundaries of religious tolerance in Europe, my Hindu neighbour in Delhi claimed with some satisfaction that Hindus were tolerant and he traced their broadmindedness to their many gods. His assumption was that a belief in many gods ought to make one more tolerant as no god could afford to be jealous.[52] So, I asked him: how did our tolerant pluralism turn into the intolerance of the Hindu Right?[53]

The source of the Hindu Right's intolerance or for that matter any fundamentalist's bigotry lies in politics and it is futile to seek answers in belief. All fundamentalists are insecure, I am convinced, and seem to take an excessive interest in others. The rise of the Hindu Right in the 1990s in India is part of a global revival of religion with a political face. Laurie Goodstein had this to say in the *New York Times* on 15 January 2005: 'Almost anywhere you look around the world . . . religion is now a rising force. Former communist countries are crowded with mosque builders, Christian missionaries and freelance spiritual entrepreneurs of every persuasion . . .' Philip Jenkins's insightful book, *The Next Christendom: The Coming of Global Christianity*, describes this in the America after 9/11. The rise in fundamentalism around the globe threatens the secular agenda everywhere.

With the rise in religious fundamentalism, it is increasingly difficult to talk about one's deepest beliefs. Liberal Hindus are reluctant to admit to being Hindu for fear they will be linked to extreme nationalists of the Right. A friend of mine is ashamed to tell her 'secularist' friends that she visits a temple regularly. I blame both sides—Right-wing nationalists for appropriating religion and culture, making it a political agenda, and intolerant secularists who behave no better than fundamentalists in their callous antipathy to religious tradition. As a liberal and secular Hindu, I oppose the entry of religion into the public domain and teaching religion in state schools. I admire the 'wall' which the American founding fathers have built. But what does one do when the great literary classics of one's country are 'semi-religious'?

In late 2005, I received a phone call from one of Delhi's best schools, asking me to speak to its students. 'Oh good!' I told the principal enthusiastically, 'I have been reading the *Mahabharata*, and I should like to speak about dharma.'

There was silence at the other end. Suddenly the voice became defensive. She finally blurted out, 'Oh don't, please! There are important secularists on our governing board, and I don't want controversy about teaching religion.'

'But surely the *Mahabharata* is a *literary* epic,' I protested, 'and dharma is about right and wrong. Where does religion come in?'

My remonstrations were to no avail. She was scared. I wondered why a successful, professional woman had reacted in this odd way. I asked myself if Italian children can proudly read Dante's *Divine Comedy* in school or English children can read Milton, why 'secularist' Indians should be ambivalent about the *Mahabharata*. True, the *Mahabharata* has many gods, and in particular the elusive divinity, Krishna, but Dante and Milton have plenty of God as well. Dante's great poem, which practically 'created' the Italian language, is a deeply religious work.

John Rawls makes the distinction between 'public reason' and 'secular reason'. Public reason limits itself to political and civic principles while secular reason is broader and concerns itself with a secular person's deepest beliefs (or 'first philosophy' as he puts it). Fundamentalists must not forget this distinction and must refrain from introducing 'secular reason' into public and civic debate.[54] Everyone, however, would gain from the unassuming, searching attitude of the *Mahabharata*, whose sceptical streak goes back to the *Nasadiya* hymn in the Rig Veda. The '*Nasadiya* temper' of the *Mahabharata* is reflected, somewhat surprisingly, at the end of the Gita, the most 'religious' part of the epic. After initiating Arjuna into the mysteries and knowledge of the holy, Krishna asks him to consider his message carefully, and having considered it, he ought *to act as he will*.[55] The searching disposition of the *Mahabharata* is a text from which fundamentalists of all hues would profit. They might even learn

the virtue of open-minded scepticism, ambiguity and tolerance—
a dharma of civic virtue that the world could profit from today.

The difficulty of being good

A.K. Ramanujan used to say, 'In India . . . no one ever reads the
Ramayana or the *Mahabharata* for the first time. The stories are
there, "always ready".'[56] He meant by this, I think, that every
generation adapts and reinterprets the Indian epics to reflect the
concerns of its time. Hence, there is a rich menu of *Mahabharata*s
on order, including Peter Brook's dramatic theatre and B.R.
Chopra's television soap opera. Each one in its own way considers
the central problem of living. It holds a mirror to our lives,
forcing us to confront a world that is 'in permanent crisis, a
world whose karmic dominoes of human weakness reach into
past and future horizons until bounded by creation and
apocalypse'.[57] Each version engages us in some way because the
epic 'is the content of our collective unconscious . . . We must
therefore grasp the great book with both hands and face it
squarely. Then we shall recognize that it is our past which has
prolonged itself into the present. We are it,' says V.S. Sukthankar.[58]

In its closing lines, the *Mahabharata* throws up its hands in
frustration:

> *With uplifted arms I cry, but no one heeds; from dharma flow
> wealth and pleasure. Then why is dharma not pursued?*[59]

A strange question you would think from a text that has been so
discouraging about the prospects of being good. It has thrown us
into a world without moral closure. No one answers Draupadi's
question in the assembly and Yudhishthira is still looking for
dharma at the epic's end. Draupadi herself remains unconvinced
by everything that Yudhishthira had said about why we must be
good. Good behaviour is not rewarded generously in the epic;
the virtuous suffer banishment and deprivation, while the wicked
flourish in their palaces. Nor does the epic seem to explain why

'good' persons, who had a strong and persuasive case to make war, could win only by unfair means? And if so, how can we still call them 'good'? It has told us that dharma is hidden in a cave, but even if it is found, it is so subtle that it slips from our grasp.

But the epic's question—why dharma is not pursued—is a rhetorical one. It pitches us into our postmodern world of doubt, its lack of certainty consistent with our temper of empirical scepticism. The epic's tentative world of moral haziness is closer to our experience as ordinary human beings in contrast to the certainty of the fundamentalist. Its dizzyingly plural perspectives are a nice antidote to the narrow and rigid positions that surround us amidst the hypertrophied rhetoric of the early twenty-first century. The epic would have had much to say to our present-day fundamentalist fanatics who undertake suicide missions, certain that they will go to heaven, and who are not unlike the kshatriyas who fought on the plains of Kurukshetra and expected to go to heaven after they died in battle.

Since the beginning, human beings have been busy denouncing each other's bad behaviour, and where has it gotten us? Like the heroes of the *Mahabharata*, we are still searching for dharma. We are a mixture of good and evil, and perfectibility is an illusion. The *Mahabharata* seems resigned to this pessimistic view, which Immanuel Kant expressed famously in these words: 'Out of timber so crooked as that from which man is made nothing entirely straight can be built.'[60] *Ahamkara*, 'the I-maker', and *kama*, 'desire', tend to enslave us. There are many ugly sides of human vanity, and we have examined a few in this book—envy, self-importance, status anxiety, a desire for revenge. If all the gods were dead, these frailties would still exist as an integral part of the human condition. The epic is saying that deliverance is not easy.[61] Its 100,000 verses have led us to an abyss with 'no exit' and a feeling that no matter what we do we shall fail.

Because the *Mahabharata* is a 'continuing repository of crisis in the public discourse of classical India',[62] I had hoped that it might throw light on the governance crises of our times and the pathetic state of our public discourse. Just as the *Mahabharata* had a problem with its kshatriya social institutions, so do we face grave deficiencies in our governance institutions—failings that are not only institutional but also moral. I had hoped that reading the epic would somehow lend a healing touch to the daily wounds inflicted by the state—to our shocked discovery in 2004, for example, that more than one in five members of the Indian parliament had criminal charges against them, and one in eighteen had been accused of murder or rape; and to my horror at learning that all major political parties in India had united to prevent political and electoral reform that might have stopped criminals from entering politics.[63] I had hoped that the *Mahabharata*'s deliberations on dharma might help one to cope with criminality and dishonesty on the part of government officials of the United States, who led their country into a disastrous war in Iraq. Or, perhaps, the pervasive failures of corporate governance—such as Enron, Satyam and others. Modern democracies expend a huge amount of energy in debates between the political Left and the Right when the greater divide is between conduct in accordance with dharma and *adharma*. Draupadi's question in the assembly about the dharma of the ruler should be an inspiration to free citizens in all democracies. When there is no other recourse to governance failures, I have concluded that citizens must be prepared to wage a Kurukshetra-like war on the corrupt to achieve accountability in public life. The purpose of the destructive war in the *Mahabharata*, as Dhritarashtra was told in the end, was to cleanse the earth, which was groaning under the accumulated iniquity of its rulers.

If our politicians would devote even a fraction of their attention to concerns that moved Yudhishthira, we might have fewer wars or acts that one regrets when it is too late. Only after President Truman saw the photographs of innocent victims of Hiroshima did he abort the plan for dropping further atomic bombs over

Japanese cities. He could not undo what had been done but at least by identifying with a common humanity of the victims, he did manage to prevent further harm. One yearns for statesmen like Yudhishthira, who not only measures the material pros and cons of going to war but also weighs the dictates of his conscience. He holds out the promise that politics need not necessarily be a dark world of *realpolitik* in which force and cunning have to be the only currency. The *Mahabharata* offers us a meaningful ideal of civic virtue in its exposition of the dharma of the king.

Yudhishthira has an abiding sense of the tragic. While striving for rationality, he senses the underlying irrationality of human existence. Having discarded the conventional *sva-dharma* of society, he is on a lonely search for true dharma. This leads him to Jajali, whose story reawakens the 'impartial spectator' within him, and he says: 'Dharma is recognized by men [to be] the ancient [quality of] compassion for the welfare of all creatures.' Thus, he arrives at the moral point of view—that is, an ability to think beyond oneself. By choosing to live in a certain way, Yudhishthira has offered us an answer that might shield us against the tragic vulnerability of life in our 'uneven' world.

Despite its dark, chaotic theme, and despite ironic reminders about how difficult it is to be good, the *Mahabharata* is able to snatch victory in the character of its 'un-hero', Yudhishthira. He teaches us that it is part of the human condition to also aspire. He shows that it is possible for good to triumph 'even in a time of cosmic destructiveness', making us realize that the theme of the *Mahabharata* is not war but peace.[64] The king 'who weeps with all creatures' demonstrates through his example that the epic's refrain—'dharma leads to victory'—is not merely an ironic hope.[65] I may not care for the ascetic streak in his character, but I do believe that ascetics rarely cause the mayhem and violence that conventional heroes do. Yudhishthira demonstrates that an act of goodness might be one of the very few things of genuine worth in this world.

DHARMA—THE STORY OF A WORD

The word 'dharma' is as complex as it is ubiquitous. It is used in a bewildering variety of ways within the Indian tradition and before closing this book, I thought it useful to trace its historical development and look at the fascinating way its meaning has evolved over time.[1]

As always, one must begin with the Rig Veda (c. 1500 BC), the oldest text of India, where we are told that the word *dharman*, the precursor to dharma, occurs sixty times and refers mostly to religious rites.[2] By performing these rituals and traditional duties, Vedic man achieved a sense of order in his world.[3] Dharman helped to preserve the identity and continuity of his tradition and established order and harmony in his universe.[4] The word comes from the Sanskrit root *dhr*, meaning to 'support' or 'uphold' like a foundation. Scholars link dharma to *dharana*, which means 'supporting' or 'maintaining', and in this sense refers to 'the eternal laws which maintain the world'.[5] A commitment to upholding the space of the world is extended to 'holding apart' in Vedic cosmogony. It is the means of holding apart heaven and earth,[6] as well as other things such as plants, rivers and the four main castes in society. Thus, the Vedic ritual of dharma re-enacts the original cosmic act of 'upholding' and 'holding apart'.

Later, in the Atharva Veda, *dharman* becomes the more abstract noun *dharma*. Here it does not refer to 'upholding' as an action or event, but to its result—a norm, a law or an established order.[7] The *Mahabharata* follows this idea, reminding us that 'the creatures are kept apart or upheld in their respective identities by dharma' and the ideal of *ahimsa* or non-violence is a form of *dharana* or 'preserving' and 'upholding'.[8] By the time we get to Manu, dharma's 'upholding' is incumbent on all qualified men; it is also the condition which preserves, is preserved, and destroys when it is violated. It protects its protectors.[9] Such a balance of 'upholding' in the cosmos and in ethics—both in 'human action' and 'natural events'—is central to the classical Indian world-view.

In Indian philosophical literature, the usage of dharma is extended to mean the essential quality or the characteristic attribute of an entity, such as the 'dharma of fire is to burn'.[10] The philosophers of the Nyaya school viewed dharma (along with its negative counterpart *adharma*) as a property or 'disposition' inherent in the soul. In the normative *Dharmashastra* literature, however, which elaborates the rules of dharma in detail, 'dharma' is not a universal law—it applies only to the Aryans, especially to brahmins. It excludes the *mleccha*, 'outcastes'. It represents the traditional Hindu dharma of the 'order of the castes and the stages of life'.[11] However, the related concept of karma did tend to mitigate dharma's particularity. Karma is, of course, always universal—its causality of retribution, which fundamentally binds the actor to the results of his action, applies to everyone.

Buddhists and Jains appropriated 'dharma' and began to use it to suit their own needs, and this led to a plurality and rivalry of usages. Soon the Vishnu and Shiva sects of Hinduism took it over, describing theirs as the only true dharma.[12] The word *yogadharma* appeared in the fifth century BC commentary by Vyasa on Patanjali's text on yoga.[13] All these represented clear challenges to the orthodox Vedic view of dharma.

The greatest challenge came from the ethical and universalistic concept of dharma in the famous edicts of the Buddhist emperor Ashoka in the third century BC, who in turn seems to have influenced the character of Yudhishthira in the *Mahabharata*.

Not only the epics but also popular texts like the *Panchatantra* began to relate dharma to universal moral ideals, *satya*, 'truthfulness', *ahimsa*, 'non-violence', and *anrishamsya*, 'compassion'. The *Mahabharata*, as we know, repeatedly calls *ahimsa* the 'highest dharma' *(paramo dharmah)*.

There was bound to be a reaction from the orthodox defenders of the Vedas, and it came from the powerful Mimamsa school. According to Kumarila, its most forceful exponent, dharma is the practise of ritual. It can only be learned from the Vedas and there is no other means of knowing it. Those brahmins who excel in sacrificial rites are 'penetrated by dharma', which is only found among Aryans and not among *mlecchas*. It is dangerous to leave dharma to reason. In the *Mimamsa* and the *Dharmashastra* texts, dharma separates the castes and distinguishes an Aryan from a non-Aryan. Clearly, in the orthodox tradition, the 'upholding' of dharma is the upholding of a social and religious status quo.

Thus, the concept of dharma kept evolving and kept being contested. Its meaning shifted from a ritual ethics of deeds to a more personal virtue based on one's conscience and back again. In Vedic times dharma meant doing visible rituals and gaining merit. These deeds were usually specific to one's caste, and this dharma is often called *sva-dharma*. With the rise of yoga sects, Buddhism and Jainism, this meaning of dharma gradually changed to mean social harmony, the cultivation of an ethical self, and actions required of all castes. In this sense, dharma has universal appeal and is called *sadharana-dharma*. In the latter sense, dharma has to do with inner traits which determine one's character. Both these senses of dharma, as we have seen, coexist in the *Mahabharata*.[14]

Let us now 'fast forward' to the early nineteenth century. For the first time we find Hindus, especially Bengali Vaishnavs of Chaitanya's school, have begun to use the word 'dharma' as *Hindudharma*, to identify their faith as something different from Islam and Christianity. Till then Hindus had never used 'dharma' to mean 'religion'. The pre-Muslim Hindu might have called himself *Arya*—the whole of his life was 'religion' in a sense. This usage was in part a reaction to the Christian missionaries in Bengal who laid claim to 'dharma', using it to proclaim Christianity as the 'true dharma'. The English–Sanskrit dictionary by Monier-Williams (1851) lists the first meaning of 'religion' as *dharma*.

That a foundational idea of the Hindus had been appropriated by Christian missionaries was clearly a challenge to Hindu self-identity. The missionaries recognized that dharma was the binding norm of Hindu life which provided legitimacy to their religious practices and society, and they capitalized on it by presenting the Christian message under the title of dharma. Hindus reacted in two ways. On the one hand, they argued that Hinduism was universal—*one* religion, *one* dharma for all, and thus distinct from other religions; on the other hand, dharma was projected as a superior idea to 'mere religion'.

Rammohan Roy (1774–1833) was one of the first Bengalis to respond to this challenge. He wished to reform Hinduism via an open, deistic organization called Brahmo Samaj. Those opposed to Rammohan and his reforms employed the word 'dharma' as a central notion of Hindu self-assertion. One of them, Kasinath Tarkapanchanana, described himself as 'one who is concerned with defending dharma'. Another critic, Radhakanta Deb, founded an association named Dharma Sabha. Following this, many dharma societies arose during the second half of the nineteenth century, often explicitly opposed to the Brahmo Samaj and other reform movements, in particular the Arya Samaj of Dayanand Saraswati in the Punjab. The expression *sanatana-dharma*, 'eternal religion', became an increasingly popular way to assert the claims of the traditional orthodoxy.[15]

At the same time, Western modern ideas began to shape the meaning of 'dharma'. Bankimchandra Chattopadhyay, the Bengali writer, under the influence of John Stuart Mill and Auguste

Comte and their religion of humanity, proposed dharma to be the link between being and duty. According to him, dharma flows from the 'essence of man', *manushyatva*, and imposes a moral obligation on each human being.[16] In his humanistic interpretation of the concept, Bankim takes us back to Yudhishthira's normative, universal concept of dharma that we have observed in the *Mahabharata*, and away from Draupadi's *varnashrama-dharma* and the hereditary order of the castes. Not surprisingly, Bankim's individualistic interpretation led him to the devotional *bhakti yoga* path of spiritual liberation in the Gita, and away from Vedic rituals of the brahmins. In this he was influenced by the eleventh century medieval saint Ramanuja's commentary on the Gita, who concluded that *bhakti* was the 'highest dharma' *(paramo dharmah)*.

Akshay Kumar Datta (1820–86), another Bengali, went further. He secularized and naturalized the concept of dharma, declaring that to observe dharma was ultimately to conform to the 'laws of nature'. Towards the end of the nineteenth century, Swami Vivekananda took this universal dharma to Europe and America. He spoke about a 'dharma of humanity', regarding dharma to be an ethical code applicable to the whole of mankind. He and other Bengali proponents of neo-Hinduism deeply influenced B.G. Tilak, Mohandas Gandhi and other leaders of India's freedom struggle in the early part of the twentieth century. This new understanding of dharma and self-representation of Hinduism, which had grown from an encounter with the West, in turn influenced Westerners like Annie Besant, the leader of the Theosophical movement. She came to India in 1893, the same year in which Vivekananda attended the Parliament of Religions in Chicago. *Sanatana-dharma* began to be increasingly associated with the Western concept of *philosophia perennis,* a 'universal or eternal religion' in search for a commonality of all religions.

The philosopher S. Radhakrishnan advanced this 'neo-Hindu' agenda in the twentieth century. He maintained that dharma 'is the norm which sustains the universe, the principle of a thing by virtue of which it is what it is'. And a 'person who follows the dharma realizes the ideal of his own character and manifests the eternal lawfulness in himself'. Thus, 'the basic principle of dharma is the realization of the dignity of the human spirit'.[17] It is quite extraordinary how a word and an idea from the ancient Rig Veda has evolved and enriched itself over three thousand years through a process of contestation and adaptation.

A SHORT BIBLIOGRAPHIC ESSAY

Following the example of Chinese mandarins, I have thought of my quest for dharma in the *Mahabharata* primarily as an exercise in self-cultivation. Since it has led to a book, however, I should like to express my debt to authors, books and friends that have helped and influenced me. The list of books and articles cited here might serve as a 'reading list' for someone similarly inclined.

The *Mahabharata* and its translations

My acquaintance with the written *Mahabharata* began with two slim paperbacks in English—one by R.K. Narayan (*The Mahabharata*, London: Penguin Classics, 2001) and the other by C.V. Narasimhan (*The Mahabharata*, Delhi and Oxford: Oxford University Press, 1996). But today my starting point would be John D. Smith's abridged translation in a single volume of Penguin Classics (2009). It is accurate, lucid, and often elegant.

Since there is no satisfactory translation of the complete *Mahabharata* in English, I have been promiscuous in my readings. The late nineteenth century, Victorian translation by K.M. Ganguli is too stilted for my taste although it has been digitized and is available on the Net (*The Mahabharata of Krishna-Dwaipayana Vyasa*, 2nd ed., 12 vols, 1884–96, Calcutta: P.C. Roy/Oriental Publishing Co; republished 1970, Delhi: Munshiram Manoharlal). The rendering by P. Lal is a 'transcreation' and the one by Ramesh Menon a 'modern rendering in prose'—they are not translations. For the first five books of the epic, I employed the translation of J.A.B. van Buitenen (*Mahābhārata*, 3 vols, Chicago: University of Chicago Press, 1975–78). For Books Eleven and Twelve, I used James Fitzgerald's in the same Chicago series (2004). W.J. Johnson has done a fine verse translation of Book Ten, and I drew upon it for my chapter on Ashwatthama's revenge (*The Sauptikaparvan of the Mahābhārata*, New York: Oxford University Press, 1998).

In the case of the epic's battle texts—Books Six to Nine—I turned to the recent, beautiful but incomplete parallel translations from the Clay Sanskrit Library/New York University Press (2005–08). Ten volumes have appeared in this series. Like the *Book of Bhishma* preceding them, the epic has named the battle books after the successive leaders of Duryodhana's army. Notable for its poetic rendering is *Drona* by Vaughan Pilikian but Adam Bowles's *Karna* and Justin Meiland's *Shalya* are also impressive.

I only wish that Clay had employed the Sanskrit Critical Edition, compiled painstakingly over half a century by comparing several hundred versions from across India and beyond. Clay follows the 'vulgate *Mahabharata*' of the seventeenth-century scholar Pandit Nilakantha Chaturdhara (R. Kinjawadekar, *The Mahābhāratam with the commentary Bharata Bhawadeepa of Nilakantha*, 2nd ed., 6 vols, New Delhi: Oriental Books Reprint Corp., 1979). Hence, its numbering of chapters and verses is different. Clay's promise to have the complete translated *Mahabharata* by 2010 has been disrupted, alas, by the illness of the philanthropist John Clay, and there is uncertainty about its future. Unless another philanthropist steps in, I fear that the potential fruits from this outstanding project may remain unfulfilled.

For the last books of the epic, I have quoted from Wendy Doniger's unpublished translation. On many occasions I have turned to the Sanskrit Critical Poona Edition to make specific modifications in the translations (Vishnu Sukthankar, S.K. Belwalkar, P.L. Vaidya, et al., eds., *Mahābhārata*, 19 vols plus 6 vols of Indexes, Poona: Bhandarkar Oriental Research Institute,

1933–72). The idea of a Critical Edition was inspired by a Viennese scholar, Moriz Winternitz, in 1899, but the colossal task did not take off until after the First World War when it was taken up by V.S. Sukthankar, who was a student of Winternitz, and did not end until the publication of the appendix, the *Harivaṃśa*, in 1970. Muneo Tokunaga rendered a machine-readable version in Kyoto in 1991. Those interested in the fascinating debates in preparing the Critical Edition (such as which scene to select and which to reject from the numerous manuscripts of the epic) should read V.S. Sukthankar's *Critical Studies in the Mahābhārata*, Bombay: Karnataka Publishing House, 1944, 77–78; Franklin Edgerton, *Sabhāparvan*: Introduction and Apparatus, vol 2 of the Critical Edition, 1944 and R.N. Dandekar, *Śalyaparvan*, vol 11, 1961, *Anuśāsanaparvan*, vol 17, 1966.

Occasionally, I have gratefully borrowed from the translations of Sanskrit scholars who have written on specific issues or characters—Alf Hiltebeitel, David Shulman, Ruth Katz, Jim McGrath, Ian Proudfoot, Nick Sutton, Norbert Klaes and others (see below).

Translations of the Gita

The Bhagavad Gita is found in Book Six of the *Mahabharata* at VI.63.23. I have quoted from Barbara Stoler Miller's translation (*Bhagavadgītā*, New York: Bantam Books, 1986). When I searched for a good English translation of this text, I discovered that there were more than thirty to choose from and like the Pandava heroes, I became confused. A fine article by Gerald Larson, 'The Song Celestial: Two Centuries of the Bhagavadgītā in English', served as a nice guide, however (*Philosophy East and West*, 31.4, October 1981, 513–41). Vedanta enthusiasts directed me to the slim Christopher Isherwood–Prabhavananda translation, which has an introduction by Aldous Huxley on 'perennial philosophy' (*Bhagavad-gita: The Song of God*, New York: Signet/Penguin Putnam Inc., 2002). While I thought it satisfying as literature, it is not the most accurate, and its interpretation is a 'de-ethnicised Shankara combined with western mysticism', according to Larson. S. Radhakrishnan's rendition is 'dull and commentarial'. Indologists recommended R.C. Zaehner's, and although his translation turned out to be stilted, his wonderful discussions on Ramanuja, Shankara and the Upanishads that run parallel in the text make it quite exciting (New York: Oxford University Press, 1973). Although an accomplished Orientalist, Zaehner is attractive because he was clearly attracted to the notion of *bhakti* and the love of a personal god.

The most poetic is still the Victorian version of Sir Edwin Arnold, and it has the virtue also of being the cheapest in the Dover Thrift edition (New York: Dover, 1993). Those seeking pure accuracy should read either Edgerton's translation or van Buitenen's, who views the Gita as an integral part of the epic and challenges the traditional idea that it was inserted later (J.A.B. van Buitenen, *The Bhagavadgītā in the Mahābhārata: Text and Translation*, Chicago: University of Chicago Press, 1981). I was told not to trust Mascaro's version, which tries unsuccessfully to be poetic. Bhaktivedanta's rendition is a dull, sectarian, Sunday school textbook, reflecting the Vaishnavite values of Chaitanya. I found Winthrop Sargeant's very useful, although relatively expensive even in paperback; it is accompanied by an interlinear Sanskrit text, a word for word grammatical commentary and vocabulary (ed. Christopher Chapple, Albany: State University of New York Press, 1994).

In the end, I chose Barbara Stoler Miller's translation because it is both accurate, poetical, and has the great virtue of simplicity. Before she died in 1993, she was professor of Sanskrit at Barnard/ Columbia and she created the translation for our generation. I have also cited a few verses from Eknath Easwaran's eloquent translation (London: Arkana/Penguin, 1985). Through this process of selecting I have come to realize that there is no right or wrong translation and each one serves its particular audience. Van

Buitenen's version is no good to a follower of Sai Baba, as Arnold's account will not interest a Sanskrit scholar. Mahatma Gandhi's or Tilak's use of the Gita in our freedom struggle is as valid as Edgerton's reading of the text as a Vaishnav brahmin document of the first century AD. Emerson and Thoreau discovered the Gita through Wilkins's translation. Hegel used Humboldt's (as well as Schlegel's and Wilkins's). Gandhi used Sir Edwin Arnold's, while post-Independence Indians turned to Radhakrishnan's.

Aspects of the *Mahabharata*

The best discussion of the moral ideas in the *Mahabharata* is by the philosopher Bimal K. Matilal, who taught at Oxford for many years but also studied earlier with Ingalls. See his *The Collected Essays of Bimal Krishna Matilal: Ethics and Epics*, ed. Jonardon Ganeri, Delhi: Oxford University Press, 2002; his edited collection, *Moral Dilemmas in the Mahābhārata*, Delhi: Motilal Banarsidass; and his essay in Arvind Sharma (ed.) *Essays on the Mahābhārata*, Leiden: E.J. Brill, 1991, 384–400. As to religious ideas in the epic, I would read Nicholas Sutton, *Religious Doctrines in the Mahabharata*, Delhi, Motilal Banarsidass, 2000 and James Laine, *Visions of God: Narratives of Theophany in the Mahābhārata*, Vienna: Gerold & Co., 1989.

Anandavardhana's *Dhvanyāloka* is a medieval classic related to the aesthetics of the epic (with the *Locana* commentary of Abhinavagupta and the *Bālapriyā* commentary of Rāmasāraka, ed. Pt. Pattābhirāma Śāstri, Kashi Sanskrit Series 135, Benares Chowkhamba Sanskrit Series Office, 1940). So is Gary Tubb's contemporary essay on Anandavardhana's 'Śāntarasa in the *Mahābhārata*' (in A. Sharma [ed], *Essays on the Mahābhārata*, Leiden: E.J. Brill, 171–203).

When it came to the overall epic, I found the following three most stimulating: V.S. Sukthankar's *On the Meaning of the Mahabharata*, Bombay: The Asiatic Society of Bombay, 1957;

Krishna Chaitanya's *The Mahabharata: A Literary Study*, New Delhi: Clarion Books, 1993 and a feisty slim work by Iravati Karve, *Yuganta: The End of an Epoch* (Hyderabad: Disha Books/ Orient Longman, 1991). I would add to this list, several essays on the epic by A.K. Ramanujan in his *The Collected Essays of A.K. Ramanujan*, gen. ed. Vinay Dharwadker, Oxford: Oxford University Press, 1999.

Individual characters in the epic

As to individual characters in the epic, I would recommend Ruth Cecily Katz's masterly discussion of Arjuna in *Arjuna in the Mahābhārata: Where Krishna Is, There is Victory*, University of South Carolina Press, 1989. Katz was also a student of Ingalls. I found her analysis of Arjuna's *aristeia* particularly interesting, especially her comparison to Achilles. For those interested in comparative lessons from Greek heroes I would recommend Werner Jaeger's classic that I read in college—*Paideia: The Ideals of Greek Culture*, New York, vol I, 1939. Worth looking at is Gregory Nagy's *The Best of the Achaeans: Concepts of the Hero in Archaic Greek Poetry*, Baltimore: Johns Hopkins University Press.

The most thoughtful analysis of Draupadi and her question is by Alf Hiltebeitel in *Rethinking the Mahābhārata: A Reader's Guide to the Education of the Dharma Kings*, Chicago: University of Chicago Press, 2001. He has also written *The Cult of Draupadi*, 2 vols, Chicago: Chicago University Press, 1988 and 1991. S.M. Kulkarni also explores issues regarding Draupadi's question in 'An Unresolved Dilemma in *Dyūta-Parvan*' in Bimal Matilal, 1989.

As for Karna, Kevin McGrath's *The Sanskrit Hero: Karna in the Epic Mahābhārata*, Leiden: E.J. Brill, Boston, 2004, is excellent. When it comes to Duryodhana, David Gitomer's essay is worth reading, 'King Duryodhana: The *Mahābhārata* Discourse of Sinning and Virtue in Epic and Drama', *Journal of the American Oriental Society*, 112. 2 (April–June 1992), 222–32. I.M. Thakur's analysis of

Bhishma, however, is uneven in *Thus Spake Bhishma*, Delhi: Motilal Banarsidass, 1992.

In Yudhishthira's case I was most influenced by Norbert Klaes's *Conscience and Consciousness: Ethical Problems of the Mahabharata* (Bangalore: Dharmaram College, 1975) and Buddhadev Bose's *The Book of Yudhishthir* (trans. Sujit Mukherjee, London: Sangam Books/Hyderabad: Orient Longman, 1986). But David Shulman clearly offered the most exciting insights in 'The Yakśa's Question' (*The Wisdom of the Poets: Studies in Tamil, Telugu and Sanskrit*, New Delhi: Oxford University Press, 2001, also appears in G. Hasan-Rokem and D. Shulman [eds.], *Untying the Knot: On Riddles and Other Enigmatic Modes*, New York: Oxford, 1996). I learned much from Gregory Bailey, 'Suffering in the *Mahābhārata*: Draupadī and Yudhiṣṭhira, *Puruṣārtha* 7.109, 109–29. Mukund Lath's 'The Concept of *ānṛśaṃsya* in the *Mahābhārata*' confirmed to me the importance of this moral idea in the epic (in R.N. Dandekar [ed.] *The Mahabharata Revisited*, Delhi: Sahitya Akademi, 1990).

The literature on Krishna's role in the epic is vast and the best way to begin is to read Alf Hiltebeitel's biographical essay, 'Kṛṣṇa and the *Mahābhārata*', in *Annals of the Bhandarkar Oriental Institute*, 60.65–107. His *The Ritual of Battle: Kṛṣṇa in the Mahābhārata* (Ithaca and London: Cornell University Press, 1976) is a classic. The genealogical table at the beginning of my book is reproduced from this book with the kind permission of the author. I would also commend Bimal Matilal's 'Krishna: in Defence of a Devious Divinity', in Arvind Sharma (ed.), *Essays on the Mahabharata*, Leiden: E.J. Brill, 1991. The accounts of Krishna in Chaitanya and Karve, noted above, are provocative.

The best account of the story of Jajali and Tuladhara in the *Moksadharmaparvan* section of Book Twelve is Ian Proudfoot's excellent monograph, *Ahimsa and a Mahabharata Story* (Asian Studies Monographs, New Series no. 9, Faculty of Asian Studies, Australian National University, Canberra, 1987).

Historical background

For those seeking a general introduction to classical India, A.L. Basham's *The Wonder That Was India* is still a good place to begin (New York: Grove Press, 1989; Delhi: Rupa, 1981). John Keay's more recent *India: A History* is a fluent, readable and balanced overview (London: HarperCollins, 2000). Romila Thapar's *The Penguin History of Early India: From the Origins to AD 1300*, Penguin Books, 2002, is an updated classic. Unlike the arid accounts of dynasties, Wendy Doniger's *The Hindus: An Alternative History* is about women, merchants, lower castes, animals, spirits and, of course, Dead Male Brahmins (New York: Penguin Press, 2009). I found Romila Thapar's voluminous collection of essays, *Cultural Pasts: Essays in Early Indian History* fascinating to read about such things as the connection of the Arya Samaj to India's independence struggle and the role of the 'renouncer' in Indian history (New Delhi: Oxford University Press, 2000).

I grew up with the notion of an 'epic period' in Indian history. C.V. Vaidya has explored this idea in *Epic India or India as Described in the Mahabharata and the Ramayana* (Bombay: Radhabhai Atmaram Sagoon, 1907). Vaidya has argued that it was the period from 3000 BC to 300 BC and he places the war in Kurukshetra between 1400 and 1250 BC; he builds his argument around the founding of Indraprastha (Delhi) by the Pandavas and the conquest of Taxila (in West Punjab) by Janamejaya among other things. Although Vaidya had a keen appreciation of the epic's literary value, I find that he was basically creating a 'national mythology' and not writing serious history. Painted Grey Ware artefacts discovered at sites identified with locations in the *Mahabharata* suggest that the great war probably occurred between 1000 BC and 400 BC (H. Kulke and E. Rothermund, *A History of India*, London: Routledge, 1986).

Similarly, E.W. Hopkins suggested the notion of an 'encyclopaedic period' for the epic's composition, from 400 BC to 400 AD when didactic portions and myths were added to it later and it became an encyclopaedia (*The Great Epic of India: Its Character and Origin*, 1901; Calcutta: Punthi Pustak, 1969) His idea of a five stage development of the epic, however, was demolished by V.S. Sukthankar, editor of the Critical Edition, who said: 'I will say candidly that for all intents and purposes this pretentious table is as good as useless' (*On the Meaning of the Mahābhārata*, Bombay: Asiatic Society of Bombay, 1957). I am inclined to go along with Alf Hiltebeitel's suggestion that the *Mahabharata* was written over a much shorter period than is usually believed, sometime from mid-second century BC and year zero (Alf Hiltebeitel, *Rethinking the Mahābhārata: A Reader's Guide to the Education of the Dharma Kings*, Chicago: University of Chicago Press, 2001).

As to the enticing issue of the relationship between Yudhishthira and the historical Buddhist king, Ashoka, I would read James Fitzgerald's outstanding introduction to his translation of the *Mahabharata*, Books 11 and 12 (vol 7, University of Chicago Press, 2004). Nick Sutton has explored this in greater depth in 'Aśoka and Yudhiṣthira: A Historical Setting for the Ideological Tensions of the *Mahābhārata*', *Religion* 27.4 (1997), 333–41. For the historical background to the Mauryan period, see Romila Thapar's *Ashoka and the Decline of the Mauryas*, as well as her *Interpreting Early India*, Delhi: Oxford University Press, 1992. See also John Strong, *The Legend of King Aśoka: A Study and Translation of the Aśokāvadāna*, Princeton: Princeton University Press, 1983. Etienne Lamotte illuminates the Buddhist period in the *History of Buddhism from the Origins to the Śaka Period* (trans. Sara Webb-Boin and Jean Dantinne, Louvain: Université Catholique de Louvain, 1988).

What led the Sanskrit poets to develop the epic genre? Romila Thapar suggests the possible influence of Alexander as the kingdom of Magadha transformed into the Mauryan empire (*From Lineage to State: Social Formations in Mid-first Millennium B.C. in the Ganga Valley*, Delhi: Oxford University Press, 1984). Alf Hiltebeitel speculates on this subject in *Rethinking the Mahābhārata:*

A Reader's Guide to the Education of the Dharma Kings, Chicago: University of Chicago Press, 2001. On the relationship between the epic and empire see David Quint's *Epic and Empire: Politics and Generic Form from Virgil to Milton*, Princeton: Princeton University Press, 1993.

Moral ideas discussed in the book

In my book I have explored a number of moral ideas as they emerged from reading the *Mahabharata*, and I give below a brief reading list related to the most important ones: envy, duty, status anxiety, war, revenge, evil, remorse, non-violence, altruism, compassion. A nice, easy way to enter the world of moral philosophy is to read one of Peter Singer's books—*How Are We to Live: Ethics in an Age of Self-interest* (London: Mandarin, 1995) or *Practical Ethics* (Cambridge: Cambridge University Press, 1979).

Envy

Although Helmut Schoeck's *Envy: A Theory of Social Behaviour* is the standard text on envy (London: Martin Secker & Warburg, 1969), I found Joseph Epstein's slim and charming book the more enjoyable (*Envy: The Seven Deadly Sins*, New York: Oxford University Press, 2003). A comprehensive survey of historical sources will be found in H. Schoeck. John Rawls's discussion on envy is most insightful in his classic *The Theory of Justice*, Cambridge, MA: Harvard University Press, 1971.

Morality of war

Two works influenced my education in the morality of war: Michael Walzer's classic *Just and Unjust Wars: A Moral Argument with Historical Illustrations* (New York: Basic Books, 1977) and Thomas Nagel's essay, 'War and Massacre' in *Moral Questions*, Cambridge: Cambridge University Press, 1979, 53–74. With regard to Arjuna's dilemma, Martha Nussbaum's eloquent essay is instructive, 'The Costs of Tragedy: Some Moral Limits of Cost-

Benefit Analysis', *Journal of Legal Studies,* XXIX (2), Pt.2, June 2000, 1005–36.

Status anxiety and caste

Although numerous philosophers have written with great insight on the insidious human craving for status, I would read an elegant, slim volume by Alain de Botton, *Status Anxiety* (New York: Vintage Books, 2005). The literature on caste in India is huge. J.H. Hutton's *Caste in India* introduced me to the subject (4th ed, London: Oxford University Press, 1963). For a historical discussion of the development of the caste system, I recommend Romila Thapar, *Early India*, 124–26, 278; Vijay Nath, *Puranas and Acculturation: A Historico-Anthropological Perspective*, New Delhi: Munshiram Manoharlal, 2001, 27ff; G. Ghurye, *Caste and Race in India* (Delhi: South Asia Books, 1986); and M.N. Srinivas, *Social Change in Modern India* (Berkley: University of California Press, 1966).

As the body of literature on American affirmative action is even larger, I would begin with a fine bibliography appended to Robert Fullenwider's entry in the on-line *Stanford Encyclopedia of Philosophy* entitled 'Affirmative Action'. The best case for the 'integration argument' is made by Elizabeth Anderson in a long article, 'Integration, Affirmative Action, and Strict Scrutiny', *New York University Law Review*, 77 (November 2002), 1195–1271. Two other books build on this case: Robert Fullenwider and Judith Lichtenberg's *Levelling the Playing Field: Justice, Politics, and College Admissions*, Lanham, Maryland: Rowman and Littlefield, 2004; and Lesley Jacobs, *Pursuing Equal Opportunities*, Cambridge: Cambridge University Press, 2004. As always, I liked Thomas Nagel's viewpoint in 'Equal Treatment and Compensatory Justice' published in 1973 in *Philosophy and Public Affairs*. Alan Goldman makes a strong argument in support of preferences in *Justice and Reverse Discrimination* (Princeton, NJ: Princeton University Press, 1979).

Duty ethics

Yudhishthira's bald reply to Draupadi, 'I act because I must', raises the question of the place of duty in the moral life. The great philosopher of 'duty ethics' (also called 'deontology') is, of course, the eighteenth century German philosopher Immanuel Kant, and I recommend two of his works that I read in college: *The Critique of Practical Reason and Other Writings in Moral Philosophy*, trans. L.W. Beck, Chicago: University of Chicago Press, 1949 and *The Metaphysics of Morals*, trans. M.G. McGregor, New York: Harper and Row. I would also read W.D. Ross who is less absolutist and more plural, *The Right and the Good*, Oxford: Clarendon Press, 1930.

Consequentialism

The British philosophers Jeremy Bentham and John Stuart Mill criticized 'duty ethics' for failing to specify which principles should take priority when rights and duties conflict—a problem that the ascetic Kaushika faced in the *Mahabharata*. Like Vidura in the epic, they proposed that the rightness of an act be judged by its consequences, based on the famous Utilitarian principle, 'the greatest good of the greatest number'. Those wishing to read more should pick up two paperback collections of essays, one edited by Philip Pettit called *Consequentialism* (Dartmouth: Aldershot, 1993) and another by Samuel Scheffler, *Consequentialism and its Critics* (Oxford: Oxford University Press, 1988).

The problem of evil

The classic on the problem of unmerited suffering is Alvin Plantinga, *The Nature of Necessary* (Oxford: Oxford University Press, 1974) and *God, Freedom, and Evil* (Grand Rapids, MI: Eerdmans, 1974). John Hick offers a creative solution in *Evil and the God of Love* (New York: Harper & Row, 1977). Eleonore Stump claims that suffering has value in 'The Problem of Evil', *Faith and Philosophy* (October 1983, 392–420). C.S. Lewis's *Mere*

Christianity (New York: Macmillan, 1943) is full of sensible ideas. Finally, Harold Kushner, a Rabbi, offers a Hindu-like answer in a widely read book, *When Bad Things Happen to Good People* (New York: Schocken Books, 1981).

Revenge, punishment and forgiveness

A good place to begin is Jeremy Bentham's *The Rationale of Punishment*, originally published in 1830 but a digitized version is available. In the past fifty years the writings of H.L.A. Hart and John Rawls, both centrist liberals, have greatly influenced thinking about retributive justice (H.L.A. Hart, 'Prolegomenon to the Principles of Punishment' [1959], reprinted in Hart, *Punishment and Responsibility*, Oxford University Press, 1968, 1–27; John Rawls, 'Two Concepts of Rules', *Philosophical Review*, 64, 1955, 3–32).

The debate on crime and punishment is divided between those who insist on revenge and retributive justice and those who believe that forgiveness has a place. On the side of retributive justice are Jeffrie G. Murphy and Jean Hampton (*Forgiveness and Mercy*, Cambridge: Cambridge University Press, 1988); Michael S. Moore, ('The Moral Worth of Retribution' in Ferdinand Schoeman ed., *Responsibility, Character, and the Emotions: New Essays in Moral Psychology*, Cambridge: Cambridge University Press, 1987; Jean Hampton, 'The Moral Education Theory of Punishment', *Philosophy and Public Affairs*, 13, 1984, 208–38; Susan Jacoby, *Wild Justice*, New York: Harper & Row, 1983; and Joram Haber, *Forgiveness: A Philosophical Study*, Lanham, Md: Rowman and Littlefield, 1991).

On the side of forgiveness are Trudy Govier (*Forgiveness and Revenge*, London: Routledge, 2002), Uma Narayan ('Forgiveness, Moral Reassessment and Reconciliation' in Thomas Magnell ed., *Explorations of Value*, Amsterdam: Rodopi, 1997, 169–78). See Mark Amstutz's inspiring account of reconciliation in the case of nations: *The Healing of Nations: The Promise and Limits of Political*

Forgiveness. For an extensive bibliography, see H.A. Bedau, 'Punishment', *Stanford Encyclopedia of Philosophy* (online), 2005.

Remorse

Raimond Gaita's *Good and Evil: An Absolute Conception* is a classic defence of remorse (London: Macmillan, 1991). However, Spinoza did not think much about this moral emotion (Benedict de Spinoza, *Short Treatise on God, Man, and His Well-Being,* in *The Collected Works of Spinoza,* vol I, trans. E. Curley, Princeton: Princeton University Press, 1985, 115). Bernard Williams has brought some clarity to it ('Moral Luck', *Philosophical Papers 1973–1980,* Cambridge University Press, 1981, 27). Martha Nussbaum offers an extensive and sympathetic account in *Upheavals of Thought: The Intelligence of Emotions* (New York: Cambridge University Press, 2001).

Non-violence

Gene Sharp's *The Politics of Non-violent Action* is in three volumes but you only have to read the first short book, *Power and Struggle,* to see that what he has done for non-violence is what Clausewitz did for war (Boston: Porter Sargent, 1973). On reflection I wish I had devoted more attention to Gandhi in my book. Obviously, there is voluminous literature on this, but I enjoyed reading the following: Suzanne and Lloyd Rudolph, *Postmodern Gandhi and Other Essays* (Delhi: Oxford University Press, 2006); Rainer Hilderbrandt, *From Gandhi to Walesa: Non-violent Struggle for Human Rights;* and George Orwell, *Collected Essays, Journalism and Letters,* vol 4, 469).

Self-interestedness

The concept of *nishkama karma* in the Gita raises the question if human beings are purely self-interested. Albert Hirschman tells us in *The Passions and the Interests: Political Arguments for Capitalism Before its Triumph,* how the idea of the self-interested human being triumphed in the West in the eighteenth century (Princeton, NJ: Princeton University Press, 1977). Adam Smith in *An Enquiry into the Nature and Causes of the Wealth of Nations* endorsed it (1776, republished Oxford: Oxford University Press, 1976). But the same Smith in *The Theory of Moral Sentiment* wrote that no matter how selfish man may be, he exhibits unselfish emotions like pity or compassion. Jean-Jacques Rousseau agreed with him in his famous *Discourse on the Origin of Inequality*. Amartya Sen in our times has also argued that 'self-interest' does not fully explain the behaviour of people, 'Rational Fools: A Critique of the Behavioural Foundations of Economic Theory', *Philosophy and Public Affairs*, 6 (1977). Jane Mansbridge brings all these arguments together in her introduction to *Beyond Self-Interest* (ed. Jane J. Mansbridge, Chicago: University of Chicago Press, 1990).

Hegel had a lot of problems with *nishkama karma* and his objections are spelled out in G.W.F. Hegel, *On the Episode of the Mahabharata Known by the Name Bhagavad-Gita by Wilhelm von Humboldt* (Berlin 1826, ed. and trans. Herbert Herring, New Delhi: Indian Council of Philosophical Research, 1995).

Selflessness and motivation

The concept of *nishkama karma* raises the question if 'self-forgetting' can enhance performance. Like Arjuna in the *Mahabharata*, Buddhists have always believed this and Eugen Herrigel shows us why in *Zen and the Art of Archery* (trans. R. Hull, New York: Pantheon Books, 1953). So does the psychologist Mihaly Csikszentmihalyi in *Flow: The Psychology of Optimal Experience* (New York: Harper, 1991). Patanjali, of course, had set the stage centuries ago for the yogic experience of 'self-forgetting' (B.K.S. Iyengar, *Light on the Yoga Sutras of Patanjali*, London: Thorsons, 1993).

Altruism

The American philosopher Thomas Nagel's *The Possibility of Altruism* (Princeton: Princeton University Press, 1978) was my starting point, but what influenced me deeply was Martha Nussbaum's discussion on altruism in *Upheavals of Thought: The Intelligence of Emotions* (Cambridge: Cambridge University Press, 2001) and in *Compassion: Human and Animal* (for the festschrift in honour of Jonathan Glover, eds. Richard Keshan and Jeffrey McMahan, Oxford University Press). Stefan Collini offers a lively account of altruism in the Victorian moral temper in *Public Moralists: Political Thought and Intellectual Life in Britain*, 1850–1930, Oxford: Clarendon Press, 1999, and it led me to read David Hume's *Treatise on Human Nature*, Book III, Part 2, section I (ed. Ernest Mossner, Harmondsworth, UK: Penguin Books, 1984) and John Stuart Mill's *Utilitarianism* (*The Collected Works of John Stuart Mill*, ed. John M. Robson, vol X, Toronto and London, 1863). I also consulted the following on altruism: C.D. Batson, *The Altruism Question: Toward a Social Psychological Answer*, Hillsdale, NJ: Lawrence Erlbaum Associates, 1991; Bernard Williams, 'Egoism and Altruism' in *Problems of the Self*, Cambridge: Cambridge University Press, 250–65; S.P. Oliner and P.M. Oliner, *The Altruistic Personality: Rescuers of Jews in Nazi Europe*, New York: Free Press, 1988; and Kristen Munroe, *The Heart of Altruism: Perceptions of a Common Humanity*, Princeton: Princeton University Press, 1996. I would also recommend Jonathan Glover's *Humanity: A Moral History of the Twentieth Century* (New Haven: Yale University Press, 2000), not so much for its discussion of altruism, but for its grand moral perspective.

Reciprocal altruism

The evolutionary idea of reciprocal altruism helped me to understand the change in Yudhishthira's character from Book Three to Book Five in the epic. Robert Wright's *The Moral Animal: Evolutionary Psychology and Everyday Life* (New York: Vintage Books, 1995) introduced me to this idea and E. Sober and D.S. Eilson's *Unto Others: The Evolution and Psychology of Unselfish Behaviour* (Cambridge: Harvard University Press, 1998), helped to amplify it. Those wishing to dig deeper should read the following key texts on the development of this nascent discipline: W.D. Hamilton, 'The Genetic Evolution of Social Behaviour I and II', *Journal of Theoretical Biology*, 7 (1964), 1–16, 17–32; George C. Williams, *Adaptation and Natural Selection*, Princeton: Princeton University Press, 1966; Robert Trivers, 'The Evolution of Reciprocal Altruism', *Quarterly Review of Biology*, 46 (1971), 35–56; E.O. Wilson, *Sociobiology: The New Synthesis*, Cambridge: Harvard University Press, 1966; Richard Dawkins, *The Selfish Gene*, Oxford: Oxford University Press, 1976; Richard D. Alexander, *The Biology of Moral Systems*, New York: Aldine de Gruyter, 1987; Robert Axelrod, *The Evolution of Cooperation*, New York: Basic Books, 1984; and Anatol Rapaport, *Fights, Games and Debates*, Ann Arbor: University of Michigan Press, 1960.

NOTES

Prelude

1. While it sounds romantic in hindsight, it was my most arduous class in college. Ingalls was an old-fashioned schoolmaster who insisted on ramming down Panini's rules of grammar. The rules, of course, are elegant; learning them is akin to learning mathematics or logic (which I was studying with W.V.O. Quine at the same time). In the spring semester, we were rewarded by Ingalls with selections from literature—the story of Nala and Damayanti from the *Mahabhurata*, animal tales from the *Hitopadesha*, selections from Manu, and others, which we read dutifully from Lanman's reader, with the help of Whitney's grammar and Apte's dictionary.

2. Association for Democratic Reforms, www.adrindia.org, jchhokar@gmail.com

3. Michael Kremer, Karthik Muralidharan, Nazmul Choudhary and Jeffrey Hammer, 'School Absences in India: A Snapshot', *Journal of European Economic Association*, III (2–3), 658–67.

4. Neesha Patel, 'Evaluating the Role of Primary Health Centres in India', *Express Healthcare Management*, 16–31 August 2005; Jishu Das and Jeffrey Hanmer, 'Money for Nothing: The Dire Straits of Medical Practice in Delhi, India', World Bank Policy Research Working Paper No. 3669 (July 2005).

5. The Dharma Sutras are the definitive texts which prescribe the four stages of life for the twice-born Hindu male in a system called *varnāśramadharma*. It is a wrong impression that the codes are unanimous in instructing all twice-born males to enter each of these stages in the given order. The earliest Dharma Sutras seemed

to value the 'one *āśrama*' view, which was focused on the householder stage that followed the period of studentship and initiation. This view recognized that the householder *āśrama* was indispensable for the viability of society in accordance with Vedic tradition. Other *āśramas* were permitted and endorsed, but there was no pressure to enter them. The four-*āśrama* view came to predominate over time and this view is reflected in the later Dharma Sutras. In the third stage the forest-dweller is expected to become celibate again, clothe himself sparsely, practise austerity, depend on nature and beg (for food). 'He is not to hoard food unduly and should provide for visitors in his forest retreat so far as he is able. He is to recite the Veda (even if it is only the sacred syllable "Om!") and keep the sacred fire. He may cook his food and, according to some early traditions, eat meat that he has not killed himself. He is expected gradually to adopt a more strict regimen, becoming more and more ascetic, refraining from all self-indulgence and cooked food, and eating only vegetarian food. He is on the threshold of the fourth and last stage, that of the renouncer.' See Patrick Olivelle, *The Āśrama System: The History and Hermeneutics of a Religious Institution*, New York: Oxford University Press, 1993. T.N. Madan focuses on the householder's life-stage in *Non-Renunciation: Themes and Interpretations of Hindu Culture*, New Delhi: Oxford University Press, 1987.

6. Patrick Olivelle, 'The Renouncer Tradition', in Gavid Flood (ed.), *The Blackwell Companion to Hinduism*, 2007; T.N. Madan (ed.), *Way of Life, King, Householder, Renouncer: Essays in Honour of Louis Dumont*, Delhi: Motilal Banarsidass, 1982; J.M. Masson, 'The Psychology of the Ascetic', *Journal of Asian Studies*, 35.4 (MJI, 1976), 611–25.

7. Rene Guenon writes: 'The term "religion" is difficult to apply strictly outside the group formed by Judaism, Christianity and Islam, which goes to prove the specifically Jewish origin of the idea that the word now expresses.' Rene Guenon, *Introduction to the Study of the Hindu Doctrines*, London: Luzac & Co., 1945, 105.

8. Some European scholars characterize Aryanism as a nineteenth century myth. See E. Leach, 'Aryan Invasions over Four Millennia', in E. Ohnuki-Tierney (ed.), *Culture Through Time*, Stanford, 1990;

L. Poliakov, *The Aryan Myth*, New York, 1974. For the connection of the Arya Samaj to India's independence struggle, see Romila Thapar, *Cultural Pasts: Essays in Early Indian History*, New Delhi: Oxford University Press, 2000, 1114–15.

9. E.H. Carr says, 'Learning from history is never simply a one-way process. To learn about the present in the light of the past also means to learn about the past in the light of the present.' E.H. Carr, *What is History?* London, 1962, 20, 31, 62.

10. I.56.34–35. (When quoting from the *Mahabharata*, I shall only mention the book, chapter and verse numbers.) The epic has good reasons to brag. It is a bit like an encyclopaedia, and often gets carried away with a delight in knowledge for its own sake. Some scholars are bothered by contradictions within it (due in part to it superimposing successive historical layers of composition over the centuries). I believe, like Ingalls, that the original story and characters have always been intact. Ingalls says: '... there are older and younger parts of the *Mahabharata*, and these can be identified by linguistic analysis. One may thus come to discover changes of custom, changes of geographical knowledge, changes in the art of warfare from passages of earlier to those of later composition. But I see in the text no reason to suppose that any real change occurred, despite the long period of composition, in the main story line or in the characters who act out the story.' Daniel H.H. Ingalls's Foreword to Ruth Cecily Katz, *Arjuna in the Mahabharata: Where Krishna Is, There Is Victory*, University of South Carolina Press, 1989, xv.

11. II.60.43, 47

12. 'The ancient Egyptian *maat* has a meaning far closer to *dharma* than anything in today's English,' says Vaughan Pilikian, the Sanskrit scholar in his Introduction to *Drona* (vol 1), Book Seven of the *Mahabharata*, Clay Sanskrit Library, New York University Press, 19.

13. In the *Brahmanas*, texts devoted to analysing and interpreting rituals, dharma is narrowly conceived as ritual excellence. Transgression is merely a ritual mistake, a blunder of negligence. The *Brahmanas* declare, for example, that the impurity of the most heinous deeds, even the killing of a brahmin (priest), can be wiped away by performing a horse sacrifice. On the other hand, another dharma text, *Vasistha Dharmasutra*, says: 'Neither austerities nor

[the study of] the Veda, nor [the performance of] rites, nor lavish liberality [to priests] can ever save him whose conduct is vile and who has strayed from the path of dharma' (VI.3).

14. Dharma can be both universal and relative to the situation and the person. Thus, there is a dharma of a husband, of a wife, of a student, of an ascetic, of a caste, even of a courtesan. There is dharma during peace and dharma at the time of war. Epistemologists speak of dharma in a descriptive (rather than a prescriptive) sense: as the essence of something. For example, the dharma of fire is to burn.

15. *kālaḥ pacati bhūtāni sarvāṇi*, XVII.1.3

16. III.313.118. (trans. David Shulman, 'The Yaksa's Question', in *The Wisdom of the Poets: Studies in Tamil, Telugu and Sanskrit*, New Delhi: Oxford University Press, 2001, 40. The essay also appears in G. Hasan-Rokem and D. Shulman (eds.), *Untying the Knot: On Riddles and Other Enigmatic Modes*, New York: Oxford University Press, 1996. Shulman employs the vulgate text of the *Mahabharata* with a commentary by the late medieval commentator Nilakantha Chaturdhara.

17. Reason = *tarka*

18. *Tarko 'pratiṣṭhaḥ śrutayo vibhinnā naiko ṛsir yasya matam pramāṇam/ dharmasya tattvam nihitam guhāyām* . . . (Shulman trans. 54).

19. Shulman, 51

20. I.56.19

21. See Christopher Minkowski, 'Snakes, *Sattras*, and the *Mahābhārata*', in Arvind Sharma (ed.), *Essays on the Mahābhārata*, Leiden: E.J. Brill, 1991, 384–400.

22. Pilikian, 18

23. XII.1.13 (J. Fitzgerald trans.)

24. Krishna may be God, but in the end he 'lives to see the ignominious destruction of his own tribe in a drunken orgy and is himself killed by a silly mistake in circumstances far from glorious'. R.C. Zaehner, Foreword to Norbert Klaes, *Conscience and Consciousness: Ethical Problems of the Mahabharata*, Bangalore: Dharmaram College, 1975, vii–viii.

25. Pilikian, 18

26. *Drona* 2.4. (Pilikian trans.)

27. Iris Murdoch says, 'A genuine sense of mortality enables us to see virtue as the only thing of worth; and it is impossible to limit and foresee the ways in which it will be required of us.' *The Sovereignty of Good*, London and New York: Routledge & Kegan Paul, 1970, 96–97.

28. The *Mahabharata*, as I explain in Chapter 10, employs the Sanskrit word *ānṛśaṃsya* ('aan ri shum sya') to describe Yudhishthira's insistence on taking a stray dog into heaven. Literally, *ānṛśaṃsya* means possessing an attitude of non-*nṛśaṃsya*, which means one who does not injure; who is not mischievous, not-noxious, not-cruel, not-malicious. The scholar Mukund Lath explains, 'the word [*ānṛśaṃsya*] has more than a negative connotation; it signifies good-will, a fellow feeling, a deep sense of the other. [It is close to] *anukrośa*, to cry with another, to feel another's pain.' (Mukund Lath, 'The Concept of *Ānṛśaṃsya* in the *Mahabharata*', in R.N. Dandekar [ed.], *Mahabharata Revisited*, New Delhi: Sahitya Akademi, 1990, 113–19). Soon after the incident with the dog the epic describes Yudhishthira as a person bestowed with '*ānṛśaṃsya*' or *ānṛśaṃsya-sāmayukta* (XVII.3.30–32). However, in the dialogue with the Yaksha at the end of Book Three, it had also described Yudhishthira's attitude by the same word: *ānṛśaṃsyaṃ paro dharmaḥ*, III.313.75–76 CSL. In the dialogue with the Yaksha, Van Buitenen translates it as 'uncruelty'; Shulman uses 'non-injury'; W.J. Johnson employs 'absence of cruelty' on the first occasion (75–76), but changes it to 'compassion' the second time.

    Eighteenth-century English texts would have used 'sympathy' to denote Yudhishthira's moral sentiments towards the dog. Today, 'sympathy' does not connote a bias for action that compassion does. While 'empathy' may reconstruct imaginatively another person's experience, it too does not require the agent to act on behalf of the sufferer. 'Pity' is not right as 'it has acquired connotations of condescension and superiority that it did not have earlier when Rousseau invoked *pitie*,' according to Martha C. Nussbaum (*Upheavals of Thought: The Intelligence of Emotions*, New York: Cambridge University Press, 2001, 12). Hence, 'compassion' is probably the right word to express Yudhishthira's insistence on taking the dog to heaven. It is more intense than the alternatives, suggesting both greater suffering of the sufferer and greater engagement of the agent.

29. XII.121.31

30. David Seyfort Ruegg's advice to the historian of ideas is: 'beware of anachronistically transposing the unsystematically imposing concepts of modern semantics and philosophy, which have originated in the course of particular historical developments, on modes of thought that evolved in quite different historical circumstances and which have therefore to be interpreted in the first place in the context of their own concerns and ideas they themselves developed.' 'Does the *Madhyamika* Have a Thesis and Philosophical Position?', in B.K. Matilal and R.D. Evans (eds.), *Buddhist Logic and Epistemology*, Dordrecht Kluwer, 1986, 236.

31. I am indebted to Professor Sheldon Pollock for encouraging me to think of the *Mahabharata* in these terms.

32. V.S. Sukthankar, *On the Meaning of the Mahabharata*, Bombay: The Asiatic Society of Bombay, 1957, 29.

33. The *Mahabharata* describes the historical period which was an interregnum between the Mauryan and Gupta empires on the Ganges plain. The period saw the rise of Buddhism as well as a Hindu brahmin reaction during the rule of the Shungas after the fall of the Mauryan empire in 185 BC. The epic refers to a quasi-Mauryan text of statecraft, *Arthashastra* (X. 1.47), particularly when seeking textual support for its *realpolitik* policy. The evolution of Hinduism is clear in the rising influence of Krishna in the epic. Krishna's role is magnified as he emerges as an earthly incarnation of the supreme Lord Vishnu. Thus, the poem becomes an important early textual source for Vaishnavism, a sectarian form of Hinduism. The triumph of the Pandavas celebrates their (especially Arjuna's) devotion to Krishna. The Bhagavad Gita, a section of the epic's sixth book, in which Krishna exhorts Arjuna to fight this righteous war and reveals himself as the all-loving God, became one of the central texts of Hindu devotionalism.

34. The epic has been translated in India and Indonesia since the eleventh century. In 1591 the Mughal emperor Akbar commissioned his chronicler, Badayuni, to translate it into Persian.

35. Van Buitenen explains: 'the *Bhārata* of 24,000 couplets grew to the

Mahābhārata of 100,000. The original story was in the first phase of complication expanded from within, in the second phase mythologized, in the third phase brahmanized. One might even discern a fourth phase, after the epic was written down, when this collection of manuscripts became, as it were, a library to which new books could be added. Almost any text of "Hindu" inspiration could be included in this expanding library, so that in the end the custodians could rightly boast that "whatever is found here may be found somewhere else, but what is not found here is found nowhere!" (I.56.34)' (*Mahābhārata* by J.A.B. van Buitenen, Chicago: University of Chicago Press, vol 1, 1975, xxiii).

36. D.D. Kosambi was satisfied that the epic took its present form between 200 BC and 200 AD. See Romila Thapar's insightful essay, 'The Historian and the Epic', in Romila Thapar, *Cultural Pasts: Essays in Early Indian History*, New Delhi: Oxford University Press, 2000, 613–29. Alf Hiltebeitel, in his Introduction to *Rethinking the Mahābhārata: A Reader's Guide to the Education of the Dharma Kings*, says: 'the *Mahabharata* was composed between the mid-second century BC and the year zero' (18) ... 'I propose further that the *Mahabharata* was written by "out of sorts" Brahmans who may have had some minor king's or merchant's patronage' (19). Van Buitenen argues that the epic evolved from 400 BC till AD 400, saying: 'Such a [long] dating ... is of course absurd from the point of view of a single literary work. It makes sense when we look upon the text not so much as one opus but as a library of opera. Then we can say that 400 BC was the founding of the library, and that AD 400 was the approximate date after no more substantial additions were made to the text.' (*Mahābhārata* by J.A.B. van Buitenen, vol 1, xxv). At the beginning of the twentieth century scholars believed that there was an 'original' epic (narrative story) and a 'pseudo' epic (didactic sections). E. Washbrook Hopkins, *The Great Epic of India*, New York, 1901.

37. The project for a Critical Edition was first inspired by a Viennese scholar, Moriz Winternitz, in 1899, but the colossal task did not take off until after the First World War when it was undertaken by V.S. Sukthankar, a student of Winternitz, and did not end until the publication of the appendix, the *Harivaṃśa*, in 1970. Curiously, the

editors gave a lot of importance to the manuscripts from 'remote and conservative Kashmir'.

38. Cited in Thomas Nagel, *Equality and Partiality*, New York: Oxford University Press, 1991.

39. F.R. Leavis, an influential British literary critic of the mid-twentieth century, wrote in his book *The Great Tradition* that works of literature are great only if they enhance our 'awareness of the possibilities of life' and show concern with the 'interests of life'. F.R. Leavis, *The Great Tradition*, London: Peregrine, 1962, 10, 16 (first published in 1948).

40. There is a large post-colonial literature on this subject beginning with Edward Said's *Orientalism* and Benedict Anderson's *Imagined Communities*. Said analysed the construction of the 'Orient' in Western imagination, and concluded: 'The Orient is an idea that has a history and a tradition of thought, imagery, and vocabulary that have given it reality and presence in and for the West.' Edward W. Said, *Orientalism*, New York: Random House, 1978; Vintage Books, 1979, 5. The most comprehensive account purely from the Indian point of view is Ronald Inden's *Imagining India*, Indiana University Press, 1990, from where I have taken Hegel's quote below. What gave 'Orientalism' a bad odour is this typical statement of John Mill (the less worthy father of John Stuart Mill): 'Our ancestors,' Mill says, 'though rough, were sincere; but under the glossing exterior of the Hindu, lies a general disposition to deceit and perfidy.' James Mill, *The History of British India*, London: 1817; republished Chicago: University of Chicago Press, 1975, 247.

41. Hegel's verdict is stereotypical when he says that the spirituality of India 'has existed for millennia in the imagination of the Europeans'. Amartya Sen says that 'this home of endless spirituality has perhaps the largest atheistic and materialist literature of all the ancient civilizations'. 'Indian Traditions and the Western Imagination', *Daedalus*, Spring 1997, American Academy of Arts and Sciences, 1. Sen adds, 'Even on religious subjects, the only world religion that is firmly agnostic (Buddhism) is of Indian origin, and, furthermore, the atheistic schools of Carvaka and Lokayata have generated extensive arguments that have been seriously studied by Indian religious scholars themselves . . .' For

example, the fourteenth-century book *Sarvadarsanasamgraha* ('Collection of All Philosophies') by Madhava Acharya (himself a good Vaishnavite Hindu) devotes the first chapter to a serious presentation of the arguments of the atheistic schools.

42. V.121.25

1. Duryodhana's Envy

1. Unless otherwise indicated, quotations from Book Two are from the University of Chicago Press translation by J.A.B. van Buitenen, based on the Critical Edition. I have also used Paul Wilmot's translation of Book Two in the Clay Sanskrit Series, CSL; it is based on pundit Nilakantha Chaturdhara's seventeenth-century 'vulgate edition' (not the Critical Edition) and its numbering of the verses is different from that of the Critical Edition's. (See my note on translation and transliteration.) In a few cases, I have edited the quotes.

2. II.43.3–8

3. In Book One, Duryodhana is described as a 'wicked soul', one 'scorched by envy' (*īrṣyayā cābhisaṃtaptaḥ*), who cannot bear anyone speaking well of the Pandavas (I.129.4–10). Like English, Sanskrit does not make a clear distinction between 'envy' and 'jealousy' in common usage. I shall have more to say on the distinction below. The online Monier-Williams Sanskrit–English dictionary offers many variants for envy and jealousy, the most common ones being: *īrṣita, mātsarya, apadhyāna, amarṣa*.

4. II.43.18

5. II.43.19, 21. Although the text describes Arjuna as '*śvetāśvasya*', I have deleted 'white-horsed' from van Buitenen's translation as it is awkward. I have modified the second part of the verse following Paul Wilmot's more idiomatic rendering: 'I am drying up like a shrunken pond in the hot season.'

6. II.47.29 CSL. '*Amarṣa*' is the word in Sanskrit, which Wilmot translates as 'jealousy', but it can also mean impatience, indignation and anger.

7. II.43.35

8. II.44.18–22

9. II. 45.6, 8–9, 12

10. II.50.1–6
11. *asamtosaḥ śriyo mūlam tasmāt* (II.50.18): 'Discontent is at the root of prosperity'.
12. II.50.22–24, 27
13. II.58.14–16 CSL
14. See footnote 20 below
15. II.55.10
16. II.58.31
17. Alf Hiltebeitel, *Rethinking the Mahābhārata: A Reader's Guide to the Education of the Dharma Kings*, Chicago: University of Chicago Press, 262.
18. II.49.40: *'niyatam tam vijeṣyāmi kṛtvā tu kapaṭam vibho/ānayāmi samṛddhim tām divyām copāhvayasva tam'*. I have quoted from Paul Wilmot's translation of Book Two ('The Great Hall'), in CSL, New York University Press, 2006. CSL follows the vulgate seventeenth century version of the epic of Nilakantha Chaturdhara; hence, the numbering of the verses is different from the Critical Edition of the earlier verses quoted in this chapter.
19. II.46.10–12 CSL. This is not in the Critical Edition.
20. Many have wondered why Yudhishthira was forced into such a catastrophic decision. Van Buitenen makes a plausible case that Yudhishthira had no choice because a game of dice was required of the king in the Vedic *rājasūya* sacrifice. Thus, when Yudhishthira replies to Vidura, 'Once challenged, I cannot refuse' (II.52.13,16), he could be thinking of the Vedic ritual. See J.A.B. van Buitenen (trans.), *Mahābhārata*, Chicago: University of Chicago Press, vol 2, 1975, 27–30). Others have pointed out that Yudhishthira was led along this ruinous path because he was addicted to gambling and he could not resist. It was a fatal flaw in his character. Julius Lipner says, 'from the story's point of view, more specifically from the point of view of tension between freedom and determinism in the context of dharma, we know perfectly well what led Yudhishthira to obey the summons. The text has been careful to tell us: Yudhishthira loves to gamble. This adharmic addiction is a chink in his dharmic armour' (*Hindus: Their Beliefs and Practices*, London: Routledge, 1994, 201). Van Buitenen's counter-argument is that although Shakuni claims that he has a passion for gambling, 'this

is disingenuous, for Yudhishthira has so far not been at all fond of gambling' (28). S.M. Kulkarni wonders why no one stopped him: 'It is noteworthy, though astonishing, that no one prevented Yudhishthira from betting . . .' S.M. Kulkarni, 'An Unresolved Dilemma in *Dyuta-parvan*: A Question Raised by Draupadi', in B.K. Matilal (ed.), *Moral Dilemmas in the Mahābhārata*, Delhi: Motilal Banarsidass, 151.

21. The 'cosmogonical rite was intended to bring about the recreation of the universe and the birth of the king'. J.C. Heesterman, *The Ancient Indian Royal Consecration*, The Hague: Mouton & Co, 1957, 153. Heesterman's is a classic study of this ritual.

22. Aaron Rester, 'Playing with Tradition: Sacrifice, Ritual, and the *Mahabharata*'s Dice Game', www.aaronrester.net/writings/mahabharatagameCCL

23. II.49.39 CSL

24. *The Rig Veda: An Anthology*, trans. Wendy Doniger O'Flaherty, London: Penguin Books, 1981, 240.

25. Protagoras, 352b–356c, *Collected Dialogues of Plato*, eds. E. Hamilton and H. Cairns, New York: Pantheon Books, 1963.

26. Ethica Nicomachea, 7.2, in *The Basic Works of Aristotle*, ed. R. Mckeon, New York: Random House, 1941.

27. Bimal K. Matilal, *The Collected Essays of Bimal Krishna Matilal: Ethics and Epics*, Oxford University Press, 2002, 63. '. . . According to classical Indian wisdom, weakness of the will is part of human nature *(svabhāva evaiṣa bhūtānām).*'

28. 'Game theory' uses the rational choices that individuals make in games to determine their interests and positions and even to unravel moral dilemmas. In 1955 the British philosopher Richard Braithwaite argued that many questions about distributive justice have the same structure as 'the bargaining problem'. R.B. Braithwaite, *Theory of Games as a Tool for the Moral Philosopher*, Cambridge: Cambridge University Press, 1955. In the late 1960s, David Gauthier used game theory to develop a moral theory (in the same way as the philosopher John Rawls derived the content of fundamental moral principles). Gauthier not only derived moral principles, but tried to show that rational agents would act morally. Most contemporary authors in ethics who use game

theory in their work are either Contractarians or Evolutionary theorists. The Contractarian tradition, with its emphasis on fully rational agents and bargaining, represents a more traditional use of game theory. The evolutionary approach, on the other hand, with its emphasis on bounded rational agents and repeated interactions, is a more recent arrival. We shall discuss it later in Chapter 3. See also Alf Hiltebeitel, 'Gambling', in *Encyclopedia of Religion*, Mircea Eliade, gen. ed., New York: Macmillan, 1987, vol 5, 469.

29. On the Vedic *rājasūya*, see J.C. Heesterman, *The Ancient Indian Royal Consecration*, The Hague: Thesis Utrecht, 1957.

30. Unevenness = *vaiṣamya*; evenness = *avaiṣamya*. After the war, Krishna tells the hermit Uttanka that he tried his best to create 'evenness' (*sauṣamya*) between the Kauravas and the Pandavas (XIV.53–55). Uttanka wants to know why Krishna, a god, could not prevent the war. Matilal concludes that Krishna was not omnipotent. Shulman questions this conclusion. He says that Krishna always took the side of the Pandavas. 'But we know that Kṛṣṇa is lying: the god works in a world that the *Mahabharata* consistently discloses to us as basically and essentially *viṣama*, uneven, inherently off balance, always spiralling downward towards destruction. Krishna himself consistently feeds this imbalance, fosters disorder, undermines surface symmetries.' David Shulman, 'The Yakṣa's Question', in *The Wisdom of the Poets: Studies in Tamil, Telugu and Sanskrit*, New Delhi: Oxford University Press, 2001, 51.

31. *kālaḥ pacati bhūtāni sarvāṇi*, XVII.1.3

32. Shulman, 40

33. Wendy Doniger, *The Hindus: An Alternative History*, New York: The Penguin Press, 2009, chapter 10.

34. Immanuel Kant, *The Metaphysics of Morals*, trans. M.G. McGregor, New York: Harper and Row, Part II, 127.

35. 'A person who is truthful (*satya*) and trustworthy must be free of envy (*amātsarya*). It is a freedom acquired by a good man, possessing the truth' (XII.156.14).

36. This quote as well as the previous one about envy's relationship with hatred is from the German philosopher Schopenhauer. Cited in Helmut Schoeck, *Envy: A Theory of Social Behaviour*, London: Martin Secker & Warburg, 1969, reprinted 1987 by Liberty Fund, 206–07.

37. Helmut Schoeck notes that envy 'is a silent, secretive process and not usually verifiable. It is surreptitious' (86).

38. Krishna Chaitanya, *The Mahabharata: A Literary Study*, New Delhi: Clarion Books, 1993, 45. No one will forget Dhritarashtra's words: 'kim jitam! kim jitam!'

39. Peter Walcot, *Envy and the Greeks: A Study of Human Behavior*, New York: Aris and Phillips, 1978; Svend Ranulf, *The Jealousy of the Gods and Criminal Law at Athens: A Contribution to the Sociology of Moral Indignation*, vol 1, London and Copenhagen, 1933, 133. The quote below of Aristides the Just is also from Peter Walcot.

40. Joseph Epstein, *Envy: The Seven Deadly Sins*, New York: Oxford University Press, 2003, 98.

41. Schoeck, 249

42. Hu Hsien-chin, 'The Chinese Concept of "Face"', *American Anthropologist*, 46 (1944), 45–64. Quoted in Schoeck, 67–68.

43. II.54.6 CSL. I have translated *svadharma* as duty here; Wilmot leaves it as *svadharma*.

44. II.55.7-8 CSL

45. II.55.11 CSL

46. *Dutavakya*, 1.24

47. II.46.20, II.50.18, 22, 27. Glaucon in Plato's *Republic* tells the story of Gyges, the shepherd, who served the king of Lydia. Gyges found a magical ring one day while tending his flock. When he accidentally turned the ring on his finger, he discovered that others could not see him. He made his way to the king's palace and used the ring to seduce the queen. He then conspired with the queen, killed the king, and assumed the throne. Glaucon argues that we act justly only because we are afraid of being punished.

48. This quote of Thucydides is from Thomas Hobbes's translation of the great Greek historian. David Greene (ed.), *The Peloponnesian War*, Chicago: University of Chicago Press, 1989, 194.

49. XII.15

50. In the myth of the flood, a tiny fish asks Manu to save him from the big fish who will otherwise devour him. The stated assumption is that without a king wielding tough punishments, the strong will devour the weak as big fish eat small fish (Manu 7.20).

51. II.62.3 CSL

52. See footnote 11 and 21.

53. Although the epic claims that the great war at Kurukshetra is a *dharma-yuddha,* a moral war, it also raises doubts in the heat of the battle if this is indeed a fight between good and evil. It keeps reminding one that dharma, the measure by which we judge good and evil, is itself contested, ambiguous and subtle. The fact is that both sides did plenty of good and bad deeds. For this and other reasons, Matilal refuses to call the Pandavas the 'good' side. He refers to them as the 'preferred' side. Bimal Krishna Matilal, 'Krishna: In Defence of a Devious Divinity', in Arvind Sharma (ed.), *Essays on the Mahabharata,* Leiden: E.J. Brill, 1991, 4.

54. Rudolph Otto pointed this out long ago and Alf Hiltebeitel more recently. Rudolph Otto, *The Original Gita: The Song of the Supreme Exalted One,* trans. J.E. Turner, London: George Allen and Unwin, 1939; Alf Hiltebeitel, *The Ritual of Battle: Kṛṣṇa in the Mahābhārata,* Ithaca and London: Cornell University Press, 1976.

55. *yūyaṃ vihatasamkalpāḥ socanto vartayiṣyatha (Salyaparvan,* 60, 50). This memorable speech includes the line, *ko nu svantatarno mayā,* 'Whose end is more admirable than mine?' Bhasa, the playwright, took this further and his plays *Pancharatra* and *Urubhanga* tended to magnify, even ennoble, the character of Duryodhana to heroic proportions. At one level, the *Mahabharata*'s war is between good and evil. Indeed, the oft-repeated first line of the Gita tells us this and the field of battle, Kurukshetra, is also a *dharmakṣetra* and the war is over dharma *('Dharmakṣetre kurukṣetre'* Gita 1.1). 'This war was for the sake of Dharma,' says V.S. Sukthankar. At this level, Yudhishthira is *Dharmarāja* or righteousness incarnate. Duryodhana, on the other side, is the incarnation of *adharma* or evil. He is also symbolic of Kali, *Kalipuruṣha,* the mark of time and death. Draupadi, on the other hand, is a symbol of Sri, the splendour of legitimate sovereignty. Therefore, not surprisingly, her humiliation by Duryodhana directs the narrative.

56. V.34.41, CSL

57. Epstein, 74

58. John Rawls, *The Theory of Justice,* Cambridge, Mass. Harvard University Press, 1971, 531.

59. This is also known as Sayre's Law, named after Wallace Stanley Sayre (1905–72), US political scientist and professor at Columbia

University. On 20 December 1973, the *Wall Street Journal* quoted Sayre as saying: 'Academic politics is the most vicious and bitter form of politics, because the stakes are so low.' Justin Kaplan, editor of *Bartlett's Familiar Quotations*, asked Henry Kissinger whether *he* had stated it. According to him, Kissinger, 'foxy as ever, said he didn't recall saying it but that it "sounded" like him. In other words, he didn't say it but wouldn't mind if we thought he did.'

60. Max Weber, 'Science as a Vocation', in H.H. Gerth and C. Wright Mills (trans. and ed.), *From Max Weber: Essays in Sociology*, New York: Oxford University Press, 1946, 129–56.

61. Epstein, 61

62. Ibid, 64

63. Rs 15,000 was roughly equal to US$2000 at the then prevailing exchange rate.

64. I have written extensively about this period in my book *India Unbound*. See especially Chapter 13, which recounts the story of the Ambani family. I knew those times well as I was working in Mumbai, selling Vicks Vaporub in the bazaars of India.

65. The phrase is from Hamish McDonald's book *The Polyester Prince: The Rise of Dhirubhai Ambani*, Allen and Unwin, 1998. He was bureau chief in Delhi for the *Far Eastern Economic Review* and his book is still banned in India.

66. See Friedrich Nietzsche's account of the 'slave revolt in morality' in *On the Genealogy of Morality*, trans. M. Clark and A. Swensen, Indianapolis: Hackett, 1998; Sigmund Freud, *Group Psychology and the Analysis of the Ego*, trans. J. Strachey, New York: Liverwright, 1949. This link can be found as far back as Aristotle. A comprehensive survey of historical sources is to be found in Schoeck, 1969. Envy receives a sympathetic treatment in R. Nozick, *Anarchy, State, and Utopia*, New York: Basic Books, 1974, though he does not explicitly endorse it. A relatively recent defence is by D. Cooper 'Equality and Envy', *Journal of Philosophy of Education*, 16, 35–47.

67. Freud, 120; see also D. Cooper, 35–47.

68. Rawls, 532

69. Loc. cit.

70. Rawls writes: 'Sometimes the circumstances evoking envy are so compelling that given human beings as they are, no one can reasonably be asked to overcome his rancorous feelings ... A person's lesser position ... may be so great as to wound his self-respect ... cause a loss of self-esteem.' Ibid, 534

71. Rawls, op. cit.

72. Richard Layard, *Happiness: Lessons from a New Science*, New York: Penguin Press, 2005.

73. Kierkegaard explains that envy will probably be greater in a society dedicated to equality than a feudal one with large differences. Adam Smith, on the other hand, was naïve in believing that envy would disappear once inequalities diminished. Smith's solution to inequalities was a state founded upon law and order. He wrote: 'Wherever there is great property, there is great inequality. For one very rich man, there must be at least five hundred poor. The affluence of the few supposes the indigence of the many, who are often both driven by want, and prompted by envy, to invade his possessions. It is only under the shelter of the civil magistrate that the owner of that valuable property, which is acquired by the labour of many years, or perhaps of many successive generations, can sleep a single night in security.' So far so good, but he was clearly wrong when he added: 'Where there is no property, or at least none that exceeds the value of two or three days' labour, civil government is not so necessary.' Adam Smith, *The Wealth of Nations*, Modern Library edition, 670.

74. Y. Olesha, *Envy* (introduction by Gleb Struve), London, 1947; reprinted New York: New York Review of Books, 2004.

75. The British socialist and Labour MP C.A.R. Crosland defended himself against allegations of envy in 1956 in *The Failure of Socialism*. In it, he discussed why his party invariably chose to leverage the envy of the lower classes even when they had become comparatively prosperous.

76. Luck egalitarians include some well-known names in philosophy: Ronald Dworkin (*Sovereign Virtue* 2000), Richard Arneson ('Equality and Equal Opportunity for Welfare', *Philosophical Studies* [1989], 77–93), G.A. Cohen ('On the Currency of Egalitarian Justice', *Ethics* [1989], 906–44), Thomas Nagel, Eric Rakowski, John Roemer and

Philippe Van Parijs. Elizabeth S. Anderson is a critic of luck egalitarianism ('What is the Point of Equality?' *Ethics* [1999], 287–337).
77. Martha Nussbaum, *The Fragility of Goodness: Luck and Ethics in Greek Tragedy and Philosophy*, Cambridge: Cambridge University Press, 1986, 1.
78. Shulman, 42–43
79. 'Poor mental hygiene' is Joseph Epstein's phrase, 98.

2. Draupadi's Courage

1. II.62.12. When quoting from the *Mahabharata*, I shall only mention the book, chapter and verse numbers. Unless otherwise indicated, the quotations from Book Two are from the University of Chicago Press translation by J.A.B. van Buitenen based on the Critical Edition. I have also employed Paul Wilmot's translation of Book Two of the epic in the Clay Sanskrit Series, which I have indicated by CSL.
2. *jitam* = won (II.58.45 in the Critical Edition; II.65.45 CSL). Van Buitenen employs 'maddened with pride' (II.60.1), but I prefer Wilmot's 'drunk' with pride in the more recent CSL translation.
3. II.59.1
4. He calls him 'Bharata' after the name of the clan to which the Kauravas and Pandavas belong. Hence, 'Mahabharata' is a story about the 'great' Bharatas (II.59.3–4). I have substituted 'fool' for van Buitenen's 'nitwit' and replaced the second line, 'You dumb deer to anger tigers', by Wilmot's more readable 'You are a deer provoking a tiger's wrath' (CSL II.66.4: *vyāghrān mrgah kopayase 'tivelam!*)
5. II.67.4 CSL
6. II.60.46
7. II.60.5. Paul Wilmot translates it more simply: 'What prince wagers his wife in a game?' II.67.5 CSL
8. II.60.7 (II.67.7 CSL: *kim nu pūrvam parājaisīr atmānam atha vāpi mām?*
9. II.60.13. After this there is a well known hiatus in the text which Hiltebeitel and Mehendale have tried to explain.
10. II.60.22
11. II.60.25
12. *Kūrun bhajasva*: 'enjoy the Kurus', II.60.20; *dāsī* = slave II.60.22–27
13. II.60.35, 36

14. Literally, 'wives always act upon a husband's orders': *striyās ca bhartur vaśatāṃ samīkṣya,* II.67.47 CSL. Manu (9.46) is more categorical—a husband owns his wife: 'Neither sale nor dismissal cuts the wife loose from the husband.'

15. II.60.40: *'na dharmasaukṣmyāt saubhage vivaktum/śaknomi te praśnam imaṃ yathāvat'* (II.60.40ab). Van Buitenen translates Draupadi's *praśnam* as riddle, but I believe 'question' is more appropriate. Bhishma, who is used to thinking about property in a legal way, says, 'One without property cannot bet another's, but considering that a wife is under a husband's authority . . .': *asvo hy aśaktaḥ paṇitum parasvam/ striyaś ca bhartur vaśatāṃ samīkṣya* (II.60.40.cd).

16. II.61.20–24; Critical Edition II.68.23–24 CSL. I have edited Vikarna's speech, using both the van Buitenen and the Wilmot translations. John Smith translates 'the world does not condone' in a better way: 'and the world holds the deeds of such a person to be of no account' (p146).

17. The text has Karna say, 'Strip the Pandavas and Draupadi of their clothes!': *pāṇḍavānāṃ ca vāsāṃsi draupadyaś cāpupāhara.* Draupadi's rejection of Karna is not in the Critical Edition but only in Neelakantha's recession. Draupadi had five husbands not only because of Kunti but of multiple layers in the text.

18. David Shulman, 'The Yaksa's Question', in Galit Hasan-Rokem and David Shulman (eds.), *Untying the Knot: On Riddles and Other Enigmatic Modes,* New York: Oxford University Press, 1996, 153. Shulman, of course, employs the transliteration of *prashna = praśna.*

19. Alf Hiltebeitel points out this anomaly. The messenger says *'kasyeśo nah parājaisīh'*, and then proceeds to repeat Draupadi's question, *'kim nu pūrvaṃ parājaisīr ātmānam mām nu'*. Alf Hiltebeitel, *Rethinking the Mahābhārata: A Reader's Guide to the Education of the Dharma Kings,* Chicago: University of Chicago Press, 242–43.

20. Among others, M.A. Mehendale discusses this legal aspect of the issue. M.A. Mehendale, 'Draupadi's Question', *Journal of the Oriental Institute,* Baroda, 35, 3–4, 183.

21. Kulkarni 1989 and Shah 1995, pp. 30–31 also come to this conclusion. Kulkarni, S.M. 1989. 'An unresolved dilemma in Dyuta-Parvan: A question raised by Draupadi', in Matilal (ed)1989, *Moral Dilemmas in the Mahabharata,* Delhi,, Motilal Banarsidass,150–53).

22. Shalini Shah makes this point eloquently in *The Making of Womanhood: Gender Relations in the Mahabharata,* Delhi: Manohar, 1995, 30–31.

23. *amārgeṇa nṛśamsavat,* II.53.3.

24. Hiltebeitel, 262. See also Hiltebeitel's discussion under 'Gambling' in the *Encyclopaedia of Religion*, 1987, editor in chief, Mircea Eliade, New York: Free Press, (5) 468–474.
25. II.60.42
26. II.62.12
27. II.61.41–43, 48
28. II.61.52: *'dharmo 'tra pīḍyate'*, II.68.59 CSL. *pīḍyate* = tormented.
29. *viddho dharmo hy adharmeṇa sabhāṃ yatropapadyate* (II.68.77 CSL)
30. II.68.78 CSL. Although the text does not name them, Vidura clearly thinks of Duryodhana as the leader, Duhshasana as the culprit, and the men in the assembly (especially the elders) who are guilty of silence.
31. II.68.89 (II.71.1. CSL)
32. II.62.7
33. II.63.27. She is called 'Panchali' because she is the daughter of King Drupada of Panchala.
34. The quote is from Hiltebeitel, 262. Mehendale does not think that Draupadi's question remained unanswered or that Draupadi regained her freedom through the intercession of bad omens. He argues that it is because Arjuna gave a decisive reply to Draupadi's question that she got the boons from Dhritarashtra. He translates Arjuna's reply in II.63.21 as follows: 'When the game of dice began Yudhishthira was our master. But once he has lost himself, whose master can he be? Kauravas take note of this' (*'īso rajā pūrvam āsīd glahe naḥ kuntīputro dharmarajo mahātmā/iśas tv ayaṃ kasya parājitātmā taj jānīdhvaṃ kuravaḥ sarva eva'*). Thus, he concludes, 'Arjuna's reply is quite clear. "Whose master defeated Yudhishthira?" Of course, of none—not even of Draupadi.' His argument rests on the translation of *jānīdhvaṃ* above, which van Buitenen translates as 'decide', and this according to him is incorrect. He gives a number of examples from the epic to prove that *vibrūta* would have been the right translation of 'decide' had the poet meant to say this. Mehendale believes that the right translation is 'realize' or 'take note'. Arjuna wants them to realize that Yudhishthira in the circumstances could not be the master of anyone. Hence, in his view, Arjuna did answer Draupadi's question, and the intercession of bad omens was unnecessary and an 'interpolation' in the Poona Critical Edition of the epic. Mehendale, 188–91.

Other scholars, however, hold the opposite view. They believe Draupadi's question remained unresolved to the end. N.R. Pathak in his 1967 Marathi translation says: 'The significant question which Draupadi had raised at this extremely critical moment could not be answered satisfactorily by anyone. Therefore, Dhritarashtra managed to somehow get out of the fix by offering boons to Draupadi' (cited in Mehendale, 181). Van Buitenen also concludes: 'There is much argument, but it remains inconclusive' (*Mahabharata*, trans. J.A.B. van Buitenen, Chicago: University of Chicago Press, vol 2, 1975, 30). Purely from a literary point of view, personally, I find it more satisfying that Draupadi's question remains unanswered. Just as I found Edgerton's notion of 'cosmic justice' more satisfying in the disrobing episode, I think the omens here vindicate her commitment to dharma, and Dhritarashtra says so when he refers to her as *dharmacārinī*.

35. Wendy Doniger, *The Hindus: An Alternative History*, New York: The Penguin Press, 2009, 793.

36. Hiltebeitel, 250–51. With regard to the disrobing, Hiltebeitel points to a parallel with Nala's story. He says the body stripped 'is a self laid bare. As Nala is stripped, so is Yudhishthira. For each, their project becomes that of restoring themselves, their kingdoms and their marriages. But the women are never stripped. Damayanti retains half a sari, and Draupadi receives endless saris ... As in Nala, it is a question of the self, as *atman*, only with the royal hero and not with the heroine' (257).

37. II.68.42–44 CSL

38. Franklin Edgerton, '*Sabhaparvan*, Introduction and Apparatus', V.S. Sukthankar et al. *Critical Edition of the Mahabharata*, Poona, 1933–70, vol 2, xxix. Julius Lipner agrees that 'Draupadi as a righteous woman was not righteously treated ... and in the final analysis dharma has vindicated Draupadi' (*Hindus: Their Beliefs and Practices*, London: Routledge, 1994, 207). Lipner adds: 'Her faith in dharma has not been void, although it has cost her dear ... whatever the solution to the riddle may be, the text implies that Draupadi as a righteous woman has been righteously treated. Otherwise her final humiliation would not have been thwarted and her modesty miraculously preserved.' Hiltebeitel also endorses the decision. 'Within the context of the passage itself the Critical Edition's accumulated evidence leaves no grounds to refute these conclusions.

The reconstituted text has continuity without Krishna's intervention and the tendency of later redactors (both northern or southern) to embroider the story is evident.'

39. Ibid, xxix

40. Purshottam Aggarwal calls the public disrobing an example of a patriarchal world view: 'Duryodhana could think of no better way than ordering the public disrobing of Draupadi to decisively emphasise the humiliating and final defeat of the Pandavas in the game of dice, and the Pandavas could not protest for the simple reason that Duryodhana, even in his reprehensible act, was justified in terms of the moral paradigm of patriarchy which was binding upon the Pandavas.' 'Savarkar, Surat, and Draupadi', in Tanika Sarkar and Urvashi Butalia (eds.), *Women and the Hindu Right: A Collection of Essays*, New Delhi: Kali for Women, 1995, 39.

41. Leo Tolstoy, *The Krentzer Sonata*, New York: Modern Library, 2003; R.F. Christian (ed.), *Tolstoy's Diaries*, abridged edition, New York: HarperCollins, 1996. I wish to thank Martha Nussbaum for this quote from Tolstoy's diaries. It appears in her article 'Body of the Nation: Why Women Were Mutilated in Gujarat', *Boston Review: A Political and Literary Forum*, Summer 2004.

42. I.99–100

43. Doniger, 346

44. See Romila Thapar, *Early India*, 193, 228; also see Doniger, 356.

45. Iravati Karve, *Yuganta: The End of an Epoch*, Hyderabad: Disha Books/Orient Longman, 1991, 101.

46. Ibid, 99

47. II.62.14, 17, 19, 20

48. This is why philosophers call moral statements prescriptive and not descriptive.

49. Philosophers call this the 'principle of universalizability' of moral judgements.

50. B.K. Matilal discusses the question of dharma's rationality in his paper, 'Dharma and Rationality', in S. Biderman and B.A. Scharfstein (eds.), *Rationality in Question: On Eastern and Western Views of Rationality*, E.J. Brill: Leiden, 1989. It is reproduced also in Bimal K. Matilal, *The Collected Essays of Bimal Krishna Matilal: Ethics and Epics*, Oxford University Press, 2002. The quote above is on 51.

51. *The Laws of Manu*, 2.6, trans. Wendy Doniger with Brian K. Smith, London: Penguin Books, 17. Wendy Doniger translates 'dharma' as 'religion' in this verse but 'law' elsewhere; Patrick Olivelle translates it as 'law' here. I think it is best to leave the word (dharma) as it is. *The Law Code of Manu*, trans. Patrick Olivelle, Oxford: Oxford University Press, 2004, 23.

52. XII.234.10

53. X.3.3

54. Kūlluka, in fact, cites Garga, another author of *The Dharmaśhastras* in support of his claim. Matilal, 57.

55. Kâlidâsa, *Abhijñāna-śākuntala*, ed. Narayana Rama Acharya, Bombay: Nirnay Sagar Press, 11th edn., 1947, I, 22.

56. Bimal K. Matilal concludes that the openness and the plurality of authorities 'bespeaks of the rational stream of the tradition as well as the lesser importance accorded to blind faith' (57).

57. XII.173.45–47. 'Atheist' translates as *nāstika*, which is usually taken to mean denial of a world to come. (Translation by Nicholas Sutton, *Religious Doctrines in the Mahābhārata*, Delhi: Motilal Banarsidass, 2000.)

58. James Fitzgerald describes this change nicely in his excellent introduction to Book Twelve of the *Mahābhārata*, vol 7, Books XI and XII, Chicago: University of Chicago Press, 2004, 101–28.

59. XII.184.15cd

60. XII.60

61. Fitzgerald explains the usage of this second sense of dharma in the *Mahābhārata* : '[It] was the result of the new religious perspectives and values of yoga that gradually emerged alongside the older Vedic ones in the middle third of the first millennium BC in northern India.' He goes on to elaborate what these 'new religious perspectives' are: 'Upanishadic brahmins worked, in meditation, to displace limited forms of desire with the bliss of the "knowledge of" *Brahman*; Jainas sought to stop the influx of fresh *karman* and ascetically "burn off" old *karman*; Buddhists sought to undermine the psychological basis of desire, thereby "extinguishing" (nirvāṇa) the erroneous idea of selfhood, desire, *karman*, and rebirth. Each tradition developed institutions of "withdrawal" (*nivṛtti*) and renunciation peculiar to itself' (109–110). (See also footnote 133 in Chapter 9.)

62. III.34.19, 22, 65. Bhima reminds Yudhishthira again in III.49.13 that *rājyam eva param dharmam kṣatriyasya vidur budhāḥ*: 'The wise know that kingship is the highest dharma of a kshatriya'.

63. Homer, *Iliad*, 24.725 ff

64. Bhagavad Gita III. 20. Krishna speaks of *loka-samgraham*, which is maintaining the world or promoting the welfare of the people, and cites King Janaka as a model monarch who acted in this manner. He repeats it in verse 25.

65. Susan Buck-Morss, 'Hegel and Haiti', *Critical Inquiry*, 26, 4 (Summer 2000), 821.

66. Indeed, Thomas McCarthy, an influential philosopher, has recently argued: 'In fact, it seems to have been Kant who first introduced the idea of explaining racial differentiation by postulating in our original ancestors a fund of four germs or seeds, each of which contained ... one set of racial characteristics.'

67. See www.antislavery.org, the website of Anti-Slavery International, for detailed statistics on present-day slavery.

68. Arun Shourie, *Governance and the Sclerosis that Has Set In*, New Delhi: ASA–Rupa, 2004, 3–7. This book is a treasure house of such examples.

69. *dharmakṣetre kurukṣetre*, Gita 1.1. Sukthankar explains as follows: 'This war was for the sake of Dharma, moral law, an abstract principle difficult even to define precisely; it is so subtle.' V.S. Sukthankar, *On the Meaning of the Mahabharata*, Bombay: The Asiatic Society of Bombay, 1957.

70. B.K. Matilal, 'Moral Dilemmas: Insights from Indian Epics', in B.K. Matilal (ed.), *Moral Dilemmas in the Mahabharata*, Delhi: Motilal Banarsidass, 1989, 2.

71. Bhishma will teach the king's dharma to Yudhishthira in Book Twelve at interminable length. The poet Kalidasa also describes this in his play *Raghuvamsha* 1.25; 17.57.

72. Kautilya, *Arthashastra*, trans. R.P. Kangle, Part II, Delhi: Motilal Banarsidass, 1972, 1.7.

73. The French playwright Jean Anouilh wrote a version of *Antigone* that was staged in German-occupied France. It was meant to be a rallying call to resist the Nazi regime, but I'm not sure that Sophocles would have sympathized with this interpretation of his play.

74. II.63.21
75. The quote is from Alfred Collins, cited in Hiltebeitel, 261–62. Alfred Collins, 'Dancing with Prakriti', Paper delivered at the annual meeting of the American Academy of Religion, 1994. Collins/ Hiltebeitel raise questions such as: Is it the sovereign self (*purusha*) that replicates itself in other selves? Or is it mind-ego-intellect (*prakriti*) that is unconscious matter, which becomes a conscious self 'for the sake of the *purusha*'?
76. Hiltebeitel, 262: 'Yudhishthira is put into the position of raising for himself and others in the court, including incarnate demons, the Pascalian/Faustian question of what it means to have "wagered one's soul".'
77. Hiltebeitel, 242. See also Hiltebeitel's discussion under 'Gambling', 468–74.
78. Walter Lippmann, *A Preface to Morals*, New York: Macmillan, 1929, reprinted Transaction, 1982, 77.

3. Yudhishthira's Duty

1. *Mahabharata* III.28.10–14. (As usual, I shall mention only the book number, chapter number and verse numbers when quoting from the *Mahabharata*.)
2. III.28.6; III.31.17–19
3. III.31.17–9
4. III.31.37–39
5. III.29.33–35
6. III.28.17–33. *manyuḥ* = anger
7. Forbearance = *kṣamā*; anger = *krodha*
8. III.32.2–5
9. III.32.15
10. Immanuel Kant, *Groundwork of the Metaphysics of Morals*, Mary Gregor (trans.), Cambridge Texts in the History of Philosophy, Cambridge: Cambridge University Press, 1998, 62.
11. 'An Enquiry Concerning the Principles of Morals', in L.A. Selby-Bigge (ed.), *Hume's Enquiries*, 2nd edn., Oxford: Clarendon Press, 1902, 272–75, first published in 1751. Hume writes, 'When a man denominates another his *enemy*, his *rival*, his *antagonist*, his *adversary*,

he is understood to speak the language of self-love. But when he bestows on a man the epithets of *vicious* or *odious* or *depraved*, he then speaks another language, and expresses sentiments, in which he expects all his audience to concur with him. He must here, therefore, depart from his private and particular situation, he must move some universal principle and touch a string to which all mankind have an accord and symphony. While the human heart is compounded of the same elements as at present, it will never be wholly indifferent to public good.'

12. Immanuel Kant, *The Critique of Practical Reason and Other Writings in Moral Philosophy*, trans. L.W. Beck, Chicago: University of Chicago Press, 1949, 193–94. Kant also wrote famously: 'Duty! Thou sublime and mighty name ... what origin is worthy of thee, and where is to be found the root of thy noble descent which proudly rejects all kinship with inclinations and ... is the indispensable condition of the only worth which men can give themselves? ... Man is certainly unholy enough, but humanity in his person must be holy to him. Everything in creation which he wishes and over which he has power can be used merely as a means; only man, and with him, every rational creature, is an end in itself. He is the subject of the moral law ... because of the autonomy of his freedom ... the autonomy of the rational being.'

13. John Locke, 'Second Treatise on Civil Government', in E. Barker (ed.), *Social Contract*, London: Oxford University Press, 1960, 7–23.

14. III.32.19

15. III.32.32

16. *The Law Code of Manu* (*Mānava Dharmaśāstra*), trans. Patrick Olivelle, New York: Oxford University Press, 2004, 2.2–4, 23.

17. III.181.35–38

18. II.55.10

19. XII.110.5–6

20. Fyodor Dostoevsky, *The Karamazov Brothers*, trans. Ignat Avsey, Oxford: Oxford University Press, 1994, I, Part 2, Book 5, Chapter 4.

21. Bhishma and Krishna are Consequentialists. A Consequentialist believes that a right act is 'one that will produce the best outcome, as judged impersonally and giving equal weight to everyone's interests'. Samuel Scheffler, *Consequentialism and its Critics*, Oxford:

Oxford University Press, 1988, 1. 'Consequentialism is the theory that the way to tell whether a particular choice is the right choice for an agent to have made is to look at the relevant consequences of the decision; to look at the relevant effects of the decision on the world,' as Philip Pettit tells us in his collection of essays *Consequentialism* (Aldershot: Dartmouth, 1993, xiii). Utilitarians, like Bentham and Mill, were among the most famous Consequentialists, who judged an action on how much it increased the happiness of the world. Hence, their famous slogan: 'the greatest good for the greatest number'.

22. Bentham said famously: 'Each to count for one and none for more than one.' Jeremy Bentham, *An Introduction to the Principles of Morals and Legislation*, New York: Hafner, 1049, chapter 1, n.4.

23. John Rawls points out elegantly the indifference of Consequentialism to considerations of distributive justice in *A Theory of Justice*, Cambridge, MA: The Belknap Press of Harvard University Press, 1971.

24. Thomas Nagel provides other ghastly examples in a fine essay, 'War and Massacre', in *Mortal Questions*, Cambridge: Cambridge University Press, 1979.

25. III.32.24

26. XII.270.20 is one of many examples of this.

27. III.34.2, 5. I have replaced 'dharma' for law, *artha* for profit and *kama* for pleasure in van Buitenen's translation.

28. III.34.38, 47

29. As a result of what Hindu philosophers called his *svabhāva*, which in turn was a result of his *guṇas*, and which also reflected his karmic balance.

30. III.35.21. This was said to Bhima. Draupadi was silent, presumably sulking.

31. III.35.1b, 21

32. Legally minded persons will recognize Yudhishthira's 'bull-headedness' in the Latin saying, *Fiat justitia et ruant coel*—'let justice be done though the heavens fall'. Van Buitenen is quite right in pointing out that one of the purposes of Book Three of the epic is to build up Yudhishthira's character, especially after his disastrous performance in the dice game: '*The Book of the Forest* serves to build the character of Yudhishthira ... Faced with all these temptations

[he] remains firm . . . he had given his word . . . [It] is the celebration of the highest value in the moral code of ancient Indians, truthfulness and faithfulness under all circumstances.' See his introduction to *The Book of the Forest (Āraṇyakaparvan), Mahābhārata,* Chicago: University of Chicago Press, 177.

33. Ibid
34. V.70.55
35. V.151.20–22
36. V.151.25–26
37. It is the sage Markandeya who calls him 'guileless': 'Do not grieve, tiger among men, you are a kshatriya, enemy burner; you are walking the road of blazing resolve that relies on the prowess of your arms; for not the strongest bit of guile is found in you' *(na hi te vrijinaṃ kiṃcid dṛśyate param aṇv api)* III.276.2.
38. V.27.1–2. The thoughts expressed by Sanjaya are those of Dhritarashtra.
39. V.27.16, 20–21
40. V.28.3–5
41. van Buitenen, 133
42. V.3.20
43. V.31.22
44. At the end of the epic Yudhishthira is referred to as a person bestowed with *ānṛśaṃsya—ānṛśaṃsya samāyukata* (XVII.3.30–32).
45. Niccolo Machiavelli, *The Prince,* Peter Constantine (trans.), New York: Modern Library, 2001, 52.
46. See, for example, W.D. Hamilton, 'The Genetic Evolution of Social Behaviour I and II', *Journal of Theoretical Biology* (1964), 7. 1–16, 17–32; E.O. Wilson, *Sociobiology: The New Synthesis,* Cambridge, MA: Harvard University Press, 1975; Richard D. Alexander, *The Biology of Moral Systems,* New York: Aldine de Gruyter, 1987; Richard Dawkins, *The Selfish Gene,* Oxford: Oxford University Press, 1976; Robert Wright, *The Moral Animal: Evolutionary Psychology and Everyday Life,* New York: Vintage Books, 1995; E. Sober and D.S. Wilson, *Unto Others: The Evolution and Psychology of Unselfish Behavior,* Cambridge, MA: Harvard University Press, 1998.
47. Charles Darwin, *The Descent of Man,* vol 1 (1871), Princeton: Princeton University Press, 1971, 80.
48. George C. Williams, *Adaptation and Natural Selection,* 1966, Princeton University Press, 1974, 94.

49. William Hamilton and Robert Axelrod connected reciprocity to evolution via kin selection based on the insight that altruism does flow towards one's relatives in their seminal paper in Robert Axelrod, *The Evolution of Cooperation*, New York: Basic Books, 1984.

50. Robert Trivers, 'The Evolution of Reciprocal Altruism', *Quarterly Review of Biology* (1971), 46.35–56.

51. Robert Axelrod, the American social theorist, conducted the Prisoner's Dilemma round-robin tournament in which Anatol Rapaport won. See Anatol Rapaport, *Fights, Games and Debates*, Ann Arbor: University of Michigan Press, 1960.

52. It is a pity that we use 'tit for tat' in unflattering ways. The *Times of India*'s headline on 6 August 2006 read: 'Tit for tat: India, Pak play spy games, expel envoys'. The *New York Times* called Pakistan's firing of the Abdali nuclear missile 'tit for tat' in response to India's Prithvi, 26 March 2003.

53. III.33.23

54. III.33.8

55. Aristotle says: 'States of character arise out of like activities. This is why the activities we exhibit must be of a certain kind; it is because the states of character correspond to the differences between these. It makes no small difference whether we form habits of one kind from our very youth; it makes a very great difference, or rather all the difference.' *Nicomachean Ethics*, 1103a.

56. III.32.37

57. Martha Nussbaum, *Upheavals of Thought: The Intelligence of Emotions*, Cambridge: Cambridge University Press, 2003, 74.

58. Mrinal Miri, *Identity and the Moral Life*, New Delhi: Oxford University Press, 2003, 98. In this essay, Miri quotes Kierkegaard, who said that the moral life is difficult because it requires the 'transformation of our whole subjectivity'.

59. M.K. Gandhi, *An Autobiography: The Story of my Experiments with Truth*, Boston: Beacon Press, 1993.

60. Joseph Conrad, *Lord Jim: A Tale*, Allan Simmons (ed.), London: Penguin Classics, 2007.

4. Arjuna's Despair

1. The offer is so appalling to Yudhishthira's brother Bhima that he is totally consumed by it in the first act of the eighth-century drama *Venisamhara*.

2. V.57.18 (As usual, I mention only the book number, chapter number and verse numbers when quoting from the *Mahabharata*.)

3. Many historians believe that the *Mahabharata*'s war did take place. Although 3102 BC is the much-cited traditional date for the war, it probably took place around 950 BC based on the evidence of Vedic texts (John Keay, *India: A History*, New York: Grove Press, 2000). Painted Grey Ware artefacts discovered at sites identified with locations in the *Mahabharata* suggest that the great war probably occurred between 1000 BC and 400 BC. (H. Kulke and E. Rothermund, *A History of India*, London: Routledge, 1986, 45.)

4. V.196.1–4

5. V.197.17ff

6. J.A.B. van Buitenen, *The Bhagavadgītā in the Mahabharata: Text and Translation*, Chicago: University of Chicago Press, 1981, 4.

7. In Book Six, *Bhishmaparvan*, the *Mahabharata* goes backwards, as we shall see in the next chapter. Sanjaya, the bard, has just told Dhritarashtra that their commander-in-chief has fallen on the tenth day of battle. Suddenly, at this point, the epic takes us back in time. The war at Kurukshetra is about to begin. The slaying of Bhishma is still on our minds when Arjuna feels confused and dejected in the first chapter of the Gita. Scholars have long debated whether the Gita belongs in the epic at all; many have called it an interpolation. But to the ordinary Indian, it belongs there incontrovertibly. A.K. Ramanujan reminds us that its central incident in which a warrior suffers a failure of nerve, an attack of cowardice, before battle, but who is then counselled and urged into battle, occurs at least five times in the epic. The most ironic of these is immediately before the big battle scenes, a comic scene in *Virataparvan*. *The Collected Essays of A.K. Ramanujan*, gen. ed. Vinay Dharwadker, Oxford University Press, 1999, 426.

8. Bhagavad Gita I.1. The Gita begins in Book Six of the *Mahabharata* at VI.63.23. I shall be quoting from Barbara Stoler Miller's translation

of the Bhagavad Gita. As I looked for a good English translation of this text, I discovered that there were more than thirty to choose from, and like the Pandavan hero, I too became confused. A fine article by Gerald Larson, 'The Song Celestial: Two Centuries of the Bhagavadgītā in English' was a good beginner's guide. Vedanta enthusiasts directed me to the slim Isherwood–Prabhavananda translation, which has an introduction by Aldous Huxley on perennial philosophy. While I thought it satisfying as literature— after all Christopher Isherwood is a great writer—I felt it was not the most accurate, and its interpretation was a de-ethnicized Shankara combined with Western mysticism. Radhakrishnan's rendition I found to be dull and commentarial. Indologists recommended Zaehner, and although his translation turned out to be stilted, his wonderful discussions on Ramanuja, Shankara and the Upanishads that run parallel in the text make it quite exciting. Although an accomplished Orientalist, Zaehner was clearly attracted to the notion of *bhakti* and the love of a personal god.

The most poetic is still the Victorian version of Sir Edwin Arnold, and it has the virtue also of being the cheapest in the Dover thrift edition. Those seeking pure accuracy should read either Edgerton's translation or van Buitenen's, who views the Gita as an integral part of the epic and challenges the traditional idea that it was inserted later. Don't trust Mascaro's version, which tries unsuccessfully to be poetic. Bhaktivedanta's rendition is a dull, sectarian, Sunday school textbook, reflecting the Vaishnavite values of Chaitanya. Since I am a beginner in Sanskrit, I found Winthrop Sargeant's very useful (but expensive); it is accompanied by an interlinear Sanskrit text, a word-for-word grammatical commentary and vocabulary.

In the end, I chose Barbara Stoler Miller's translation because it is both accurate, poetical, and has the great virtue of simplicity. Before she died in 1993, she was professor of Sanskrit at Barnard/ Columbia and she created the translation for our generation. Through this process of selecting I have come to realize that there is no right or wrong translation and each one serves its particular audience. Van Buitenen's version is no good to a follower of Sai Baba, as Arnold's account will not interest a Sanskrit scholar.

Mahatma Gandhi's or Tilak's use of the Gita in India's freedom struggle is as valid as Edgerton's reading of the text as a Vaishnav brahmin document of the first century AD. Emerson and Thoreau used the Wilkins translation. Hegel used Humboldt's (as well as Schlegel's and Wilkins's). Gandhi used Sir Edwin Arnold's, while post-Independence Indians turned to Radhakrishnan's.

9. Bhagavad Gita 1.14
10. Bhagavad Gita I.21–22
11. Bhagavad Gita I.26
12. Bhagavad Gita I.29, 30, 31
13. Bhagavad Gita I.47
14. Bhagavad Gita II.1–2
15. Bhagavad Gita II.5, 9
16. Karl von Clausewitz, *On War*, trans. Michael Howard and Peter Paret, Princeton: Princeton University Press, 1976, 76.
17. V.70.58
18. '700 fratricidal verses' are the words of the Marxist historian D.D. Kosambi, *An Introduction to the Study of Indian History*, 2nd edition, Bombay: Popular Prakashan, 1975, 128. See Kunal Chakrabarti, 'The Lily and the Mud', *Economic and Political Weekly*, 26 July 2008, 60–70; Romila Thapar, 'The Contribution of D.D. Kosambi to Indology', *Interpreting Early India*, Delhi: Oxford University Press, 1993.
19. Bhagavad Gita II.31
20. Bhagavad Gita II.37
21. Bhagavad Gita II.19
22. Bhagavad Gita II.21
23. Bhagavad Gita II.47: *karmany evādhikāras te mā phaleṣu kadācana*. Eknath Easwaran translates this line as: 'you have the right to work, but never to the fruit of work' (*The Bhagavad Gita*, trans. Eknath Easwaran, London: Arkana/Penguin, 1986, 66). Van Buitenen explains that 'the right to work' (*adhikāra*) or 'entitlement' as he translates it, is a technical term among Mimamsa philosophers, who would not necessarily have agreed with Krishna's advice: 'it is his desire for fruit that is the person's entitlement. But Krishna condemns such *kāmya* (desire motivated) acts as conducive to rebirth, and he upholds as ultimately beneficial only those acts that

are naturally incumbent on one' (J.A.B. van Buitenen, *The Bhagavadgītā in the Mahābhārata*, 163, footnote 13).

24. 'Preserve the world' is the celebrated notion of *lokasaṃgraha*. Bhagavad Gita III.20 and 25 = *Mahabharata* VI.25.25.

25. Bhagavad Gita III.35; XVIII.47 = *Mahabharata* VI.25.20 and 35.

26. Martha Nussbaum has eloquently pointed this out in an essay, 'The Costs of Tragedy: Some Moral Limits of Cost-Benefit Analysis', *Journal of Legal Studies*, XXIX, 2, Part 2 (June 2000), 1005–36.

27. See the discussion between 'duty' (or deontological) ethics and Consequentialism in Chapter 3.

28. From Pat Parker's novel *Regeneration*, London: Penguin, 1992. Robert Graves is one of the historical characters in this first part of a trilogy on World War I.

29. Bhagavad Gita XI.12–13

30. Bhagavad Gita XI.23, 25

31. Bhagavad Gita XI.32–33

32. Bhagavad Gita XVIII.63

33. VI.102.36

34. VI.102.37

35. T.S. Eliot, *Four Quartets*, London: Faber and Faber, 1944, 31.

36. Thomas Nagel explains how a person can feel strongly both types of moral intuitions and how it can lead to an unsolvable moral dilemma. See his essay 'War and Massacre' in *Mortal Questions*, Cambridge: Cambridge University Press, 1979, 53–74.

37. Amartya Sen, 'Consequential Evaluation and Practical Reason', *The Journal of Philosophy*, XCVI. 9 (September 2000), 485.

38. Nussbaum, 1009

39. V.60.1–3

40. Nussbaum, 1011

41. VII.34.19. Learning in the womb is not in the Critical Edition.

42. VII.49.14–16, 22–23 CSL

43. VII.49.32–35 CSL

44. VII.50.1–4 CSL

45. XI.20.32

46. VII.51.20ff. 'Oaths [in the *Mahabharata*] are connected directly with the proper functioning of world order, insofar as their fulfilment depends upon and helps to preserve that order; likewise, to frame

it as an oath raises any act to the level of action in support of *dharma* and truth.' Ruth C. Katz, *Arjuna in the Mahabharata: Where Krishna Is, There is Victory*. Columbia, SC: University of South Carolina Press, 1989, 140.

47. VII.56.6ff

48. VII.75.28

49. VII.121.15

50. Poona Critical Edition, 7, Appendix 1, 16, 5–10. This impressive moment is not recorded in the Critical Edition, but is found in Bengali and Devanagari texts.

51. VII.121.30ff

52. I shall return to the dubious moral quality of Krishna's advice in killing Jayadratha in Chapter 7.

53. *Iliad* XVIff. I am indebted to Ruth Katz's interesting discussion of Arjuna's *aristeia*, and her comparison of Arjuna and Achilles. See Katz, 137–39; 151, footnote 14.

54. VII.125.1–2. Gregory Nagy, *The Best of the Achaeans: Concepts of the Hero in Archaic Greek Poetry*, Baltimore: Johns Hopkins University Press, 26ff. Cited in Katz, 144, footnote 44.

55. Literally: *kshetra* = field; *dharma* = righteousness.

56. The literature on the Western realist tradition in international affairs is vast. A good starting point for the uninitiated might be Robert Kaplan's entertaining article, 'Kissinger, Metternich and Realism', *Atlantic Monthly* (June 1999), 73–82, which is a longish review of Kissinger's masterly book, *The World Restored*.

57. M.A. Mehendale discusses this subject insightfully in *Reflections on the Mahābhārata War*, Simla: Institute for Advanced Studies, 1995. He reaches the same conclusion. With reference to the third criterion above, 'the Kuruksetra war turns out to be a *dharmayuddha* for the Pandavas, but not for the Kauravas' (2). As to the second criterion, he says, 'the conclusion . . . can only be that from the point of view of the observance of the rules of war, the *Mahābhārata* cannot be called a *dharmayuddha*, the heroes of both sides having to share the responsibility for this' (23).

58. IX.60.39–46

59. Such as Francisco de Vitoria (1486–1546), Francisco Suarez (1548–1617), Hugo Grotius (1583–1645), Samuel Pufendorf (1632–1704), Christian Wolff (1679–1754) and Emerich de Vattel (1714–67).

60. Sheldon Pollock comments that unlike the *Mahabharata*, Homer, Virgil, Tasso and other pre-modern writers of the Western narrative poetry were sensitive to the pity of war but not as much to the possibility of its injustice.

61. Michael Walzer discusses this issue in *Just and Unjust Wars: A Moral Argument with Historical Illustrations*, New York: Basic Books, 1977, 81, 90.

62. Vaughan Pilikian's Introduction to his translation of *Drona* (vol 1), Book Seven of the *Mahabharata*, Clay Sanskrit Library, New York: New York University Press, 18.

63. V.70.55–58

64. V.26.3 CSL

65. Romila Thapar, *The Penguin History of Early India: From the Origins to AD 1300*, New Delhi: Penguin Books, 2002, 278.

5. Bhishma's Selflessness

1. Ralph Waldo Emerson's quote is from Frederic Carpenter, *Emerson and Asia*, New York: Haskell House, 1968. Emerson also wrote a famous and influential poem, 'Brahma', which Friedrich read out to us in class. Thoreau's is from his *Journal*, vol 1, reproduced in Paul Friedrich's fine book, which he wrote some years later, *Gita within Walden*, New York: State University of New York Press, 2008, 1.

2. Bhagavad Gita II.47: *karmany evādhikāras te mā phaleshu kadācana*. As in Chapter 4, I shall be quoting mostly from Barbara Stoler Miller's translation.

3. Bhagavad Gita III.8

4. *vimatsarah* = free from envy. Bhagavad Gita IV.22. The previous quotes are from IV.20 and IV.21.

5. Bhagavad Gita II.48. The previous quote about 'unattached and free' is at IV.23. Barbara Stoler Miller translates the word 'yoga' as 'discipline'. In the main epic, 'yoga' also means a trick or fraud, as in Krishna's suggestion to use yoga in Dronavadha (7.164.68). Van Buitenen mostly leaves it as yoga, but he clarifies the problem: 'Any translator will have difficulty in giving a satisfactory rendering of the word yoga. First of all, let the reader not mistake the yoga of the *Bhagavadgītā* for the Yoga of Patanjali

or, worse, Hatha-Yoga or even Kundalini Yoga. The word yoga and cognates of it occur close to 150 times in the *Gītā*, and it needs attention ... When yoga occurs by itself it is oftentimes an abbreviation for *karma-* or *bhakti-yoga*. Yoga, then, implies (1) the process of a difficult effort; (2) a person committed to it; (3) the instrument he uses; (4) the course of action chosen; and (5) the prospect of a goal.' J.A.B. van Buitenen, *The Bhagavadgītā in the Mahābhārata: Text and Translation*, Chicago: University of Chicago Press, 1981, 17–18.

6. Bhagavad Gita II.50. In the second line, I have substituted 'yoga' for 'discipline' in Miller's translation. Zaehner translates the second line, *yogaḥ karmasu kauśalam*, as: 'for Yoga is skill in [performing] works'. Van Buitenen translates 'yoga' here as 'singleness of purpose', which also makes sense. When one acts with singleness of purpose one is 'intent on the act' and is not distracted by the 'fruits of the act'. Swami Prabhavananda and Christopher Isherwood render this less literally, but in keeping with the spirit of the text: 'Work done with anxiety about results is far inferior to work done without anxiety.' This classic translation with an introduction by Aldous Huxley is still in print. *Bhagavad-Gita: The Song of God*, New York: New American Library, a division of Penguin Putnam, 41.

7. My father's mystic way was the Gita's favourite way of salvation. The Gita's religion is a compromise between the speculation of the intellectuals and the emotionalism of popular religion, which in later times comes to play a great role; the cult of Krishna (identified with the Vedic god Vishnu in the Gita XI.24 and 30) must have originated in such local popular circles. The impersonal Brahman is still the First Principle, devotion to God is preferred. As the Gita says, it is not so easy to feel a mystic's warm personal devotion for an abstract, impersonal Absolute. The mystic vision of God in the eleventh chapter is the climax of the poem.

8. Barbara Stoler Miller, Afterword to her translation of the *Bhagavadgītā*, New York: Bantam Books, 1986, 155.

9. In making the connection of Arjuna's dilemma and Bhishma's death in the preamble of the *Bhagvadgitaparvan*, van Buitenen concludes: 'In the light of all this it cannot be reasonably argued that the setting of the *Gītā* is a random choice dictated by purely

dramatic (read melodramatic) considerations. The preamble tells us that Bhīsma is dead, that Arjuna's reluctance to fight in this war was therefore fully justified, and that consequently a need existed to override Arjuna's reluctance with a higher truth, so that in fact *that* will come about which we know is *already* the case. This is a very subtle narrative weaving that requires the preamble so often forgotten and that also masterfully contrasts the high dilemma of the *Gītā* with the chapter following immediately—the formal approval-seeking by Yudhisthira' (3). Although Van Buitnenen did not consider the *Gītā* to be part of the 'original' epic, he believed that 'it was conceived and created in the context of the *Mahabharata*. It was not an independent text that somehow wandered into the epic.' (5)

10. V.23.7

11. I.94.91

12. VI.41.36ff

13. Iravati Karve, *Yuganta: The End of an Epoch,* Hyderabad: Disha Books/Orient Longman, 1991, 15-16. Others have also condemned Bhishma's behaviour. M.A. Mehendale, 'Draupadi's Question', *Journal of the Oriental Institute, Baroda,* 35 (1985), 3–4.194; I.M. Thakur, *Thus Spake Bhishma,* Delhi: Motilal Banarsidass, 1992, 141–47.

14. I.M. Thakur has expressed concern about the possible political implications of exposing Shakuni in public and the potential damage to the alliance between the Gandhara and Hastinapura states. Gandhara was an ally of the Kauravas through Gandhari's marriage to Dhritarashtra. *Thus Spake Bhishma,* 145–46.

15. Karve, 8

16. Adam Smith, *An Enquiry into the Nature and Causes of the Wealth of Nations,* 1776; republished by Oxford: Oxford University Press, 1976; also in the *Collected Edition of the Works and Correspondence of Adam Smith,* London: Dent, 1910, vol 1, 13.

17. Albert Hirschman describes in his classic, *Passions and Interests*, that the idea of the basic self-interested nature of beings originated with statecraft in the seventeenth century, and gradually it grew to cover all human conduct by the eighteenth century. Albert O. Hirschman, *The Passions and the Interests: Political Arguments for Capitalism Before its Triumph,* Princeton, NJ: Princeton University Press, 1977, 42.

18. Amartya Sen points out in a famous essay, 'Rational Fools', that 'self-interest' does not fully explain the behaviour of real people, and it is inaccurate to identify Smith's 'prudence' with 'self-interest'. See *On Ethics and Economics*, Oxford: Basil Blackwell, 1987, 22; 'Rational Fools: A Critique of the Behavioural Foundations of Economic Theory', *Philosophy and Public Affairs*, 6 (1977).

19. Adam Smith in *The Theory of Moral Sentiments* (I.I.I.), writes: 'Howsoever selfish man may be supposed, there are evidently some principles in his nature, which interest him in the fortune of others, and render their happiness necessary to him, though he derives nothing from it except the pleasure of seeing it. Of this kind is pity or compassion, the emotion which we feel for the misery of others, when we either see it or are made to conceive it in a very lively manner.'

20. Jean-Jacques Rousseau, *Discourse on the Origin of Inequality*, in *The Collected Writings of Rousseau*, vol 3, ed. Roger D. Masters and Christopher Kelly, trans. Judith R. Bush, Roger D. Masters, Christopher Kelly, and Terence Marshall, Hanover, NH: University Press of New England, 1992, 36. See also Pierre Force, *Self-Interest before Adam Smith: A Genealogy of Economic Science*, Cambridge: Cambridge University Press, 2003, 8. Amartya Sen makes the point that an emotion like Smith's sympathy (or Rousseau's pity) is laudable but it is still egoistic for 'one is pained at others' pain', such as in seeing a child tortured, 'and the pursuit of one's own utility is helped by sympathetic action'. Therefore, he proposes 'commitment' as a better option since 'it does not make you feel personally worse off, but you think it is wrong and you are ready to do something to stop it'. 'Rational Fools', 6.

21. Donald Hall, the American poet, recounts that Henry Moore, the sculptor, was perpetually in this state, and his wife had to drag him home from his studio at midnight because he had forgotten lunch and dinner, and also to send bills to his customers. Donald Hall, *Life Work*, Boston: Beacon Press, 1993.

22. See Mihaly Cziksentmihalyi, *Flow: The Psychology of Optimal Experience*, New York: Harper, 1991; Abraham Maslow, *Motivation and Personality*, New York: Harper, 1954.

23. I.123.60–64

24. Eugen Herrigel, *Zen in the Art of Archery*, New York: Taylor & Francis, 1953, republished New York: Vintage, 1989, 6.

25. John Stuart Mill, *Utilitarianism* (1863), *The Collected Works of John Stuart Mill*, ed. John M. Robson, 31 vols, Toronto and London, 1965–91, vol x, 215, 231.

26. Bhagavad Gita IV.22

27. This appeared in an essay on war and action in the *Cambridge Review* in 1920, when E.M. Forster was writing *A Passage to India*. Cited by Barbara Stoler Miller in her Afterword to her translation, 158.

28. David Riesman, the American social thinker, characterized persons as 'inner directed', who tend to set their own standards and seem to care less about what others think of them. On the other hand, 'outer directed' persons let others set the mark and are less in control of their actions and feelings. David Riesman and Nathan Glazer, *The Lonely Crowd: A Study of the Changing American Character*, 1950.

29. See note 27 above.

30. T.N. Madan, *Non-renunciation: Themes and Interpretations of Hindu Culture*, New Delhi: Oxford University Press, 1987, 2; Louis Demont, 'World Renunciation in Indian Religions', *Contributions to Indian Sociology*, 9 (1960), 67–89.

31. Romila Thapar explains this in a fascinating essay, 'Renunciation: The Making of a Counter-culture?' in *Cultural Pasts: Essays in Early Indian History*, New Delhi: Oxford University Press, 2000, 877–79.

32. Van Buitenen says, 'Krsna's argument for action is two-pronged: he defends the right kind of action against, on the one hand, the overzealous advocates of Vedic ritualism and, on the other, the propounders of the doctrine that all acts should be given up. His argument is at once simple and complex: simple, because he finds cause to propose that action is both necessary and unproductive of rebirth; complex, because he attempts to hold on to the orthodoxy of social action while revolutionizing it from within, and at the same time to demolish the heterodoxy of renunciation-at-any-price without discarding the value of renunciation per se. These were the issues of the time, and Krsna addresses them before going on to the consolations of personal religion' (16–17).

33. Bhagavad Gita III.30–31. I have used van Buitenen's translation here as it is more effective, partly because he has not translated *karman* into 'action' as Miller does. Van Buitenen says, '[Krsna's] overriding concern is that a person can act without *karman*, however one might philosophically confront this issue. His Vedanta successors recognize the distinction and hold, with *Mīmāṃsā*, the self/soul/person is not the agent of his acts and the experient of their fruits (*kartr* as well as *bhoktr*) and reject the *Sāṃkhya* view that only *prakrti* acts, and that the *puruṣa* is solely the experient (*bhoktr*)' (23).

34. Bankimchandra Chattopadhyay, *Dharmatatva*, trans. Apratim Ray, New Delhi: Oxford University Press, 2003. See also Sudipta Kaviraj, *The Unhappy Consciousness: Bankimchandra Chattopadhyay and the Formation of Nationalist Discourse in India*, Delhi: Oxford University Press, 1995.

35. Shankara (c. 788–820) offered an influential *Advaita Vedanta* reading of this concept; Ramanuja (c. 1017–37) had an attractive 'modified non-dualist' interpretation, closer to the *bhakti* or devotional spirit of the Gita.

36. G.W.F. Hegel, *On the Episode of the Mahabharata Known by the Name Bhagavad-Gita by Wilhelm von Humboldt*, Berlin, 1826, ed. and trans. Herbert Herring, New Delhi: Indian Council of Philosophical Research, 1995.

37. Ibid, 15

38. Hegel's other major objection is that 'to act means nothing else than achieving some purpose; one acts to achieve something, some result. The realization of the purpose is success; that the action is successful gives some satisfaction, a fruit inseparable from the performed action' (ibid, 47). Hence, Hegel is dubious about Krishna's principle about remaining indifferent to the fruits of action. In fact, he says, 'the more senselessly and stupidly an action is performed, the greater the involved indifference towards success.' Certainly, it is normal to feel satisfaction for a job that is completed, but Krishna's advice to act without attachment to reward does not preclude, I think, this sense of satisfaction that a disinterested person feels at a job well done. The agent's satisfaction when achieving the purpose of the activity is not the same thing as the

agent's yearning for personal advancement or material rewards. Hegel is right in thinking that an action cannot exclude its result or goal. But an agent who acts in a disinterested manner is fully aware of those results. There is a difference between fulfilling the purpose of an activity and desiring personal rewards from it. The *karma yogi* is focused on doing the job well but not on what it means for his personal advancement. So, I think this objection of Hegel's is unsustainable.

39. Hannah Arendt, *Eichmann in Jerusalem*, London: Faber and Faber, 1963, 120–23. Hannah Arendt, a Jew who fled Germany before Hitler's rise to power, and who reported on Eichmann's trial for the *New Yorker*, concluded that aside from a desire for improving his career, Eichmann showed no trace of an anti-Semitic personality or of any psychological damage to his character. She called him the embodiment of the 'banality of evil', as he appeared at his trial to have an ordinary and common personality, displaying neither guilt nor hatred. To her mind, he discredits the idea that the Nazi criminals were manifestly psychopathic and different from ordinary people.

40. Peter Singer, *How Are We to Live?* Amherst, New York: Prometheus Books, 1995, 186. Singer quotes from R. Hilberg, *The Destruction of the European Jews*, Chicago: Quadrangle, 1961, 218–19.

41. Posted on the web on 4 December 2004 under Comments to the Speaking Tree on http://www.timesofindia.indiatimes.com.

42. Aristotle, *Politics*, Book II, trans. Benjamin Jowett, Oxford: Clarendon Press, 1905, 61–63.

43. Isaiah Berlin pointed this out in a classic essay called 'The Pursuit of an Ideal' in *The Crooked Timber of Humanity* (first published in 1959), New York: Knopf, 1991. The title of the collection comes from Immanuel Kant's line: 'Out of timber so crooked as that from which man is made nothing entirely straight can be built.'

44. Jane Mansbridge discusses these issues in her introduction to *Beyond Self-Interest*, ed. Jane J. Mansbridge, Chicago: University of Chicago Press, 1990.

45. The expression 'general benevolence' belongs to Henry Sidgewick, the nineteenth century moral philosopher, who also emphasized the importance of achieving an impartial perspective in moral acts.

In rather dramatic words, he called it the ability to adopt 'the point of view of the universe'. Henry Sidgewick, *The Methods of Ethics*, 7th edn., London: Macmillan, 1907, 379–83.

46. Rudolf Hoess, *Commandant of Auschwitz: The Autobiography of Rudolf Hoess*, ed. Constantine Fitz Gibbon, London: Pan, 1961.

47. Benedict R. Anderson, *Mythology and the Tolerance of the Javanese*, Cornell Modern Indonesia Project, Dept. of Asian Studies, Cornell University, 1965.

48. Claude Adrien Helvetius, *A Treatise on Men*, trans. W. Hooper, New York: Burt Franklin, 1969, vol 2, 18.

49. Martha Nussbaum explains this in *Upheavals of Thought: The Intelligence of Emotions*, Cambridge: Cambridge University Press, 2003.

50. T.S. Eliot, 'Little Gidding', in *Four Quartets*, Faber and Faber: London, 1944.

51. Ibid, 31

52. This is a rough paraphrase of Patanjali's *Yoga Sutra* 1.5–22, 29–35.

53. Steven Collins, *Selfless Persons: Imagery and Thought in Theravada Buddhism*, Cambridge: Cambridge University Press, 1982, 4.

54. Contemporary Buddhist scholars are divided. The monks of the orthodox Southern Buddhism (Theravada) believe in *anatta* literally. However, many scholars, such as the flamboyant Mrs Rhys Davids, felt the original teaching of the Buddha did not contain this doctrine. Zaehner agreed with her, arguing that in denying the self, the Buddha merely meant the 'elimination of the ego'. The renowned Austrian Buddhist scholar Frauwallner also regarded *anattā* merely as the 'strategic denial of any description of the self'. Steven Collins believes that the way the texts present *anattā* is in opposition to an aspect of the human experience; for example, 'consciousness is not-self', and he concludes that 'Buddhist metaphysics could be reduced to a kind of pragmatic agnosticism in which the self is not so much denied as declared inconceivable.' Collins, 10.

55. David Hume, 1739, *Treatise on Human Nature*, London.

56. Rene Descartes, *Discourse on Method*, 1637. Descartes wrote: 'I next considered attentively what I was; and I saw that while I could pretend that I had no body, that there was no world, and no place for me to be in, I could not pretend that I was not; on the contrary,

from the mere fact that I thought of doubting the truth of other things it evidently and certainly followed that I existed. On the other hand, if I had merely ceased to think, even if everything else that I had ever imagined had been true, I had no reason to believe that I should have existed. From this I recognized that I was a substance whose whole essence or nature is to think and whose being requires no place and depends on no material thing.'

57. Virginia Woolf, *The Common Reader*, First Series, New York: Harvest/Harcourt, Brace & World, 1960, 154.

58. Daniel C. Dennett, *Consciousness Explained*, Boston: Little Brown and Co., 1991, 429. Dennet writes: '"Call me Ishmael" is the beginning sentence of *Moby Dick*. But who do we call Ishmael? Call Melville, Ishmael? No. Call Ishmael, Ishmael. Melville has created a fictional character named Ishmael. As you read the book you learn about Ishmael, about his life, about his beliefs and desires, his acts and attitudes. You learn a lot more about Ishmael than Melville ever explicitly tells you. Some of it you can read into the character as the story progresses by our own imagination. The self in the same way is rather like a fictional character. Let us imagine a novel-writing machine, and the first sentence of the novel reads, "Call me Gilbert". It is an autobiography of some fictional character, Gilbert. This thought experiment is to condition us to the fact that we are a consciousness-creating machine; there is no "thinker" sitting behind our thoughts. The same is true of your brain: it doesn't know what it's doing either.'

59. *Muṇḍakopaniṣad* III. The image can also be found in the *Mahabharata* in *Dronaparvan* (VII. 201.76). The poet, A.K. Ramanujan, has rendered this passage freely and elegantly into English. A.K. Ramanujan, *The Collected Essays of A.K. Ramanujan*, ed. Vinay Dharwadker, Oxford University Press, 1999, 181.

60. Antonio Damasio, *The Feeling of What Happens: Body, Emotion, and the Making of Consciousness*, London: Heinemann, 1999.

61. Ibid

62. Robert Kirk, *Raw Feeling: A Philosophical Account of the Essence of Consciousness*, New York: Oxford University Press, 1994.

63. Thomas Metzinger (ed.), *Conscious Experience*, Schoningh: Imprint Academic, 1995, 9. Joseph Levine is credited by the *Oxford Companion*

to the Mind for having called attention to *qualia* in a well known paper in 1983, 'Materialism and Qualia: The Explanatory Gap'. His examples were the smell of fresh ground coffee, or the taste of pineapple. The most celebrated literary example of *qualia* is the moment in Marcel Proust's novel, *A la Recherche du Temps Perdu*, when the taste of the Madeleine dipped in tea triggers in the narrator a vivid and intense childhood memory of another time and place. Only Proust's narrator will ever know the exact taste of the Madeleine on that day, and only *his* memory can transport him to his childhood.

64. Thomas Nagel, 'What Is It Like to Be a Bat?', *Philosophical Review* (1974), 435–50.

65. Quoted in David Lodge, *Consciousness and the Novel*, London: Secker and Warburg, 2002, 18.

66. Metzinger, 3

67. Jacob Burckhardt, *The Civilization of the Renaissance in Italy*, trans. S.C. Middlemore, 2 vols, New York: Harper, 1958, vol 1, 143.

68. William Shakespeare, *Hamlet* 3.1.58.

69. Ibid 3.1.85

70. Cynthia Marshall gives a fine account of the emergence of this new subjectivity in the early modern texts. Cynthia Marshall, *The Shattering of the Self: Violence, Subjectivity, and Early Modern Texts*, Baltimore: Johns Hopkins University Press, 2002.

71. Lodge, 16.

6. Karna's Status Anxiety

1. *Mahabharata* I.127.15: *katham ādityasamkāsam mrgī vyāghram janiṣyati*. As usual, I mention only the book number, chapter number and verse numbers when quoting from the *Mahabharata*. I gratefully acknowledge the use of the following translations in this chapter: (1) K.M. Ganguly, *Mahabharata*, Calcutta: P.C. Roy (1883 to 1896), reprinted New Delhi: Munshiram Manoharlal, Book Eight. (2) Adam Bowles, *Mahabharata*, Book Eight, *Karna*, vol 1, Clay Sanskrit Library, New York: New York University Press, 2006. (3) Kevin McGrath, *The Sanskrit Hero: Karna in the Epic Mahabharata*, Lieden and Boston: E.J. Brill, 2004. (4) Quotes from the *Adiparvan*, Book

One of the epic, are from van Buitenen's Chicago University Press translation.

2. William James, *The Principles of Psychology*, Boston, 1890. William's equally famous bother, Henry James, wrote great novels such as *Portrait of a Lady* and *Wings of the Dove*, which also explore the anxiety of human beings about their status.

3. The epic employs the Sanskrit word *vidhāna* for this trial of martial skills.

4. I.124.18–25

5. Although this is Karna's official entry in the epic, we have already been informed of his inborn attributes (earrings and breastplate) that make him invincible. Book One, *Adiparvan*, mentions that the earrings made his face shine and his breastplate distinguished him from ordinary beings: *sahajaṃ kavacaṃ bibhrat kuṇḍaloddyotitānanaḥ* (I.57.82).

6. One of the meanings of the word 'Karna' is 'the one with ears' or 'the ear-ringed one'. Kevin McGrath explains that it is entirely fitting for a hero who is intensely preoccupied with fame ('that which is heard') should have his name connected with 'hearing'. *The Sanskrit Hero: Karna in the Epic Mahabharata*, Leiden: E.J. Brill, 2004, 31.

7. Do it 'better', *viśeṣavat: pārtha yat te kṛtaṃ karma viśeṣavad ahaṃ tataḥ/ kariṣye paśyatāṃ nṛnām mātmanā vismayaṃ gamaḥ* (I.126.9). During his dramatic entry in the epic, Karna is also described as *pādacārīva parvataḥ*, 'like a walking mountain'. This and the subsequent translations of the specific verses are by Kevin McGrath. Kripa, like Drona, is a teacher of the princes. He is also the 'match referee' of this tournament.

8. *yat kṛtaṃ tatra pārthena tac cakāra mahābalaḥ*: 'What was done by Arjuna—that the mighty one [Karna] has done' (I.126.12).

9. *vrīḍāvanatam ānanam*: 'his face [was] bowed down by shame' (I.126.33).

10. *bhayam arjunasaṃjātam kṣipram antaradhīyata*: 'The fear born of Arjuna quickly vanished' (I.127.23), when Duryodhana realizes that he may have found a match in Karna.

11. Duryodhana says there are three classes of king: *ācārya trividhā yonī rājñāṃ śāstraviniścaye tatkulīnaś ca śūras ca senāṃ yas ca prakarṣati*

('Master, in the opinion of sacred teaching, the origin of kings is threefold; one, of family; [the second is] a hero; and [third] whoever leads an army') (I.126.34).

12. I.127.1–4

13. *sūtaputra* or the 'son a charioteer' is the epithet that attaches to Karna for all his life. The Pandavas and the Kauravas, sometimes from meanness and at other times just unthinkingly, address him thus throughout the epic. And so do others. Practically every Indian child today seems to know that *sūtaputra* is the derogatory way to refer to a low-caste person.

14. *katham ādityasaṃkāsam mṛgī vyaghram janiṣyati* (I.127.15). Although the epic uses both words *vīra* and *śūra* to describe Karna, McGrath translates *śūra* as 'hero', saving *vīra* for 'warrior'. In this instance, Duryodhana uses the grander *śūra* to describe Karna.

15. I.127.10

16. Draupadi says: *nahāṃ varayāmi sūtam* (I.1827.3). This incident is located at I.174–85 in the Critical Edition. The rejection by Draupadi was not included in the Critical Edition of the epic because according to the editor, V.S. Sukthankar, it is from 'late and inferior or conflated manuscripts'. Nevertheless, he says that 'this seemingly beautiful little passage ... won its way into people's hearts'. Sukthankar adds, 'the brave little Draupadi ... snubs openly ... the semi-divine bastard, the understudy of the villain ... the unwanted suitor'. V.S. Sukthankar, *Critical Studies in the Mahābhārata*, Bombay: Karnataka Publishing House, 1944, 77–78.

17. James Tod depicts Karna as 'the Hindu Apollo', because of his radiance. This is similarly an aspect of Achilles. *Annals and Antiquities of Rajasthan*, 1929, vol II, 9.637, Reprinted in 1990 by Low Price Editions.

18. *yad ayaṃ katthate nityam hantāhaṃ pāṇḍavān iti/nāyaṃ kalāpi sampūrṇa pāṇḍavānāṃ mahātmanām.*

19. *garjitvā sūtaputra tvaṃ śaradābhram ivājalam.*

20. *śūrā garjanti satataṃ prāvṛṣīva balāhakāḥ phalaṃ cāśu prayacchanti bījam uptam ṛtāv iva* (VII.133.25).

21. A.K. Warder, *Indian Kavya Literature*, Delhi: Motilal Banarsidass, 1989, 89.

22. Adam Smith throws light on Karna's anxiety about his social

position when he asks: 'To what purpose is all the toil and bustle in the world?' in *The Theory of Moral Sentiments*. 'What is the end of avarice and ambition, of the pursuit of wealth, of power, and pre-eminence? To be observed, to be attended to, to be taken notice of with sympathy, complacency and approbation . . . To feel that we are taken no notice of necessarily disappoints the most ardent desires of human nature.' Adam Smith, The Theory of Moral Sentiments, ed. Knud Haakonssen, Cambridge: Cambridge University Press, 2002, 61.

23. Alain de Botton, *Status Anxiety*, New York: Vintage, 2005, 5.

24. Ibid, 9

25. The apt phrase, 'leaky balloon', is de Botton's. See note above.

26. J.H. Hutton, *Caste in India*, 4th edn., London: Oxford University Press, 1963, 1.

27. VIII.32.44–48 CSL

28. The body of literature on American affirmative action is large. I would commend the reader to the fine bibliography appended to Robert Fullenwider's entry in the online *Stanford Encyclopedia of Philosophy* entitled 'Affirmative Action'. The best case for the 'integration argument' is made by Elizabeth Anderson in a long article, 'Integration, Affirmative Action, and Strict Scrutiny', *New York University Law Review*, 77 (November 2002), 1195–1271. Two other books build on this case: Robert Fullenwider and Judith Lichtenberg's *Levelling the Playing Field: Justice, Politics, and College Admissions*, Lanham, MD: Rowman and Littlefield, 2004, and Lesley Jacobs, *Pursuing Equal Opportunities*, Cambridge: Cambridge University Press, 2004. The most insightful piece I have read from the viewpoint of moral philosophy is Thomas Nagel's 'Equal Treatment and Compensatory Justice' published in 1973 in *Philosophy and Public Affairs*. He argues that affirmative action might be beneficial and not necessarily be unjust because the system of linking of rewards to credentials might itself be wrong. Alan Goldman, in support of preferences, argues that the rule of competences should normally apply in selection. However, if the application of this rule might compound existing injustice where opportunities are unequal, then violation of the rule is justified. *Justice and Reverse Discrimination*, Princeton: Princeton University Press, 1979.

29. My friend, the historian Rajat Kanta Ray, burst into song one day over dinner with this Bengali song from Tagore's *Gitabitan*. Ray then graciously wrote down this translation on a paper napkin for me.

30. Thomas Nagel explains these in his 'A Defence of Affirmative Action', Testimony before the Subcommittee on the Constitution of the Senate Judiciary Committee, 18 June 1981.

31. Amartya Sen, in a book, *Meritocracy and Economic Inequality*, edited by Kenneth Arrow and others, points out that merit is a dependent idea and its meaning depends on how a society defines a desirable act.

32. 'You will be king': *rājā bhaviṣyasi* (V.138.9); 'royal fan': *vyajana;* 'great white umbrella': *chatram* ... *mahac chvetam; pādau tava grahīṣyanti*: 'they will touch your feet' (V.138.12).

33. *vijayaṃ vasuṣenasya ghoṣayantu ca pāṇḍavāḥ/sa tvaṃ parivṛtaḥ pārthair nakṣatrair iva candramāḥ* (V.138.26–27).

34. *ṣaṣṭhe tvāṃca tathā kāle draupadī upagamiṣyati* (V.138.15).

35. *anṛtaṃ notsahe kartuṃ dhārtarāṣṭrasya dhīmataḥ* (V.139.17). David Shulman has pointed out that Karna is the quintessential hero and his hero's dharma is different from that of a king. '[Karna] is wholly identified with the ethos of the hero's ... path to fame ... His world is closed, relatively static, locked into meaning.' He would be endangering the hero's eternal fame were he to switch sides. *The King and the Clown in South Indian Myth and Poetry*, Princeton: Princeton University Press, 1985, 399.

36. Karna's elegantly crafted reply is at V.139.3–22: 'inauspicious': *yathā na kuśalam* (V.139.3–4); 'from affection': *sauhārdāt;* 'not from birth': *saṃjātaṃ kāmabandhanam* (V.139.9–11).

37. Yudhishthira then 'will not uphold the kingdom': *na sa rājyam grahīṣyati* (V.139.21); 'be forced to pass the kingdom on to Duryodhana': *prāpya* ... *mahad rājyam* ... *sphitaṃ duryodhanāya* ... *sampradayām* (V.139.22); 'Let conscientious Yudhishthira be king forever': *sa eva rājā dharmātmā śāśvato stu yudhiṣṭhiraḥ* (V.139.21).

38. *kuṇḍalī baddhakavaco devagarbhaḥ śriyā vṛtaḥ* (V.143.5).

39. *asādhyam kiṃ nu loke syād yuvayoḥ sahitātmanoḥ* (V.143.10).

40. 'obey his mother's wishes': *mātṛvacaḥ kuru;* 'does not make him waver': *cacāla naiva karṇasya matiḥ satyadhṛtes tadā* (V.144.3).

41. 'abandoned by her': *avakīrṇo smi te*; 'denied fame and glory': *yaśahkīrtināśanam* (V.144.5). 'I was born a kshatriya, but never received what was due to a kshatriya/What enemy would do anything so evil': *ahaṃ ca kṣatriyo jāto na prāptaḥ kṣatrasatkriyām/ tvatkṛte kiṃ nu pāpīyaḥ śatruḥ kuryān mamāhitam* (V.144.60).

42. *kiṃ mām kṣatram vadiṣyati* (V.144.10).

43. 'She will thus always have her five sons': *na te jatu naśiṣyanti putrāh pañca* (V.144.22). Iravati Karve chastises Karna for this answer. Although not mean-hearted, she does not think that his answer stands up to moral scrutiny: 'On the face of it it appears to be a generous gesture. It seems like one of the exaggerated gestures he [Karna] was so fond of making ... He had neither love nor pity for Kunti. He was equally indifferent to his so-called brothers. When he said he would not kill the others, it was not generosity or love which prompted him, but extreme contempt. The meaning of his promise was that he would engage with the one he thought his equal. He was not concerned with the others. This contempt and overconfidence was not misplaced in a kshatriya. But it was certainly not appropriate in this context. This was a real war, not a tournament. It was his duty to help Duryodhana win the war and not to engage in an empty boast. He was hurting Duryodhana's cause in promising not to kill the others, especially Dharma [Yudhishthira]. It has to be said that he ignored Duryodhana's need and was carried away by a false notion of his own greatness.' Iravati Karve, *Yuganta: The End of an Epoch*, Hyderabad: Disha Books, 1991, 151.

44. I.123.10–39

45. For a historical discussion of this process of assimilation in the development of the caste system, see Romila Thapar, *Early India*, 124–26, 278; Vijay Nath, *Puranas and Acculturation: A Historico-Anthropological Perspective*, New Delhi: Munshiram Manoharlal, 2001, 27ff; M.N. Srinivas, *Social Change in Modern India*; Ghurye, *The Scheduled Tribes*.

46. Shashikant Hingonekar, 'Ekalavya', cited in Gail Omvedt, *Dalit Visions: The Anti-caste Movement and the Construction of an Indian Identity*, New Delhi: Orient Longman, 8.

47. III.284.10–18

48. III.284.35
49. III.285.4; 6–7
50. 'One whose vow is true': *satyavrata*.
51. In the previous sentence: 'Karna reminds him laughingly' (*prahasan* III.294.9); 'he would become vulnerable' ('accessible', *gamanīya*); 'If I would give you, O deity, both my ear-rings and breastplate/I would give myself a death sentence': *yadi dāsyāmi te deva kuṇḍale kavacaṃ tathā/vadhyatām upayāsyāmi* (III.294.16).
52. 'celestial creatures': *dānavas* and *siddhas* (III.294.36).
53. *karṇaṃ loke yaśasā yojayitvā* (III.294.40).
54. Kevin McGrath concludes, 'Without his ear-rings, Karna is a hero without himself'. He is dead, or soon to be dead—the earrings being an emblem for 'the identity of his life' (31–32). Hence, Karna is referred to as *kuṇḍalī kavāci śūro*, a hero with 'earrings and breastplate' (III.291.17).
55. In return Karna receives a missile from Indra, *śakti*, which is flawless. Thus, although he is no longer invincible, he still has the potential to destroy Arjuna. But he will never be able to use the weapon against Arjuna, thanks to a clever strategy of Krishna's, who never underestimated Karna's capabilities and reminded the Pandavas on more than one occasion, 'What man is there in the world who can withstand Karna/with a missile in his hand?': *śaktihastaṃ punaḥ karṇaṃ ko lokesti pumān iha/ ya enam abhitiṣṭhet . . .* (VIII.155.13).
56. *bibhemi na tathā mṛtyor yathā bibhye' nṛtād aham* (III.296.6).
57. For Bhishma's vilification of Karna, see V.16–21; 48.32–41; 6.94, 6–9; 61.15–17; 165.2–7). McGrath discusses the antagonism between Bhishma and Karna, 100–11.
58. Earlier, Duryodhana had told his warriors something very similar in the *Karnaparvan: jayo vāpi vadho vāpi yudhyamānasya saṃyuge:* 'For one fighting in battle, there is either victory or death' (VIII.2.9).
59. VIII.32.49–52 CSL. Note that the Shalya episode follows the vulgate and not the Critical Edition.
60. He likens Karna to the sun: *Ādityasadṛśa*.
61. *nāpi sūtakule jātaṃ karṇaṃ manye kathaṃcana* (VIII.24.151).
62. 'Just as Shalya is superior to Krishna, so am I superior to Arjuna. As [Krishna] knows horsemanship . . . so does Shalya. Just as no

one bears bows as I do, so no one can match Shalya in leading horses' (VIII.22, 53–56).

63. The interchange between Shalya and Karna takes place from VIII.26 to VIII.29. '. . . an enemy with the face of a friend': *mitramukhah satruh.* He also refers to Shalya as a 'betrayer of friendship': *mitradroh* (VIII.29.22).

64. The epic fight is described in VIII.66. See Georges Dumezil's work on the opposition of Surya and Indra, *Mythe Et Epopee*, I, II and III, Paris: Gallimard, 1968–73, reprinted in one volume, 1995. See vol I (1965), chapters 1–4. Kevin McGrath also writes about the dualism, explaining how this binarism is part of the kshatriya world view (72, 85, 95ff).

65. Karna charged his arrow with a speech act. *hato' si vai phalguna:* 'You are dead, Arjuna' (VIII.66.9).

66. Then, 'the earth swallowed the wheel': *agrasan mahī cakram* (VIII.66.52).

67. 'I think dharma does not always protect': *manye na nityam paripāti dharmah* (VIII.66.43).

68. 'Karna weeps in anger': *kopād aśrūny avartayat;* 'wait a moment': *muhūratam ksama pāndava.*

69. *yaśaś ca dharmas ca jayaś mārisa/priyāni sarvāni ca tena ketunā . . . apatan* (VIII.67.16). McGrath explains this verse thus: '"Glory", because no other hero in the poem is as passionate about glory as Karna is, and one could reasonably aver that no other hero possesses or obtains such glory as Karna held. "Dear things", because this was a younger brother slaying an older half-brother. As for "dharma", perhaps dharma here collapses because the Pandavas made use of deceptive stratagems in order to win the battle—much as the Kauravas had behaved illicitly in the gambling match—and their claim to dharma is somewhat counterfeit' (98).

70. This translation is from K.M. Ganguly's *Mahabharata,* Calcutta: P.C. Roy, 1883 to 1896, reprinted New Delhi: Munshiram Manoharlal, 1970, Book Eight, 249–51, 255.

71. *dehāt tu karnasya nipātitasya/ tejo dīptam kham vigāhyāciren* (VIII.67.27).

72. Rajmohan Gandhi, *Revenge and Reconciliation,* New Delhi: Penguin Books India, 1999, 4.

73. XII.5.11–13

74. Adam Bowles, *Mahabharata*, Book Eight, *Karna*, vol 1, trans. Adam Bowles, Clay Sanskrit Library, New York: New York University Press, 2006, 32, 23. The metaphor of the 'sacrifice' is developed in the *Udyogaparvan* (V.29.57). See David Shulman, *The King and the Clown in South Indian Myth and Poetry*, Princeton: Princeton University Press, 1985, 384–96.

75. His *tejovadhas*, V.8.27 and V.41.81.

76. *tat . . . karṇaṃ prati mahad bhayam* (III.284.3).

77. VIII.30.6, VIII.57.38

78. *sakhitvaṃ tvayā* (I.126.15)

79. Hiltebeitel examines the importance of 'friendship' in epic culture. See Alf Hiltebeitel, 'Brothers, Friends, and Charioteers: Parallel Episodes in the Irish and Indian Epic', in Edgar Polome (ed.), *Homage to Georges Dumezil, Journal of Indo-European Studies*, 3, 85.

80. Karna is 'happy': *hṛṣta*, II.60.38; he calls her *bandhakī*, 'harlot', II.61.35, 81; and *dāsī*, 'slave', II.63.1–4; '. . . she be disrobed': *vāsāṃsi . . . upāhara*, II.61.38.

81. *na hi me śāmyate duḥkhaṃ karṇo yat prāhasat tadā* (III.13.113). She repeats the same words at V.93.11.

82. 'It was terrible to Arjuna's heart, a stab in the vitals, cutting to the bone, arrogant; an arrow, from Karna, made of words, sharply caustic that stuck in his heart' (V.29.37): *yo bībhatsor hṛdaye prauḍha āsīd asthipracchin marmaghātī sughoraḥ/karṇāc charo vāṅmayas tigmatejāḥ pratiṣṭhito hṛdaye phalgunasya.*

83. *mitramukhaḥ śatrur* or the 'betrayer of friends' (*mitradrohin*), VIII.27.28; VIII.27.68.

84. Alf Hiltebeitel also notes the irony: 'Śalya is thus put to the test of friendship and fatefully accepts, [which] is a reflection of the symbolism of Karna's fall' (IX.5. 23). Alf Hiltebeitel, *The Ritual of Battle: Krishna in the Mahābhārata*, Albany: State University of New York Press, 1990, 250.

85. X.23.4–5

86. 'breakdown of social order': *varṇasaṃkara*; 'customary behaviour': *dharmasaṃkara*. See Adam Bowles's Introduction to his translation of Book Eight, 43, footnote 3.

87. For a discussion of Shalya and Karna, and friendship and betrayal, see Hiltebeitel, 256–59.

88. *yato dharmas tato jayaḥ* (V.141.33). It is totally out of Karna's character to make a Vaishnav devotional statement: 'Where there is dharma there is Krishna, and where there is Krishna, there is victory' (V.41.55). This seems to be the work of later 'mischievous'. Bhargava brahmin editors. See Kevin McGrath, 153, footnote 48.

89. Alf Hiltebeitel is referring to a contemporary Tamil drama. See *The Cult of Draupadi*, 2 vols, Chicago: University of Chicago Press, 1988, 412. The lyrical lament of the women in the *Striparvan* is also a touching example. An example of Karna's continuing popularity in contemporary India is the *Song of Karna* sung in Gujarat by Muslim members of the Tragada Bhavaya caste, who perform the rural folk theatre, in which Hindu and Muslim cultural practices are combined.

7. Krishna's Guile

1. IX.60.27. I am indebted to Alf Hiltebeitel's analysis and translation of specific verses in the episode relating to the death of Drona in his book, *The Ritual of Battle: Krishna in the Mahābhārata*, Delhi: Sri Satguru Publications, 1991, 250–54. Unless otherwise indicated, references are to the Critical Edition of the epic.

2. IX.60.27–38, IX, 61.27–37 CSL

3. Ruth Katz, *Arjuna in the Mahabharata: Where Krishna Is, There is Victory*, Columbia, SC: University of South Carolina Press, 1989, 168–69. Katz also provides many examples of deceptions in Greek epics, 189, footnote 40. The episode of Athena posing as Hector's brother to put him off guard is from the *Iliad*, XXII.227ff.

4. *The Mahabharata of Krishna-Dwaipayana Vyasa*, trans. K.M Ganguli and Pratap Chandra Roy, 2nd ed., vol 6, Calcutta: Oriental Publishing Co., 1962, 447. The context is to find a 'strategy' to kill Drona.

5. IX.126.1, 6, 10, IX, 61.43–44 CSL

6. Michael Walzer, *Just and Unjust Wars: A Moral Argument with Historical Illustrations*, New York: Basic Books, 1977, 32.

7. Ibid, 32–33

8. VI.1.28–32

9. Bhishma reminds us about this rule, 'One does not fight a person who has laid down his weapons or armour, nor a woman or one who bears a woman's name, or one who is injured . . .' (VI.103.72–73).

10. 'I shall cast down my weapons after hearing bad news' (*sumahadapriyam*) (VI.41.61).

11. Arun and Vasanti Jategaonkar argue that Krishna was unaware of *vadhopaya*. 'Remarks on the Dronavadha Episode', Annals of the Bhandarkar Oriental Research Institute, 2009. 'Cast aside virtue' (*dharmamutsrjya*) . . . 'let a device be adopted for victory' (*āsthīyatām jaye yogo*) (VII.164.68). I am indebted to Alf Hiltebeitel's analysis and the translation of this verse (and other verses below) from the episode relating to the death of Drona, in his book, *The Ritual of Battle: Krishna in the Mahābhārata*, Delhi: Sri Satguru Publications, 1991, 250–54.

12. Yudhishthira accepts the advice 'with difficulty' (*krcchrena*) (VII.164.70).

13. 'Drona had firm knowledge (*sthirā buddhir*) that Yudhishthira would not speak an untruth (*anrtam*), even for the sake of the sovereignty of the three worlds (*trayānām api lokanam aisvāryārthe*). Therefore, he asked him especially, and no one else, for in this Pandava, beginning with childhood, Drona surely had his hope for truth (*satyasa*)' (VII.164.95–96).

14. *tasya pūrvam rathah prthvyās caturāṅgula uttarah babhūvaivam tu tenokte tasya vāhāsprsanmahīm* (VII.164.106–07).

15. VI.154.70

16. VI.165.51

17. 'Untruth may be better than truth (*satyājjyāyo 'nrtam bhavet*). By telling an untruth for the saving of life, untruth does not touch one (*na sprśyate 'nrtah*)' (VII.164.98–99).

18. 'Sunk is the fear of untruth (*atathyabhaye magno*) but clinging to victory (*jaye sakto*)' (VII.164.105).

19. 'For someone who is conversant with dharma': *dharmajñena satā*; 'untruth in the garb of truth': *satyakakañcukam . . . anrtam*; 'for the sake of sovereignty': *rājyakāranāt* (VII.167.33–35, 47). Alf Hiltebeitel makes a good point that Arjuna believes that the *adharma* committed by Yudhishthira attaches to all the Pandavas (254).

20. VII. 118.13–15

21. VIII.66.62–63

22. V.S. Sukthankar, *On the Meaning of the Mahabharata*, Bombay, 1975, 95.

23. VI.61.14ff

24. VII.168.3–5
25. VII.168.9; 'immorally': *adharmataḥ*.
26. II.61.11ff
27. VI.78.45ff
28. XV.15.19ff
29. Even though Bhishma's sympathies are for the Pandavas, he fights like a professional. He tells Duryodhana, as he lies dying on the battlefield, 'O tiger among men, today I am fulfilling my obligation to you based on the food you have provided me' (VI.105.27). It is a moment of pathos that the grandfather, who brought up these Kauravas and Pandavas, should feel so dependent, so vulnerable, so powerless. Ruth Katz makes an interesting observation: 'Insofar as Bhishma, Drona, and Kripa are all viewed as incarnations of gods, not demons (I.61.63) their participation on the demonic side in the war makes better sense in human rather than heroic terms' (173–74). She cites the pioneering work of Madeleine Biardeau, 'Salvation of the King in the *Mahābhārata*', *Contributions to Indian Sociology*, NS 15 (1981), 191, 81ff, footnote 67.
30. Krishna Chaitanya makes this point eloquently in his stimulating study, *The Mahabharata: A Literary Study*, New Delhi: Clarion Books, 1993.
31. Adolf Holzmann the Younger propounded an extravagant 'Inversion Theory' (subsequently discredited) to explain the sins of the Pandavas, arguing that it was, in fact, the Kauravas (rather than the Pandavas) who were the embodiments of righteousness in the original epic.
32. 'A Cloak of Clever Words: The Deconstruction of Deceit in the *Mahābhārata*', published in Chong Kim Chong and Yuli Liu (eds), *Conceptions of Virtue East and West*, Singapore: Marshall Cavendish Academic, 2005, and in Frederic Squarcini (ed), *Boundaries, Dynamics and Construction of Traditions in South Asia*, Florence: Florence University Press, 2005.
33. XII.156.22–24. The epic also refers to truth as 'indeed imperishable, eternal and unchanging. Not in conflict with any moral duty' (XII.156.3–10). In a similar vein, Bernard Williams, the philosopher, has an insightful discussion of truthfulness as an intrinsic value. He notes two aspects of the virtue of truth—sincerity and accuracy.

A sincere person says what he or she believes in. Thus, sincerity makes one trustworthy and reliable. Accuracy ensures that one's beliefs are based on the way things really are. Bernard Williams, *Truth and Truthfulness*, Princeton: Princeton University Press, 2002, 92–93.

34. I.210

35. *udyoga*: 'effort'. 'The effort in Sanskrit, *Udyoga*, may be understood both as a peace effort ... and a war effort,' says J.A.B. van Buitenen. 'It is to the latter meaning that the etymology of the word points: yoking up of the horses, chariots, and elephants of the army in preparation for making an attack; also, simply *yoga*, "the yoking".'

36. The tree 'whose ... trunk is Karna, its ripe fruit Duhshasana, and the ignorant king Dhritarashtra its root' (I.I.65; V.31.20).

37. Bhagavad Gita XI.28–29, 40.

38. Barth is one of the scholars who suggested the *kuladevatā* theory; Hopkins said he was 'patron god of the Pandavas'. E. Washburn Hopkins, *The Great Epic of India*, New York, 1901, 63.

39. Sukthankar also interprets the epic in terms of Hindu psychology and refers to Krishna as the 'Inner Self' (*paramātman*) or the divine inside each one of us. Taking off from Sukthankar, Alf Hiltebeitel adds, 'After all, such a psychology becomes intelligible in a religious tradition which places such regular emphasis on the belief that the divine is found in every man, the centre to which all else relates.' Sukthankar concludes sensibly: 'We must, therefore, be content with taking Sri Krsna to be a person of the same order of reality as the other heroes of the epic, the Pāndavas and the Kauravas ... As I said, there is no passage in the epic which does not presuppose, or which contradicts, his character as an incarnation of the Supreme Being, who is generally called in our epic, Visnu or Narayana.' V.S. Sukthankar, *On the Meaning of the Mahabharata*, Bombay: Asiatic Society, 1957, 47.

40. Bankimchandra Chattopadhyay, *Krishna-charitra*, trans. Pradip Bhattacharya, Calcutta: MP Birla Foundation, 1991. According to Buddhadev Bose, Bankimchandra 'strung term after legal term in order to convert Krishna into a law-abiding person untouched by blame or fault'. Buddhadev Bose, *The Book of Yudhishthir*, trans.

Sujit Mukherjee, London: Sangam Books/Hyderabad: Orient Longman, 1986, 157.

41. Peter Brook's essay in P. Lal (ed), *Vyasa's Mahabharata: Creative Insights,* Calcutta: Writers' Workshop, 1985/1992, 308.

42. I am indebted to Chakravarthi Ram-Prasad for this interpretation of 'Krishna's mystery'.

43. The exchange takes place at V.70.49–64; 'a sin': *vrjinam* (V.70.53).

44. Krishna's argument is at V.29.5–29; 'duty to family': *kuladharma*; 'duty to kingship': *rājadharma*; 'duty to society': *svadharma*; 'it is improper and cowardly to lead the life of non-activity': this is the classical distinction between *nivṛtti* (non-activity) and *pravṛtti* (path of works); 'even the gods have to engage in work': *karma*.

45. V.31.19f

46. V.138–49. 'His first strategy is reconciliation': V.148.7; 'the tactic of fear': *bheda*; 'policy of generosity and gifts': *dāna*; 'only recourse is force': daṇḍa.

47. II.62.7, 9

48. See Chapter 1 for an explanation of the game of dice.

49. Instead it was meant to be a friendly game. *Suhrddyuta*: II.51.21.

50. In thinking about *Kali Yuga,* Vidura says, 'When brothers are split, [you are bound to] have a quarrel' (*kalahaḥ*) (II.51.24).

51. II.60.40

52. III.148. The French scholar Madeleine Biardeau also found comfort in the *Kali Yuga* theory. Madeleine Biardeau, vol 80.8, 131ff; vol 82, 90. Another scholar, Dahlmann, also regarded the epic as the victory of good over evil. Ruth Katz, however, finds both these views optimistic. She believes quite sensibly that 'Yudhishthira and his successors ... are destined to be good kings in a bad world'. Certainly, the downswing in the epic's mood after the war seems to support Katz. She accepts the *Kali Yuga* theory and argues that since time has declined in the 'human age' from the earlier 'heroic age', Krishna has to be deceptive in order to win: 'At the heroic level there is no doubt that human effort will succeed: fate and human effort will not be in opposition to one another. At the human level, the *Kali Yuga* represents the interference of fate. What has been fated is the destruction of the ksatriyas (the heroes), as prophesied at the time of Draupadi's birth ... One might say that

the allowance of trickery by the good side in the battle books [of the epic] marks an attempt to outwit opposing fate by human effort; but fate cannot really be outwitted.' Ruth Katz, *Arjuna in the Mahabharata: Where Krishna Is, There is Victory*, Columbia, SC: University of South Carolina Press, 1989, 179. She expresses her disagreement with Biardeau and Dahlmann in footnotes 87, 93, 193–94. Luis Gonzales-Reimann argues in 'The Mahabharata and the Yugas' that Kali Yuga is a later invention and was interpolated into the epic to give legitimacy.

53. IX.59.21

54. *yatah krishnas tato dharmo yato dharmas tato jayah* (VI.62.34; XIII.153.39). Madeleine Biardeau agrees with the believer's perspective. She too felt that the *Mahabharata*'s purpose was to advocate *bhakti* or devotion to Krishna. This she felt was related to Krishna's conception in the Gita, and in particular of *nishkāma karma* (desireless action). Krishna teaches that action which is free from selfish desires, and in the name of God, is true moral action. Thus, she felt the epic's morality is subordinate to Krishna the God. See her *Etudes V; Etudes IV*, 173; *Etudes V*, 195; *Salvation*, 88. The epic tells us in the first book that the war in the *Mahabharata* was needed because demons began to oppress the world. The earth appealed to Brahma, who asked the gods to help. Thus, many gods assumed human forms. One of them was Krishna (as an *avatāra* of Vishnu), another was Indra, in the form of Arjuna. Many scholars have seen this blatant attempt to make Krishna (Vishnu) supreme over all the other gods as a way to 'Vaishnavize' the epic.

55. I.155.44

56. Chandogya Upanishad III.27.6

57. R.G. Bhandarkar, the Indologist, says in an essay, 'Krsna, the son of Devakī, was still regarded in the Vedic period as a wise man enquiring into the highest truth, and only at a later time was he put on an equality with Visnu. Vāsudeva, the god, and Krsna, the sage, were originally different from each other, and only afterwards became by a process of syncretism, one deity, thus giving rise to a theory of incarnation.' R.G. Bhandarkar, 'Vaisnavism and Śaivism', *Works*, vol II, 58. Elsewhere, he adds, 'It thus appears that a religion of devotion arose in earlier times, but it received a definite shape when Vāsudeva [Krishna] related the Gita to Arjuna and led to the formation of an independent sect . . .' (13).

58. The epic narrates the important myth of Daksha, which shows how the Vedic gods were replaced by sectarian gods—the example of Shiva in this case (XII.274.2–58). 'Once upon a time, when Shiva was living on Mount Meru with his wife Parvati, the daughter of the mountain Himalaya, all the gods and demigods thronged to him and paid him homage. The Lord of Creatures named Daksha began to perform a horse sacrifice in the ancient manner, which Indra and the gods attended with Shiva's permission. Seeing this, Parvati asked Shiva where the gods were going, and Shiva explained it to her, adding that the gods had decided long ago not to give him any share in the sacrifice. But Parvati was so unhappy about this that Shiva took his great bow and went with his band of fierce servants to destroy the sacrifice. Some put out the sacrificial fires by dousing them with blood; others began to eat the sacrificial assistants. The sacrifice took the form of a wild animal and fled to the skies, and Shiva pursued it with bow and arrow. The gods, terrified, fled, and the very earth began to tremble. Brahma begged Shiva to desist, promising him a share of the sacrificial offerings forever after, and Shiva smiled and accepted that share.' I have quoted above from Wendy Doniger's account of this famous myth, which is repeated at several places in the epic. Wendy Doniger, *Hinduism*, New York: Penguin Books, 2009, 260.

59. Jayadeva Goswami's *Gita Govinda*, or 'Song of the Cowherd', is a twelfth century poem about Krishna's romance with Radha and the gopis. This work is of great importance in the development of *bhakti* or the devotional tradition of Hinduism. There are rich traditions of painting and music associated with this theme.

60. Katz, 241

61. IX.61.60–63, 68 CSL

62. Michael Walzer, *Just and Unjust Wars*, 44.

63. See Jorg Friedrich, *The Fire: The Bombing of Germany, 1940–45*, trans. Allison Brown, Columbia University Press, 2006.

64. At a joint press conference with Tony Blair on 26 May 2006, George W. Bush finally conceded that this scandal was the biggest mistake of the Iraq War. 'We've been paying for a long period of time,' he said. Not surprisingly, this act of contrition came when both leaders' popularity rating had plunged to its lowest depths.

'They looked like two defeated men in the twilight of their careers,' reported the *Times of India*'s Chidanand Rajghatta from Washington. The *Washington Post*'s story was headlined 'Blair and Bush are Duo Even in Descent'.

65. Michael Walzer expressed his views in a programme on the Australian Broadcasting Company with the reporter Mark Colvin on 4 August 2005. The print version of the story is available at http://www.abc.net.au/pm/content/2005/s1430514.htm.

66. Walzer, 38

67. Ronald Lewin, *Rommel as Military Commander*, New York, 1970, 294, 311.

68. The discussion between Uttanka and Krishna takes place in Book Fourteen, *Ashvamedhikaparvan*, immediately following the *Anugita* section (XIV.53–55). The Sanskrit word *pāpa* comes closest to sin or evil and it appears in the Rig Veda with a moral meaning—for example, adultery is a sin, incest is evil. See Wendy Doniger O'Flaherty, *The Origins of Evil in Hindu Mythology*, Delhi: Motilal Banarsidass, 1976; Arthur L. Herman, *The Problem of Evil and Hindu Thought*, Delhi: Motilal Banarsidass.

69. Epicurus, as quoted in *2000 Years of Disbelief*. Epicurus himself did not leave any written form of this argument. It can be found in Lucretius's *De Rerum Natura* and in Christian theologian Lactantius's *Treatise of the Anger of God* where Lactantius critiques the argument. In *Essais de Théodicée sur la bonté de Dieu, la liberté de l'homme et l'origine du mal*, a well-known essay written in 1710, Leibniz introduced the term 'theodicy' to describe the formal study of this subject. This term is also used for an explanation of why God permits evil to exist without it being a contradiction of his perfect goodness.

70. III.31.39

71. Bimal K. Matilal, 'Krṣna: In Defence of a Devious Divinity', in *The Collected Essays of Bimal Krishna Matilal*, vol 2, New Delhi: Oxford University Press, 2002, 91–108. Max Weber argued that 'the most complete formal solution of the problem of theodicy is the special achievement of the Indian doctrine of karma. Max Weber, *The Sociology of Religion*, trans. E. Fischoff, 4th edn., London, 1963, 145.

72. After Duryodhana's fall, Krishna tells Yudhishthira: 'thus it was meant to be': *diṣṭyā vardhase*.

73. Shankara, *Brahmasutra* II.1.34: 'No partiality and cruelty [can be charged against God] because of [His] taking other factors into consideration.' In II.1.35, he adds: 'If it be argued that it is not possible [to take karma into consideration in the beginning], since the fruits of work remain still undifferentiated, then we say, no, since the transmigratory state has no beginning.' The opponent now argues that there could have been no 'previous birth' at the very beginning of creation, before which karma could not have existed. Shankara replies that it is not so, for the number of creation cycles is beginningless. See Swami Gambhirananda, *Brahma Sutra Bhasya of Shankaracharya*, Ramakrishna Math; J.N. Mohanty, *Classical Indian Philosophy*, Oxford: Rowman & Littlefield, 2000. According to A.B. Keith, the theory of karma does not appear until the later period of the Upanishads. A.B. Keith, *The Religion and Philosophy of the Vedas and Upanishads*, Harvard Oriental Series, vols 31–33, Cambridge, MA: Harvard University Press, 570 ff.

74. Alvin Plantinga, *The Nature of Necessary*, Oxford: Oxford University Press, 1974; *God, Freedom, and Evil*. Grand Rapids, MI: Eerdmans, 1977. Other solutions to the problem include John Hick's, who rejects the traditional view of the Fall, wherein human beings were created perfect but fell disastrously. Instead, he thinks human beings are unfinished and evolving. Although capable of reasoning and responsibility, they must now (as individuals) go through a second process of 'soul-making'. Natural evil presumably helps them to become humble and 'spiritual'. John Hick, *Evil and the God of Love*, revised edn., New York: Harper & Row, 1977. Eleonore Stump claims that a world full of evil and suffering has value: 'Natural evil—the pain of disease, the intermittent and unpredictable destruction of natural disasters, it tends to humble him, show him his frailty, make him reflect on the transience of temporal goods, and turn his affections towards other-worldly things.' Eleanore Stump, *The Logic of Disputation in Walter Burley's Treatise on Obligation*, Netherlands: Springer, 1985, 409.

75. C.S. Lewis, *Mere Christianity*, New York: Macmillan, 1943, 52. Plantinga (1974) agrees with this. God can create free creatures, but

He cannot ensure that they do only the right thing. If He did, then they would not be free (166–67). Harold Kushner, a Rabbi, offered a Hindu-like answer. In a widely read book in 1981, *When Bad Things Happen to Good People*, he argued that God does not ignore suffering; He knows about it and feels the pain. He can't do anything about it because He's not omnipotent. He is kind-hearted and would like to help, but He does not have the power to do it. (This answer did not go down too well with many believers.) Harold S. Kushner, *When Bad Things Happen to Good People*, New York: Schocken Books, 1981.

76. XI.25.36ff
77. *Mausalaparvan* 2
78. Buddhadev Bose, 165
79. V.S. Sukthankar, *On the Meaning of the Mahabharata*, 95.
80. A.K. Ramanujan, *The Collected Essays of A.K. Ramanujan*, gen. ed., Vinay Dharwadker, New Delhi: Oxford University Press, 1999.

8. Ashwatthama's Revenge

1. *Mahabharata*, X.4.21, 23
2. I shall be quoting from the verse translation of the *Sauptikaparvan* (Book Ten of the *Mahabharata*) by W.J. Johnson. (*The Sauptikaparvan of the Mahabharata*, New York: Oxford University Press, 1998). James Fitzgerald says 'the word Sauptika is unusual, and its meaning is not obvious on its face. [It is derived from the participle *supta* ("fallen asleep")] . . . Of the word's seven occurrences in Book X, one in particular allows us to determine that it signifies "an attack upon some who are asleep", *jijñāsamānās tattejaḥ sauptikaṃ ca didṛkṣavaḥ* (X.7.48ab). This sentence refers to the hordes of preternatural beings who had gathered outside the Pandava camp after Asvatthama worshipped Mahadeva just prior to getting his blessing and receiving a sword from him (X.7.64). These beings "were eager to ascertain his [Asvatthama's] fiery energy *(tejas)* and see the *sauptika*." The word *sauptika* here is a noun that refers to the upcoming attack upon and slaughter of those asleep.' *The Mahābhārata*, ed. and trans. James Fitzgerald, vol 7, Chicago: University of Chicago Press, 2004, xxix, footnote 25.

3. X.1.32, 34, 36, 37–40, 43–44
4. X.1. 64–65
5. X.4.5
6. X.4.21, 23–24
7. I.1.143
8. X.4.26, 31
9. X.5. 9, 11–12, 15
10. X.5.25
11. X.6.3–4, 6, 8
12. X.6.30, 31
13. X.8.12–21
14. X.8.39–40, 78
15. The epic's mood (*rasa*) has been famously discussed by Anandavardhana, who calls it *Santarasa*. See Gary Tubb's essay, 'Śantārasa in the *Mahābhārata*', in A. Sharma (ed.), *Essays on the Mahābhārata*, Leiden: E.J. Brill, 171–203.
16. Alexander the Great, the Macedonian king, uttered similar words to his generals, when they thought they were drowning in the Indian monsoon. Arrian recounts that a single narrow boat carried history—the king himself with his great captains, who would one day rule vast parts of the world: Ptolemy, the future king of Egypt; Lysimachus, the future king of Thrace; Perdiccas, the future Regent; and Seleucus, who would inherit Alexander's vast Asian empire. They were afraid that they would drown in the Jhelum river that stormy night before engaging Raja Puru (Porus) of the Punjab, but Alexander reassured them that their fame was secure back in Greece, and their grandchildren would sing their praises.
17. *Virataparvan*, chapter 50.
18. *Dronaparvan*, chapter 150.
19. X.4.27
20. Charles Malamound, *Cooking the World: Ritual and Thought in Ancient India*, trans. David White, Delhi: Oxford University Press, 1996, 156–57.
21. Pietro Marongiu and Graeme Newman, *Vengeance*, New York: Rowman & Littlefield, 1987, 47.
22. Karen Horney, *Feminine Psychology*, New York: Norton, 1967, 102.
23. Jeffrie Murphy, *Getting Even: Forgiveness and Its Limits*, New York: Oxford University Press, 2003.

24. This is also the position of Susan Jacoby, *Wild Justice: The Evolution of Revenge*, New York: Harper and Row, 1983, 4.

25. XII.121.8–9, judicial process = *vyavahāra*.

26. Jeremy Bentham, *The Rationale of Punishment*, originally published in 1830, digitized version at http://www.la.utexas.edu/labyrinth/rp/. In the past fifty years the writings by H.L.A. Hart (1959) in England and John Rawls (1955) in the United States, both centrist liberals, have had much influence in thinking about retributive justice in the Anglo-Saxon world. Herbert L.A. Hart, 'Prolegomenon to the Principles of Punishment', reprinted in Hart, *Punishment and Responsibility*, Oxford: Oxford University Press, 1968, 1–27; John Rawls, 'Two Concepts of Rules', *Philosophical Review*, 64, 3–32.

27. Michael S. Moore, 'The Moral Worth of Retribution', in Ferdinand Schoeman (ed), *Responsibility, Character, and the Emotions: New Essays in Moral Psychology*, Cambridge: Cambridge University Press, 1987.

28. Jean Hampton, 'The Moral Education Theory of Punishment', *Philosophy and Public Affairs*, 13 (1984), 208–38.

29. Robert Martinson, 'What Works?—Questions and Answers About Prison Reform,' *The Public Interest* (10), 1974, 22–54.

30. It is worth remembering what the Indian political leader Mahatma Gandhi also said about this: 'An eye for an eye makes the whole world blind.'

31. XII.122.40–42

32. H.A. Bedau, 'Punishment', *Stanford Encyclopedia of Philosophy* (online), 2005. See also his 1978 paper, 'Retribution and the Theory of Punishment,' *Journal of Philosophy*, 75, 601–20.

33. Ibid

34. X.11.13–14. W.F. Johnson tells us in a note to his translation of the *Sauptikaparvan* about Madeleine Biardeau's consistent reminder about the connection 'between the princess [Draupadi] and the goddess Earth: the latter calls on the gods to restore *dharma*, but that very restoration involves, inevitably, the death of her human "children"' (119–20).

35. Some Indians believe, as did the director Peter Brook, that when Ashwatthama's weapon of mass destruction entered the wombs of the Pandava women and destroyed their foetuses, it was a foretelling of the nuclear threat in the world today. According to Tibor de

Viragh, King Dhritarashtra's inability to see symbolizes the metaphorical blindness towards nuclear weapons of our present-day political leaders.

36. X.16.9–12

37. III.40.42. The good Vidura repeats these words of Yudhishthira's in the *Udyogaparvan*: 'forgiveness is the strength of the virtuous', during his interminable moral teaching to the insomniac Dhritarashtra (V.34.75).

38. III.28.10–14; *manyuḥ* = anger; forbearance = *ksamā*; anger = *krodha*.

39. Jeffrie G. Murphy and Jean Hampton, *Forgiveness and Mercy*, Cambridge: Cambridge University Press, 1988.

40. Joram G. Haber, *Forgiveness: A Philosophical Study*, Lanham, Md: Rowman and Littlefield, 1991.

41. Trudy Govier in her influential book *Forgiveness and Revenge*, catalogues why revenge is immoral. Trudy Govier, *Forgiveness and Revenge*, London: Routledge, 2002, 11. She adds: 'Any satisfaction an avenging party might feel would be morally objectionable because it would amount to satisfaction at having brought about the suffering of another human being.'

42. Jean Hampton, 208–38

43. V.3.20

44. XII.121.34–35. Bhishma recounts a story about punishment to Yudhishthira: 'Once upon a time the rod of force disappeared because Brahma was in a happy mood. After the rod disappeared, people became mixed up ... Lawlessness prevailed, and they harmed one another: They tore at each other like dogs fighting over a piece of meat, the strong killing the weak. Then the Grandfather [Brahma] paid his respects to the everlasting blessed Vishnu and said to the Great God, the God who grants wishes, "You absolutely have to relieve the virtuous here. You must devise a way for there to be no confusion here" ... Eventually, [Vishnu] created his own self as the rod of force' (XII.122.18–19, 22–23, 25).

45. XII.121.2

46. X.10.9

47. X.8.144–45

48. XI.10.15–30

49. XII.41.4–7

50. William O. Stephens draws this distinction in his review of Trudy Govier's book on Forgiveness, in *Essays in Philosophy*, 4.2 (June 2003). Also see Patrick Boleyn-Fitzgerald, 'What Should "Forgiveness" Mean?' *The Journal of Value Inquiry*, 36 (2002), 483–98.

51. See Mark Amstutz's excellent account of this subject in his book, *The Healing of Nations: The Promise and Limits of Political Forgiveness*, New York: Rowman & Littlefield, 2004.

52. David A. Crocker, 'Retribution and Reconciliation', Report from the Institute for Philosophy and Public Policy 20 (Winter/Spring 2000), 6.

53. Amy Gutmann and Dennis Thompson, 'The Moral Foundations of Truth Commissions', in Robert I. Rotberg and Dennis Thompson (eds), *Truth v. Justice: The Morality of Truth Commissions*, Princeton: Princeton University Press, 2000, 35–36.

54. Quoted in Gary Jonathan Bass, *Stay the Hand of Vengeance: The Politics of War Crimes Tribunals*, Princeton: Princeton University Press, 2000, 286–95.

55. 'Jaime Malamud-Goti, a senior legal advisor to President Alfonsín, has argued that the prosecutions tended to undermine the existing legal order, rather than strengthen the rule of law and emerging democratic institutions,' according to Mark Amstutz.

56. The quote belongs to the theologian Walter Wink.

57. Amstutz, 104.

58. Murad Ali Baig, 'Revenge', *Times of India*, 9 August 2007.

9. Yudhishthira's Remorse

1. X.10.13. Unless otherwise indicated, the English translation employed in this chapter is by James Fitzgerald, *Mahābhārata*, Books Eleven and Twelve, 2004. It is volume 7 of the University of Chicago Press series. I have also quoted from the recent translation of Book Seven, *Drona*, vol 1 by Vaughan Pilikian, Clay Sanskrit Library (CSL), New York: New York University Press, 2006. The translation of the Tuladhara and Jajali story is from the monograph *Ahimsa and a Mahābhārata Story* by Ian Proudfoot, Asian Studies Monographs, new series no. 9, Faculty of Asian Studies, Australian National University, Canberra, 1987. Finally, quotes from Book One of the epic are from van Buitenen's Chicago Press translation.

2. XI.15.3–4

3. James Fitzgerald writes: '*The Book of Peace* (the *Śāntiparvan*) and its companion, Book XIII, *The Book of Instructions* (the *Anuśāsanaparvan*), make up the first canonical library of "Hinduism". This library covers a very wide range of ancient Indian intellectual history and was intended to serve as a comprehensive, Brahmin-inspired basis of living a Good Life in a Good Society in a Good Polity.' James L. Fitzgerald, Introduction to Book Twelve of the *Mahābhārata*, trans. James Fitzgerald, vol 7, Chicago: University of Chicago Press, 2004, 79.

4. *śoka*, from the root *śuc*, related to 'burning too hot' from the Vedic ritual for a king who is made ready for ruling (ibid, 94–100).

5. XI.9.19–21

6. XI.16.11–15

7. XI.16.55cd–56

8. 'She caresses his body with sexual hunger', according to James Fitzgerald in his Introduction, 15.

9. XI.20.15–16ab, 17cd

10. XII.1.38

11. I.137

12. III.36

13. 8.90.106, 108, 112–15 CSL: *smṛtvā dharmopadeśaṃ tvaṃ/mūhurtaṃ kṣama pāṇḍava.*

14. XI.27.18, 20

15. XII.6.9cd–10

16. XII.7.8–10

17. XII.7.33. 'Now this grief holds me in check': *śoko māṃ rundhayaty ayam!*

18. XII.7.37

19. XII.9.3–4

20. XII.9.12–19. I have added 'hurting' to Fitzgerald's translation to emphasize the ethic of non-violence which is driving Yudhishthira.

21. XII.8.3-5. The only other time that Arjuna spoke thus to his elder brother was in the middle of the war in VIII.48–50, when he had called him a *dharmabhīruka,* a 'coward because of his commitment to dharma'. Whereas in this dialogue *vaiklavya* means 'feebleness', Fitzgerald defends his use of the sexual innuendo in calling him a

'sissy' because Arjuna had immediately followed up these exclamations with explicit accusations that Yudhishthira was unmanly. Arjuna also calls him *klība*, a eunuch. 'Daft' is a fair translation for *buddhilāghavāt*, 'light-minded'. See notes XII.8.3 and 4 (681–82) in Fitzgerald's translation.

22. XII.14.36, 35b
23. XII.7.5–8
24. XII.14.15–16
25. V.70.53–57. In the *Udyogaparvan*, while preparing for the war, Yudhishthira repeatedly argued for peace. He called the dharma of the warrior sinful——*pāpaḥ ksatriyadharmo yam* (V.70 46) and warriors always wicked—*sarvathā vrjinam yuddham* (V.70.53).
26. *śham āgaskarah pāpaḥ* (XII.27.22); *mayā hy avadhyā bahavo ghātitā rājyakāraṇāt* (XII.32.10).
27. XII.27.4, 12–13; Yudhishthira makes it clear that he coveted kingship and hence he is guilty of sin: *sa mayā rājyalubdhena pāpena gurughātinā/ alpakālasya rājyasya krte mudhena ghātitaḥ*.
28. XII.27.14–17. 'I put a little jacket on the truth': *satyakañcukam āsthāya*. Fitzgerald explains that 'a *kañcuka* is a small tight-fitting garment worn on the upper body . . . Sometimes the word means "disguise" and that translation may be more apposite. But I think the point here is a *kañcuka* covers half the body . . . and Yudhishthira spoke only half the truth.' Note to 27.17 (702). As to the lie itself, Yudhishthira is right to be afraid, for at the end of the epic he will have to visit hell, albeit briefly (XVIII.3.14).
29. *idāṃ tu me mahad-duhkhaṃ vartate hrdi nitya* (XII.1.13). Apart from an occasional perfunctory remark, the other Pandavas do not appear to express much regret. Like good kshatriyas, they assume that killing is a natural part of warfare. See XII.7–19 where the family tries to persuade Yudhishthira to change his disastrous decision to give up the throne.
30. Raimond Gaita, *Good and Evil: An Absolute Conception*, London: Macmillan, 1991, 45.
31. Ibid, 47
32. Ibid, 34
33. This is a variant to the philosopher Bernard Williams's example of a lorry driver and a passenger, which first introduced me to the

difference between regret and remorse. He writes that when a child is accidentally hit by a truck, the passenger feels regret, wishing that the accident had not happened. The driver, however, feels remorse even if it was not his fault—when he was neither legally nor morally culpable. Williams uses slightly different terminology— he distinguishes between 'regret' and 'agent-regret'. Bernard Williams, *Moral Luck: Philosophical Papers 1973–1980*, Cambridge: Cambridge University Press, 1981, 27.

34. Benedict de Spinoza, *Short Treatise on God, Man, and his Well-Being*, in *The Collected Works of Spinoza*, vol I, trans. E. Curley, Princeton: Princeton University Press, 1985, 115. He writes, '[Some] might perhaps think that Remorse and Repentance would bring them to the right path, and conclude, as the whole world does, that these are good. But if we consider them correctly, we shall find that they are not only not good, but on the contrary, injurious, and consequently evil. For it is manifest that we always come to the right path more through reason and love of truth than through Remorse and Repentance. And because they are species of sadness, which we have already proven to be injurious, and which we must therefore strive to avoid, as an evil, these two are injurious, evil, and to be shunned and fled.'

35. Aldous Huxley, Foreword to *Brave New World*, Harmondsworth: Penguin Books, 1950, 7.

36. Bernard Williams, 'Utilitarianism and Moral Self-Indulgence', in *Moral Luck: Philosophical Papers 1973–1980*, 44f.

37. Nussbaum claims that moral emotions, far from being irrational distractions, are 'intelligent responses to the perception of value'. They proceed from judgements we make concerning objects and people that are beyond our control but important to our flourishing, and as such are 'part and parcel of the system of ethical reasoning'. She believes that human beings enter the world dependent on objects beyond their control, most notably their mothers, and emotional development is a response to this fact. Recognizing our common vulnerability, our inevitable victimization by fate should lead us to an ethics of empathy and compassion. The pain and partiality of emotion are a value-laden mode of thinking that must be acknowledged if we are to create a just and compassionate

world. In taking this position Nussbaum courageously stands up to the weight of the Western philosophical establishment. Not only Spinoza (whom I have quoted above), but Plato, the Stoics, Kant and others felt that emotions are dangerous, arising from parochial needs and interests, and they subvert human reason. Kant was particularly dismissive of moral sentiments—he felt that they had to be subordinated to reason for achieving a rational grasp of moral principles.

38. *dharmacaryā ca rājyaṃ ca nityam eva virudhyate* (XII.38.4). See James Fitzgerald's analysis of *śoka* and *śānti* in his introduction to vol 7, 86–100. The cooling, he explains, is via a time-honoured process called *praśamana* and *śānti* in the Vedas. See D.J. Hoens, *Śanti: A Contribution to Ancient Indian Religious Terminology*, Granvenhage: N.V. De Nederlandsche Boek en Steendrukkerij v.h., H.L. Smits, 1951.

39. Many Indians accuse Yudhishthira of being indulgent and tender-minded. Alf Hiltebeitel, Buddhadev Bose and James Fitzgerald offer three different views of Yudhishthira's character, his role in the war and his sorrow. Alf Hiltebeitel, *The Ritual of Battle*, 229–86; James Fitzgerald, Introduction to Book Twelve of the *Mahābhārata*, vol 7, 86–100; Buddhadev Bose, *The Book of Yudhisthir*.

40. 'The *śānti* of the *Śāntiparvan* is basically an apotropaic *śānti* that functions first of all to render Yudhiṣṭhira, the king, fit to rule,' James Fitzgerald, Introduction to vol 7, 98.

41. Van Buitenen points out that Bhishma's instruction of Yudhishthira before dying at the solstice 'must be the longest deathbed sermon on record'.

42. Sheldon Pollock reminds us that 'the integral theme of Sanskrit epic literature is kingship itself'. In Robert Goldman (ed), *The Rāmāyaṇa of Vālmīki: An Epic of Ancient India*, vol 2, Princeton: Princeton University Press, 1991. 10.

43. XII.91.3, 4

44. Thomas Hobbes, *Leviathan*, London: JM Dent, 1973, 49.

45. Ibid, 64–65

46. Romila Thapar, *Ashoka and the Decline of the Mauryas*, Delhi: Oxford University Press, 255–56; Nikam and McKeon, *The Edicts of Ashoka*, Chicago: University of Chicago Press, 1978, 27–29.

47. John Strong writes, 'Aśoka seems to have been obsessed with Dharma. The Aśokan state was to be governed according to Dharma. Wars of aggression were to be replaced by peaceful conquests of Dharma. Special royal ministers were charged with propagation of Dharma. True delight in the world came only with delight in Dharma, and the old royal pleasure tours and hunts were replaced by Dharma-pilgrimages ... Dharma seems to have meant for Aśoka a moral polity of active social concern, religious tolerance, ecological awareness, observance of common ethical precepts and the renunciation of war.' *The Legend of King Aśoka*, Delhi: Motilal Banarsidass, 2nd edn., 2008, 4.

48. Nick Sutton, 'Aśoka and Yudhiṣṭhira: A Historical Setting for the Ideological Tensions of the *Mahābhārata*', *Religion*, 27.4 (1997), 333–41, points out that 'the extended debates that surround [Yudhishthira's] dharma reflect controversy that arose in the reigns of Aśoka and other rulers of similar disposition.' Sutton's suggestion is that 'it was reinterpretation of dharma, and in particular royal dharma, that lies behind the characterization of Yudhiṣṭhira and the debates in the epic on the use of violence, with the fictional Yudhiṣṭhira representing the historical Aśoka and other kings of similar inclination.' Another scholar has noted the similarity between Arjuna and Ashoka. Israel Selvanayagam in his article 'Asoka and Arjuna as Counterfigures Standing on the Field of Dharma: A Historical Hermeneutical Perspective', *History of Religions*, 32 (1992–93), 59–75.

49. Romila Thapar places Ashoka's accession date as 269–68 BC in *Asoka and the Decline of the Mauryas* (33); John Strong offers the more cautious 'circa 270 BC' (*The Legend of King Aśoka*, 3). Magadha was the most prominent of the early monarchical states, ruled by low-caste Nandas from their capital Pataliputra (modern-day Patna in Bihar) from 340 BC. They were supporters of the new sect of Jains. Soon after Alexander the Great's invasion in 326 BC, the Nandas were overthrown by the Mauryas, who created the first empire to cover large parts of the then known India. Chandragupta Maurya, founder of the dynasty, also became a Jain, but grandson Ashoka converted to Buddhism.

50. Strong, 4

51. Thapar, 255–57. The word 'Dhamma' means dharma in Pali, the common language of the people adopted by the Buddha. Although John Strong thinks Ashoka renounced violence, James Fitzgerald disagrees. He believes that this very twelfth Major Rock Edict, which expresses remorse over the Kalinga war, 'has a clear ultimatum directed at the "forest tribes of the empire" ... Aśoka's edicts represent a remarkably aggressive policy of attempting to shape the thinking and behavior of his subjects' (118–19).

52. Ibid, 255

53. See Lamotte, *Histoire*, 388. According to Panini, the Shungas were descendants of the seer Bharadvaja, as was Drona, the famous brahmin teacher who taught the martial arts to the Pandavas and the Kauravas (ibid, 389). The Shungas were succeeded in paramountcy in northern India by another brahmin dynasty, the Kanvas, whose four rulers reigned from 75 BC to 30 BC (ibid, 388). James Fitzgerald argues that the Mauryan empire and the deliberate effort to spread Buddhist ideas by Ashoka 'were profound challenges to pious Brahmins. These may well have influenced the development and redaction of the *Mahabharata*.' See his Introduction to vol 7, 120. In footnote 172, he elaborates the views of Haraprasad Shastri, Romila Thapar and others.

54. James Fitzgerald writes: 'I have no doubt that the Suṅga revolution contributed a great deal to the development of our *Mahabharata*: however, one very important trait of the *Mahabharata* does not fit with the Suṅga era and may be a reaction against it. I refer to the critically important insistence in the *Mahabharata* upon rule being appropriate to ksatriyas and not brahmins. For these reasons, I have suggested that the first major written Sanskrit redaction of the *Mahabharata* was post-Suṅga and post-Kāṇva as well as post-Mauryan' (122).

55. Sheldon Pollock writes about a 'politically incapacitating bifurcation' in Ashoka's situation in his introduction to *Ayodhyākāṇda*, in Robert Goldman (ed), *The Rāmāyaṇa of Valmiki*, 2.10. The bifurcation relates to the dilemma of a monarch who believes that violence is sinful. How then does he respond to external military threats and internal lawlessness? This was the central problem crucial to the survival of the ancient Indian state.

56. 'Thus, the *Mahabharata*'s narrative tension lies in its effort to combine a hugely violent story based on the older sense of right and wrong with the new ethics of *yoga* and *ahimsa* that had caught the Indian imagination at the time. The ambivalent Yudhishthira is at the centre of this tension' (Fitzgerald, 122).

57. 'pacifying instruction': *praśamana anuśāsana*.

58. XII.98.1

59. The complete quote goes thus: 'The highest dharma is non-violence; look upon on all creatures equally': *ahiṃsā paramo dharmaḥ sarvaprāṇabhṛtāṃ smṛtaḥ*.

60. Ashoka's fourth Rock Edict regards non-violence as the special ideal of the ascetic: *avihisa bhutanam* (Bloch, *Inscriptions d'Asoka* [99]), whereas the *Arthashastra* sees *ahimsa* as a social ideal (I.3.13–14).

61. XII.253.6. I am indebted to Ian Proudfoot's excellent monograph *Ahimsa and a Mahabharata Story* for the translation and a wise retelling of this story from the *Moksadharmaparvan* section of Book Twelve (XII.252–56). Ian Proudfoot, *Ahimsa and a Mahabharata Story*, Asian Studies Monographs, new series no. 9, Faculty of Asian Studies, Australian National University, Canberra, 1987.

62. Phrases like *tulyanindāstuti* suggest indifference to blame or praise and a devaluing of the ego, Ian Proudfoot notes (99).

63. XII.253.2, 35ff. Proudfoot's translation: 'O Jajali, a [truly] wise man would immediately grasp [the distinction between] dharma and a mode of behaviour: [it would be] thus {with one] who is restrained, [and] acts properly, without enmity.'

64. Ian Proudfoot adds this elegant, classical liberal twist to this story: 'The petty trader, with a multiplicity of suppliers and a multiplicity of buyers, is not dependent for his livelihood upon the grace and favour of any individual. His gains or losses need not be made directly at the expense of others, but as a result of the impersonal action of market forces' (105).

65. XVIII.116.37–41. Scholars have speculated if vegetarianism in India emerged from the concept of *ahimsa*, from a belief in the immanence of God in all living beings. Gerard Manley Hopkins writes, 'The Brahman soon rose above the old savage notion that "the eater will hereafter be eaten by the eaten", as a reason for not killing animals.

He began to see life as a whole and ... he declared that "to take oneself as the norm" in ethics was the inevitable corollary of "every soul is part of the All-soul" in philosophy. Love any neighbour as thyself, in a new interpretation, became his rule. Moralizing his law of retribution he turned it for himself into a law of mercy. As I suffer (said he), so suffers the one whom I hurt; and the animal pleading for life suffers as well as the man injured and dying. To injure this other life, which in reality is one with my life, as both our lives are one with divine life, what could be more sinful?' G.M. Hopkins, *Ethics of India*, 231.

66. 'not taking life', III.199.27–29; 'not causing pain', XII.269.5; 'not causing injury', XII.285.23–24. In the *Laws of Manu*, *ahimsa* connotes 'not having an aggressive attitude' *(Manusmriti* 11.223); 'not having an unstilled spirit', Patanjali, *Yoga Sutra* 2.30–31.

67. Ian Proudfoot, 1. I owe the different senses of *ahimsa* to Proudfoot.

68. Mark Kurlansky, *Nonviolence: The History of a Dangerous Idea*, London: Jonathan Cape, 2006.

69. Gene Sharp, *The Politics of Non-Violent Action*, Boston: Porter Sargent, 2.

70. George Orwell, *Collected Essays, Journalism and Letters*, vol 4, 469. Originally published in 1949 in the *Partisan Review*.

71. With regard to the limitations of *ahimsa*, Lloyd Rudolph made this interesting observation in Mahatma Gandhi's defence in an e-mail to the author: 'The default position here is Gandhi's view that it is better to resist and die than to give your consent to violent death. You will have my body but not my consent [my will]. Most Jews in Germany went to their death in places such as Auschwitz without resisting. They were complicit in their death. Vikram Seth's *Two Lives* recounts how his Aunt Henny's sister served as a top official of the main German *gemeinde* in Berlin but, like all such officers of Jewish welfare organizations, ended by being sent to the gas chambers. She was among the very last of the German Jews to go but go she did.

'The question is, when and how could German Jews have resisted. Some say that *krystal nacht*, November 9, 1938, when SA Brown Shirts, the lumpen "storm troopers" of the Nazi party, attacked Jewish shops, homes and synagogues, was a moment when resistance might have made a difference. The event made clear that Hitler's threats to annihilate the Jews had to be taken seriously. At the same time, educated, middle class Germans were shocked by this evidence of the regime's encouragement of lawlessness and violence. But it was not to be. Although Jews were being deported and fleeing the general view among assimilated, educated professional Jews was one of denial and avoidance of "disorder". That is where the *gemeinde* fit in; they provided a sense of "order", a way to cooperate rather than to resist.

'If, in Hitler's Germany, non-violent resistance was not contemplated, much less tried, it was tried with considerable success in the countries of Soviet-occupied Eastern Europe, particularly in Poland where Lech Walesa is given much credit and in Czechoslovakia where Vaclav Havel is featured. (See Rainer Hilderbrandt, *From Gandhi to Walesa: Non-Violent Struggle for Human Rights*.) Similarly, Nelson Mandela's leadership of the struggle against the apartheid regime in South Africa was influenced by Gandhi's ideas about inclusiveness and commitment to non-violence, a commitment that after the Sharpesville massacre in 1960 was modified to allow violence against property but not persons. And there are quite a few other examples of the effectiveness of non-violence against oppressive regimes. Martin Luther King, of course, learned from Gandhi not only about non-violence but also about inclusiveness. The point is that Gandhi launched an idea and a practice that can succeed under a broader array of circumstances than those posed by a "civilized" British colonial regime. In any case, and more important, is the Gandhian lesson that it is better to die resisting, non-violently and even violently if courage requires it, than to die consenting.' See Lloyd Rudolph and Susanne Rudolph, *Postmodern Gandhi and Other Essays*, New Delhi: Oxford University Press, 2006.

72. Gene Sharp, *Exploring Nonviolent Alternatives*, Boston, 1971, 52. Michael Walzer makes the same point in *Just and Unjust Wars*, 330.

73. The expression 'bath of tears' is used by James Fitzgerald in the introduction to his translation of Book Eleven of the *Mahabharata*; he may or may not have got it from the English poet John Donne's famous poem, 'An Anatomy of the World':

> For in a common bath of tears it bled,
> Which drew the strongest vital spirits out . . .

74. See note 15 to Chapter 8.

75. The expression belongs to Werner Jaeger, the great scholar of classical Greece, who contrasted public and private spheres and did not think that the rules of private morality applied to the public sphere: 'the principle of force forms a realm of its own, with laws of its own, as distinct from the laws that inform the moral life of ordinary human beings.' Werner Jaeger, *Paideia: The Ideals of Greek Culture*, New York, 1939, vol I, 402.

76. The quotes from Thucydides are from Thomas Hobbes's translation of Thucydides's *History of the Peloponnesian War*, ed. Richard Schlatter, New Brunswick, NJ, 1975, 377–85. See Michael Walzer, 9.

77. Buddhadev Bose, *The Book of Yudhisthir: A Study of the Mahabharata of Vyasa*, trans. Sujit Mukherjee, London: Sangam Books, 1986, 20. Bose adds that even Yudhishthira's archery teacher, Drona, thought him incompetent in the martial arts. 'Give up, you are worthless,' he says in *Adiparvan*, I.132.

78. *Economist*, 4 February 2009. The comparison in the previous sentence to the French aristocracy was suggested to me by John Gapper of the *Financial Times* in January 2009.

79. The *Mahabharata* says that only human beings have the 'freedom' to choose whereas the lower orders behave through instinct. Hence, only human beings can be blamed or praised in the practise of dharma. 'Dharma and adharma apply only to human beings, O king. They do not exist in the world among creatures, other than man' (XII.283.28). For an excellent discussion of this subject, see Julian F. Woods, *Destiny and Human Initiative in the Mahābhārata*, Albany: State University of New York Press, 2001. Immanuel Kant also believed that human beings become conscious of their freedom at the moment of making a decision and this perception of autonomy results in their capability for leading moral lives.

80. Alexander Solzhenitsyn, 'One word of truth . . .': The Nobel Speech on Literature 1970, trans. BBC Russian Service, London: The Bodley Head, 1972, 27.

10. Mahabharata's Dharma

1. XV.28.10f
2. XV.46.8
3. XVI.8.52–64
4. XVII.1, 2
5. The text says that they 'desired to circumambulate the earth, with *yoga* as their dharma' (XVII.1.44); the Pandavas finally turn northward and ascend into the Himalayas (XVII.2.1).
6. 17.3.1, 7–8, 10–11. My gratitude to Wendy Doniger for allowing me to use her unpublished translation of Books Seventeen and Eighteen of the *Mahabharata*. According to some versions of the epic (though not the Critical text), Yudhishthira insists on taking the dog into heaven because of a vow never to abandon one who is frightened, devoted, afflicted, or for whom 'there is no other [recourse]' (Poona Critical Edition, XVII.13).
7. XVII.13.16–17
8. XVII.3.18–19
9. The incident of the fire sticks is at III.295–99 in the Critical Edition. I have also quoted from William J. Johnson's translation, *Mahabharata, Book Three, The Forest*, vol 4, Clay Sanskrit Library, New York: New York University Press. In the Poona Critical Edition the incident is at III.311–15.
10. III.311.22–25. W. Johnson's translation in CSL. In the Critical Edition it is at III.295.18–20.
11. III.296.13 in the Critical Edition.
12. David Shulman explains, 'The praśna points to a baffling, ultimately insoluble crystallization of conflict articulated along opposing lines of interpretation … Both questions and answers tend to the metaphysical, with the latent centre of meaning—the ultimate reality that is the true object of the quest—usually present only as a suggested power situated somewhere between the two explicit poles of the contest.' David Shulman, 'The Yaksa's Question', in *The Wisdom of the Poets: Studies in Tamil, Telugu and Sanskrit*, New Delhi: Oxford University Press, 2001 and *Untying the Knot: On Riddles and Other Enigmatic Modes*, New York: Oxford, 1996.
13. David Shulman adds, 'The Yaksa fulfils all three of the major

conditions for what might be called, abstracting and generalizing to some extent, the classical Upaniṣadic "riddling" scenario: (1) the situation of the contest on the border between life and death, so that wrong answers (and also other wrong moves, such as excessive questioning) may prove fatal; (2) the presence, within the contest, of a concealed ultimacy' (ibid).

14. III.313.115 CSL. The dialogue between the Yaksha and Yudhishthira is a long one, with dozens of questions and answers. I have used only a few questions and answers to illustrate my point.

15. *bhūtāni kālaḥ pacatī vārttā* (III.313.118d).

16. *ānṛśaṃsyyaṃ paro dharmas* is at III.313.75–76 CSL; Yudhishthira repeats it at III.313.129 CSL.

17. Transliterated properly as *ānṛśaṃsya*.

18. A few lines later the epic describes Yudhishthira as a person 'bestowed with *ānṛśaṃsya*' or *ānṛśaṃsya-samāyukta*, XVII.3.30–32. The word occurs three times in four verses (XVII.3.7, 8, 10, 30).

19. In the dialogue with the Yaksha, van Buitenen translates it as 'uncruelty'; David Shulman uses 'non-injury'; W.J. Johnson employs 'absence of cruelty' on the first occasion (75–76), but changes it to 'compassion' the second time at III.313.129 (CSL) in the Clay Sanskrit version. Nilakantha Chaturdhara, the famous commentator of the *Mahabharata* in the seventeenth century, glosses 'cruelty' as 'lack of pity' (*nirdayatvam*) and so, according to Wendy Doniger, '"lack of cruelty" which is the form that occurs in the text (*a-nr-samsya*), would be "pity"'. She adds in her inimitable way: '"Anti-cruelty", for the abstract noun, has the dubious advantage of conjuring up, for a contemporary American reader, the name of a prominent society concerned with animals.' Wendy Doniger, *The Hindus*, New York: Penguin Books, 2009, footnotes 2 and 3.

20. Mukund Lath, 'The Concept of *Anrsamsya in the Mahabharata*', in R.N. Dandekar (ed.), *Mahabharata Revisited*, New Delhi: Sahitya Akademi, 1990, 113–19.

21. English also has its own verbal confusions. It is important to get the word right in English to describe Yudhishthira's attitude. 'Pity' is obviously not right, for, as Martha Nussbaum explains, 'it has acquired connotations of condescension and superiority that it did not have earlier when Rousseau invoked *pitie*.' Eighteenth-century

texts would have used 'sympathy' to denote Yudhishthira's sentiments towards the dog. Today, however, 'sympathy' no longer suggests the bias for action that compassion does. Similarly, while 'empathy' may reconstruct imaginatively another person's experience, it too does not require the agent to act on behalf of the sufferer. Hence, 'compassion' is probably the right word to express Yudhishthira's insistence on taking the dog to heaven. It is more intense than the alternatives, suggesting both greater suffering of the sufferer and greater engagement of the agent. See Nussbaum's discussion on this in *Upheavals of Thought*, 12.

22. *divaṃ spṛśati bhūmiṃ ca śabdaḥ puṇyasya karmāṇaḥ/yāvat sa śabdo bhavati tāvat puruṣa ucyate* (III.313.120 CSL, III.297.63 in the Critical Edition). I have followed J.A.B. van Buitenen's translation. The connection between 'man' and 'deed' becomes clearer in David Shulman's literal translation of this verse: 'The word [or sound] touches heaven and earth together with [in association with, through] a good deed, as long as that word exists, one may be called a man.'

23. *ānṛśaṃsya samāyukta* (XVII.3.30–32).

24. XVIII.1.4–5

25. XVII.3.33

26. XVIII.2.12

27. XVIII.2.22

28. XVIII.2.26

29. XVIII.2.29

30. XVIII.3.32

31. XVIII.3.10–19

32. 'human condition' is *mānuṣo bhāvaḥ* (XVIII.3.34).

33. XVIII.1–5

34. *Mokṣadharmaparvan* section of Book Eighteen (XVIII.252–56). I have employed with gratitude the translation from Sanskrit of Tuladhara and Jajali's story from the monograph *Ahimsa and a Mahabharata Story* by Ian Proudfoot. The portions quoted below are from Proudfoot's deconstruction of the text into two alignments, whose authors (Proudfoot speculates) might have been different.

35. XII.254.6, 7ab, 8bd

36. XII.253.12

37. XII.253.18ff
38. XII.256.2
39. This is the wise conclusion of Ian Proudfoot, 116.
40. XII.254.15cd
41. Proudfoot, 116
42. Wendy Doniger, *The Hindus: An Alternative History*, New York: Penguin Books, 2009, 267.
43. Martha C. Nussbaum, *Compassion: Human and Animal*, festschrift in honour of Jonathan Glover, edited by Richard Keshan and Jeffrey McMahan, Oxford University Press. Also recounted in her book *Upheavals of Thought*.
44. Stefan Collini, *Public Moralists: Political Thought and Intellectual Life in Britain 1850–1930*, Oxford: Clarendon Press, 199. Collini provides an excellent account of the moral temper of the Victorian age.
45. Hume wrote: 'there is no such passion in human minds as the love of mankind, independent of personal qualities, of services, or of relation to ourself.' David Hume, *A Treatise on Human Nature*, Book III, Part 2, section i, ed. Ernest Mossner, London: Penguin Books, 1984.
46. David Hume, *Enquiry Concerning the Principles of Morals*, 1751.
47. John Stuart Mill, *Utilitarianism* (1863), *The Collected Works of John Stuart Mill*, ed. John M. Robson, 31 vols, Toronto and London, 1965–91, vol x, 215, 231.
48. Beatrice Webb, *My Apprenticeship*, London, 1926; reissued by Cambridge: Cambridge University Press, 1979, 143.
49. I am indebted to the American philosopher Thomas Nagel for this idea. See *The Possibility of Altruism*, Princeton: Princeton University Press, 1978, 82.
50. Ibid, 84
51. Loc cit, 84
52. Ibid, 85
53. Immanuel Kant, *Groundwork for the Metaphysics of Morals*, trans. James W. Ellington, Indianapolis, IN: Hackett, 1993.
54. Martha C. Nussbaum, *Upheavals of Thought*, 400.
55. Vinit Haksar, 'Ideals of Perfection', in John Skorupski (ed.), *Routledge Companion to Ethics*, London: Routledge, 2009 (forthcoming).
56. J.S. Mill, *Utilitarianism, On Liberty, Representative Government*, Letchworth: The Aldine Press, 1957.

57. J. Urmson makes this distinction between moral rules and ideals in his essay, 'Saints and Heroes', in A. Melden (ed.), *Essays in Moral Philosophy*, Seattle: University of Washington Press, 1958.

58. XVIII.3

59. *vaiṣamya* = unevenness. David Shulman points out this possibility in his essay, 'The Yakṣa's Question', 51.

60. W.J. Johnson, Introduction, *The Sauptikaparvan of the Mahābhārata: The Massacre at Night*, New York: Oxford University Press, 1998, xxviii.

61. James Fitzgerald explains this background: 'The *Mahābhārata* is a "myth of the *avatāra*", that is a tale of the divine "unburdening" ... of the beleaguered Earth who has taken refuge with the celestial Gods. The *Mahābhārata* tells this story, narrating the divinely planned purging from the Earth of a demonic *kṣatra*, and the subsequent chartering of proper [brahmin guided] kingship ... Draupadi in the *Mahābhārata* is an incarnation of Sri; she was born directly from the earthen altar during a sacrifice. As soon as she was born, a bodiless voice announced, "This most splendid of all women, this Dark One (Kṛṣṇa) will tend to lead the *kṣatra* to destruction. She with her lovely figure will in time do the business of the Gods. Because of her, a tremendous danger for the *kṣatriyas* will develop' (I.155.44–45), Fitzgerald, 5.

62. Martha Nussbaum explains how we learn compassion from our vulnerability: 'The recognition of one's own related vulnerability is, then, an important and frequently an indispensable epistemological requirement for compassion in human beings—the thing that makes the difference between viewing hungry peasants as beings whose sufferings matter and viewing them as distant objects whose experiences have nothing to do with one's own life. Such a judgment is psychologically powerful in moving other people into one's own circle of concern.' *Upheavals of Thought*, 32.

63. Vaughan Pilikian, 'Like Suns Risen at the End of Time: Metaphor and Meaning in the *Mahabharata*', *Journal of Vaishnava Studies*, 14.2, Spring 2006.

64. *kālaḥ pacati bhūtāni sarvāṇi* (XVII.1.3).

65. I had originally employed *pratinayaka*, 'anti-hero', but clearly *anayaka*, 'un-hero', is a better way to describe Yudhishthira. I owe this clarification to Sheldon Pollock.

66. Martha Nussbaum, *The Fragility of Goodness: Luck and Ethics in Greek Tragedy and Philosophy*, Cambridge: Cambridge University Press, 1986.

67. *Dhvanyāloka* (Kākā 5): *Mahāmuninā vairāgyajananatātparyam prādhānyena svaprabandhasya darśayatā mokṣalakṣaṇaḥ puruṣārthaḥ śānto rasaś ca mukhyatayā vivakṣāviṣayatvena sūcitaḥ. Ānandavardhana, Dhvanyāloka*, with the *Locana* commentary of Abhinavagupta and the Bālapriyā commentary of Rāmasāraka, ed. Pt. Pattābhirāma Śāstri, Kashi Sanskrit Series 135, 1940, 4.5 9 533, cited in Gary A. Tubb, 'Śāntarasa in the *Mahābhārata*', ed. Arvind Sharma, *Essays on the Mahābhārata*, Leiden and New York: E.J. Brill, 1991, 199.

Conclusion

1. Apropos a child's engagement with narrative, Friedrich Nietzsche says in the *The Gay Science* that 'art saves us from nausea at human life by giving us a good will toward things that we have made. We can relax the demand for omnipotence and perfection because we find that we enjoy something that is fully human' (107).

2. The *Mahabharata* is generally regarded in Indian tradition as *itihasa*, 'history', while the other epic, *Ramayana*, is known as *kavya*.

3. If she were alive, I would be tempted to defend myself and my project in the words of Andre Malraux, who declared in a conversation with Jawaharlal Nehru in the 1950s, 'I am endowed with a sacred spirit without faith, which seeks to grasp the irony behind the spiritual'.

4. Some societies seem to do a better job of it. Students in both England and Scandinavia were asked a few years ago, 'Are most of your classmates kind and helpful?' Only 43 per cent said 'yes' in the UK while 75 per cent of Scandinavian youth answered in the affirmative. Richard Layard, *Happiness: Lessons from a New Science*, London: Allen Lane (Penguin), 2005.

5. Gurcharan Das, *India Unbound*, New Delhi: Penguin Books, 2000, xiii, xiv, 233.

6. *bhūtāni kālaḥ pacati vārttā* (III.313.118d).

7. XII.262.9; *The Mahābhārata: An Enquiry into the Human Condition*, trans. Chaturvedi Badrinath, New Delhi: Orient Longman, 2006.

8. Too much harm is done, T.S. Eliot pointed out, because of human vanity and of 'people who want to feel important'. T.S. Eliot, *The Cocktail Party*, New York: Harcourt Brace, 1950.

9. Plato, *Apology*, 38a.

10. IX.2.1–15

11. In recent times the French existentialist Jean-Paul Sartre has made the strongest plea for the human agent to choose 'authentically' in order to avoid a life of 'bad faith'. Sartre did not believe in a divine plan, and hence, according to him, our choices are arbitrary. Nevertheless, he passionately declared, 'you are free . . . therefore choose—that is to say, invent'. Jean-Paul Sartre, 'Existentialism is a Humanism', in Walter Kaufman (ed.), *Existentialism from Dostoevsky to Sartre*, New York: New American Library, 1975, 356.

12. Ruth Katz makes an excellent comparison of Arjuna to Achilles in her book, *Arjuna in the Mahabharata: Where Krishna Is, There is Victory*, Columbia, SC: University of South Carolina Press, 1989, 6.

13. *Laws of Manu* VI. Also *Mahabharata* XII. 236f. Scholars have suggested that vested interests may have influenced the ending of the epic. Bhargava brahmins may have 'brahminized' the character of Yudhishthira in later redactions of the text, making him the real hero of the epic. Whereas Arjuna, Krishna's devotee, was committed to the path of devotion or *bhakti*, the brahmins favoured Yudhishthira's path of knowledge. Thus, they turned the epic's message to one of philosophical peace (instead of a mystical union with God). Ruth Katz provides a number of examples. 'The Sauptikaparvan Episode in the Structure of the *Mahābhārata*', in Arvind Sharma (ed), *Essays on the Mahābhārata*, Leiden and New York: E.J. Brill, 1991, 149. The Bhargava brahmins might have hijacked the epic at a certain point in its history by adding to it the Rāma Jāmadagnya episode and some obviously pre-brahmin elements, such as in the *Anusasanaparvan* section of the epic, where brahmins shamelessly advise the listener to give gifts of food, money and cows to brahmins. See also V.S. Sukthankar, 'The Bhṛgus and the Bharata: A Text-Historical Study', in *Critical Studies in the Mahābhārata*, vol 1 of *Sukthankar Memorial Edition*, ed. P.K. Godse, Bombay: Karnataka Publishing House, 1944, 278–337; also see Robert P. Goldman, *Gods, Priests, and Warriors: The Bhṛgus of the Mahābhārata*, New York: Columbia University Press, 1977.

14. Indra says: 'Amongst the virtuous, the great feature of *dharma* is compassion—*anukroso hi sādhūnāṃ sumahad—dharmalakṣaṇam* and compassion always pleases those who are virtuous' (XIII.5.23).

15. Max Weber, who gave much thought to prophecy, distinguished between 'ethical prophecy' which was characteristic of the Judaic–Christian tradition and 'exemplary prophecy' which is characteristic of India. Yudhishthira is an example of the latter. I want to thank the sociologist Andre Bétéille for bringing this to my attention.

16. Iris Murdoch, *The Sovereignty of the Good*, London: Routledge & Kegan Paul, 1970.

17. Graham Greene makes this point brilliantly in his novel, *The Power and the Glory*, in which the 'whisky priest' strives to overcome physical and moral cowardice in order to find redemption: 'Without thinking what he was doing, he took another drink of brandy. As the liquid touched his tongue he remembered his child, coming in out of the glare: the sullen unhappy knowledgeable face. He said, "Oh God, help her. Damn me. I deserve it, but let her live for ever." This was the love he should have felt for every soul in the world: all the fear and the wish to save concentrated unjustly on the one child. He began to weep; it was as if he had to watch her from the shore drown slowly because he had forgotten how to swim. He thought: This is what I should feel all the time for everyone ...' Graham Greene, *The Power and the Glory*, New York: Penguin Classics, 1992, 208.

18. V.60.2–3 CSL

19. Ibid, V.26.3 CSL

20. V.31.22

21. XII.121.34

22. These expressions—'ethic of ultimate ends' and 'ethic of responsibility'—belong to the sociologist Max Weber. See his essay, *Politics as a Vocation,* and *From Max Weber: Essays in Sociology*, ed. Hans Gerth, C.W. Mills, New York: Routledge & Kegan Paul, 1970.

23. The notion that societies are held together by 'laws, customs and moral habits' was articulated by Edmund Burke in the eighteenth century in his critique of the French Revolution as well as in his other writings.

24. The temper of the *Mahabharata* is closer to that of David Hume

than of Immanuel Kant, the two philosophers who have most deeply influenced the modern ethical sensibility. When Yudhishthira tells Draupadi in the forest, 'I act because I must', he is reflecting an uncompromising world of absolute moral standards, similar to Kant's. Chastened, however, by Duryodhana's betrayal, he slowly becomes a reciprocal altruist, and decides to go to war. Later he learns the art of statecraft from Bhishma and he recognizes the need for punishment in public life. David Hume believed that one's reason for doing something had to link to some desire or emotion that human beings possess. Similarly, Bhishma speaks of *svabhava*, 'human inclination'. Hume's world of sociable beings, who find moral reward in the nobility of character, is not dissimilar to the prudent ethical life of the good king that Yudhishthira pursues after he becomes king. It recognizes the place of both *danda* and benevolence.

25. N. Machiavelli, *The Prince*, 1513, ed. P. Bondanella, Oxford: Oxford University Press, 1984, 52.

26. III.31.39

27. XIV.53–55

28. III.32.19, 24, 30

29. I am indebted to Sheldon Pollock for these words of caution. He warned me not to try and seek a single meaning, nor excessive coherence from the epic, while reassuring me about my own quest for dharma in the epic, saying that it 'is not only permissible but a hermeneutic necessity'.

30. Scholars have long been perplexed at this moral confusion. As already noted, Adolf Holtzmanns proposed a complex inversion theory, suggesting that the Pandavas might have been villains in an earlier version of the epic. Adolf Holtzmanns (the younger), *Arjuna: Ein Beitrag zur Reconstruction des Mahābhārata*, Strassburg: Karl J. Trubner, 1879. Another scholar, E. Washbrook Hopkins, treated the Pandava deceits as examples of an earlier morality in the epic's historical development. E. Washbrook Hopkins, *The Great Epic of India: Its Character and Origin*, New York: Scribner, 1901.

31. This was the late Professor Bimal Krishna Matilal's verdict. See his essay, 'Krishna: In Defence of a Devious Divinity', in Arvind Sharma (ed.), *Essays on the Mahabharata*, Leiden: E.J. Brill, 1991, 4.

32. Bimal Matilal, *The Collected Essays of Bimal Krishna Matilal: Ethics and Epics*, ed. Jonardon Ganeri, New Delhi: Oxford University Press, 65.

33. III.148. The three ages prior to Kali Yuga are *Krta*, followed by *Treta* and *Dvapara*.

34. Sir Stuart Hampshire, Address to Second Meeting of the UNESCO Universal Ethics Project, Naples, 1997.

35. XIII.74.22–27

36. A.K. Ramanujan, 'Repetition in the *Mahābhārata*', *The Collected Essays of A.K. Ramanujan*, gen. ed., Vinay Dharwadker, New Delhi: Oxford University Press, 1999, 176–77. He adds: 'Because *dharma-sukshmata* is one of the central themes that recur in an endless number of ways, the many legal discussions are a necessary part of the action.'

37. XII.252.36ab, 13, 17, 50ab

38. J.A.B. van Buitenen, *Mahabharata*, Introduction to Book Two, 29.

39. The value system designated by the epic as *nivrtti* had been influenced by the philosophical ideas of Samkhya and Yoga. These can be found in the epic's sections called *Mokshadharma*, *Ashvamedhika*, and in the didactic portions of *Vanaparvan*. The epic's *pravrtti* value is best illustrated in the concept of *sva-dharma*, one's caste duty (also called *varna dharma*). There is also a third way in the epic, of *bhakti*, devotion to a loving and all-powerful God (with a capital G). The world view of *bhakti* is different from that of the Vedas and the Upanishads. Its God is much more exalted, referred to in later redactions of the epic as Narayana or Shiva. That these three ways might be contradictory does not seem to bother the epic. Nor is any particular character a perfect representative of one or the other strand of thinking. Krishna praises Yudhishthira, for example, for upholding both *pravrtti* and *nivrtti* values: '*Dharma* is greater than the winning of a kingdom and they describe the execution of it as a penance. By executing the duties of *sva-dharma* with truth and honesty, you have conquered both this world and the next. In the beginning you engaged in study, following various vows, and absorbed the complete science of warfare; having gained possessions and wealth through *kshatriya-dharma*, you have executed all the traditional sacrifices. You take no delight in licentious

pleasures and you do not strive in any way after the objects of enjoyment. You never abandon *dharma* because of greed, and thus, because of your nature, you are the *dharma-raja*. Having won lands, riches and objects of pleasure, your greatest delight is always in charity, truthfulness, austerity, faith, tranquility, determination and tolerance' (III.180.16–19).

40. *Drona*, trans. Vaughan Pilikian, vol 1, Clay Sanskrit Series, New York: New York University Press, 2006, II.4.

41. Vaughan Pilikian, Introduction to *Mahabharata*, Book Seven, 22.

42. Deussen and Strauss include *Sanatsujatiya* in their *Vier Philosophischen Texte des Mahabharatam*. Paul Deussen and Otto Strauss, *Vier Philosophischen Texte des Mahabharatam*, Leipzig, 1906.

43. Vidura says, 'The ancient and eternal youth Sanatsujata had proclaimed that there is no death' (V.41.2). Dhritarashtra presses his brother to reveal this wisdom. Vidura demurs: he is the son of a shudra woman and thus not entitled to speak. But he calls Sanatsujata with his mind and asks him, 'Pray do speak to [Dhritarashtra], so that upon hearing it this Indra among kings may be translated beyond happiness and misery . . . so that old age and death do not overwhelm him . . .' (V.41.8).

44. Recall Yudhishthira did offer the incentive of heaven for being good to Draupadi: 'He who resolutely follows dharma, O beautiful woman, attains to infinitude hereafter' (III.32.19).

45. This is also Derek Parfit's position in *Reasons and Persons*, Oxford: Oxford University Press, 1984, 453–54.

46. Thomas Nagel, *What Does It All Mean?*, New York: Oxford University Press, 1987; he makes the same point in *The Possibility of Altruism*, Princeton: Princeton University Press, 1978.

47. *Dhvanyāloka* (Kākā 5). Gary Tubb and Sudipta Kaviraj have elaborated on this verse (DE 690–91). Sudipta Kaviraj was kind enough to share with me his unpublished paper, 'The Second *Mahabharata*', presented in a seminar at Columbia University in honour of Professor Sheldon Pollock in 2008.

48. David Gitomer, 'King Duryodhana: The *Mahābhārata* Discourse of Sinning and Virtue in Epic and Drama', *Journal of the American Oriental Society*, 112.2, (April–June) 1992, 223.

49. It has been suggested that the idea of Hindu pluralism is grounded

in its earliest text, the Rig Veda. See Wendy Doniger, 'Many Gods, Many Paths: Hinduism and Religious Diversity', *Religion and Culture Web Forum*, February 2006. An earlier draft of this article appeared as 'Do Many Heads Necessarily Have Many Minds? Tracking the Sources of Hindu Tolerance and Intolerance,' *Parabola*, 30.4 (Winter 2005), 10–19.

50. The poet doubts if even the gods know how the world was created: 'Whence this creation has arisen—perhaps it formed itself, or perhaps it did not—the one who looks down on it, in the highest heaven, only he knows—or perhaps he does not know.' This famous 'Nāsadīya' verse is at X.129. Wendy Doniger, *The Rig Veda: An Anthology*, London: Penguin Books, 1981, 25. There are many translations of the Rig Veda to choose from; my favourite is by Raimundo Panikkar, *The Vedic Experience: Mantramañjarī* (Berkeley and Los Angeles, 1977). Of the complete text, I recommend Ralph T.H. Griffith, *The Hymns of the Rig Veda* (London, 1889; reprinted Delhi, 1973). Of the partial text, I also like A.A. Macdonell, *A Vedic Reader for Students* (Oxford, 1917); *Hymns from the Rigveda* (Calcutta, London, 1922). This simple verse about the creation of the universe has provoked dozens of complex commentaries by Indian theologians and Western scholars. The open-mindedness of this verse is in contrast to the certainty of other verses in the Rig Veda, according to Stephen Phillip. See, for example, W. Norman Brown, 'Theories of Creation in the Rig Veda', *Journal of the American Oriental Society*, 85 (1965), 23–34; Jwala Prasad, 'The Philosophical Significance of Rigveda X.129.5 and Verses of an Allied Nature', *Journal of the Royal Asiatic Society* (1929), 586–98; W.D. Whitney, 'The Cosmogonic Hymn, Rig-Veda X.129', *Proceedings of the American Oriental Society* (1882), 109. As a general study of the Rig Veda, I would suggest Jan Gonda, *The Vision of the Vedic Poets* (The Hague, 1963).

51. *Aitareya Brahmana* (with the commentary of Sayana), Calcutta: M.N. Sarkar, 1895, 3.21.

52. 'David Tracy explains that one of the chief dangers in monotheism is an exclusivism that can (though it need not) lead to intolerance by falsely suggesting that the one-ness of God requires totality thinking. A polytheistic religion, by this argument, might be

expected to be more tolerant of the worship of other gods than a monotheistic religion would be. A monistic religion, characterized by infinity thinking rather than totality thinking, stands in the middle, more tolerant than monotheism but less tolerant than polytheism. The Hindu evidence supports this correlation. And it reflects this skeptical attitude in the charming way as open-minded kings in the Upanishads invite holy men of various schools to debate religious issues.' Wendy Doniger, 'Many Gods, Many Paths: Hinduism and Religious Diversity', *Religion and Culture Web Forum*, February 2006.

53. Hindutva or 'Hindu-ness' is the creed of the political groups at the right wing of the Indian political spectrum, the most prominent being the Bharatiya Janata Party (BJP), which rose to power in India in the 1990s and ruled the country as a part of the National Democratic Alliance (NDA) from 1999 to 2004, and was the chief opposition from 2004 to 2009.

54. John Rawls, *Political Liberalism*, New York: Columbia University Press, 1993, 216–20. The debate on teaching the *Mahabharata* in our schools is relevant for another reason, which I found upon reading Michael Oakeshott. It is the idea that there are things to be enjoyed, but that enjoyment is almost heightened by one's awareness that what one is enjoying is in danger of being lost. It is the combination of enjoyment and fear that stimulates conservative thoughts. The epic has given me so much enjoyment that I have become a *Mahabharata* addict. I feel deeply sad that many young boys and girls in India are growing up rootless, and they will never have access to these forbidden fruits of pleasure. My fears of the loss of tradition may appear exaggerated. Perhaps they are. Certainly in the villages of India, where the vast majority of Indians live, the *Mahabharata* is well and alive in the oral traditions. But the future of India does not lie in the villages but in the cities. It is there, especially with the powerful onslaught of the global culture, that we have to concern ourselves with to preserve continuity with the past.

55. Bhagavad Gita XVIII.63, *vimṛśyāitad aśeṣeṇa/yathecchasi tathā kuru*: 'Having reflected on this fully/Then act as you choose.'

56. A.K. Ramanujan, 'Three Hundred Rāmāyaṇas', *The Collected Essays*

of A.K. Ramanujan, ed. Vinay Dharwadker, New Delhi: Oxford University Press, 158.

57. David Gitomer, 222

58. V.S. Sukthankar, *On the Meaning of the Mahabharata*, republished by Motilal Banarsidass, 2003, 24.

59. XVIII.5.49

60. Immanuel Kant, 'Idee zu einer allgemeinen Geschichte in welbürgerlicher Absicht' (1784). German translation by Isaiah Berlin in *The Crooked Timber of Humanity: Chapters in the History of Ideas*, ed. Henry Hardy, New York: Vintage Books, 1992, 1. At another point, Berlin translates it as follows: 'Out of the crooked timber of humanity no straight thing was ever made' (19), which provided the famous title to his book of essays.

61. George Orwell, I think, best captures the *Mahabharata's* belief in the lack of human perfectibility in the following famous lines: 'The essence of being human is that one does not seek perfection, that one is sometimes willing to commit sins for the sake of loyalty, that one does not push asceticism to the point where it makes friendly intercourse impossible, and that one is prepared in the end to be defeated and broken up by life, which is the inevitable price of fastening one's love upon other human individuals.' Richard Rovere (ed.), *The George Orwell Reader: Fiction, Essays, and Reportage*, New York: Harcourt, 1961, 332. He could have been describing Yudhishthira.

62. David Gitomer, 223: 'The Sanskrit *Mahabharata* is a continuing repository of crisis in the public discourse of classical India.'

63. Association for Democratic Reforms, www.adrindia.org, jchhokar@gmail.com.

64. The expression 'in a time of cosmic destructiveness' is Barbara Stoler Miller's, in her Introduction to *The Bhagavad-Gita: Krishna's Counsel in Time of War*, New York: Bantam Books, 1986, 3.

65. Under the powerful influence of Vaishnavism, 'dharma leads to victory' was modified over time in some versions of the epic to read, 'Krishna leads to dharma, and this in turn leads to victory.' From depending on oneself and one's conscience to know right from wrong, the devotees of Krishna surrendered themselves to Krishna, the God, with the full expectation that He would lead them to dharma and to victory.

Dharma—The Story of a Word

1. I am indebted to many scholars for this story of dharma and I wish to acknowledge my gratitude to R. Lingat, *The Classical Law of India*, trans. J.D.M. Derrett, Berkeley: University of California Press, 1973; P.V. Kane, *History of the Dharmaśāstras* vol 1; Franklin Edgerton, 'Dominant Ideas in the Formation of Indian Culture', *Journal of the American Oriental Society*, 62 (1942), 155–56; J.A.B. van Buitenen, 'Dharma and Moksha', *Philosophy East and West*, 7 (1956–57), 33–40; D.D.H. Ingalls, 'Dharma and Mokṣa', Loc cit 41–48; Wilhelm Halbfass, *India and Europe: As Essay in Understanding*, State University of New York Press, 1988, 312–43; G.J. Larson, 'The Trimūrti of Dharma in Indian Thought: Paradox or Contradiction', *Philosophy East and West* 22 (1972), 145–53; Bankim Chandra Chatterjee, *Dharmatattva*; S. Radhakrishnan, 'The Hindu View of Life', *Indian Philosophy*, 1, 7th edn., 1962; Rabindranath Tagore, *The Religion of Man*; J.M. Koller, 'Dharma: An Expression of a Universal Order', *Philosophy East and West* 22 (1975), 133–44.

2. P.V. Kane, *History of the Dharmaśāstras*, vol 1, Poona: Bhandarkar Oriental Research Institute, 1962–75.

3. P. Hacker, 'Dharma im Hinduisms', quoted in Wilhelm Halbfass, *India and Europe: As Essay in Understanding*, 314. *The Concept of Duty*, ed. W.D. O'Flaherty and J.D.M. Derrett, New Delhi, 1978.

4. J. Gonda, 'Dharma, Karman, Samsaara, bilden einen Komplex, ein weltanschauliches System', 1, 292, quoted in Wilhelm Halbfass, 312.

5. R. Lingat, *The Classical Law of India*, 3.

6. According to the Rig Veda VI.70.1, *dharnan* is the means of separating heaven and earth (*dyāvāpṛthivī*).

7. The Atharva Veda refers to the *dharma purāṇa*, the 'ancient law' (XVIII.3.1).

8. *Mahabharata* XII.10.10; VII.49.49 (*dharmeṇa vidhṛtāḥ prajāḥ*).

9. *Manavadharmasastra* II.75ff.

10. Such usages are found since the time of the *Brāhmaṇa* (XIV.7.3.15) and they are conspicuous in the Nyāya and Vaiśeṣika systems.

11. The *varnāśramadharma* allocates, as we have seen, the duties of the four castes and the stages of life as *sva-dharma*.

12. The Nārāyaṇīya section of the *Mahabharata* tells us about the development of the Hindu sects. It deals with the dharma of the *ekantin,* i.e. the 'exclusive' worshippers of Vishnu-Narayana; their dharma, whose focus is monotheistic devotion, is also described as 'venerable', 'eternal dharma' (*dharmah sanatanah*).

13. *Yoga Sutra* II.33

14. James Fitzgerald describes this change in his excellent introduction to Book Twelve of the *Mahābhārata,* vol 7, Books Eleven and Twelve, Chicago: University of Chicago Press, 2004, 101–28.

15. Manu had also used *sanatana-dharma* in his classic text to refer to particular statutes or norms.

16. R. Antoine, 'A Pioneer of Neo-Hinduism, Bankim Chandra Chatterjee', *Indica,* The Indian Historical Research Institute Silver Jubilee Commemorative Volume, Bombay, 1953, 5–21.

17. S. Radhakrishnan, *Religion and Society,* London: George Allen and Unwin, 1952, 107–08.

INDEX

421